Classical Music
ON COMPACT DISC
A CRITICAL GUIDE TO THE BEST RECORDINGS

ON COMPACT DISC
A CRITICAL GUIDE TO THE BEST RECORDINGS

PETER HERRING

Harmony Books/New York

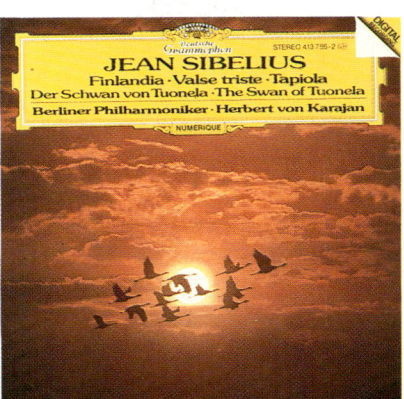

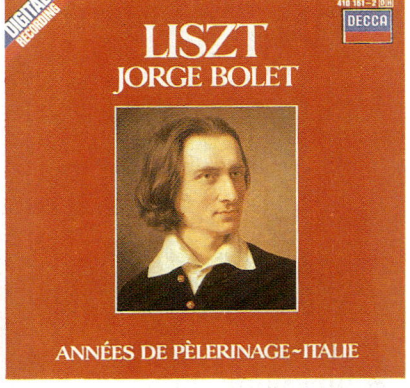

A SALAMANDER BOOK

Copyright © 1986 by Salamander Books, Ltd.

All rights reserved. No part of this book may be reproduced or transmitted in any form or by any means, electronic or mechanical, including photocopying, recording, or by any information storage and retrieval system, without permission in writing from the publisher.

Published in the United States in 1987 by Harmony Books, a division of Crown Publishers, Inc., 225 Park Avenue South, New York, New York 10003 and represented in Canada by the Canadian MANDA Group.

Originally published in Great Britain by Salamander Books Limited, 52 Bedford Row, London WC1R 4LR

HARMONY and colophon are trademarks of Crown Publishers, Inc.

Manufactured in Italy

Library of Congress Cataloging-in-Publication Data
Herring, Peter.
  Classical music on compact disc.
  1. Compact discs—Reviews. 2. Music—Discography.
I. Title.
ML156.9.H42   1987   016.7899′13   86-18341
ISBN 0-517-56493-9

10 9 8 7 6 5 4 3 2 1

First American Edition

CREDITS

Editor:
Philip de Ste. Croix

Designer:
Philip Gorton

Picture researcher:
Julia Hanson

Filmset:
Poole Typesetting Ltd, England

Color and monochrome reproduction:
Rodney Howe Ltd, England

Printed in Italy:
Sagdos SpA, Milan

ACKNOWLEDGMENTS

The author would like to thank the record companies and importers who supplied Compact Discs for evaluation and sleeve photography, and acknowledge his indebtedness to two of London's leading CD retailers, Music Discount Centre of Rathbone Place W1 and Covent Garden Records of Charing Cross Road WC2 for 'filling the gaps' and assisting us in the preparation of this book. My thanks, too, to David G Präkel and Robert Dearling for their skilful editing and proof-reading of the text and ever-helpful comments.

CONTENTS

Introducing Compact Disc	6	Claude Debussy	52
A Few Thoughts on Recording	10	Frederick Delius	56
One Hundred Best Recordings	12	Antonin Dvořák	58
Notes on the Reviews	13	Edward Elgar	61
		Manuel de Falla	65
Johann Sebastian Bach	14	Gabriel Fauré	66
Béla Bartók	22	César Franck	67
Ludwig van Beethoven	25	George Gershwin	68
Hector Berlioz	34	Edvard Grieg	70
Johannes Brahms	36	George Frideric Handel	72
Benjamin Britten	42	Franz Joseph Haydn	78
Anton Bruckner	44	Gustav Holst	84
Frédéric Chopin	46	Leoš Janáček	85
Aaron Copland	51	Franz Liszt	86

THE AUTHOR

Peter Herring has been writing and commenting upon music and the art of recording and reproduction for some thirteen years, over ten of them as editor of a leading UK hi-fi journal. Over twenty years and more, he has built up a wide-ranging library of music, in the past four years augmenting LPs with an equally representative collection of Compact Discs. He contributes regular reviews and comments – not always reverent! – on the subject of Compact Disc to several music and hi-fi publications.

NOTES ON THE CATALOGUE NUMBERS

For our American readers: the US **Angel** and **London** labels are here referred to by their European names, **EMI** and **Decca** respectively. When a Decca recording appears on the London label, the DH2 suffix changes to LH2. EMI (Angel) also change the catalogue numbers for their US box sets: the CDS7 prefix is replaced by CDC, and American readers should delete the last digit from the number given here and subtract one from the penultimate digit. By way of example, the Haitink *Tannhäuser*, UK listing CDS7 47296-8, becomes US number **3-Angel** CDC-47295.

Gustav Mahler	90	Robert Schumann	140
Felix Mendelssohn	96	Dmitri Shostakovich	144
Wolfgang Amadeus Mozart	100	Jean Sibelius	148
Modest Mussorgsky	112	Johann Strauss II	152
Carl Nielsen	113	Richard Strauss	153
Jacques Offenbach	114	Igor Stravinsky	156
Serge Prokofiev	115	Pyotr Ilyich Tchaikovsky	159
Sergei Rachmaninov	119	Georg Philip Telemann	164
Maurice Ravel	123	Giuseppe Verdi	165
Ottorino Respighi	127	Ralph Vaughan Williams	166
Nicolai Rimsky-Korsakov	128	Antonio Vivaldi	168
Gioacchino Rossini	130	Richard Wagner	174
Camille Saint-Saëns	132		
Franz Schubert	134	Index	176

INTRODUCING COMPACT DISC

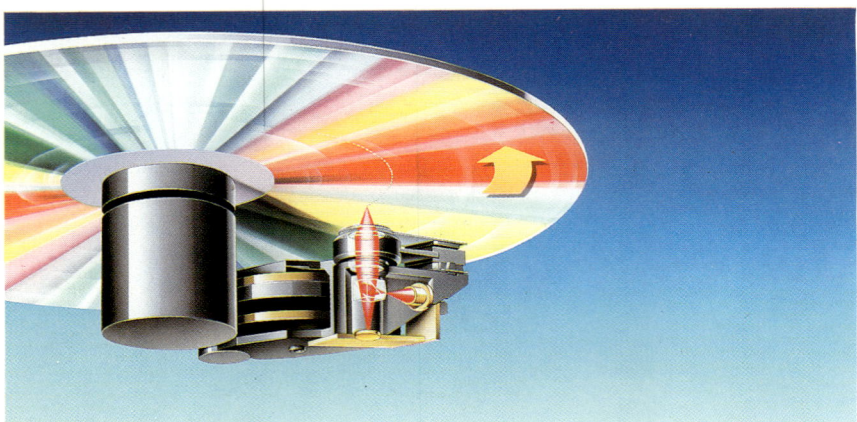

Since the worldwide launch of the Compact Disc digital audio system between the autumn of 1982 and the Spring of 1983, the catalogue of discs has expanded enormously, nowhere more so than in the classical field where record-buyers have been only too eager to embrace the benefits of the new medium.

However, while all Compact Discs share the same basic advantages, the artistic and technical differences between them can be just as great as those between LPs and cassettes. The CD itself is no absolute guarantee of quality: all that you can be assured of is that it faithfully conveys what is on the master tape, and CD captures a bad performance every bit as well as a good one.

With so many titles on budget labels, LPs give classical music lovers the chance to gamble a little on what they buy; a 'bad buy' is not too great a loss. That gamble is considerably greater with Compact Disc, yet the choice in the classics is almost as bewildering, and the chances of buying an inferior recording every bit as high.

The basic Compact Disc catalogues, by definition, give no indication of quality; this book, however, most certainly does.

Research shows that many people are discovering classical music for the first time

As this diagram shows, laser light is focussed onto the disc's surface. The varying signals reflected back are converted into digital code by a photodiode, via a prism.

through the medium of Compact Disc, relishing the many advantages it brings. The following reviews are, therefore, a first attempt to present the basis of a library of classical music, chosen from the many thousands of Compact Discs now available. There are some exceptions: a few major works will be conspicuous by their absence simply because no recommendable CD issue has yet appeared. Other works, perhaps slightly out of the mainstream, but nonetheless rewarding, are included simply because the CD issue is of such high quality. The opportunity has been taken to introduce this less-familiar music, and – briefly – the lives of the composers encompassed.

As any Compact Disc buyer will know, there is still a shortfall in the supply of discs worldwide. Demand for the new medium,

Theoretical illustrations of the digital audio encoding of the original musical waveform, and its subsequent decoding from CD into an exactly similar analogue signal for hi-fi reproduction.

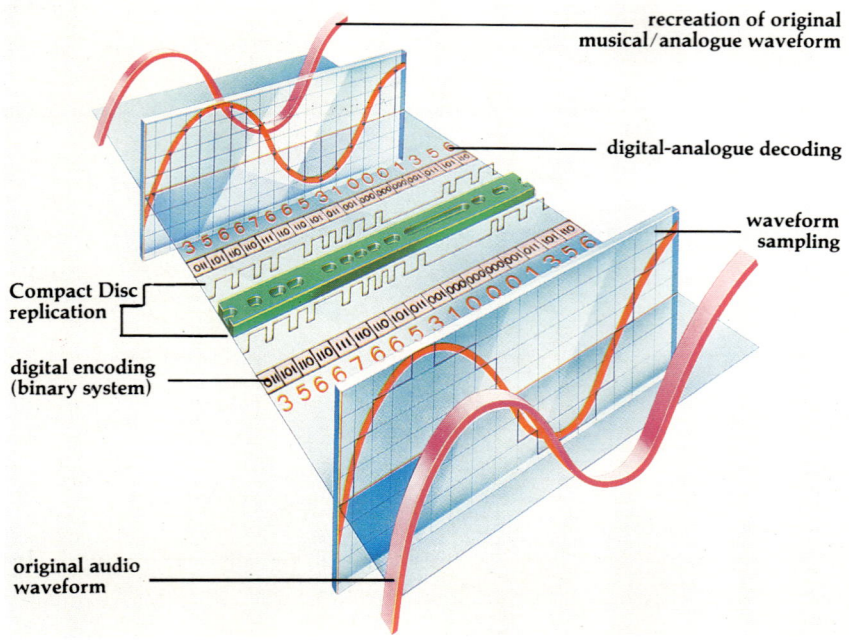

INTRODUCING COMPACT DISC

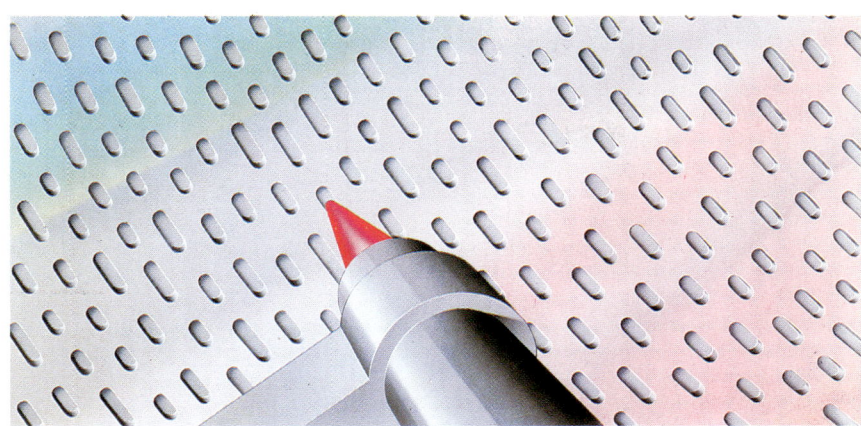

As the laser scans the alternating 'pits' and 'flats' of the disc surface, the beam will switch between being scattered and reflected back along its original path.

especially with ever-decreasing player prices, outstrips supply. The number of new production plants is set to increase considerably in the coming months, and the situation should therefore improve. However, for the time being, it can only be suggested that if you spy a Compact Disc you want, don't hesitate – buy it! If it is among those included here, you should not be disappointed.

The Coming of Compact Disc
There have been a number of 'false starts' in hi-fi over the past twenty years (which goes a long way to explain the initial reluctance of some record labels to embrace this new medium), but Compact Disc has now established itself as the first viable alternative to the LP record. Technically, it only

Cross-section through the lens photodiode/prism/laser system, which is the key to CD technology. The laser, at the base of the component, is a miniature diode type and of course, totally safe.

resembles its predecessor in being circular: for the rest, it is a wholly new technology, exploiting ideas unimagined when the LP was first developed – laser optics and digital information storage (essentially the technique used to store computer data).

With Compact Disc, the 'data' – in other words, the music – is contained on the disc in a type of code, (it actually resembles a series of microscopic 'pits') which has been derived from the original music signal. This is read by the laser which feeds what it sees through electronic circuits designed to convert the signal from its digital form into an 'analogue' one, or the kind of 'waveform' which can be translated into sound by any normal amplifier and loudspeakers.

None of this, of course, would be of any value unless the end result brought significant improvements over existing media, LPs and cassettes. However, CD offers substantial benefits in several distinct ways.

Generally, a much-improved sound quality can be expected although, like LPs and cassettes, the system is only as good as the performers and technicians that employ it. At its best, Compact Disc offers a noticeable increase in dynamic range (higher 'highs' and lower 'lows'!), and can reveal

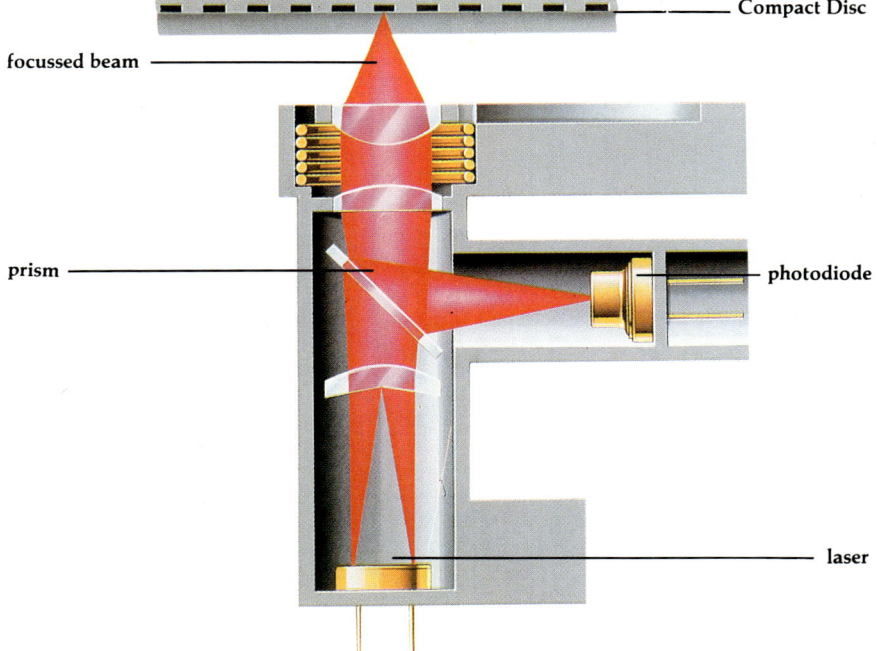

INTRODUCING COMPACT DISC

Above: The Marantz CD65: this player uses the new 16-bit oversampling system.

Below: Philips' CD150 is typical of current high-performance, good value CD players.

detail in an original recording which, by virtue of the limitations inherent in the technology, was lost on vinyl records.

There is also a noticeable lessening of the distortions which, if not always apparent on LP, are pleasantly noticeable by their absence on Compact Disc: the pitch variations and low-level 'wow' which afflicted the best of piano recordings, for example, or the inability of even the best pickup cartridges unwaveringly to reproduce high choral and solo voices.

Since the disc is not touched in any way while it is being played, it suffers no wear no matter how often you listen to it, and therefore has a prolonged lifespan, unlike the LP which, by the very nature of the reproduction process, suffers a degree of wear each time it is played.

Compact Discs are also much less susceptible to accidental handling damage – those clicks and scratches which seem to materialise on LPs no matter how carefully they are handled. All CDs are protected by a lacquer coating and, even if this becomes scuffed, the fact that the laser is finely-focussed on the substrate of the disc, not its surface, should ensure that such blemishes will not be 'seen' and therefore have no effect on the sound.

The convenience of Compact Disc should also not be overlooked. Playing is a simple push-button operation: no problems with a dirty stylus, or adjustment of the pickup cartridge or tone arm. Compact Discs are free from static, too, and since they are totally enclosed while playing, should attract no dust and dirt if properly stored in the plastic 'caddy' which accompanies each one.

Most Compact Disc players offer a variety of track selection and repeat functions

Loading discs into the metalliser to receive their aluminium coating at Nimbus' plant.

INTRODUCING COMPACT DISC

which, using the 'index points' programmed on to the discs themselves, will enable you to choose the sequence of music you wish to hear from a disc. Merely punching the appropriate number into the player will direct the laser to the relevant section of the disc (no more shaky lowering of the stylus into the barely-visible gap between LP tracks!)

Compact Disc Basics

CD technology derives little from existing audio principles. Instead, the musical waveform is analysed into easily-stored digits (binary digits or bits), which by virtue of the way they are stored cannot be degraded in the transfer process from recording to reproduction. Moreover, such encoding offers the facility for correction should the need arise, whether through storage errors or even missing 'information'.

Like its analogue predecessor, the digital signal is stored on tape, although the requirements of recorder and processor are considerably greater. This master tape is used to make the basic disc master, a plain glass disc with a light-sensitive surface. Modulated by the signal coming off-tape, a laser traces the recording photographically on the disc. After development, this master disc then goes through various stages to produce the stampers from which the Compact Discs themselves are made. At this stage, the CDs are transparent, but are then given the reflective metallic coating (necessary for the laser to do its job) and an outer protective layer applied. And there is no reason why that disc should not be an accurate replica of what was contained on the digital master tape.

It is now up to the player to decode the contents of the Compact Disc and re-create the original musical waveform which will be acceptable to any hi-fi amplifier and loudspeakers.

This is probably a good moment to mention the compatibility of Compact Disc players with hi-fi systems. First, it is vital to remember that the player does *not* use the same socket on an amplifier as a record turntable. It does not have the same

The transparent, but 'pressed' CD is taken from injection moulding by a robot arm.

electrical characteristics, and instead should be plugged into the socket marked 'tape', 'tuner', 'cassette' or 'auxiliary' (although more recent amplifiers will have an input specifically designated for CD).

It should also be borne in mind that the output level from the average CD player, in hi-fi terms, is unusually high (up to two volts) and, consequently, may cause overloading problems with the pre-amplifier sections of some older amplifiers. The problem may only be apparent (if at all) at high volume levels, but can readily be solved by attenuating the CD output. Any good hi-fi dealer will be able to advise you on this.

Of course, if you buy a stacking system or similar, containing a CD player, such problems should not arise since all the electrical matching will have been taken care of by the manufacturer.

With any system, however, do take care over volume levels. After the background noise that accompanied even the best of LPs, the total silence of CD can be deceptive: a shattering opening chord could prove expensive in terms of damage to loudspeakers or amplifier.

Something of a mythology has grown up about the level of abuse that the Compact Discs themselves can withstand! The simple fact is that, yes, they are far more resistant to accidental handling damage than LPs, but the surface is not wholly impervious to misuse. Some players are better than others at overcoming blemishes, but it frequently needs only a sizeable dust particle or surface scratch to put a laser literally off-beam.

It is also worth bearing in mind that not all CDs are pressed to the highest standards, although with the kind of stringent quality control employed in every pressing plant, the number of failures slipping through is very low and constantly decreasing.

Along with the development of magnetic tape recording, and that of the microgroove LP, Compact Disc is one of the few *genuine* revolutions in hi-fi. But it is not solely an astonishing piece of digital and optical technology, more importantly it can – at its best – add to the enjoyment and appreciation of music by eliminating the distractions inherent in other mediums. Assisting that enjoyment and appreciation is also the ultimate aim of this book.

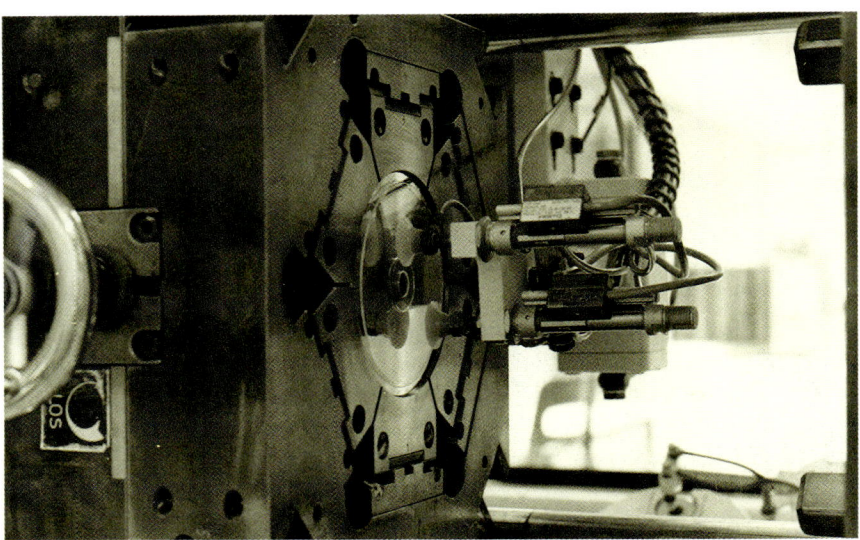

A FEW THOUGHTS ON RECORDING

Apart, perhaps from some avant-garde electronic compositions, it is unlikely that any classical music has been written with the microphone in mind, as opposed to the human ear. It may seem an obvious assumption, but it is one that has an important bearing on the way any recording is made and, of course, on the final outcome, be it LP, cassette or, most relevantly here, Compact Disc.

Equally, little if any classical music has been composed for the acoustic of a recording studio: composers have expected it to be performed and heard in concert halls, churches, even drawing rooms, and have therefore allowed for the advantages and disadvantages of the intended surroundings in their scores.

It follows, therefore, that any music should be recorded in an acoustic which is responsive and sympathetic, and not one that is actively conspiring to detract from it. A glance through the reviews here will reveal a number of venues that are regularly responsible for outstanding recordings: the Concertgebouw in Amsterdam; the Sofiensaal in Vienna; the Church of St Eustache in Montreal; Kingsway Hall in London.

Increasingly, engineers are favouring the lively sound of a church acoustic, not solely for sacred works, but for all forms of instrumental music, too. Notable examples in London are St John's, Smith Square, All Saints', Tooting, and the 'de-sanctified' church which became the Henry Wood Hall and is now given over entirely to recording.

A less-than-sympathetic acoustic is but one of the factors which can complicate the otherwise simple business of stereo recording. Some are technical, while others are purely artistic, but all have assumed a greater importance with the coming of digital audio and Compact Disc.

To return to the first observation, if a recording is to convince the ear that it offers something approaching 'the real thing', it should obviously possess the characteristics of the sound that would be heard from an 'ideal' listening position. These can be generally summed up as clarity, or transparency; separation and definition; scale and perspective; and, of course, a sense of 'presence' and acoustic.

Given a good acoustic, in theory it should only be necessary to sit the stereo microphone in the best seat in the hall and allow it to capture what it hears.

As many 'purist' recordings prove, the simple technique can work wonderfully well, but conditions are not always all they should be and frequently some kind of reinforcement is required to ensure that clarity is maintained, that each instrument gets a fair hearing, and that a suitable degree of reverberation is caught.

It is often the way this 'reinforcement' is achieved that makes the difference between a good and a bad recording. The best engineers have a knack of introducing extra microphones where required without destroying the overall integration and balance of the sound. If they do feel that an instrument needs a little help, it is done discreetly, and certainly not by planting a microphone in the mouthpiece! Every instrument needs space in which to 'breathe' if it is to reproduce with the correct timbre, bloom and 'shape' of sound.

They will also have learned to set the microphone levels at the start of a performance and then to leave well alone. Sadly, the habit of using a mixing desk to 'pull up' various instruments from the orchestral texture when, say, they are playing a solo still prevails in some quarters. Not only is it unnatural, it is a practice which contradicts the intentions of the composer, who would have elected to obtain any 'highlighting' required simply by ensuring that the overall sound was sufficiently transparent, or the particular instrument playing loud enough.

The musicians themselves can also modify the internal balance of sound, and often problems can be solved simply by moving instruments around!

Mercifully, the fading-up, fading-down habit seems to be on the decline, but there is still a tendency to emphasise the solo instrument throughout concerted works. Again, with any solo player of competence, this should hardly be necessary, and it can

At one of the sessions for the Taverner Consort's recording of Monteverdi's Vespers *(EMI): a variety of vocal and instrumental forces, and not at all easy to balance.*

A FEW THOUGHTS ON RECORDING

A single-point stereo microphone was used by Nimbus for this session with the English String Orchestra in the Great Hall of Birmingham University: simple, but effective.

also be detrimental to the sound the soloist produces.

Unfortunately, decisions about the relative placing of soloist and orchestra are sometimes taken out of the hands of the recording engineer and taken on a commercial, or even egotistical basis! By no means all performers leave the technicalities to the technicians, and by no means all performers are astute judges of sound balances.

There is a similar urge, it seems, to give too 'forward' a balance to chamber ensembles and solo instrumentalists. Not only is a sense of acoustic then excluded from the sound, but it can be very difficult for the listener to set an acceptable replay level: the level at which the softer sounds are satisfactorily revealed can prove excessively loud for the *fortes*.

It is all a question of judgement and taste. The character of any instrument is affected by the acoustic in which it is played. The degree of reverberation can present the engineer with a few headaches: too much and the sound may become blurred and ill-defined – 'washy' is the most frequently used term; too little, and it becomes dry and constricted. Very few venues have the kind of acoustic that suits orchestral, chamber and instrumental music in equal measure. Some seem suitable for none of them, yet are still used – presumably at the behest of others than the sound engineers!

And even the best locations can be plagued by other problems: traffic noise is a common bugbear, and one that assumes even greater importance with digital recording, which is as adept at capturing *unwanted* sounds with as much accuracy and clarity as it does wanted ones. It picks up extraneous noises such as creaking floors and shuffling musicians with only-too-audible fidelity.

Indeed, although digital recording has released the engineer from many constraints imposed by the analogue tape and LP mediums – no worries about overloading the signal, for example – its analytical quality is wholly revealing of both the good and the bad in a recording.

Some recording engineers have had the measure of digital since the outset, while in many other cases it is now forcing an all-too-apparent change of attitude, and for the better. There will always be those who need the 'safety net' of a battery of microphones and a multi-track recorder (which permits adjustment of the sound balance *after* the recording), but it is heartening to see the number of recordings now being taped straight down to the basic two-track stereo format, the one that has always been advocated by the finest exponents of the recording art.

It is not difficult to make an impressive recording, but it is those that impress by their very naturalness that generally remain a genuine source of listening pleasure after repeated hearings.

These are, of course, only personal observations on the techniques of classical recording and would no doubt be disputed by those who make the kind of productions that have come in for criticism: they would no doubt point to a certain naivity about the 'needs of the market'. However they are also opinions shared by many leading recording engineers, and there are plenty of successful recordings which evidence their validity, too.

It is to be hoped that these comments will assist in understanding the criticisms, adverse or otherwise, made in the following reviews on the subject of sound quality. However, do remember to let your own ears, and your own experience of music, be the final judges. Digital recording, just like analogue, is only as good as those who employ it and, as mentioned earlier, if anything it is yet more critical, to the extent that it may often take the blame for *introducing* faults when in fact it is merely *revealing* them.

ONE HUNDRED BEST RECORDINGS

From the three-hundred-and-fifty-and-more Compact Discs discussed in these pages, one hundred have been singled out for special mention as outstanding performances combined with, in the main, technically excellent recordings and, therefore, forming an ideal basis of any classical CD collection.

However, it remains an undeniably personal choice and, inevitably, cannot encompass all the works which would be regarded as essential to a 'classical library'. Given that the music appeals, none of the discs listed should disappoint in any way.

Johann Sebastian Bach
1 Orchestral suites Nos1-4/Gardiner/Erato ECD88048/9
2 Violin concertos/Laredo/Pickwick IMP Red Label PCD808
3 Organ works/Koopman/Archiv 410 999/2AH
4 Sonatas and partitas for violin/Mintz/DG 413 810-2GH3

Béla Bartók
5 Concerto for orchestra/Two pictures/Dorati/Philips 411 132-2PH
6 Music for strings, percussion, celesta/Divertimento/Rolla/Hungaroton HCD12531-2

Ludwig van Beethoven
7 Symphony No5/Kleiber/DG 415 861-2GH
8 Symphony No6 (Pastoral)/Ashkenazy/Decca 410 003-2DH
9 Symphony No7/Ashkenazy/Decca 411 941-2DH
10 Piano concerto No5 (Emperor)/Arrau/Philips 416 215-2PH
11 String quartets Nos12-16/Alban Berg/EMI CDS7 47135-8
12 Piano sonatas Nos2 and 4/Gilels/DG 415 481-2GH
13 Piano sonatas Nos7 and 23/Perahia/CBS MK39344
14 Piano sonata No29 (Hammerklavier)/Gilels/DG 410 527-2GH

Hector Berlioz
15 Symphonie Fantastique/Davis/Philips 411 425-2PH

Johannes Brahms
16 Symphony No4/Kleiber/DG 400 037-2GH
17 Piano concerto No2/Ashkenazy/Decca 410 199-2DH
18 Violin concerto/Mutter/DG 400 064-2GH

Benjamin Britten
19 Bridge variations, Simple Symphony/Boughton/Nimbus NIM5025

Anton Bruckner
20 Symphony No4/Böhm/Decca 411 581-2DH
21 Symphony No9/Haitink/Philips 410 039-2DH

Frédéric Chopin
22 24 Preludes/Pollini/DG 413 796-2GH

Claude Debussy
23 Nocturnes/Jeux/Haitink/Philips 400 023-2PH
24 Preludes Book II/Rouvier/Denon C37-7043
25 Suite Bergamasque, etc/Kocsis/Philips 412 118-2PH

Frederick Delius
26 Song of the High Hills, etc/Fenby/Unicorn-Kanchana DKP (CD) 9029

Antonin Dvořák
27 Symphony No8/Dohnanyi/Decca 414 422-2DH
28 Serenades Op22 and Op44/Marriner/Philips 400 020-2PH

Edward Elgar
29 Violin concerto/Kennedy/EMI CDC7 47210-2
30 'Cello concerto/de Pré/EMI CDC7 47329-2
31 Concert overtures/Gibson/Chandos CHAN8309

Manuel de Falla
32 The Three-cornered Hat/Love the Magician/Dutoit/Decca 410 008-2DH

Edvard Grieg
33 Peer Gynt suites (c/w Sibelius Pelléas et Mélisande Suite)/Karajan/DG 410 026-2GH

George Frideric Handel
34 Concerti Grossi Op3/Pinnock/Archiv 413 727-2AH
35 Fireworks Music, Concerti/Pinnock/Archiv 415 129-2AH
36 Water Music/Pinnock/Archiv 410 525-2AH

Franz Josef Haydn
37 Symphonies Nos94 (Surprise) and 96 (Miracle)/Hogwood/L'Oiseau-Lyre 414 330-2OH
38 Symphonies Nos100 (Military) and 104 (London)/Hogwood/L'Oiseau-Lyre 411 833-2OH
39 String quartets Op76 Nos4 and 6/Orlando Qt/Philips 410 053-2PH

Gustav Holst
40 The Planets-suite/Previn/EMI CDC7 47160-2

Leos Janáček
41 String quartets/Smetana Qt/Supraphon C37S-7545

Franz Liszt
42 Années de Pelerinage; Italie/Bolet/Decca 410 161-2DH
43 Piano recital/Bolet/Decca 410 257-2DH
44 Piano recital/Bolet/Decca 411 803-2DH
45 Piano sonata, etc/Brendel/Philips 410 040-2PH

Gustav Mahler
46 Symphony No4/Maazel/CBS MK 39072
47 Symphony No6/Rückert Lieder/Karajan/DG 415 099-2GH2
48 Symphony No8/Solti/Decca 414 493-2DH2
49 Symphony No9/Karajan/DG 410 726-2GH2

Felix Mendelssohn
50 Symphonies Nos1-5, etc/Abbado/DG 415 353-2GH4
51 Midsummer Night's Dream/Marriner/Philips 411 106-2PH

Wolfgang Amadeus Mozart
52 Clarinet and Oboe Concertos/Hogwood/L'Oiseau-Lyre 414 339-2OH
53 Piano concertos Nos8 and 27/Serkin/DG 410 035-2GH
54 Piano concertos Nos17 and 18/Perahia/CBS MK 36686
55 Piano concertos Nos19 and 23/Perahia/CBS MK 39094
56 Symphonies nos38 and 39/Hogwood/L'Oiseau-Lyre 410 233-2OH
57 Symphonies Nos 40 and 41/Tate/EMI CDC7 47147-2
58 Violin concertos Nos4 and 5/Shumsky/Nimbus NIM 5009
59 Piano sonata K457, Fantasia K475, etc/Uchida/Philips 412 617-2PH
60 String quintets/Grumiaux/Philips 416 486-2PH3

Modest Mussorgsky
61 Pictures at an Exhibition (piano version)/Rouvier/Denon C37-7177

Serge Prokofiev
62 Symphony No5/Järvi/Chandos CHAN 8450
63 Symphony No6/Järvi/Chandos CHAN 8359
64 Violin concertos Nos1 and 2/Mintz/DG410 524-2GH

12

ONE HUNDRED BEST RECORDINGS

Serge Rachmaninov
65 Piano concertos Nos2 and 4/Ashkenazy/ Decca 414 475-2DH
66 Symphony No1/Ashkenazy/Decca 411 657-2DH
67 Symphonic Dances/Isle of the Dead/ Ashkenazy/Decca 410 124-2DH
68 Preludes/Piano sonata No2/Ashkenazy/ Decca 414 417-2DH2

Maurice Ravel
69 Rapsodie Espagnole, La Valse, etc/ Dutoit/Decca 410 010-2DH
70 Le Tombeau de Couperin, etc/Dutoit/ Decca 410 254-2DH
71 Daphnis et Chloé/Dutoit/Decca 400 055-2DH

Ottorino Respighi
72 The Fountains of Rome, etc/Dutoit/ Decca 410 145-2DH

Nicolai Rimsky-Korsakov
73 Scheherazade/Dutoit/Decca 410 253-2DH

Gioacchino Rossini
74 Overtures/Chailly/Decca 400 049-2DH

Camille Saint-Saëns
75 Symphony No3 *(Organ Symphony)*/ Dutoit/Decca 410 201-2DH
76 Carnival of the Animals (c/w Ravel)/ Previn/Philips 400 016-2PH

Franz Schubert
77 Symphonies Nos5 and 8 *(Unfinished)*/ Solti/Decca 414 371-2DH
78 Symphony No9/Solti/Decca 400 082-2DH
79 Rosamunde-incidental music/Masur/ Philips 412 432-2PH
80 Piano quintet *(The Trout)*/Hagen/Schiff/ Decca 411 975-2DH
81 String quintet/Alban Berg/EMI CDC7 47018-2
82 Impromptus D899/D935/Lupu/Decca 411 711-2DH

Robert Schumann
83 Kinderszenen/Waldszenen, etc/Pires/ Erato ECD 88092

Dmitri Shostakovich
84 Symphony No5/Haitink/Decca 410 017-2DH
85 Symphony No10/Karajan/DG 413 361-2GH
86 'Cello concertos/Schiff/Philips 412 526-2PH

Jean Sibelius
87 Symphony No1/Järvi/BIS CD-221
88 Symphony No2/Ashkenazy/Decca 410 206-2DH
89 Symphony No5/Night-Ride and Sunrise/ Rattle/EMI CDC7 47006-2
90 Symphony No7/Tapiola/Ashkenazy/ Decca 411 935-2DH

Richard Strauss
91 Also Sprach Zarathustra/Don Juan/ Karajan/DG 410 959-2GH
92 Don Juan/Tod und Verklärung, etc/ Haitink/Philips 411 442-2PH

Igor Stravinsky
93 The Firebird/Davis/Philips 400 074-2PH
94 Petrushka/Scenes de Ballet/Bernstein/ DG 415 996-2GH
95 Apollon Musagète (c/w Copland)/ Dorati/Decca 414 457-2DH

Pyotr Tchaikovsky
96 Symphony No4/Jansons/Chandos CHAN8361
97 Symphony No5/Jansons/Chandos CHAN8351
98 Symphony No6/Ashkenazy/Decca 411 615-2DH
99 Piano concerto No1 (c/w Prokofiev Piano concerto No3)/Argerich/DG 415 062-2GH

Antonio Vivaldi
100 Violin concertos Op8 Nos1-4 *(The Four Seasons)*/Parrott/Denon C37-7283

NOTES ON THE REVIEWS
All Compact Discs discussed in these pages have been evaluated for both technical and artistic merit and, in addition to the detailed comments, a basic assessment of each has been given by a 'star rating' system. Stars have been awarded for both performance and recording, three indicating a Compact Disc of outstanding merit; two stars, a disc that is of very good standard; and one, a disc that is generally acceptable (often a one-star recording will accompany a three-star performance, the quality of the latter outweighing the disadvantages of the former).

As their titles suggest, our two volumes are complementary: *Classical Music on Compact Disc* covering the fields of symphonic, concerted, and other orchestral works, chamber and instrumental music, while *Opera on Compact Disc* encompasses the fields of opera, choral music and song. There are a couple of exceptions to this rule: the song cycles of Gustav Mahler, being symphonic in nature and closely allied to his symphonies have been included in *Classical Music on Compact Disc*; similarly the orchestral songs of Frederick Delius have been included in that volume.

Wherever appropriate, opus numbers have been appended to the works evaluated, or generally accepted catalogue numbers (i.e., the Köchel numbering for Mozart (K), and Peter Ryom's (RV) system for Vivaldi).

In listing the alternatives available on Compact Disc (where applicable) space has sometimes precluded a full listing and an abbreviated personal choice has been included.

Inevitably, additions have been made to the CD catalogue since these books were compiled, although we have attempted to be as up-to-date as possible – even recommending some likely 'winners' that experience of the LP version suggested would make successful CDs! Suffice to say, however, that the majority of Compact Discs reviewed here are unlikely to be surpassed in the foreseeable future, and should prove wholly rewarding.

Generally, the sequence adopted for reviews in *Classical Music on Compact Disc* commences with symphonies, concertos and other orchestral works and continues through chamber music and instrumental music.

Abbreviations used are listed below, and throughout we have prefixed composers and works other than the principal compositions on a disc with c/w (coupled with). Additionally, in the listings of alternatives, for reasons of space, the Deutsche Grammophon label has been abbreviated throughout to **DG**.

In common with most record labels, we have adopted the international standard coding for the description of the mastering process employed for Compact Disc issues. **DDD** therefore indicates that the recording has been produced entirely digitally: digital recording and digital mastering. **ADD** indicates an original analogue recording which has been digitally remastered in its transfer to Compact Disc. **AAD** refers to an analogue recording processed through analogue transfer equipment before the making of the Compact Disc master. This last system is decreasing in use as more and more record labels acquire digital remastering equipment.

COMMON ABBREVIATIONS USED IN THIS BOOK
AAM — Academy of Ancient Music; **arr** — arranged; **ASMF** — Academy of St Martin-in-the-Fields; **b.** — born; **BPO** — Berlin Philharmonic Orchestra; **CBSO** — City of Birmingham Symphony Orchestra; **CE** — Chamber Ensemble; **CO** — Chamber Orchestra; **cpte** — complete; **d.** — died; **ECO** — English Chamber Orchestra; **ed.** — edited; **exc.** — excerpt(s); **FNO** — French National Orchestra; **LAPO** — Los Angeles Philharmonic Orchestra; **LPO** — London Philharmonic Orchestra; **LSO** — London Symphony Orchestra; **NYPO** — New York Philharmonic Orchestra; **Op.** — Opus; **PO** — Philharmonia Orchestra; **Qt.** — Quartet; **rec.** — recorded; **RPO** — Royal Philharmonic Orchestra; **RSO** — Radio Symphony Orchestra; **SNO** — Scottish National Orchestra; **SO** — Symphony Orchestra; **SRO** — Suisse Romande Orchestra; **trans.** — transcribed; **VCM** — Vienna Concentus Musicus; **VPO** — Vienna Philharmonic Orchestra.

JOHANN SEBASTIAN BACH
(b. Eisenach, Thuriniga, Germany, 21 March 1685;d. Leipzig, 28 July 1750)

The provision of music for the courts and churches of protestant Northern Germany had become something of a family business by the time that most renowned of the musicians to carry the Bach name was born in 1685. Johann Sebastian belonged to the fifth generation to make a life in music; his sons and grandchildren would ensure the continuance of the tradition for yet another two.

When his parents died within a year of one another, in 1694 and 1695, the young Bach went to live with his elder brother, Johann Christoph, and from him learnt the clavichord. A three-year scholarship to the Benedictine school of St Michael's at Lüneberg continued his development as an all-round instrumentalist.

By 1703, he was organist and choirmaster at Arnstadt, and had become a great admirer of the Danish organist and composer, Diderik Buxtehude whom, legend has it, Bach once trekked two hundred miles to hear play.

Marriage to his second cousin, Maria Barbara, in 1707 was followed by a nine-year tenure at the court of Weimar, a period that saw his genius truly flourish: many of the great organ works date from this time. However, it was the open-minded and receptive establishment at Cöthen, his source of employment from 1717, which stimulated Bach to produce much of his finest instrumental music, including the most famous of his concerted works, the *Brandenburg Concertos*.

He was stunned by the death of his beloved wife in 1720, but soon after married Anna Magdalena Wilcken, whose chronicles of their life together fill in much of the detail about Bach that we would otherwise lack. What we do know is that he was a short-tempered character, and not one to fight shy of an argument. At one time, he was even imprisoned, albeit briefly, for his insolence towards his employers. He was also a prodigious father as well as composer, being responsible for twenty children by his two wives, although several failed to survive infancy.

Where the need at Weimar and Cöthen was for instrumental music, it is to Bach's next – and final – appointment that we owe the bulk of the religious masterpieces, the cantatas, passions, masses and motets.

In June 1722, the post of cantor to St Thomas' Church and School in

Johann Sebastian Bach, most renowned member of a German musical family that encompassed seven generations of composers and performers.

J. S. BACH

Leipzig, where as cantor of St Thomas', Bach was inspired to his greatest choral works.

Leipzig became vacant. There were six applicants, including Bach, and first choice was a fellow composer, but a lesser one, Georg Philipp Telemann. Bach, incredible though it seems now, was no more than third choice.

Ironically, he probably would not have thought about leaving Cöthen at all had it not been for the marriage of his patron there, Prince Leopold, to a wife who had little time or taste for music.

There followed twenty-seven productive years at Leipzig and Bach died still holding the office (notwithstanding now total blindness) he was originally given so reluctantly. Despite an obituary notice that described him as *'the greatest organ and clavier player that ever lived'*, no one yet regarded Bach as one of the few imperishable giants of music, so not a single monument was erected to his memory. Further, his music fell into almost total neglect for some eighty years until revived by the enthusiastic advocacy of, among others, Felix Mendelssohn and Robert Schumann.

The tercentenary celebrations of 1985 have ensured very good representation for Bach on Compact Disc, certainly in the instrumental field. Moreover, a great many of the performances are by ensembles such as The English Concert, whose quest for authenticity has produced fascinating and refreshing results.

BRANDENBURG CONCERTOS: NO1 IN F MAJOR BWV1046*/NO2 IN F MAJOR BWV1047*/NO3 IN G MAJOR BWV1048†/ NO4 IN G MAJOR BWV1049†/NO5 IN D MAJOR BWV1050†/NO6 IN B FLAT MAJOR BWV1051*
Linde Consort
Director: Hans-Martin Linde
EMI Reflexe CDC 7 47045-2*; CDC 7 47046-2† (two discs, available separately)
DDD Running time: 96.44
Performance: ★ ★ ★   Recording: ★ ★ ★

There is no want for alternatives in these most popular of Baroque concertos. They were written between 1717 and 1721, during Bach's Cöthen period, for Christian Ludwig, Margrave of Brandenburg.

Interpretatively, there is little to choose between Trevor Pinnock's lively and refreshing performances on Archiv and these comparably well-judged and well-played readings from Hans-Martin Linde and his colleagues.

Where the Linde set does score, however, is in the recording which allows a degree more 'air' around the instruments and is not so vividly 'up-front' as the Archiv sound, which as a consequence can become somewhat fatiguing.

Although both sets employ original instruments (or copies) and seek authenticity of scale in the Concertos, neither seems lightweight or tonally abrasive. Linde's sparkling performances are very stylish indeed and should satisfy most seeking a set of the *Brandenburgs* to live comfortably with.

Other recordings on CD (selection):
English Concert/Trevor Pinnock/Archiv 410 500-2AH/410 501-2AH
VCM/Nikolaus Harnoncourt/TelDec

J. S. BACH

ZK8.42823/ZK8.42840
Amsterdam Baroque Orch/Ton Koopman/
Erato ECD88054/5
AAM/Christopher Hogwood/L'Oiseau-Lyre
414 187-2OH2

CONCERTOS FOR TWO HARPSICHORDS: NO1 IN C MINOR BWV1060/NO2 IN C MAJOR BWV1061/ NO3 IN C MINOR BWV1062
Kenneth Gilbert, Trevor Pinnock: Harpsichords
The English Concert
Archiv 415 131-2AH
DDD Running time: 47.45
Performance: ★ ★ (★)   Recording: ★ ★

Two of these concertos began life in other guises, the C minor in a version for two violins or violin and oboe, while BWV1062 is nothing less than an arrangement for two keyboards of the great Double Violin Concerto BWV1043. It is interesting enough, but cannot match the stringed instruments in bringing out the beauty of the score, especially in the poetic slow movement.
   Three fairly vigorous and forceful performances receive an appropriately forward and bright-ish balance, although the sheer clarity of texture is striking. The no-nonsense approach will not suit everyone's idea of how Bach should be played, but there is no denying its validity, or its freshness and crispness.

Other recordings on CD:
Christoph Eschenbach/Justus Franz/
   Hamburg PO/DG 415 655-2GH

CONCERTOS FOR THREE HARPSICHORDS: NO1 IN D MINOR BWV1063/NO2 IN C MAJOR BWV1064/ CONCERTO FOR FOUR HARPSICHORDS IN A MINOR BW1065*
Trevor Pinnock, Kenneth Gilbert, Lars Ulrik Mortensen, Nicholas Kraemer*: Harpsichords
English Concert
Director (from the harpsichord): Trevor Pinnock
Archiv 400 041-2AH
DDD Running time: 39.42
Performance: ★ ★ ★   Recording: ★ (★)

Sparkling performances, with lithe, immaculate playing from all the soloists, which might even persuade those who believe the multiple harpsichord concertos to be something of a passing aberration on the part of Bach, to re-consider. A pity, therefore, that the recording does them less than justice. The harpsichords, each a different type of instrument, are not sufficiently clearly defined, the whole a somewhat confused collage of sound. The fourteen-piece string orchestra behind them fares little better. A missed opportunity, in some respects, although an enjoyable enough disc overall. A few less microphones on the session might have produced a much better result.

Other recordings on CD:
Michel Beroff/Jean-Phillipe Collard/Gabriel
   Tacchino/Bruno Rigutto/Paris Orch Ens/
   Jean-Pierre Wallez/EMI CDC 7 47063-2
Christoph Eschenbach/Justus Franz/Gerhard
   Oppitz/Hamburg PO/DG 415 655-2GH

VIOLIN CONCERTOS: NO1 IN A MINOR BWV 1041/NO2 IN E MAJOR BWV1042/ CONCERTO FOR TWO VIOLINS BWV1043*
Jaime Laredo: Violin
John Tunnell: Violin*
Scottish Chamber Orchestra
Director (from the violin): Jaime Laredo
Pickwick IMP Red Label PCD808
DDD Running time: 46.48
Performance: ★ ★ ★   Recording: ★ ★ ★

There are some excellent bargains to be had on Pickwick's budget CD label, and this is most certainly one of them. The lively, detailed recording is ideal for these works, spacious and pleasantly reverberant and with a finely-judged balance between soloist (and soloists) and orchestra.
   Without opting for the full period instrument approach, the performances are 'authentic' in scale, although not eschewing all opportunities for expressive touches. As a compromise between the severity of some 'big-name' recordings of the Violin Concertos, and the self-indulgence of others, these stylish and effortlessly enjoyable readings by the under-valued Jaime Laredo, and his Scottish players come highly recommended.

VIOLIN CONCERTOS: NO1 IN A MINOR BWV1041/NO2 IN E MAJOR BWV1042/ CONCERTO FOR TWO VIOLINS BWV1043*
Jaap Schröder: Violin
Christopher Hirons: Violin*
The Academy of Ancient Music
Director: Christopher Hogwood
L'Oiseau-Lyre 400 080-2OH
DDD Running time: 45.09
Performance: ★ ★ (★)   Recording: ★ ★

These products of Bach's fascination with the Italian concerto style (especially that of Vivaldi), like the *Brandenburgs*, date from his service with Prince Leopold of Cöthen (1717–21). Here Hogwood and Schröder attempt to perform them in the manner of that period – in other words, before they were over-sweetened by successive generations of romantically-inclined fiddlers! Those who prefer the latter style would be advised to steer clear of these brisk, taut, but undoubtedly refreshing readings.
   The recording is good, if fairly forward and starkly analytical and, given the inherently 'sour' quality of the instruments themselves, there is a danger this one might 'fizz' on bright-sounding systems. Some

J. S. BACH

traffic rumble is discernible, and the sound, if anything, is a touch light and dry in the bass.

The complete antithesis of the Academy's approach is that of Anne-Sophie Mutter and Salvatore Accardo on EMI: here the warmth and richness of expression verges on the glutinous. 'Authenticity' is on offer in versions by the English Concert on Archiv and La Petite Bande on Deutsche Harmonia-Mundi; for a 'modern' version that is not indulgently romantic, that of the Scottish Chamber Orchestra (reviewed above) can be recommended.

Other recordings on CD (selection):
Sigiswald Kuijken/Lucy van Dael/La Petite Bande/Deutsche Harmonia-Mundi 1C 157 199743-2

THE MUSICAL OFFERING BWV1079
(edited and orchestrated by Neville Marriner)
Iona Brown, Malcolm Latchem, Roger Garland: Violins/Stephen Shingles: Viola/Denis Vigay: 'Cello/William Bennett: Flute/Nicholas Kraemer: Organ and Harpsichord
Academy of St Martin-in-the-Fields
Director: Neville Marriner
Philips 412 800-2PH
DDD Running time: 48.51
Performance: ★ ★ ★
Recording: ★ ★ (★)

Bach's improvisations on a theme devised by the monarch himself so impressed King Frederick II of Prussia, a finished score along the same lines was requested and duly despatched on 7 July 1747. Bach certainly took a lot of trouble over the work, incorporating thirteen pieces in all, including ten canons on the 'royal' theme of staggering complexity and workmanship, and further flattering the recipient (who was a flautist) by incorporating a sonata for flute, violin and continuo.

Marriner has produced his own arrangement of the work for this recording, quite legitimately as Bach left this aspect of performance fairly fluid. And what a fine performance it is, with superb solo contributions all round. The 1979 recording – rich, tonally excellent and detailed, if lacking a little in 'real' atmosphere – comes up well in this digital transfer.

Other recordings on CD:
Leipzig Bach Collegium/Capriccio 10032
Musica Antique Köln/Reinhard Goebel/ Archiv 413 642-2AH3

ORCHESTRAL SUITES: NO1 IN C MAJOR BWV1066*/NO2 IN B MINOR BWV1067*/NO3 IN D MAJOR BWV1068†/NO4 IN D MAJOR BWV1069†
English Baroque Soloists
Conductor: John Eliot Gardiner
Erato ECD88048*; ECD88049† (two discs, available separately)
DDD Running time: 96.42
Performance: ★ ★ ★
Recording: ★ ★ (★)

The Baroque orchestral suite was a development of the French *ouverture*, a creation of the composer, Jean-Baptiste Lully. A stately, dignified opening movement (although punctuated by a lively central section where the orchestra's principals could display their skills) was followed by a series of shorter, dance sections. Bach followed this pattern, but not slavishly, introducing many novel features of his own and by no means obeying the 'rules' about the composition of the dance sequences.

Considering these four works contain some of Bach's most engaging and, these days, most popular music – the *Badinerie* of No2 and the *Air* of No3 for example – it is astonishing that the first published edition did not appear until 1835, such was the neglect of the composer after his death.

Overall, Gardiner's performances are currently the best on offer, lively, elegantly pointed and unmannered and he receives a well-balanced and well-integrated recording. It is sweet-toned and, if slightly forward, faithfully presents the excellent playing of the English Baroque Soloists. Both discs are immensely enjoyable.

Other recordings on CD (selection):
La Petite Bande/Sigiswald Kuijken/Deutsche Harmonia Mundi 1C 157 199930/1-2

GOLDBERG VARIATIONS BWV 988
Trevor Pinnock: Harpsichord
Archiv 415 130-2AH
AAD Running time: 56.50
Performance: ★ ★ ★
Recording: ★ ★ (★)

Johann Gottlieb Goldberg was one of Bach's most talented pupils, and this demanding set of thirty variations was written for him (between 1741 and 1742) to play at the behest of an insomniac nobleman who could only get to sleep to the sound of music. However, this complex work, scored for double-keyboard harpsichord hardly qualifies as soporific, especially in a performance as brisk and articulate as Trevor Pinnock's. It is full of imaginative touches, wholly responsive to the varying demands of mood and rhythm, and Pinnock sensibly opts to take the repeats in about half the variations, not outstaying his welcome.

The rather close 1980 recording of the restored two-manual Rückers harpsichord of 1646 is a realistic one though a little blurred at the edges and lacking some of the crystalline quality that enhances many newer recordings of such instruments.

Other recordings on CD:
Glenn Gould/CBS MK37779
Fernando Valenti/Sine Qua Non 79045-2

J. S. BACH

DIE KUNST DER FUGE (THE ART OF FUGUE) BWV1080
Davitt Moroney: Harpsichord
Harmonia-Mundi HMC90 1169/70 (2 discs)
DDD Running time: 98.47
Performance: ★ ★ ★   Recording: ★ ★ ★

This extraordinary amalgam of music and science was left unfinished at Bach's death, the open score devoid of any indication as to the instrument (or instruments) for which it had been written. In a total of fourteen fugues and four canons, a simple theme is subjected to a consummate metamorphosis, the whole as symmetrically balanced as any piece of classical architecture.

In the absence of any clear direction in the score, *The Art of Fugue* has been transcribed for chamber ensemble, clavichord, piano, organ, and as here, harpsichord. Davitt Moroney's teacher, the great keyboard player Gustav Leonhardt, made a convincing argument some years ago for the latter instrument, and Moroney eloquently restates the case, both in words and music.

It is a well-conceived and convincing interpretation, with a deft completion of the final, unfinished fugue (although omitting the two-harpsichord transcription of Contrapunctus 13) and the degree of flexibility Moroney allows himself is welcome in music that is far from 'easy'.

The harpsichord looms large, centre-stage, although in a pleasant pool of ambience.

Other recordings on CD:
Musica Antiqua Köln/Reinhard Goebel/
  Archiv 413 642-2AH3

TOCCATA AND FUGUE IN D MINOR BWV565/TOCCATA, ADAGIO AND FUGUE IN C MAJOR BWV564/TOCCATA AND FUGUE IN F MAJOR BWV540/ TOCCATA AND FUGUE IN D MINOR 'DORIAN' BWV538
Ton Koopman: Organ
Archiv 410 999-2AH
DDD Running time: 46.13
Performance: ★ ★ (★)
Recording: ★ ★ ★

It is ironic that doubts should remain about the attribution of the famous D minor work, since it ranks as one of the three or four pieces by Bach with which just about everyone is familiar. It is certainly the earliest of the toccatas and fugues here, the other three probably dating from the early-to-middle Weimar years, given that those in C and F betray a noticeable Italian influence.

Ton Koopman is well-recorded at the organ of the Maassluis Grotekerk in Holland, an instrument built between 1730 and 1732, but restored in 1975. The inner clarity of the fugues to BWV540 and BWV564 is quite remarkable, although the unrelieved brilliance of the sound does make the ear wish for more of the kind of contrast afforded by the latter's central *adagio* movement. However, with a satisfying sense of space, a good balance between pedals and manuals, and the kind of fine delineation of texture that CD – given the right recording – can bring to the most densely woven organ scores, this is one of the most recommendable of the currently-available Bach recitals.

Other recordings on CD:
(Toccata and Fugue BWV538)
Peter Hurford/Argo 411 824-2DH
(Toccata and Fugue BWV540)
Michael Murray/Telarc CD80049
Pierre Bardon/Pierre Verany PV710811
(Toccata, Adagio and Fugue BWV564)
Peter Hurford/Argo 411 824-2
Herbert Tachezi/TelDec ZK8.43191
(Toccata and Fugue in D minor – see below)

TOCCATA AND FUGUE IN D MINOR BWV565/PASSACAGLIA AND FUGUE IN C MINOR BWV582/FANTASIA AND FUGUE IN G MINOR BWV542/ CONCERTO IN A MINOR (AFTER VIVALDI) BWV593/FUGUE IN G MINOR BWV578
Marie-Claire Alain: Organ
Erato ECD88004
DDD Running time: 49.36
Performance: ★ ★ ★   Recording: ★ ★ ★

A good investment for those wanting three of the major organ works on one disc, with generally fine performances pleasingly recorded. Additionally, the Vivaldi transcription and the exquisite G minor fugue come over exceptionally well.

The engineers have allowed a good measure of air around the Schwenkendel organ, giving a strong sense of space and ambience to the recording. Distancing also takes care of any mechanical noise which might intrude, giving an end result which is tonally attractive without losing impact.

Other recordings on CD:
(Organ Concerto No2 only: see other reviews for remainder)
Michael Murray/Telarc CD80088
Daniel Chorzempa/Philips 412 116-2PH

J. S. BACH

TOCCATA AND FUGUE IN D MINOR BWV565/SIX SCHUBLER CHORALES BWV645-650/PRELUDE AND FUGUE IN G MINOR BWV535/TRIO IN C MINOR BWV585/PRELUDE AND FUGUE IN C MAJOR BWV545/FUGUE IN G MINOR BWV578/FANTASIA IN C MAJOR BWV570/TRIO IN D MINOR BWV583
Hans Otto: Organ
Denon C37-7004
DDD Running time: 55.37
Performance: ★ ★ (★)
Recording: ★ ★ ★

The focus of interest here is the instrument itself, the 18th Century Silbermann organ of Freiburg Cathedral. And what a splendid sound it makes, especially when recorded as faithfully as this, firmly-imaged, but allowed to expand into the acoustic and become an integral part of it. It is not hard (with the right volume setting) to imagine yourself in a seat somewhere towards the middle of the nave, and the recording does not tamper with that perspective at all.

The programme, apart from the obligatory BWV565, has a reasonably fresh look. Although it is virtually certain that the C minor Trio, BWV585, is not by Bach at all, but one of his Leipzig students, Johann Ludwig Krebs, it nevertheless remains, an enjoyable enough piece, as is its lyrical and richly ornamented companion BWV583. The Fantasia BWV570 and the 'little G minor' Fugue, BWV578, are both delightful pieces, and the six transcriptions of Protestant chorales, which gained their nickname through being published by one of Bach's pupils, Johann Schubler, are justly famous. Is there a more joyful melody than that of BWV650?

These are generally good performances from Hans Otto – his Toccata and Fugue in D minor has impact and virtuosity in abundance, although a slightly slower, gentler pulse for *Wachet auf* would have been preferable. He misses some of the warmth in the other pieces, too.

Mechanical noise from the organ is audible during the quieter passages, although the ear readily adjusts to it. It should be noted that the back cover of the booklet gives the correct indexing numbers, not, as appears at first glance, the list of works on the third page.

Other recordings on CD:
(Schubler Chorales)
Maire-Claire Alain/Erato ECD88030
Daniel Chorzempa/Philips 412 117-2PH
Ton Koopman/Archiv 413 638-2AH3
(Prelude and Fugue BWV545 – selected alternative)
Michael Murray/Telarc CD80097
(Fugue in G minor BWV578)
Marie-Claire Alain/Erato ECD88004
Helmuth Rilling/Denon C37-7039
(Toccata and Fugue in D minor BWV565 – selected alternatives)
Ton Koopman/Archiv 413 638-2AH3 and Archiv 410 999-2AH
Marie-Claire Alain/Erato ECD88004
Pierre Bardon/Pierre Verany PV710811
Michael Murray/Telarc CD80088
Peter Hurford/Argo 411-824-2

FANTASIA AND FUGUE IN G MINOR BWV542/TOCCATA IN F MAJOR BWV 540/PASSACAGLIA AND FUGUE IN C MINOR BWV582/TWO CHORALE PRELUDES: VATER UNSER IN HIMMELREICH BWV737, ALLE MENSCHEN MÜSSEN STERBEN BWV643
Michael Murray: Organ
Telarc CD80049
DDD Running time: 39.51
Performance: ★ ★ ★   Recording: ★ ★ ★

Of particular interest here is the instrument itself, a mid-nineteenth century, German-built Walcker (rebuilt by Methuen), and the first concert organ to be installed in the United States. It certainly possesses a splendid sound, rich and full-bodied, but with that degree of brilliance which suits the Baroque repertoire.

Good, unmannered performances from Michael Murray in a well-balanced programme where the cool serenity of the two chorale preludes provides the perfect 'dessert' to the rich main course: the elaborate Gothic majesty of the G minor Fantasia and Fugue, written in 1715 when Bach was at the height of his virtuoso powers, and the sublime Passacaglia with its magnificently-woven tapestry of variations. The recording is excellent, but playing time is mean.

Other recordings on CD:
(Fantasia and Fugue in G minor BWV542)
Marie-Claire Alain/Erato ECD88004
Helmuth Rilling/Denon C37-7039
Pierre Bardon/Pierre Verany PV710811
Herbert Tachezi/TelDec ZK8.43119
(Passacaglia and Fugue in C minor BWV582)
Ton Koopman/Archiv 413 638-2AH3
Marie-Claire Alain/Erato ECD88004
Pierre Bardon/Pierre Verany PV710811
Peter Hurford/Argo 411 842-2ZH

J. S. BACH

TRIO SONATAS: NO1 IN E FLAT MAJOR BWV525/NO2 IN C MINOR BWV526/NO3 IN D MINOR BWV527/NO4 IN E MINOR BWV528/NO5 IN C MAJOR BWV529/NO6 IN G MAJOR BWV530
Marie-Claire Alain: Organ
Erato ECD88146
DDD Running time: 67.15
Performance: ★ ★ ★   Recording: ★ ★ ★

The six Trio Sonatas were intended as teaching pieces for the eldest of the Bach sons, Wilhelm Friedemann, who had proved a talented keyboard player. Composed between 1723 and 1727, they make few concessions to the youth of the intended player, being both complex and varied.

These affectionate and enjoyable performances by Marie-Claire Alain were recorded at the organ of St Hilaire de Nätels, Glaris, Switzerland, and benefit from a warm acoustic that comfortably 'embraces' The organ is decently distanced, and the whole is convincingly atmospheric.

On the strength of her recordings for the French Erato label, Marie-Claire Alain proves a consistently fine Bach interpreter.

INVENTIONS AND SINFONIAS (complete) BWV772-801
Huguette Dreyfus: Harpsichord
Denon C37-7566
DDD Running time: 49.49
Performance: ★ ★ ★   Recording: ★ ★ ★

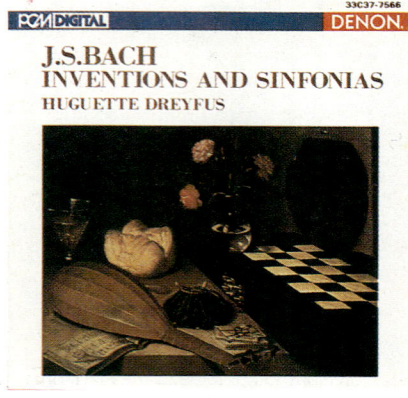

The autograph manuscript of what are mere teaching pieces, but fascinating ones, was completed in 1723 the intended pupil being Bach's son, Wilhelm Friedemann. Encompassing the full range of keys, from C Major through to B minor, there is hardly a musical device, or facet of expression, left unrepresented among these thirty miniatures, and French harpsichordist Huguette Dreyfus graces each one with playing of precision and refinement. She has a worthy ally in the pleasantly warm-toned Hemsch harpsichord, which is tastefully set back in a subtle acoustic (often the harpsichord is recorded far too closely, which not only distorts the instrument's sound, but amplifies its inevitable mechanical noise to a distracting degree).

A benefit of Compact Disc is that it allows the listener to programme his player for the alternative arrangements of the pieces suggested by Bach and others, such as pairing each 'invention' with the 'sinfonia' of equivalent key. The accompanying booklet thoughtfully provides numbered charts for just this purpose. This is a disc that rewards exploration.

CHROMATIC FANTASIA AND FUGUE IN D MINOR BWV903/CONCERTO IN F MAJOR BWV971/FANTASIA IN C MINOR BWV906/PRELUDE AND FUGUE IN A MINOR BWV894
Huguette Dreyfus: Harpsichord
Denon C37-7233
DDD Running time: 39.33
Performance: ★ ★ ★
Recording: ★ ★ (★)

There are many good things about this collection of some of the finest solo harpsichord compositions, and some not-so-good, especially the short playing time.

That said, Huguette Dreyfus offers dazzling playing in the faster movements, especially of the Chromatic Fantasia and Fugue (BWV903), where it seems Bach wanted to explore the full potential of the new instrument acquired by the Cöthen household around 1719. Equally arresting is the *Concerto in the Italian Style* (BWV971) from Klavierübung I of 1735.

The 1976 recording (Denon were early into digital) of the Schütze harpsichord is a little on the dry side, and although the instrument has a rich-toned and weighty bass register, a certain brittle quality affects the mid-band. But these are minor criticisms and, overall, there is much to relish in these performances.

Other recordings on CD:
(Chromatic Fantasia and Fugue BWV903)
Trevor Pinnock/Archiv 413 638-2AH3
Alfred Brendel/Philips 412 252-2PH
(Italian Concerto BWV971)
Trevor Pinnock/Archiv 413 638-2AH3 and 413 591-2AH
Alfred Brendel/Philips 412 252-2PH

SUITE IN E MINOR BWV996/FANTASIA AND FUGUE IN A MINOR BWV904/ TOCCATA IN E MINOR BWV914/ CAPRICCIO IN B FLAT MAJOR BWV992/ PRELUDE, FUGUE AND ALLEGRO BWV998
Gustav Leonhardt; Harpsichord
Philips 416 141-2PH
DDD Running time: 53.32
Performance: ★ ★ ★
Recording: ★ ★ (★)

There are some rare delights here, not least the *Capriccio* which Bach wrote as a farewell present for his brother who was leaving home to join a military band. This genial, six-part offering contrasts with the darker timbres of the E minor Toccata and the mature style of the E flat Prelude, Fugue and Allegro, the latter originally written for lute, like the Suite in E minor. However, both fit comfortably into the compass of the harpsichord and are beautifully realised by Leonhardt, whose playing these days is more yielding than it once was.

The recording fully captures the wonderful sound of the harpsichord, a William David of 1984, after an 18th Century Mietke. If anything, it is a little too full, although solidly imaged. A little more distancing might have been preferable, especially when Leonhardt's sniffles are so audible!

However, there is no denying that this is a rewarding recital in every way.

SIX SUITES FOR SOLO 'CELLO BWV1007-12: NO1 IN G MAJOR/NO2 IN D MINOR/NO3 IN C MAJOR/NO4 IN E FLAT MAJOR/NO5 IN C MINOR/NO6 IN D MAJOR
Paul Tortelier: 'Cello
EMI CDC 7 47090/1/2-2 (3 discs, available separately)
DDD Running time: 144.49
Performance: ★ ★ (★)   Recording: ★ ★

It was the great Spanish 'cellist Pablo Casals who rescued these visionary works from relative obscurity and introduced them to a wide audience through performances which, although now regarded as fairly free interpretations. Although he takes no such textural liberties, Tortelier's view is a similarly romantic one, his readings robust and strongly-projected, and the recording, too, is on the grand scale. It was made in the lively resonance of London's Temple Church and, although there is no blurring of detail, even in the quicker movements where

Tortelier is at his most dazzling, a drier acoustic might have been preferable. There is no questioning the lovely sound of the instrument, however, which is vividly captured – along with bowing noise and other sundry intrusions! That said, a little more warmth would not have gone amiss.

Despite the reservations, Tortelier's remains the most recommendable of current Compact Disc versions, although not for Bach purists. Interestingly, the most satisfying recording in any medium is also in the EMI catalogue: that by Heinrich Schiff. Were it to appear on CD, assuming a competent transfer, it would undoubtedly displace Tortelier both technically and artistically.

Other recordings on CD:
Mari Fujiwara/Denon C37-7373/5
Lynn Harrell/Decca 414 163-2DH2
Mischa Maisky/DG 415 416-2GX3

SONATAS AND PARTITAS FOR SOLO VIOLIN BWV1001-6: SONATAS NO1 IN G MINOR/NO2 IN A MINOR/NO3 IN C MAJOR/PARTITAS NO1 IN B MINOR/ NO2 IN D MINOR/NO3 IN D MAJOR
Shlomo Mintz: Violin
Deutsche Grammophon 413 810-2GH3 (3 discs)
DDD Running time: 144.25
Performance: ★ ★ ★   Recording: ★ ★ ★

The Cöthen years proved a high-water mark in Bach's instrumental writing, responsible among other works for the Suites for Solo 'Cello and this set of Sonatas and Partitas for Solo Violin. Both have become the ultimate test for exponents of the two instruments, not solely in the technical skill required, but in the ability to obtain the fullest emotional and intellectual expression from just a single instrument.

On both counts, Shlomo Mintz, playing a Guarnarius of 1742, succeeds marvellously, his performances enhanced by an outstandingly natural recording. It was made in a church cloister, and in terms of timbre, balance and presence is nothing less than ideal. The whole makes for compelling listening: Bach's invention and imagination can rarely have sounded so utterly persuasive, although if Deutsche Harmonia-Mundi were to release Sigiswald Kuijken's recent version on Compact Disc, it would present formidable artistic and technical competition. It, too, brings revealing insights to these works and makes fascinating listening.

Other recordings on CD:
Jean-Jacques Kantorow/Denon C37-7405/7

BÉLA BARTÓK
(b. Nagyszentmiklós, Hungary, 25 March 1881; d. New York, 26 September 1945)

East meets West in the music of Béla Bartók. In synthesising the folk music of his native Hungary with formal classical disciplines, he created a host of compositions where outward sophistication and ordered construction enclose and enhance a motivation that is frequently elemental and primitive. From the rhythms, textures and sonorities of his music, even those of the rigorously 'classical' string quartets, it is easy to detect an empathy with things Eastern, even if the remarkable craftmanship which has shaped it owes all to the West.

Bartók's interest in folk music was first aroused during his early life in the country, where his mother was his first 'music teacher'. Later, at Budapest Conservatoire, where he studied until the age of twenty-two, major influences were Liszt and Wagner – as they were for just about every young composer of the period. Then came the impact of Richard Strauss' tone poems, *Zarathustra* and *Heldenleben*, which inspired the young Bartók to return to composition after a couple of years spent developing his impressive skills as a pianist.

Equally important was the discovery in 1905 of the *true* Hungarian folk music, the music which had evolved naturally among peasant communities, rather than the popular 'gypsy melodies', which had been consciously composed in a folk idiom. Together with his friend, the composer Zoltan Kodály, Bartók researched and collected peasant music throughout Hungary, Rumania, Czechoslovakia and the Balkan states, travelling as far afield as Algeria before the First World War put an end to his journeying.

Through such research, Bartók discovered archaic musical scales and from them developed new, startling harmonies of his own. Gradually, he abandoned the orthodox major and minor scale altogether, although many of the works that resulted were greeted with loud disapproval in Budapest, where he had been appointed a professor at the Conservatoire. Among compositions from this period were the ballet *The Wooden Prince*, and *Bluebeard's Castle*, his only venture into opera. He became fascinated by the potential of percussion instruments, and the percussive qualities of the piano, as is very evident in the first two piano concertos. Bartók also nurtured a keen ear for natural sounds, especially nocturnal ones: a number of his slow movements, the 'night musics', bear witness to this preoccupation.

A thoughtful Bartók portrayed on the cover of a score published in Budapest during 1935 five years before he left Hungary.

In discussion with the violinist, Rudolph Kolish while rehearsing Music for Strings, Percussion and Celesta *in 1940.*

In 1940 the Second World War drove the composer, along with many other artists, into exile in the United States. There he took up a temporary post at Columbia University and was awarded a Doctorate of Music. Despite failing health, he completed some of his finest work in this period, the Concerto for Orchestra and Third Piano Concerto among them. One was left unfinished, the lovely Viola Concerto, when he died on 26 September 1945 after a year in hospital.

The Viola Concerto is one of Bartók's major compositions as yet unrepresented on CD. Surprisingly, so is the Second Violin Concerto, and the first two piano concertos (although Deutsche Grammophon are rumoured to be reissuing Maurizio Pollini's recording of these with Claudio Abbado and the Chicago Symphony). Alternative versions of the String Quartets – in temperament, ambition and sense of searching 'inner communion' so akin to the late quartets of Beethoven – would also be very welcome.

CONCERTO FOR ORCHESTRA SZ116
TWO PICTURES SZ46(OP10)
Concertgebouw Orchestra, Amsterdam
Conductor: Antal Dorati
Philips 411 132-2PH
DDD Running time: 54.05
Performance: ★ ★ ★   Recording: ★ ★ ★

The *Concerto for Orchestra*, a work derived from the concertante style of the 18th Century in which instruments were each given prominence within a group of players as a whole, was composed in 1943 to a commission from the conductor, Serge Koussevitzky. Bartók, by then living in the United States, was already suffering from the leukaemia which was to prove fatal two years later. But despite the illness, he was still composing as well as ever, as the *Concerto* demonstrates. It was enthusiastically received at the first performance in Boston in 1944, and has since become his most popular work. With its fund of melody and strong folk-dance influence, that is hardly surprising.

It is the folk element, as well as the genial and witty side of the music, which shines through in Dorati's amiable reading. And in this way, he surely gets closer to the heart of the score than the altogether tougher, more incisive Solti. He is also better recorded than Solti, whose Chicago recording is over-lit and lacking in depth. No such problem here: the clarity is still there, but so is a satisfactory distancing and layering of the orchestra, and the warm ambience of the Concertgebouw. The *Two Pictures* are not as desirable a 'filler' as the *Dance Suite* that Solti offers, but Dorati steals it with his splendid performance of the main work.

Other recordings on CD:
CSO/Georg Solti/Decca 400 052-2DH
BPO/Herbert von Karajan/DG 415 322-2GH

PIANO CONCERTO NO3* Sz119
(c/w PROKOFIEV PIANO CONCERTO NO3 IN C MAJOR OP26†)
Vladimir Ashkenazy: Piano
London Philharmonic Orchestra*
Conductor: Georg Solti*
London Symphony Orchestra†
Conductor: Andre Previn†
Decca 411 969-2DH
AAD Running time: 53.09
Performance: ★ ★ (Bartok)
★ ★ ★ (Prokofiev)   Recording: ★ ★

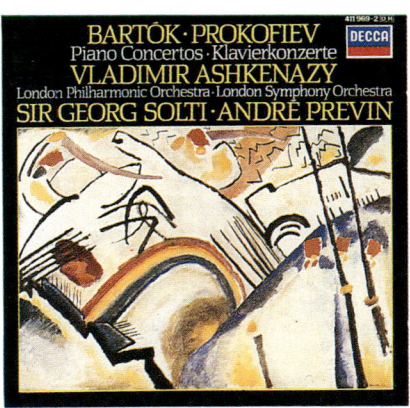

The connection between these two concertos is more than numerical: both were written after their composers had sought refuge in the United States, Bartók's in 1945, Prokofiev's in 1921. Both eschewed the aggressive modernism of their predecessors for something altogether more conventional in melody and mood – and more immediately accessible. Whatever their artistic qualities, the plain fact is that both concertos were composed with the intention of earning money; in Bartók's case for his wife, soon to become a widow. Indeed, Bartók just failed to complete the work before he died: the last seventeen bars were added by Tibor Serly.

If Bartók absorbed any influences while in the United States, they are to be heard in this enchanting work, with its slow movement reminiscent of a mysterious, sultry night,

BARTOK

punctuated by birdsong and insect noises. It also harks back, in its profound serenity, to the *Hymn of Thanksgiving* from Beethoven's Quartet Op132, and it is in this movement that Ashkenazy is at his best. A fast tempo loses some of the sense of wonderment in the first movement, but the Slav temperament of both soloist and conductor comes into its own in the third. The recording is good, but not helped by the forward balance of the piano, which becomes clangorous at times.

In the Prokoviev, the most classically traditional of his concertos, the rapport between Ashkenazy and Previn produces a marvellous result; the recording is better, too.

Other recordings on CD:
(Prokofiev Piano Concerto No3)
Martha Argerich/BPO/Claudio Abbado/ DG 415 062-2GH

**MUSIC FOR STRINGS, PERCUSSION AND CELESTA SZ106
DIVERTIMENTO FOR STRINGS SZ113**
Ferenc Liszt Chamber Orchestra, Budapest
Director: Janos Rolla
Hungaroton HCD12531-2
DDD Running time: 53.28
Performance: ★ ★ ★   Recording: ★ ★ ★

Even in his most avowedly neo-classical works, Bartók (unlike, say, Stravinsky) never wholly discarded the East European folk music idiom which he had so painstakingly researched in the early years of his life. The *Music for Strings, Percussion and Celesta* is a case in point: formal and symmetrical in structure, yet unmistakably elemental in motivation, from the turbulent rhythms of the second and fourth movements to the haunting, even sinister 'night music' of the first and third.

Boldly experimental in its colours, sonorities, and instrumental dialogues, the work is also notable for developing almost entirely from a single, darkly pregnant theme.

Bartók was quite emphatic about the effects he wanted from the combination of piano, harp, percussion, double string orchestra and the celesta (the latter resembling the glockenspiel in its use of hammered steel plates, but with the addition of a wooden resonator to each one, giving a distinctly ethereal quality to the sound). He was very specific about the layout and spatial relationships of the instruments, which makes the balance in a recording all the more important. This Hungarian production is most successful in this respect and the performances, both of the main work and of the contemporary (but slightly less remarkable) *Divertimento*, are mellow, affectionate and succeed in being exciting without being exaggerated; the tempi are nicely judged.

Other recordings on CD:
(*Music for strings, percussion and celesta* only)
Tokyo Metropolitan SO/Moshe Atzmon/ Denon C37-7122
Philadelphia O/Eugene Ormandy/EMI CDC7 47117-2
Detroit SO/Antal Dorati/Decca 411 894- 2DH
BPO/Herbert von Karajan/DG 415 322-2GH

STRING QUARTETS: NO1 OP7 SZ40, NO2 OP17 SZ67, NO3 SZ85, NO4 SZ91, NO5 SZ102, NO6 SZ114
Tackács Quartet
Hungaroton HCD12502/4-2 (3 disc set)
DDD Running time: 154.26
Performance: ★ ★ (★)
Recording: ★ ★ ★

Taken overall, the six quartets of Béla Bartók, like those of Beethoven, constitute an autobiographical essay. The composer's development can be charted through them, in Bartók's case from late Romanticism, through the powerful influence of folk music, to the search for new forms of expression and the exploration of a host of startling new sonorities within the medium.

The results are often sharp-edged, sour, even grotesque; some are mysterious and elusive, such as the opening movement of No2, others bizarre, the most memorable example being the sudden appearance of an 'out-of-tune barrel organ' effect punctuating the scurrying *presto* of the Fifth. There are also numerous echoes of Beethoven's last quartets, the obvious debt to the *Grosse Fuge* Op133 in No6 for one.

The youthful Tackács Quartet has the field virtually to itself on CD, but does offer performances of a standard that could only be challenged by the likes of the Tokyo ensemble (DG) or the passionate and authoritative Vegh Quartet (TelDec) should they appear in the medium. But it would be unfair to suggest that the Tackács versions, especially of the tougher, later works, are anything less than satisfying. For one thing, it is pleasing to have a recording that does not over-project the quartet and narrow its range. The players are set in a lively acoustic, with crisp imaging and inner clarity (no blurring of the instrumental lines), while managing to retain essential unity.

Invariably, a result of the close-up recording of chamber music is the distracting intrusion of noises made by the performers themselves, as is evident here. More specifically, much of Bartok's writing would benefit from a less oppressive presentation.

Hopefully, choice in these important works will eventually be enhanced on Compact Disc. The Tokyo set certainly deserves to be high on Deutsche Grammophon's list of analogue masters eligible for CD transfer, while there is always the newer, digital series by the Eder Quartet on TelDec, although this has still to be issued complete on LP in Britain.

Other recordings on CD:
(Quartet No3 only)
Sequoia Quartet/Delos/D-CD3004

LUDWIG VAN BEETHOVEN
(b. Bonn, Germany, 16 December 1770; d. Vienna, 26 March 1827)

Just as life was never easy for Beethoven, nor was composing. Not for him the astonishing facility of a Mozart, or dependable craftsmanship of a Bach; but, then, Beethoven was intent on 'breaking the musical rules' in a way none of his distinguished predecessors had attempted. As with most innovators, the creative process was a difficult, often tortuous one.

It was with Beethoven that music first became truly unpredictable. True, Mozart and Haydn had injected a good many surprises into their music – in the latter's case, many a good joke, too – but it was never so radical as to upset the underlying logic of the composition.

This was seldom the case with Beethoven, and in his mature works, he pointed the way, through Berlioz and Liszt, to Wagner, for like them, Beethoven's music was a direct and unrestrained response to the strong feelings and emotions that stirred within him.

This was just as well, for in childhood, the learning and practice of musical theory was abhorrent to him. Early music lessons from his father were a case of a tyrannical teacher attempting to hammer instruction into an unwilling pupil.

His first eight years in Vienna produced works which, for all their qualities, were not startlingly original. However, in the years 1801–9, he left his contemporaries far behind with the likes of the *Eroica* symphony, the Fourth and Fifth Piano Concertos and the *Rasumovsky* quartets.

Beethoven had no family of his own: he had been thwarted in love on a number of occasions (he was, in truth, a most unprepossessing figure) and, by the time of his last and greatest compositions, was leading an increasingly squalid and isolated life.

Ludwig van Beethoven died in Vienna on 26 March 1827 and, perhaps typifying the impact he had had on the city and on music, the most violent of thunderstorms raged over the city at the time.

Superficially, Beethoven appears to have been done well by Compact Disc, but analysis reveals no wholly recommendable version of the Ninth Symphony, and a lack of choice in the piano concertos, and in some of the greatest of the piano sonatas, too.

An irascible and unsociable character but capable of producing music of sublime humanity.

BEETHOVEN

**SYMPHONY NO1 IN C MAJOR OP21/
SYMPHONY NO2 IN D MAJOR OP36**
The Academy of Ancient Music
Director: Christopher Hogwood
L'Oiseau-Lyre 414 338-2OH
DDD Running time: 59.31
Performance: ★ ★   Recording: ★ ★

After their successful re-assessments of, among others, Haydn and Mozart, Hogwood and his colleagues are now extending their quest for 'authenticity' to the Beethoven symphonies. The intention, however, is not simply to employ period instruments (or copies thereof), but to recreate the whole performance in the manner of the composer's time, which, as well as using a smaller orchestra than most modern recordings employ, means there is no conductor in the sense of someone laying an expressive interpretation on the music. Instead, Christopher Hogwood 'directs' from the fortepiano, his rôle simply to set the tempo for each movement and little else.

Tempos are brisk, and while the precise and emphatic pulse produces effective and likeable results in the faster movements, the slower ones seem to pale a little from the expressive austerity. Overall, the Second fares the better of the two.

Other recordings on CD (selection):
Dresden PO/Herbert Kegel/Capriccio
  CAPR1001
BPO/Herbert von Karajan/DG 415 505-2GH

**SYMPHONY NO2 IN D MAJOR OP36
SYMPHONY NO4 IN B FLAT MAJOR
OP60**
Philharmonia Orchestra
Conductor: Otto Klemperer
EMI CDC 7 47185-2
AAD Running time: 73.13
Performance: ★ ★ ★   Recording: ★ ★

To commemorate the centenary of the birth of one of this century's greatest conductors, in 1985 EMI remastered Klemperer's entire stereo cycle of the Beethoven symphonies, issuing them on CD as well as LP.

Klemperer's slower-than-usual tempi were always a subject of debate in his day, but surely no one could argue that he misses the radiant geniality of these works, first performed in 1803 and 1807 respectively. The *scherzi* are as vigorous and earthily boisterous as one could want; the lovely slow movements never drag.

The 'sixties sound is clean and firmly-defined, if not as sweet as we are now accustomed to (but it should be borne in mind that orchestral opulence was well down the list of Klemperer's priorities, some way below rhythmic accuracy and clarity).

Other recordings on CD:
(Symphony No2)
AAM/Hogwood/Oiseau-Lyre 414 338-2OH
Dresden PO/Herbert Kegel/Capriccio
  CAPR1001
Berlin Staatskapelle/Otmar Suitner/Denon
  C37-7367
BPO/Herbert von Karajan/DG 415 505-2GH
Leipzig Gewandhaus O/Kurt Masur/Philips
  416 274-2PH6
Columbia SO/Bruno Walter/CBS MK42009
(Symphony No4)
Bavarian State SO/Carlos Kleiber/Orfeo
  CRFC100841
Berlin Staatskapelle/Otmar Suitner/Denon
  C37-7077
BPO/Herbert von Karajan/DG 415 121-2GH
Dresden PO/Herbert Kegel/Capriccio
  CAPR1006/7
Columbia SO/Bruno Walter/CBS MK42011

**SYMPHONY NO3 IN E FLAT MAJOR
OP55
GROSSE FUGE OP133 (orchestral version)**
Philharmonia Orchestra
Conductor: Otto Klemperer
EMI CDC 7 47186-2
AAD Running time: 70.02
Performance: ★ ★ ★   Recording: ★ ★

'*I am not contented with my works so far, henceforth I shall take a new path.*' And so Beethoven most assuredly did after making this promise to a friend in 1802. With the Third Symphony, written during 1803, he finally loosed the ties with Haydn and Mozart, establishing a style uniquely his own and thereby changing the nature of the symphony forever.

With Klemperer, there is no doubting the titanic nature of the Third: the performance of the great *Marcia Funebre*, surely the core of the work, is awesome in its unrelenting intensity. With characteristically slow, but far from unyielding, tempi in the remaining movements – and a total grasp of structure – Beethoven's argument unfolds.

This *Eroica*, from 1961, comes up well in remastering, apart from a truncation of the decaying ambience at the end of the movements. The 1957 *Grosse Fuge* fares less well, but remains a substantial bonus.

Other recordings on CD:
(Symphony No3)
Berlin Staatskapelle/Otmar Suitner/Denon
  C37-7011
ASMF/Neville Marriner/Philips 410 044-2PH
Cleveland O/Christoph von Dohnanyi/
  Telarc CD80090
Dresden PO/Herbert Kegel/Capriccio 1002
VPO/Leonard Bernstein/DG 413 778-2GH
Leipzig Gewandhaus O/Kurt Masur/Philips
  416 274-2PH6

SYMPHONY NO5 IN C MINOR OP67
Vienna Philharmonic Orchestra
Conductor: Carlos Kleiber
Deutsche Grammophon 415 861-2GH
ADD Running time: 33.10
Performance: ★ ★ ★
Recording: ★ ★ (★)

If your view of the Fifth is that of a heroic struggle, intense and urgent, yet triumphantly resolved, then Kleiber's is the version to have. The electricity it generates, often with ferocious power, is rare indeed among recordings of the symphony in this day-and-age, although evoking strong recollections of the version made by the conductor's father, Erich Kleiber, in 1952.

True, the disc offers poor value playing time alongside the likes of Karajan, who offers nothing less than the *Pastoral* Symphony as a coupling, and Klemperer, where the Eighth is a substantial bonus. But the performance is everything here, and such considerations are of passing significance.

However, if a wholly digital version is

sought, then Ashkenazy on Decca is the best alternative.

Other recordings on CD (selection):
Philharmonia O/Vladimir Ashkenazy/Decca 400 060-2DH
LAPO/Carlo Maria Giulini/DG 410 028-2GH
Hanover Band/Monica Huggett/Nimbus NIM5007
BPO/Herbert von Karajan/DG 413 932-2GH
Leipzig Gewandhaus O/Kurt Masur/Philips 416 274-2PH6

SYMPHONY NO6 IN F MAJOR OP68 (PASTORAL)/SYMPHONY NO9 IN D MINOR OP125 (CHORAL)*
Jessye Norman: Soprano*/Brigitte Fassbaender: Contralto*/Placido Domingo: Tenor*/Walter Berry: Baritone*
Concert Association of the Vienna State Opera Chorus*
Vienna Philharmonic Orchestra
Conductor: Karl Böhm
Deutsche Grammophon 413 721-2GX2
(2 discs)
ADD/DDD* Running time: 124.39
Performance: ★ ★ (★)
Recording: ★ ★ ★ (6th)/★ ★ (9th)

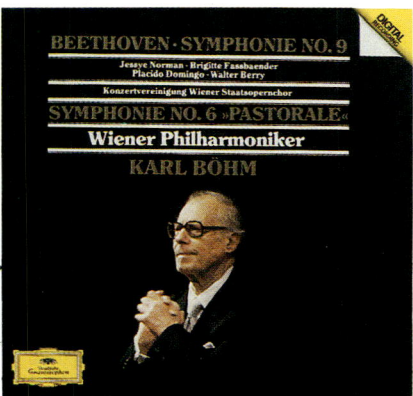

It was an inspired piece of programming to combine Böhm's classic 1972 account of the *Pastoral* with the last recording of his long and distinguished career, the Ninth, made in 1980. What is immediately apparent is that, despite the range and excellent definition, the latter cannot compete with its predecessor in terms of warmth and opulence of sound, where the rich bloom of the Vienna Philharmonic is captured in a glorious acoustic. Lovingly played, this is an unsurpassed performance of the Sixth.
The *Choral* is more controversial, a measured view which, while commanding in the first movement, brings the *scherzo* dangerously close to outstaying its welcome. However, the tenderness of the *adagio* is beautifully caught, and the steady pace of the finale builds to a splendid conclusion, with impressive contributions from both soloists and choir (how satisfying to hear the high voices in the *Über Sternen* passage uninhibited by the imperfections of record pressing, or the limitations of pickup cartridges).

Other recordings on CD (selection):
BPO/Herbert von Karajan/DG 410 897-2GH
VPO/Karl Böhm/DG 413 721-2GX2
Cleveland O/Christoph von Dohnanyi/Telarc CD80120
Concertgebouw O/Bernard Haitink/Philips 410 036-2PH
Leipzig Gewandhaus O/Kurt Masur/Philips 416 274-2PH6

SYMPHONY NO6 IN F MAJOR OP68 (PASTORAL)
Philharmonia Orchestra
Conductor: Vladimir Ashkenazy
Decca 410 003-2DH
DDD Running time: 60.21
Performance: ★ ★ ★
Recording: ★ ★ (★)

Beethoven thought the *Pastoral* more 'an expression of feelings rather than a painting in sound' – feelings generated by pleasant summer days spent in the countryside around Vienna. The smiling, untroubled nature of the symphony reflects the composer's contentment at the time, and to this day there are few pieces of music more capable of raising the spirits. Despite that, the Sixth is far from easy to bring off well.
Ashkenazy's fresh, direct approach scores handsomely here. It is genial and relaxed but flows, – not too briskly though – the concluding *Hymn of thanksgiving* being superbly conveyed.
The familiar bloom and comfortable acoustic of the Kingsway Hall, London, plays its part in giving the performance radiant character. Although violin tone could be fuller (and the basses perhaps less so), the orchestral sound is very good, in terms of tonal balance, depth and a well-defined presence.

Other recordings on CD (selection):
BPO/Herbert von Karajan/DG 413 932-2GH
VPO/Leonard Bernstein/DG 413 779-2GH
VPO/Wilhelm Furtwangler/EMI CDC 7 47121-2 (historic recording)
VPO/Karl Bohm/DG 413 721-2GX2

SYMPHONY NO7 IN A MAJOR OP92 OVERTURES: EGMONT OP84/ CORIOLAN OP62
Philharmonia Orchestra
Conductor: Vladimir Ashkenazy
Decca 411 941-2DH
DDD Running time: 59.32
Performance: ★ ★ ★   Recording: ★ ★ ★

Beethoven wrote nothing more confidently exuberant than his Seventh Symphony. Dominated by muscular rhythmic patterns, the vitality never slackens throughout the four movements.
Ashkenazy wisely avoids any temptation to over-drive here: the result is spontaneous and exciting without becoming overwhelming. Nothing is forced – if anything, the *allegretto* is a little too measured – but with full, spacious sound (Kingsway Hall again) bestowing a lively presence, this is a performance that can be lived with. The disc offers good value with a better-than-usual bonus in the shape of two overtures, including the tautly-conceived *Egmont* equally well-played and recorded.

Other recordings on CD (selection):
BPO/Herbert von Karajan/DG 415 121-2GH
VPO/Carlos Kleiber/DG 415 862-2GH
Berlin Staatskapelle/Otmar Suitner/Denon C37-7032

BEETHOVEN

SYMPHONY NO9 IN D MINOR OP125 (CHORAL)
Elisabeth Schwarzkopf: Soprano/Elisabeth Höngen: Contralto/Hans Hopf: Tenor/Otto Edelmann: Bass
Bayreuth Festival Chorus and Orchestra
Conductor: Wilhelm Furtwängler
EMI CDC 7 47081-2
AAD Running time: 74.42
Performance: ★ ★ ★
Recording: ★ (MONO)

The circumstances of the performance, as well as the performance itself, have contributed to the 'legendary' stature of this recording. It was made in the Festspielhaus, Bayreuth, in 1951 during a concert to re-inaugurate the Bayreuth Festival after the Second World War. During the Hitler years, Bayreuth had been under the control of the pro-Nazi, Winifred Wagner, the composer's daughter-in-law, and if there were ghosts to be exorcised, surely Beethoven's triumphant affirmation of the human spirit, freedom and brotherhood would be the ideal means.

And so it proved. It would be wrong to suggest this is a 'perfect' performance of the Ninth: there are lapses of ensemble and intonation, the soloists are not at their best, and there are some quirks of tempo, but the cumulative result is undeniably exhilarating.

Furtwängler's reading is an expansive one, although he whips up the excitement in the last movement. Allowing for the obvious limitations imposed by its vintage, the recording is surprisingly clear and smooth.

PIANO CONCERTO NO1 IN C MAJOR OP15/PIANO CONCERTO NO2 IN B FLAT MAJOR OP19
Alfred Brendel: Piano
Chicago Symphony Orchestra
Conductor: James Levine
Philips 412 787-2GH
DDD Running time: 67.36
Performance: ★ ★   Recording: ★ ★

The brisk tempi of the outer movements of No1 on this recording, incisive to the point of brusqueness, will not be to all tastes, although the performance of the central *largo* is spellbinding. The Second Concerto (actually the first to be written – around 1793 – but numerically transposed by its later publication) fares better in these live recordings from concerts given in Chicago during 1983. At times, it seems Brendel and Levine are a little too determined to avoid all unnecessary elaboration in the quick movements, losing some of the magic.

The sound is warm and full, although the acoustic is on the dry side and piano and wind balances are fairly close. However, such is the paucity of competition on Compact Disc, these thoughtfully-conceived performances earn a recommendation – if somewhat by default!

Other recordings on CD (selection):
Vladimir Ashkenazy/VPO/Zubin Mehta/ Decca 411 900-2DH
Mary Verney/Hanover Band/Nimbus NIM5003
(Piano Concerto No2)
Vladimir Ashkenazy/VPO/Zubin Mehta/ Decca 411 901-2DH
Maurizio Pollini/VPO/Eugen Jochum/DG 413 445-2GH

PIANO CONCERTO NO2 IN B FLAT MAJOR OP19/PIANO CONCERTO NO4 IN G MAJOR OP58*
Maurizio Pollini: Piano
Vienna Philharmonic Orchestra
Conductor: Eugen Jochum/Karl Böhm*
Deutsche Grammophon 413 445-2GH
ADD*/DDD Running time: 60.58
Performance: ★ ★ (★)   Recording: ★ ★

Pollini's is a noble, glittering account of the G Major, aloof in some respects, but missing none of the poetry in this most romantic of the five concertos. This is nowhere better heard than in the slow movement's remarkable dialogue between piano and orchestra.

Yet there is an element of charm and humour missing from the performance of the B flat, although there is no shortage of drama and electricity. This recording is marginally less satisfying technically, despite being a digital taping made several years after the Fourth (with a change of conductor following Karl Böhm's death in 1981). There is a rather hard, metallic quality to both piano and strings; similarly, the remastering of the Fourth, while producing a clearer image, also results in a harder sound than was obtained from LP.

Other recordings on CD (selection):
(Piano Concerto No4)
Vladimir Ashkenazy/VPO/Zubin Mehta/ Decca 411 901-2DH

PIANO CONCERTO NO3 IN C MINOR OP37/ANDANTE FAVORI IN F MAJOR WoO57/BAGATELLE NO25 IN A MINOR WoO59 (FÜR ELISE)
Vladimir Ashkenazy: Piano
Vienna Philharmonic Orchestra
Conductor: Zubin Mehta
Decca 411 902-2DH
DDD Running time: 49.19
Performance: ★ ★ (★)
Recording: ★ ★ (★)

The Third is the 'plum' from Ashkenazy's most recent cycle of the Beethoven concertos, just as the Fourth was the star of the previous series under Solti. He and Mehta take a broad view of the first movement, the latter bringing in the orchestra on tip-toes at the start and evoking an unusually mysterious atmosphere. The lovely slow movement is sheer poetry here, and the finale, impressively articulated, fairly sparkles. Warm and full, the recording is well-balanced.

It is good to have Ashkenazy's playing of

two popular items from the solo repertoire as a bonus, but the sum total is not over-generous: Brendel and Levine offer nothing less than the Fourth Concerto.

Other recordings on CD:
Rudolf Serkin/BSO/Seiji Ozawa/Telarc CD80063 and CD80061 (set)
Alfred Brendel/CSO/James Levine/Philips 412 788-2PH and 411 189-2PH3 (set)
Maurizio Pollini/VPO/Karl Böhm/DG 413 446-2GH

PIANO CONCERTO NO5 IN E FLAT MAJOR OP73 (EMPEROR)
Claudio Arrau: Piano
Staatskapelle Dresden
Conductor: Colin Davis
Philips 416 215-2PH
DDD Running time: 40.33
Performance: ★ ★ ★   Recording: ★ ★ ★

It will be surprising if this is not acknowledged as one of the very greatest recordings of the *Emperor*, as Claudio Arrau – now in his eighties – brings both the wisdom of experience, and a technique that pianists of any age would envy, to this most regal of the concertos. His vision is unimpeded by precedent, or familiarity, and this same freshness is shared by Davis and the Dresden Orchestra, unquestionably now one of Europe's finest.
    Tempi seem absolutely right, and the spirit of the performance is irresistible. The recording, spacious, with natural, well-defined perspectives and, at times, revelatory in illuminating the orchestration, is an ideal vehicle for the performance. And to complement Arrau's playing, the piano has a crystalline quality that is simply outstanding. No question, this one is special.

Other recordings on CD:
Vladimir Ashkenazy/VPO/Zubin Mehta/Decca 411 903-2DH
Alfred Brendel/CSO/James Levine/Philips 412 789-2PH and 411 189-2PH3 (set)
Radu Lupu/Israel PO/Zubin Mehta/Decca 400 050-2DH
Rudolf Serkin/BSO/Seiji Ozawa/Telarc CD80065 and CD80061 (set)
Maurizio Pollini/VPO/Karl Böhm/DG 413 447-2GH
Artur Rubinstein/LPO/Daniel Barenboim/RCA RD89389

VIOLIN CONCERTO IN D MAJOR OP61/ROMANCES FOR VIOLIN AND ORCHESTRA: NO1 IN G MAJOR OP40/NO2 IN F MAJOR OP50
Henryk Szeryng: Violin
Concertgebouw Orchestra, Amsterdam
Conductor: Bernard Haitink
Philips 416 418-2PH
ADD Running time: 63.34
Performance: ★ ★ ★   Recording: ★ ★ ★

Coupling a performance of both power and poetry with a gloriously open sound quality that takes full advantage of the Concertgebouw acoustic, this 1974 recording emerges as currently the most recommendable of the several competing versions of Beethoven's solitary Violin Concerto of 1806.
    There is impressive weight and scale, Haitink shaping the orchestral contribution with enormous skill; the balance between it and the soloist has been finely judged. It is this aspect which lets down the otherwise outstanding version by Perlman and Giulini. Technically taxing as it is, the Beethoven is one fiddle concerto which is not an unabashed virtuoso showpiece. Equanimity between soloist and orchestra is vital to the whole mood of the work.

Other recordings on CD:
(Violin Concerto – selection)
Kyung-Wha Chung/VPO/Kyril Kondrashin/Decca 400 048-2DH
Itzhak Perlman/Philharmonia O/Carlo-Maria Giulini/EMI CDC 7 47002-2
Anne-Sophie Mutter/BPO/Herbert von Karajan/DG 413 818-2GH
(Romances for Violin and Orchestra)
Isaac Stern/BSO/Seiji Ozawa/CBS MK37204

CONCERTO FOR VIOLIN, 'CELLO AND PIANO IN C MAJOR OP56/OVERTURES: EGMONT OP84/CORIOLAN OP62/FIDELIO OP72B
Anne-Sophie Mutter: Violin
Yo-Yo Ma: 'Cello
Mark Zeltser: Piano
Berlin Philharmonic Orchestra
Conductor: Herbert von Karajan
Deutsche Grammophon 415 276-2GH
ADD Running time: 60.54
Performance: ★ ★ ★   Recording: ★ ★ ★

While the Triple Concerto may not scale the heights of, say, the *Emperor* or the Violin Concerto, it certainly emerges as no lightweight from this strongly-characterised performance. Karajan brings drama and intensity with the first bars of the orchestral introduction, and the soloists maintain that pulse throughout (although Yo-Yo Ma's playing is not as immaculate as is his companions').
    The result is a compelling performance which emerges as one of DG's best concerto recordings of recent times (it was one of their last analogue tapings). Although each solo part is clearly defined, no one overwhelms another, and combined, they do not swamp the orchestra either.
    Equally powerful readings of three overtures, in recordings of varying vintage – and quality – make for a well-filled disc.

Other recordings on CD:
(Triple Concerto)
Kalichstein, Laredo, Robinson Trio/ECO/Alexander Gibson/Chandos CHAN8409

BEETHOVEN

STRING QUARTETS OP18 NO1 IN F MAJOR/NO2 IN G MAJOR/NO3 IN D MAJOR/NO4 IN C MINOR/NO5 IN A MAJOR/NO6 IN B FLAT MAJOR
Alban Berg Quartet
EMI CDS 7 47127-8 (3 discs)
ADD Running time: 151.34
Performance: ★ ★ ★
Recording: ★ ★ (★)

This first set of quartets, composed around 1797–1800, predictably shows the influence of the established masters, Haydn and Mozart and – more surprisingly – that of a lesser-known Viennese composer, Emanuel Alois Förster, a good friend whom Beethoven called his *'alter Meister'*. However, they are far from being mere competent imitations, and already suggest an emotional force pushing classical conventions and disciplines to the limit.

That vitality and tension is evident in the Alban Berg Quartet's performance, one of awesome technical precision and polish, here recorded with good definition and immediacy, if with a rather wiry string tone.

These nigh-on immaculate renderings currently stand alone in the Compact Disc catalogue, but would undoubtedly face the strongest challenge if ASV get round to transferring the Lindsay Quartet's deeply-considered readings to CD.

STRING QUARTETS OP59 (RASOUMOVSKY QUARTETS): NO1 IN F MAJOR/NO2 IN E MINOR/NO3 IN C MAJOR/STRING QUARTET NO10 IN E FLAT MAJOR OP74 (HARP)/STRING QUARTET NO11 IN F MINOR OP95 (SERIOSO)
Alban Berg Quartet
EMI CDS7 47131-8 (3 discs)
ADD Running time: 153.18
Performance: ★ ★   Recording: ★ ★ ★

This group of five quartets represents one of the major achievements of Beethoven's 'middle period'. All these works are technically and intellectually demanding, none more so than the Op95. Beethoven, aware that he was dealing in subtleties of thought and emotion at the time believed to be beyond the compass of the medium, kept the work back from publication for some six years. It does indeed point in a new, revolutionary direction, its inwardly-searching, visionary character a foretaste of the extraordinary world of the late quartets, then a decade away.

Although the recording wants for little, with a clear, well-defined, natural balance and sumptuous tonal quality, this is ultimately the least satisfying of the Alban Berg's cycle of the quartets. Against the admirably polished ensemble, rhythmic sense, and crisp precision of attack must be set a tendency to exaggerate and to over-point dynamic contrasts in a somewhat self-conscious way.

However, the set has much to commend it and remains preferable to the recently-issued Melos set on DG. There is little doubt, though, that the appearance on Compact Disc of a classic account, such as that of the Vegh Quartet, would take precedence here.

Other recordings on CD (complete):
Melos Quartet/DG 415 342-2GH3

STRING QUARTET NO14 IN C SHARP MINOR OP131
Smetana Quartet
Supraphon C37S-7312
DDD Running time: 39.43
Performance: ★ ★ (★)
Recording: ★ ★ (★)

For many, the C sharp minor represents the crowning glory of the late quartets, an assessment with which it is hard to disagree, as the aching sadness of the first movement reaches out to touch both heart and mind. Is there a more transcendentally spiritual utterance in all music?

Despite the composer's remark that the work was, *'cribbed together variously from this and that,'* the seven-movement structure, with its fulcrum the fourth variation movement, possesses a well-developed symmetry. The outer pair are the most profound, while the combination of the lighter second and third deftly balances that of the sixth and fifth.

The Smetana Quartet's performance is keenly responsive, yet unforced, a description that also applies to the recording: sensitive to dynamic contrast, and with a light but telling ambience. Again, like the playing, it puts nothing untoward in the way of the listener.

Other recordings on CD:
Alban Berg Quartet/EMI CDS7 47135-8

STRING QUARTETS: NO12 IN E FLAT MAJOR OP127/NO13 IN B FLAT MAJOR OP130/NO14 IN C SHARP MINOR OP131/NO15 IN A MINOR OP132/ GROSSE FUGE IN B FLAT MAJOR OP133/ NO16 IN F MAJOR OP135
Alban Berg Quartet
EMI CDS7 47135-8 (4 discs)
DDD Running time: 192.32
Performance: ★ ★ ★   Recording: ★ ★ ★

From 1824, despite increasing illness and total deafness, Beethoven was somehow able to attain fresh heights of inspiration, devoting himself exclusively to the string quartet and in the process producing five works which represent not only the summation of his own art, but arguably the highest pinnacle of musical expression.

In many ways, they are far from 'beautiful' in the accepted musical sense: had he ever been able to hear the works performed, Beethoven would no doubt have corrected some of the harsh sonorities and tonal imbalances: the *vivace* of Op135 is surely an example. Yet much is among the most sublime music ever written: the *cavatina* of Op130, and the *molto adagio* of Op132, that poignant *Hymn of Thanksgiving*. At the opposite extreme is the formidable *Grosse Fuge* Op133, originally the finale of the Op130 quartet.

The Alban Berg quartet are at their very best here, and the recording (now digital) is also noticeably better than its predecessors, with fine clarity, openness and realistic presence. The pleasantly reverberant acoustic of the church used for the recording, and the burnished mahogany tone of the quartet are a delight to listen to.

Their playing is indeed beautiful, with marvellous ensemble, and tempi are generally well-judged although some of the quicker movements sound rushed. The Op131 and Op132 are perhaps the best accounts, along with the masterly playing of the *Grosse Fuge*, but it would be wrong to suggest the whole set emerges as less than satisfying.

STRING QUARTET NO13 IN B FLAT MAJOR OP130/GROSSE FUGE IN B FLAT MAJOR OP133
Fitzwilliam Quartet
Decca 411 943-2DH
DDD Running time: 63.47
Performance: ★ ★ ★   Recording: ★ ★ ★

In every respect, this is an improvement on their previous issue of Op132. Both players and engineers appear to have sorted out the problems of dynamics and tone which marred that recording and the result is a thoughtful, intense performance that displays notable grasp of structure. Appropriately, the lovely *cavatina* comes off best of all, while the leisurely-paced finale is most convincing.

The addition of a trenchant reading of the *Grosse Fuge* allows Beethoven's first and second-thoughts on concluding the Quartet to be selected at will.

Other recordings on CD:
Vermeer Quartet/TelDec ZK8.42982
Alban Berg Quartet/EMI CDS 7 47135-8

VIOLIN SONATA NO5 IN F MAJOR OP24 (SPRING)/VIOLIN SONATA NO9 IN A MAJOR OP47 (KREUTZER)
David Oistrakh: Violin
Lev Oborin: Piano
Philips 412 255-2PH
ADD Running time: 58.47
Performance: ★ ★ ★   Recording: ★ ★

We do not know who gave the F Major sonata its nickname *Spring*, but it was an apt choice for this light and lyrical work the opening theme of which, had it been used in an orchestral work rather than a chamber composition, would surely have become one of Beethoven's best-loved melodies.

The A Major, however, is an altogether grander piece and it is difficult to believe that just five years separate the *Kreutzer* from the first, fairly unambitious, violin sonatas of Op12. Here the source of the nickname is not in doubt: the work was dedicated to the French violinist, Rodolphe Kreutzer, yet he apparently never played it!

Although recorded in the early 'sixties, tape hiss fails to intrude on these finely-shaped, elegant performances. There is a subtlety to them which is in sharp contrast to the more extrovert Ashkenazy and Perlman on Decca. Although the latter offer undeniably impressive performances, Oistrakh and Oborin seem to come closer to the spirit of these sonatas.

The Decca is technically superior, but the Philips recording, if a little over-wide and lacking ambience, is nevertheless wholly acceptable.

Other recordings on CD:
Itzhak Perlman/Vladimir Ashkenazy/Decca 410 554-2DH
Uto Ughi/Wolfgang Sawallisch/RCA RD70430

SONATAS FOR 'CELLO AND PIANO: NO1 IN F MAJOR OP5 NO1/NO2 IN G MINOR OP5 NO2/NO3 IN A MAJOR OP69/NO4 IN C MAJOR OP102 NO1/NO5 IN D MAJOR OP102 NO2
Mstislav Rostropovich: 'Cello
Sviatoslav Richter: Piano
Philips 412 256-2PH2 (2 discs)
ADD Running time: 109.09
Performance: ★ ★ ★
Recording: ★ ★ (★)

As with the string quartets, part of the fascination of the Beethoven 'Cello Sonatas is that they date from each of the creative periods of his life. When the Op5 pair was composed, the 'cello had only recently emerged as suitable to take the lead in chamber compositions, and Beethoven breaks new ground with remarkable daring. There is also an equality between the instruments which is maintained in the later Op69 – probably the most immediately attractive and popular of the five – and the two deeply-felt sonatas of Op102.

Altogether a rewarding musical journey, especially with performances of this quality. The sheer technique, and the subtlety of expression that Rostropovich and Richter bring to the sonatas has assured vintage status for these 1961 recordings, and with consistently good balancing and fine tonal quality, the transfer to Compact Disc is well-merited.

Other recordings on CD:
(Sonatas Nos 1 and 2)
Christophe Coin/Patrick Cohen/Harmonia-Mundi HMC90.1179
Yo-Yo Ma/Emanuel Ax/CBS MK37251
(Sonatas Nos 3 and 5)
Yo-Yo Ma/Emanuel Ax/CBS MK39024

BEETHOVEN

PIANO SONATA NO2 IN A MAJOR OP2 NO2
PIANO SONATA NO4 IN E FLAT MAJOR OP7
Emil Gilels: Piano
Deutsche Grammophon 415 481-2GH
DDD Running time: 58.28
Performance: ★ ★ ★   Recording: ★ ★ ★

With Emil Gilels' untimely death in October 1985, his recorded cycle of the thirty-two sonatas of Beethoven, potentially the most consistently rewarding of any modern interpretation, was left incomplete. This was the penultimate release (a coupling of the Op109 and Op110 awaited issue at the time of writing), and it more than ever illustrates the incomparable understanding Gilels was able to bring to Beethoven. There is formidable technique, of course, but much more: a wisdom and humanity that seem to be at one with Beethoven. Gilels does not so much interpret as communicate, without mannerism or affectation.

This is a compelling recording, the kind of music-making that confounds the passing of time. The two sonatas, complementary in temperament and their often bold originality, date from Beethoven's mid-twenties, yet the Op7 was to prove the second longest of his piano sonatas, exceeded only by the mighty *Hammerklavier* Op106.

The sound here is a marked improvement on that evident in the Op106; much less bright and edgy, and less 'up-front', too. The image is of realistic width and depth, and the rounded, crystalline tone of the instrument, with the usual benefits CD brings to solo piano, is lovely to hear. All that is missing is a degree more ambience.

Other recordings on CD (selection):
(both sonatas: all boxed sets)
Alfred Brendel/Philips 412 575-2PH11
Daniel Barenboim/DG 413 759-2GX6

PIANO SONATA NO7 IN D MAJOR OP10 NO3/PIANO SONATA NO23 IN F MINOR OP57 (APPASSIONATA)
Murray Perahia: Piano
CBS MK39344
DDD Running time: 47.12
Performance: ★ ★ ★   Recording: ★ ★ ★

Predictably, Murray Perahia proves as rewarding and illuminating an interpreter of Beethoven as he has already proved himself to be of Mozart and Schubert. These are compelling performances from first bar to last, both in the well-known *Appassionata* of 1804, part of that trilogy of most popular sonatas which includes the *Moonlight* and the *Pathétique*, and in the early D Major of 1797/8.

The recording comes from the 'new school' of CBS engineering: truthful in timbre and scale, and bathed in a warm ambience. This is an auspicious beginning to what will, one hopes, become a complete cycle of the sonatas.

Other recordings on CD:
(Piano Sonata No7)
Alfred Brendel/Philips 412 575-2PH11 (set)
Daniel Barenboim/DG 413 759-2GX6
Friedrich Gulda/Amadeo/415 193-2
(Piano sonata No23 – selection)
Vladimir Ashkenazy/Decca 410 260-2DH
Carol Rosenberger/Delos D/CD3009
Alfred Brendel/Philips/412 575-2PH11 and 411 470-2PH
Daniel Barenboim/DG 413 766-2GX6

PIANO SONATAS: NO8 IN C MINOR OP13 (PATHETIQUE)/NO13 IN E FLAT MAJOR OP27 NO1/NO14 IN C SHARP MINOR OP27 NO2 (MOONLIGHT)
Emil Gilels: Piano
Deutsche Grammophon 400 036-2GH
DDD Running time: 52.06
Performance: ★ ★ ★
Recording: ★ ★ (★)

Without resorting to perversities of interpretation, Gilels invests the two most popular (and often most mistreated) of the sonatas with an unexpected freshness and perception: the fiery opening movement of the *Pathétique*, and the measured tread of its slow movement are but two examples. Such is Gilels' fine control, the first movement of the *Moonlight* succeeds in being serene without erring towards the lugubrious as does Rudolf Buchbinder on TelDec.

Although possessing a stunning presence, the close recording, as well as giving a rather over-wide image, produces a bright edge to the piano tone in *fortissimos*. But this does little to detract from the performance, which is just as compelling in the E flat sonata as in its better-known companions.

Other recordings on CD (selection):
Vladimir Ashkenazy/Decca 410 260-2DH (Nos 8/14 only)
Alfred Brendel/Philips 411 470-2PH and 412 575-2PH11 (set)
Daniel Barenboim/DG 413 759-2GX6 (set)
Friedrich Gulda/Amadeo 415 193-2
(Piano sonata No13 only)
Shura Cherkassky/Nimbus NIM5021

PIANO SONATAS: NO11 IN B FLAT MAJOR OP22/NO21 IN C MAJOR OP53 (WALDSTEIN)/NO27 IN E MINOR OP90
Rudolf Buchbinder: Piano
TelDec ZK8.43111
DDD Running time: 58.48
Performance: ★ ★ (★)
Recording: ★ ★ ★

Over and above playing of quite breathtaking fluency and precision, this disc offers finely-wrought performances of three sonatas, including the magnificent Op53 of 1803/4. This remarkable work, dedicated to Count Waldstein, hence the nickname, was originally intended to have an *andante* in F Major as its slow movement, but Beethoven replaced it with the *adagio* which serves to introduce the *rondo finale*.

The original *andante* was not discarded, however: now known as the *Andante favori*, it has become a staple part of the popular piano literature.

With rock-steady imaging and impressive transparency, the sound quality here is startlingly truthful.

Other recordings on CD (selection):
(Piano sonatas Nos 11, 21, 27)
Alfred Brendel/Philips 412 575-2PH11 (set)
Daniel Barenboim/DG 413 759-2GX6 (set)
(Piano sonatas Nos21 and 27)
Vladimir Ashkenazy/Decca 414 630-2DH

PIANO SONATA NO29 IN B FLAT MAJOR OP106 'HAMMERKLAVIER'
Emil Gilels: Piano
Deutsche Grammophon 410 527-2GH
DDD Running time: 48.38
Performance: ★ ★ ★   Recording: ★ ★

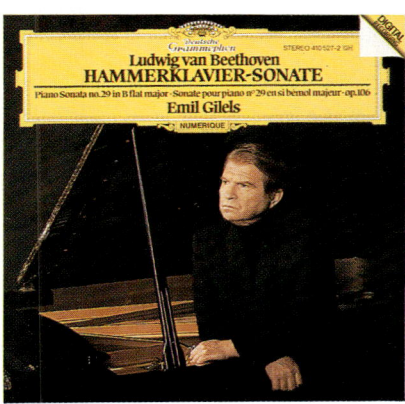

Beethoven's powerful piano style was often too much for the more frail instruments of his day: broken strings were a frequent occurrence. He was therefore delighted when, in 1818, the English firm of John Broadwood and Sons offered to supply him with a much more robust instrument than those he previously had access to, and with a compass extended to six octaves. It was almost certainly the capabilities of this instrument which encouraged him in the composition of his most ambitious and most demanding piano work, the so-called *Hammerklavier* sonata, on which he worked simultaneously with the Ninth Symphony.

However, the sonata taxes the player every bit as much as the instrument, both physically and intellectually, from the dazzling musical invention of the first movement, through the profound sorrow of the *adagio*, to the formidable complexities of the final fugue. Few successfully rise to this challenge. But Emil Gilels' performance is of rare integrity and insight, coupled to an ability to view the work as a unified whole. The lofty repose of the slow movement is particularly moving.

A fairly close recording certainly allows every note to be heard, although at the expense of creating an over-wide image and excluding any ambience. There is also a brightness to the sound which could become fatiguing on some equipment. But such criticisms pale into insignificance beside playing of this stature.

Other recordings on CD:
Rudolf Buchbinder/TelDec ZK8.42761
Alfred Brendel/Philips 412 557-2PH11
Daniel Barenboim/DG 413 766-2GX6
Friedrich Gulda/Amadeo 415 193-2

PIANO SONATAS: NO30 IN E MAJOR OP109/NO31 IN A FLAT MAJOR OP110/ NO32 IN C MINOR OP111
Rudolf Buchbinder: Piano
TelDec ZK8.43027
DDD Running time: 66.41
Performance: ★ ★ (★)
Recording: ★ ★ ★

Beethoven's sketchbooks for the period 1820-22 reveal a dual preoccupation with both the Mass in D Major, the *Missa Solemnis*, and what were to prove his last three piano sonatas, Op109-111. But, as before, it is the piano compositions that are precursors of a new stylistic phase, all three breaking new ground, not least in the way each ends. Not one leaves us with the usual feeling of matters debated and triumphantly resolved. Instead, questions are left unanswered: Op109 withdraws with a sigh of resignation; Op110 seems to shatter as notes pound down upon each other, and most enigmatic of all, Op111 extinguishes its final glittering cascade in expectant silence.

There is much to admire in Rudolf Buchbinder's performances, which are thoroughly well-thought-out. Op109 is clearly-executed, its contrasts of temperament and dynamics well-judged, and a feature of all three sonatas is the attention given to Beethoven's numerous and diverse expression marks. The playing of the fugue of Op110 and the variations of Op111 is quite stunning, as indeed is the recording itself, faithfully capturing the tonal quality and range of the instrument in a lively acoustic: that marvellous sensation, obtainable from the best CDs, that nothing is obscuring the listener's appreciation of the performer, is amply evident here.

Other recordings on CD:
Alfred Brendel/Philips 412 575-2PH11
Daniel Barenboim/DG 413 766-2GX6
Friedrich Gulda/Amadeo 415 193-2
(Piano Sonata No30 Op109 only)
Yukie Nagai/BIS CD-281
(Piano Sonata No31 Op110 only)
Alfred Brendel/Philips 412 789-2PH
Maurizio Pollini/DG 413 446-2GH
(Piano Sonata No32 Op111 only)
Ivo Pogorelich/DG 410 520-2GH
Carol Rosenberger/Delos D/CD3009
Friedrich Gulda/Philips 412 114-2PH

HECTOR BERLIOZ
(b. Côte St André, Grenoble, France, 11 December 1803; d. Paris, 8 March 1869)

Romanticism, the reaction of the 19th Century art to the Classicism which preceded it, came naturally to Hector Berlioz. It entirely suited his temperament which was excitable, impetuous and imaginative. He was quite unsuitable for the study and practice of medicine, the original reason he left home for Paris at the age of eighteen.

Berlioz' passion for music, which had started as a hobby but which now became a full-time study, was matched by an interest in literature. He befriended writers such as Balzac, Dumas and Hugo, as well as the painter, Delacroix – all men committed to the Romantic movement. Chopin and Liszt became influential acquaintances, too, but he found acceptance by the Paris conservatoire less forthcoming, having to wait until 1826 for entry.

Soon afterwards, he developed an infatuation for the Irish actress, Harriet Smithson, who was touring France with a Shakesperian company. Berlioz loved Shakespeare, and in Harriet he had found his Ophelia. His feelings, however, were not reciprocated (although he and Harriet later married), but found expression in the *Symphonie Fantastique*, a remarkable composition for a twenty-six-year-old and notable both for its bizarre 'programme', and use of the *'idée fixe'*, here a musical motif common to all the symphony's movements and is wildly varied in shape and treatment according to the music's mood. In truth, all Berlioz' love affairs were influential on his music.

When the need came for his own epitaph two years later, Berlioz had already suggested an appropriate line from Shakespeare: what was life if not *'a tale told by an idiot, full of sound and fury, signifying nothing'*.

There are those who would pass this judgement on his music. They cite it as naive and inflated, while others see it as simple and sincere. What is indisputable is Berlioz' intuitive mastery of orchestral instru-

SYMPHONIE FANTASTIQUE OP14
Concertgebouw Orchestra, Amsterdam
Conductor: Colin Davis
Philips 411 425-2PH
ADD Running time: 56.31
Performance: ★ ★ ★   Recording: ★ ★ ★

The twelve or so current Compact Disc versions of Berlioz' *Episode in the life of an artist* can soon be whittled down to three or four contenders worthy of final consideration. Muti, Dutoit and Abbado are all good in their different ways, but in performance none quite matches Colin Davis on Philips, whose recording has been a first choice on LP for over ten years now, and which continues that pre-eminence newly remastered for CD. The sound quality concedes little to its latter day rivals – the inner detail may be more sharply defined with Abbado, and Dutoit's is yet another outstanding Decca effort from Montreal. But for a performance that brings out all that is weird and wonderful about Berlioz' unique conception, while retaining an absolute command of line and structure, Davis remains unsurpassed.

Other recordings on CD (selection):
Cleveland O/Lorin Maazel/Telarc CD80076
CSO/Claudio Abbado/DG 410 895-2GH
Montreal SO/Charles Dutoit/Decca 414 203-2DH
Philadelphia O/Riccardo Muti/EMI CDC 7 47278-2

OVERTURES: KING LEAR OP4/ROB ROY/LE CORSAIRE OP21/BEATRICE ET BENEDICT/LE CARNAVAL ROMAIN OP9
Scottish National Orchestra
Conductor: Alexander Gibson
Chandos CHAN8316
DDD Running time: 52.33
Performance: ★ ★ ★   Recording; ★ ★ ★

The influence of literature on Berlioz is evident in this attractive selection of overtures, especially that of his beloved Shakespeare: *King Lear* was composed while convalescing in Nice in 1831, and ideas for an opera based on the two lovers in *Much Ado About Nothing* were formed around this time, although *Beatrice and Benedict* was not completed until some thirty years later. However, links between *Le Corsaire* and Byron's poem are tenuous to say the least.

The composer and 'Nipper', the unmistakeable trademark of His Master's Voice, illustrate this 1920s production of Berlioz' Faust.

Reflecting on a life whose intensity was so accurately mirrored in his music, Berlioz is portrayed in 1865, four years before his death.

mentation and colour, which had a universal impact on composition, and his contribution to the cause of programme music. He also worked on vast canvases, many of his compositions requiring unprecedented choral and orchestral forces. The *Symphonie Fantastique* offers a bewildering choice of conductors and orchestras, and it is a pity that, so far, none of the recording companies have acknowledged the equally fine *Romeo and Juliet* Symphony.

This CD features exhilarating performances from the Scottish players, and clear, well-detailed recording, with excellent stereo imaging and presence. The brilliance may be a little too much for some listeners, though, and a treble cut may prove judicious.

Other recordings on CD:
(*Le Carnaval Romain* only)
BPO/Lorin Maazel/Deutsche Grammophon 415 109-2GH
NPO/Leopold Stokowski/PRT CDPCN6

HAROLD IN ITALY OP16*
OVERTURE: LE CARNAVAL ROMAIN OP9
Wolfram Christ: Viola*
Berlin Philharmonic Orchestra
Conductor: Lorin Maazel
Deutsche Grammophon 415 109-2GH
DDD Running time: 51.05
Performance: ★ ★ ★   Recording: ★ ★

Like the *Symphonie Fantastique*, Berlioz' second exploration of symphonic form has a well-defined programme, this time based on the notion of the hero as observer who contemplates various colourful facets of Italian life, including an *Orgy of Brigands*. The borrowing of the name is the only true connection with Byron's poetic creation Harold: the central figure of Berlioz' work is the composer himself, and what he translates into music are his own experiences.

Maazel's well-paced, poetic and finely-judged performance certainly does justice to

this fascinating piece of *sinfonie concertante* writing. In ascribing the role of hero to the solo viola (here eloquently played by Wolfram Christ) Berlioz comes the closest he would ever get to the concerto form.

Ten years after *Harold*, Berlioz produced a concert overture drawing on music from his opera, *Benvenuto Cellini*, and a marvellous performance of this alternately exuberant and languidly romantic piece completes the programme here.

The symphony, incidentally, was recorded at a live concert (with a mercifully silent audience) something Deutsche Grammophon seems to encourage now from its major conductors – Karajan, Bernstein, Maazel among them (although presumably only when they, too, feel it would be beneficial). It has certainly paid off here; the sound quality is very good indeed.

JOHANNES BRAHMS
(b. Hamburg, Germany, 7 May 1833; d. Vienna, Austria, 3 April 1897)

The younger Brahms: the swansong of German classicism, deeply-felt yet nobly restrained.

If lyrical and romantic in temperament, the music of Johannes Brahms nevertheless remains firmly rooted in the German classical tradition. In a commitment to 'pure', orthodox forms such as the four-movement symphony, the concerto, quartet and sonata, it is Brahms more than any of his contemporaries, who inherited the mantle of Haydn, Mozart and Beethoven. And, like Beethoven, he spent the greater part of his creative life in the congenial atmosphere of Vienna, surroundings very different from the slum tenement in the port of Hamburg where he was born.

Brahms' father, an impecunious horn and double-bass player with a Hamburg theatre orchestra, somehow managed to pay for the very best piano teacher for his son, with the result that Brahms became a fine keyboard artist, if – unlike some of his counterparts – no virtuoso showman. That simply was not in his character.

The young Brahms earned a living the hard way: entertaining customers in Hamburg's waterfront cafés and dance-halls. He also toured Germany accompanying a Hungarian violinist (a source of inspiration which was to prove fruitful later) and on his travels encountered the violinist, Joseph Joachim, eventual dedicatee of his Violin Concerto. He also met, and earned the praise of, Liszt. By far his greatest allies, however, were Robert and Clara Schumann; they were also his closest friends and Brahms repaid that friendship generously during his fellow composer's harrowing mental illness (he also long harboured a hopeless passion for Clara, fourteen years his senior).

It was in the Autumn of 1862 that Brahms visited Vienna for the first time, and immediately fell in love with the city. The following year he returned to take up a post at the Singakademie and, although that was to be a short tenure, the city became home for the rest of his life, and from 1868, composition was his prime occupation.

With the increasing appreciation of his music, Brahms acquired celebrity status, and a fiercely loyal following. He became the focus of attention for those opposed to the 'new' music of Liszt and Wagner and was persuaded, perhaps unwisely, to put his name to a 'manifesto' declaring 'war' on the works of his two contemporaries. In truth, Brahms preferred to remain aloof from these bitter divisions, and had even expressed an admiration for Wagner's later operas, the antithesis of his classical disciplines.

An honest, sincere personality, one that remained unspoilt by success, Brahms lived very simply, never marrying, and devoting his time and energy to music. The result was four great symphonies, a similar number of concertos, many chamber masterpieces, solo piano and organ music of high quality, choral works (including the awesome *German Requiem*), and a large quantity of exceptionally fine songs.

His concern with melodic development and fulfilment – and what sublime melodies he could conjure – has led to Brahms' orchestrations being described as comparatively dull and rudimentary, yet it is difficult to conceive such a master musician being less than fully aware of the results he would obtain – and wanting those results. There is a nobility and humanity to his mature works, the symphonies, the Second Piano Concerto, the Clarinet and Piano Quintets, the String Quartets and the Horn Trio to name a few of the more famous, which confounds any criticism.

With the death of this last of the Viennese classicists in 1897, an important era in music drew to a close. If anyone assumed the mantle of Brahms, it was a composer from a country where his music has been admired as much as in his native Germany – England's Edward Elgar.

SYMPHONY NO1 IN C MINOR OP68
National Philharmonic Orchestra
Conductor: Carlos Paita
Lodia LO-CD779
DDD Running time: 43.06
Performance: ★ ★ ★   Recording: ★ ★ ★

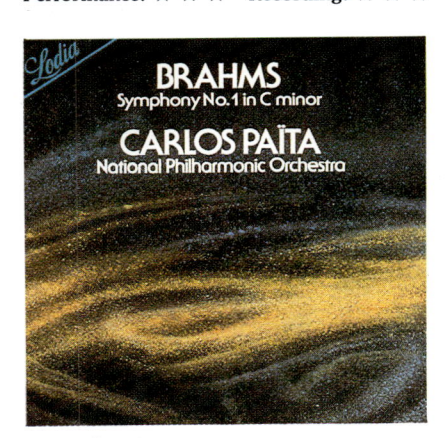

Exactly why Brahms waited until 1876, his forty-third year, before publishing a First Symphony has been a continuing source of speculation. The theory that the 'shadow of Beethoven' inhibited him falls down once it is remembered Brahms had no difficulty producing three piano sonatas very early in his composing career, a form as much dominated by Beethoven as the symphony. And the scale of those sonatas gives the lie to the notion that Brahms was reluctant to work on a large canvas during his formative years. Most likely, however, he did feel a rather inhibiting responsibility to continue the tradition of the German symphony.

Brahms described the C minor as '*long and not particularly amiable*', which underestimates the smiling nature of the two middle movements, much shorter and lighter than the rock-hewn structures which surround them. The tragic urgency of the first movement may hark back to the profound impact of the death of Brahms' friend and champion, Robert Schumann in 1856 (the earliest sketches for a symphony were made about that time), while the 'big tune' of the fourth has long suffered from its similarity to the '*Joy*' theme of Beethoven's Ninth Symphony, and a casual remark that Brahms' First was 'Beethoven's Tenth'. Whether meant as praise or condemnation, it is best ignored, and the finale enjoyed for the stirring, inspirational music that it is.

Carlos Paita directs a refreshingly unmannered and spontaneous performance, which is also an extremely well-recorded one apart from some over-prominent tympani. It is certainly preferable to some of the better-known names below, though the radically-different, highly-charged version by Gunter Wand will appeal to those who like the challenge of originality.

Other recordings on CD:
LAPO/Carlos Maria Giulini/DG 410 023-2GH
VPO/Leonard Bernstein/DG 410 081-2GH
LPO/Klaus Tennstedt/EMI CDC 7 47029-2
North German RSO/Gunter Wand/
  Deutsche Harmonia-Mundi 1C 567 199774-2

**SYMPHONY NO2 IN D MAJOR OP73/
TRAGIC OVERTURE OP81**
Chicago Symphony Orchestra
Conductor: Georg Solti
Decca 414 487-2DH
AAD Running time: 58.48
Performance: ★ ★ (★)   Recording: ★ ★

Given the tough, hard-driven nature of his readings elsewhere in the symphonic repertoire, Solti's Brahms is surprisingly mellow and genial in its approach, as is his Schubert. This warm, easy-going performance of the Second is a prime example, although it wisely stays the right side of the rather ponderous quality that lets down Giulini's otherwise radiant interpretation.

With Bernstein on DG, although performance is good, the live recording disappoints – not that Solti's is wholly acceptable: it is close enough to become quite glaring and has a certain portly quality. The *Tragic Overture* fares better in this respect.

In the final analysis, a wholly recommendable Second has yet to appear on

Compact Disc and EMI could do worse than remaster one of their three vintage analogue recordings: the Boult, Klemperer, and early stereo Karajan, all of which are preferable to the three CD versions.

Other recordings on CD:
LAPO/Carlo Maria Giulini/DG 400 066-2GH
VPO/Leonard Bernstein/DG 410 082-2GH

SYMPHONY NO3 IN F MAJOR OP90
VARIATIONS ON A THEME BY HAYDN OP56A
Columbia Symphony Orchestra
Conductor: Bruno Walter
CBS Masterworks MK42022
ADD Running time: 51.44
Performance: ★ ★ ★   Recording: ★ ★

In the 'Indian summer' of his long career, Bruno Walter made a large number of recordings for CBS in America, with the specially-formed Columbia Symphony Orchestra. The repertoire was that for which he had become justly famous on the concert platform: principally Mozart, Beethoven, Mahler and Brahms. Very sensibly, CBS have remastered much of this unique material for Compact Disc, the four Brahms symphonies included. All are great performances, but the Third is the plum: affectionate, lyrical, warmly played and recorded.

Few concessions need be made for the 1960 sound, which is full-bodied, wide-ranged and in no way under-nourished. Indeed, the agreeable sense of a real orchestra playing in front of the listener is matched by very few more modern productions.

First performed in 1883, the Third is the shortest of the symphonies, and perhaps the most romantic of the set, the poignant, nostalgic theme of the third movement justly famous in this respect. The whole work is unified by a motto theme (a variant of Brahms' youthful three-note motif, *F-A-F*: in German, *frei aber froh* (*free but happy*) and, as well as the most concentrated of the four, the Third is also the most introspective, ending quietly and undramatically.

A well-played performance of the Haydn Variations makes an appropriate and satisfying filler for the symphony.

Other recordings on CD:
VPO/Leonard Bernstein/DG 410 083-2GH
CSO/Georg Solti/Decca 414 488-2DH

SYMPHONY NO4 IN E MINOR OP98
Vienna Philharmonic Orchestra
Conductor: Carlos Kleiber
Deutsche Grammophon 400 037-2GH
DDD Running time: 39.20
Performance: ★ ★ ★   Recording: ★

The Fourth Symphony followed hard on the heels of the Third, Brahms himself conducting the first performance in 1885. Whatever inhibitions had kept him from symphonic composition a decade earlier had now been conquered four times over. The last symphony, however, has more in common with the First than its immediate predecessor. It has the air of a swan-song, a lyric tragedy on a grand scale, yet the movements themselves have very little in common, especially the blustering *scherzo*,

its feeling of forced jollity epitomized by the incongruous jangling of the triangle. It makes a curious partner for the finale, Brahms' ultimate homage to his musical lineage: a tightly-knit set of thirty variations on an eight-bar ground bass (a theme from Bach's Cantata No150) which forms an awesome monument in music. In this way, in his last symphony, Brahms triumphantly reconciled the classical ideal with the romantic vision.

That is something that comes across strongly in Carlos Kleiber's gripping performance, which is one of great individuality and distinction. Searching, questioning, the approach fresh and unhampered by tradition, the result is compelling, and certainly the most recommendable CD version despite the uncomfortably dry, enclosed, and one-dimensional sound quality. That, presumably, was approved by Kleiber, although the clipping of the reverberation at the end of each movement no doubt occured in the later mastering stages. You will also note the poor-value playing time, but on this occasion the performance is everything.

Other recordings on CD:
VPO/Leonard Bernstein/DG 410 084-2GH
CSO/Georg Solti/Decca 414 563-2DH
North German RSO/Gunter Wand/ Deutsche Harmonia-Mundi 1C 567 169530-2

PIANO CONCERTO NO1 IN D MINOR OP15
Vladimir Ashkenazy: Piano
Concertgebouw Orchestra, Amsterdam
Conductor: Bernard Haitink
Decca 410 009-2DH
DDD Running time: 48.38
Performance: ★ ★ ★
Recording: ★ ★ (★)

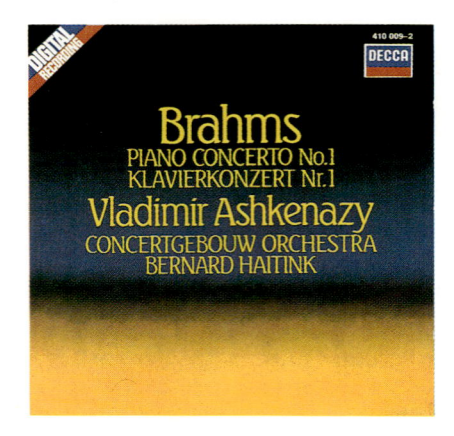

The First Piano Concerto integrates solo instrument with orchestral texture in a composition of epic scale, as befits its origins as a symphony. The first movement depicts a mighty struggle, the usually decorative piano trill here employed to the most dramatic effect. Again, the death of Robert Schumann had left its mark, the moving *adagio* originally bearing the opening words of the *Benedictus* from the Latin rite, but also described by Brahms as a reflection of Schumann's wife, Clara, for whom he had a deep affection. The torment and conflict is hardly resolved by the storming finale, which may go some way to explaining the work's indifferent reception after its initial performances in 1859.

The Decca recording is generally successful in unifying soloist and orchestra, as the work demands, although the piano remains well-projected. Tonally, both piano and strings could be better, but there can be no denying the quality of the Concertgebouw playing: the horns are in especially fine form. Masterly playing, too, from Ashkenazy, after a slightly hesitant start. He proves equal to the capricious moods of the piece, and both he and Haitink are fully responsive to the constant interplay between soloist and orchestra. This is a performance that succeeds in being dramatic, without becoming hysterical, as can so easily happen in this concerto.

Other recordings on CD:
Krystian Zimerman/VPO/Leonard Bernstein/DG 413 472-2GH
Emmanuel Ax/CSO/James Levine/RCA RCD84962

PIANO CONCERTO NO2 IN B FLAT MAJOR OP83
Vladimir Ashkenazy: Piano
Vienna Philharmonic Orchestra
Conductor: Bernard Haitink
Decca 410 199-2DH
DDD Running time: 50.58
Performance: ★ ★ ★   Recording: ★ ★ ★

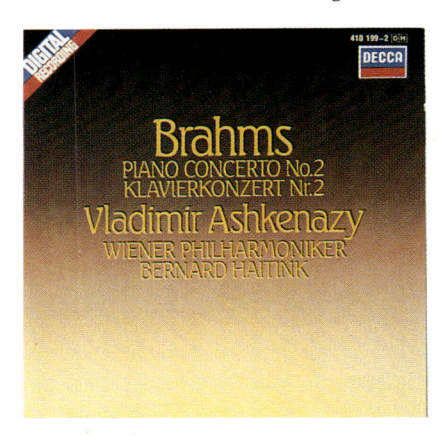

For the Second Concerto, Decca took Ashkenazy and Haitink to Vienna and results were predictably every bit as good as those obtained in Amsterdam. If anything, the balancing is a little better, and there can be no quibbles here about tonal quality. The whole performance is most sensitively moulded, measured yet supple in its responses. The slow movement is quite magical, with a lovely solo 'cello contribution from Robert Scheiwein.

Much less stress-laden and highly-strung than the First, the B-flat Concerto dates from 1881, when Brahms, at forty-eight, had received the acclaim due him. It is undoubtedly reflected in the noble and confident style of the work, the finale being positively playful. In all this is a radiant performance of a genial and heart-warming work.

Other recordings on CD:
Wilhelm Backhaus/VPO/Karl Bohm/Decca 414 142-2DH
Krystian Zimerman/VPO/Leonard Bernstein/DG 415 359-2GH

CONCERTO FOR VIOLIN AND 'CELLO IN A MINOR OP102/ACADEMIC FESTIVAL OVERTURE OP80
Gidon Kremer: Violin
Mischa Maisky: 'Cello
Vienna Philharmonic Orchestra
Conductor: Leonard Bernstein
Deutsche Grammophon 410 031-2GH
DDD Running time: 45.26
Performance: ★ ★ ★   Recording: ★ ★

Like the Violin Concerto, the Double Concerto of 1887 was dedicated to Joseph Joachim, who duly gave the first performance with the 'cellist from his own quartet, Robert Haussman. It did not prove an easy combination for which to compose, giving Brahms his fair share of worries.

Solo contributions are strongly characterised here, and Bernstein is with them all the way, in a well-defined recording which, although it tends to crowd at climaxes, possesses a preferable balance to the over-projected Karajan version.

Other recordings on CD:
Anne-Sophie Mutter/Antonio Meneses/ BPO/Herbert von Karajan/DG 410 603-2GH

VIOLIN CONCERTO IN D MINOR OP77
Anne-Sophie Mutter: Violin
Berlin Philharmonic Orchestra
Conductor: Herbert von Karajan
Deutsche Grammophon 400 064-2GH
DDD Running time: 40.04
Performance: ★ ★ ★   Recording: ★ (★)

Brahms' solitary violin concerto was written for his friend, Joseph Joachim, whom he consulted on the more technical aspects, although by no means always deferring to Joachim's suggestions which were mostly aimed at reducing the work's difficulties! Brahms makes bold use of the violin's potential in a work firmly in the 'symphonic' style of the Beethoven and Mendelssohn concertos, rather than the unashamed showpieces of, for example, Paganini.

Originally in four movements, Brahms finally replaced the middle two with a new *adagio*, a serene interlude between the muscular and dramatic opening movement and the exhilarating swagger of the Hungarian-flavoured *rondo*. From the very first performance in 1879, the concerto joined its distinguished predecessors among the immortal masterpieces of the genre.

There is no doubting the stature and appeal of Anne-Sophie Mutter's performance

BRAHMS

here: it is the recording which poses some fundamental questions about the balancing of concerto compositions. Mutter, who plays with much expressive warmth and considerable flair, is very closely recorded, so much so that on occasions she seems as loud as the orchestra, which certainly was not Brahms' intention. Another by-product of the close-miking is the coarseness of the sound in climaxes, causing the solo image to 'swim' about the stereo stage, and giving the whole sound an inflated quality. It is all so unnecessary, as naturally-balanced concerto recordings amply demonstrate.

In performance terms, though, Mutter leads the field at present.

Other recordings on CD:
Uto Ughi/PO/Wolfgang Sawallisch/RCA RCD70072
Gidon Kremer/VPO/Leonard Bernstein/DG 410 029-2GH
Boris Belkin/LSO/Ivan Fischer/Decca 411 677-2DH

PIANO QUINTET IN F MINOR OP34
Andre Previn: Piano
Musikverein Quartett, Vienna
Philips 412 608-2PH
DDD Running time: 41.16
Performance: ★ ★ ★   Recording: ★ ★ ★

The richly melodic, complex, yet mellowing Piano Quintet passed through a remarkable metamorphosis before attaining its final form. It was originally scored as a string quintet along the lines of Schubert's C Major, but Brahms had to concede that this form would be altogether too thickly-layered. He therefore transferred it to his favoured two-piano medium, only after that publishing the work as a quintet for piano and strings in 1865. However, he did not relinquish the two-piano version, which appeared as Op34b.

It is not an easy work to record: the piano can easily become oppressively dominant. Ensuring that it does not do so is as much the responsibility of the player as the recording engineer, and here both judge its contribution to perfection. Fairly close, but not without atmosphere, the recording offers crisply-focussed imaging of the five instruments, no loss of detail, but (on the 'minus side') just a little edginess to the sound.

The performance is a fine one, Previn revealing an unexpected empathy with the work. With well-adjusted tempi throughout, the result is immensely satisfying.

HUNGARIAN DANCES NOS1-21:
orchestrations
Leipzig Gewandhaus Orchestra
Conductor: Kurt Masur
Philips 411 426-2PH
DDD Running time: 53.01
Performance: ★ ★ ★
Recording: ★ ★ (★)

Brahms' wrote this series of dances, based on popular Magyar and gypsy tunes, over a seventeen-year period between 1852 and 1869. All were originally for piano, four hands, but various orchestrations were subsequently made, including some by the composer himself.

One of two complete recordings on Compact Disc, Kurt Masur scores over his rival, Claudio Abbado, by injecting a degree more affection and charm into the performances. Although played with tremendous verve, Abbado's readings are a little straight-faced by comparison.

There is no lack of impact in the Leipzig sound, with a full, ripe resonance to basses and timpani. Generally the sound is clean and atmospheric with the imaging well-preserved and, with responsive playing from the Leipzig orchestra, the result is thoroughly enjoyable. Brahms is nowhere so immediately accessible and entertaining as here.

Other recordings on CD (complete):
VPO/Claudio Abbado/DG 410 615-2GH

CLARINET TRIO IN A MINOR OP114/ HORN TRIO IN E FLAT MAJOR OP40*
Andras Schiff: Piano
Members of the New Vienna Quartet:
Peter Schmidl: Clarinet
Friedrich Dolezal: 'Cello
Günter Högner: Horn*
Erich Binder: Violin*
Decca 410 114-2DH
DDD Running time: 55.20
Performance: ★ ★ (★)
Recording: ★ ★ (★)

It is the predominantly melancholy Clarinet Trio, one of Brahms' last great chamber works, which emerges best here, with a sensitive but not overtly maudlin performance that manages to be well-defined without despatching the performers to the extreme edges of the sound-stage and losing the essential homogeneity of sound. Tonal quality is generally good, especially the burnished resonance of the 'cello.

The unsentimental approach works less

well in the Horn Trio, especially when remembering Brahms' grief at the death of his mother, and its likely expression in the elegaic third movement. However, it remains a satisfying account, better balanced than the only alternative version with Tuckwell, Ashkenazy and Perlman (also on Decca), if missing a little of their heartfelt eloquence.

Other recordings on CD:
(Horn Trio Op40)
Barry Tuckwell/Vladimir Ashkenazy/Itzhak Perlman/Decca 414 128-2DH

SCHERZO IN E FLAT MINOR OP4/ BALLADES OP10: NO1 IN D MINOR/NO2 IN D MAJOR/NO3 IN B MINOR/NO4 IN B MAJOR/PIANO PIECES OP76 NOS1-8
Stephen Bishop-Kovacevich: Piano
Philips 411 103-2PH
DDD Running time: 49.33
Performance: ★ ★ ★   Recording: ★ ★ ★

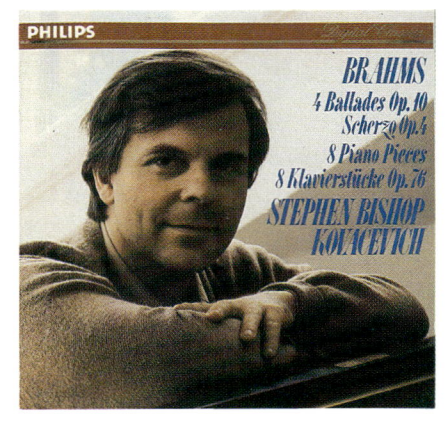

Both the *Scherzo* and the set of *Ballades* were composed before Brahms was twenty-one, at a time when a career as a concert pianist was still on the cards for him. The more intimate Piano Pieces Op76 date from his mid-forties and display a remarkable concentration of ideas. The youthful works are similarly notable for furnishing ample evidence that Brahms had a greater feel for textural lucidity than is often acknowledged.

Demanding works, therefore, but Bishop-Kovacevich is equal to their widely contrasting moods and, needless to say, plays impeccably. The recording, although fairly close, allows the piano nicely to excite the hall ambience. Accuracy and clarity are maintained throughout, and the lustrous tone, as well as being realistic, is lovely to hear.

Other recordings on CD:
(Ballades)
Arturo Benedetti Michelangeli/DG 400 043-2GH
Glenn Gould/CBS MK37800

'CELLO SONATAS: NO1 IN E MINOR OP38/NO2 IN F MAJOR OP99
Steven Isserlis: 'Cello
Peter Evans: Piano
Hyperion CDA66159
DDD Running time: 50.15
Performance: ★ ★ ★   Recording: ★ ★ ★

Perhaps with Beethoven at the back of his mind, Brahms laboured some three years (1862–5) over the First 'Cello Sonata. The outcome was a work of sombre, reflective mood which relies heavily on the lower register of the 'cello, and presents formidable problems of balance in its complex, almost Bach-like, third movement.

It was not until the summer of 1886 that he completed a second sonata, one of three major chamber works to emerge from that period, and quite different in temperament to its predecessor, mirroring Brahms' own happiness and confidence.

Steven Isserlis and Peter Evans respond ably to the demands of both works, and offer performances every bit as profound and satisfying as their 'superstar' rivals.

With a clearly-defined, equable balance between the two instruments, enabling the sound of Isserlis' gut-stringed 'cello to be fully enjoyed, this is yet another notable issue from the comparatively small Hyperion label.

Other recordings on CD:
Mstislav Rostropovich/Rudolf Serkin/DG 410 510-2GH
Rama Jucker/Werner Giger/Accord 149049
Lynn Harrell/Vladimir Ashkenazy/Decca 414 558-2DH

FANTASIEN NOS1-7 OP116/THREE INTERMEZZI OP117/KLAVIERSTÜCKE NOS1-4 OP119
Stephen Bishop-Kovacevich: Piano
Philips 411 137-2PH
DDD Running time: 51.19
Performance: ★ ★ ★   Recording: ★ ★ ★

In his later piano writing, Brahms avoided the large-scale sonata and variation formats and devoted his attention to groups of miniatures, not least because they were all that the ailing Clara Schumann had the stamina to play. In the *Fantasias* of 1891, he contrasted four tender, plaintive pieces, with three of volatile mood, calling the former *Intermezzi* and the latter, *Capriccios*. The following year, the *Three Intermezzi*, Op117, were almost unrelievedly filled with an air of deep sadness and regret, while the Op119 pieces were to be Brahms' last compositions for solo piano.

There is an unerring rightness about these performances: only in the fifth of the *Fantasien* does Bishop-Kovacevic seem rather too headstrong, elsewhere displaying scrupulous judgement in matters of tempo and expression. There can have been few better interpretations of Brahms' sometimes elusive keyboard musings, and certainly none better recorded.

BENJAMIN BRITTEN
(b. Lowestoft, Suffolk, 22 November 1913; d. Aldeburgh, Suffolk, 4 December 1976)

Such were the gifts of Benjamin Britten, he was composing at the age of five and writing string quartets and piano sonatas at ten. By twelve he was studying with the much-underrated English composer, Frank Bridge, after a performance of the latter's marvellous tone poem, *The Sea*, had left an indelible impression on Britten. His admiration for Bridge never waned, nor that for his two teachers at the Royal College of Music, John Ireland and Arthur Benjamin. But his early choral works and songs indicated the development of a style that owed little to that of his tutors, or any other composer, although influences as diverse as Purcell and Mahler much attracted him.

The *Bridge Variations* of 1937 first brought him to wide public notice, and in subsequent years, soundtrack music for some twenty documentary films, including the famous *Night Mail* and *The Instruments of the Orchestra* (1945), which in concert performance became the justly popular *Young Person's Guide to the Orchestra*.

When war was declared in 1939, Britten and his lifelong companion, Peter Pears, were in North America. They returned in 1942, when Britten, a registered conscientious objector, was forced to face a tribunal to justify his exemption from the armed services.

During the war years, he displayed his increasing mastery of word-setting with the *Serenade for Tenor, Horn and Strings*, and in 1945, brought it to full flower with his first opera, *Peter Grimes* (discussed in our companion volume). Many ambitious compositions followed, operatic, choral and instrumental: including the Church Parables; the *War Requiem*; the *Spring Symphony*, and *Curlew River* – a unique combination of medieval music drama and Japanese Noh play.

Britten also did much to promote the love of music among children – the delightful *Noye's Fludde* is a prime example – and in 1948 he founded the annual Aldeburgh Festival, based around the concert hall created within a disused maltings in the Suffolk village of Snape. He received several honours in his career, culminating in a life peerage just before his death, after a three-year illness, in 1976.

From the few titles mentioned above, it is obvious that much more of Britten's output, in all fields of music, deserves to appear on Compact Disc. As we go to press, the Pears/Britten recordings of those two magnificent orchestral song cycles, the *Serenade for Tenor, Horn and Strings* and the Rimbaud settings, *Les Illuminations*, were due for Compact Disc release in ADRM transfers from Decca. It was for that label, of course, that Britten made so many recordings of his own music and it would be encouraging to think that similarly definitive issues as the *Spring Symphony*, and the *Young Person's Guide to the Orchestra* and the *Bridge Variations* are in the pipeline for CD issue.

Then, of course, there are those marvellous recordings Britten made conducting others' music, notably Mozart.

VARIATIONS ON A THEME OF FRANK BRIDGE OP10/SIMPLE SYMPHONY OP4/LACHRYMAE – REFLECTIONS ON A SONG OF DOWLAND*/PRELUDE AND FUGUE FOR STRING ORCHESTRA OP29
Roger Best: Viola*
English String Orchestra
Conductor: William Boughton
Nimbus NIM5025
DDD Running time: 65.18
Performance: ★ ★   Recording: ★ ★ ★

There is no doubt that Britten's set of variations on a theme from the second of three *Idylls* composed by his teacher, Frank Bridge, is one of the greatest compositions for string orchestra this century. It is also one of the most innovative in its treatment of the string ensemble, a remarkably confident and well-crafted work which was premiered in 1937, just before Britten's twenty-fourth birthday. There is an equal freshness in the robust *Simple Symphony*, which the composer said was evolved from themes first thought of in childhood. The *Prelude and Fugue* of 1943 is an altogether more demanding work. The most recent composition here is the orchestration of the *Lachrymae*, originally scored for viola and piano, which Britten produced just before his death in 1976. This is the first recording, and it is a fine one. However, alongside Britten's own, the otherwise wholly enjoyable performance of the *Bridge Variations*, the most important work here, seems a little under-characterized.

Splendidly and naturally recorded, and giving generous measure, this is a welcome issue in an under-represented area of the 20th Century musical repertoire.

Other recordings on CD:
Bournemouth Sinfonietta/Ronald Thomas/
  Chandos CHAN8376

SYMPHONY FOR 'CELLO AND ORCHESTRA OP68*
DEATH IN VENICE: suite from the opera OP88
Raphael Wallfisch: 'Cello*
English Chamber Orchestra
Conductor: Steuart Bedford
Chandos CHAN8363
DDD Running time: 60.55
Performance: ★ ★ (★) Recording: ★ ★

The *'Cello Symphony*, one of several works Britten wrote for his close friend, the Russian 'cellist Mstislav Rostropovich, was, when completed in 1963, his first large-scale intrumental work for nearly two decades. It is called a symphony, rather than a concerto, because the solo intrument is intended to be on equal terms with the orchestra, and integrated with it, not, as is usual in a concerto, to be the dominant partner. The one drawback with this recording is that the 'cello balance is rather forward, as if it *were* a concerto, and therefore it does not entirely communicate the effect Britten intended.

That said, the solo instrument still has plenty of space to 'breathe' in a pleasantly full and resonant acoustic, and Raphael Wallfisch must be congratulated on producing a performance that generally stands comparison with that of the dedicatee.

It was at the suggestion of Peter Pears that the conductor, Steuart Bedford arranged an instrumental suite from Britten's last opera, *Death in Venice*, and a worthwhile one it proved to be since the score so effectively conveys imagery of place and character. No quibble about the recording here, with the sparkling percussion writing, a product of the composer's interest in Indonesian 'gamelan' music, utterly beguiling.

SINFONIA DA REQUIEM OP20/ OCCASIONAL OVERTURE OP38/AN AMERICAN OVERTURE OP27/SUITE ON ENGLISH FOLK TUNES: 'A TIME THERE WAS. . .' OP90
City of Birmingham Symphony Orchestra
Conductor: Simon Rattle
EMI CDC7 47343-2
DDD Running time: 53.12
Performance: ★ ★ ★ Recording: ★ ★ ★

An enterprising programme that enhances the Britten CD discography considerably, principally by adding one of his most profound orchestral compositions to the catalogue: the *Sinfonia da Requiem* of 1939/40. It was originally written to a commission from the Japanese government, although they took the Christian overtones of the work as an insult and finally rejected it. The *Sinfonia* is imbued throughout with the foreboding and despair that Britten felt at the time, as the world descended inexorably into the abyss of war.

There are few more prescient openings in music than the first movement of the *Sinfonia*, and few more chilling than the *scherzo* which follows. It is a powerful and disquieting work, one which needs the light relief of the two brilliant and colourful overtures which follow. Britten preferred not to acknowledge them during his lifetime, so both have had to wait until recent years for performance and recording.

Two years before his death, Britten's last orchestral work was a suite on English folk tunes, which took its sub-title – and, subconsciously, possibly more – from Thomas Hardy. It is certainly no bucolic romp, as the haunting lament for cor anglais in the best of the movements, *Lord Melbourne*, amply proves.

Simon Rattle demonstrates again what a sensitive Britten interpreter he has become, and the recording is very good indeed, especially in its dynamic range which, for example, allows the very soft, but vital, taps on the bass drum in the *Lacrymosa* of the *Sinfonia* to come over in the way the composer undoubtedly intended.

ANTON BRUCKNER
(b. Ansfelden, near Linz, Austria, 4 September 1824; d. Vienna, 11 October 1896)

A series of symphonies on epic scale was the principal outcome of the diligent study, not to mention self-criticism, which Bruckner thought vital if his music was to command respect.

Gauche, ingenuous, socially inept, perhaps, but Bruckner was never quite the 'country bumpkin' described by some critics. No simpleton could have conceived the vast 'cathedrals of sound', as his symphonies have been aptly described, nor undertaken the arduous course of study which contributed much towards their creation.

He was the son of a schoolmaster, and became one himself at seventeen, remaining so for fifteen years despite the decision in his mid-twenties that composition should be his life's work. He was a devout Catholic, and organist of several village churches before gaining the coveted post of organist of Linz Cathedral. Yet that was mainly due to the persistent encouragment of his friends – Bruckner's opinion of his own abilities was low. He needed the reassurance of the considerable number of academic musical distinctions which his studies earned him, although his creative powers were slow to flourish. Some choral works, and three symphonies (the third of which is now numbered as his First), were completed before he left Linz for Vienna in 1868.

A turning point for him had been hearing Wagner's *Tannhäuser* in 1863, and his subsequent admiration for the composer bordered on glorification. This put him somewhat out-of-step with the Vienna of the 1870s which was largely pro-Brahms in the great debate between the two schools of music. Bruckner, rather unwittingly, found himself heading the pro-Wagner movement, hardly an ideal position for someone sensitive to criticism and whose self-assurance was quickly sapped by adverse comment.

A by-product of this was his willingness to allow others to amend and alter his scores, no doubt with the best intentions, with the result today that the symphonies are published in different editions.

There are naive aspects to his music: in repetition of phrase, for instance, and awkward discontinuities, but much that is very beautiful and often deeply spiritual. If ever there were such things as 'religious symphonies', surely Bruckner's qualify, especially the glorious Eighth and Ninth.

In sharp contrast to the first years of the LP record, when Bruckner's symphonies enjoyed little popularity, Compact Disc offers recommendable alternatives in all the major symphonies, although the choral music, some of which is very fine indeed, lacks representation.

BRUCKNER

SYMPHONY NO3 IN D MINOR
Berlin Philharmonic Orchestra
Conductor: Herbert von Karajan
Deutsche Grammophon 413 362-2GH
DDD Running time: 57.09
Performance: ★ ★ (★)
Recording: ★ ★ ★

Ample in both width and depth, this recording is one of the most expansive to come from Berlin, although some harshness is still evident when things get loud and the Brucknerian brass makes its presence felt. Mostly, though, it proves an ideal stage for Karajan's dramatic and often mercurial performance.

Opting for the revised 1889 score rather than the 1873 original, he makes no attempt to beautify some of the rough-edged and decidely rustic material Bruckner employs, and the result is all the better for it.

Other recordings on CD:
Frankfurt RSO/Eliahu Inbal/TelDec ZK8.42922
Bavarian Radio Sym O/Rafael Kubelik/CBS MK39033
Berlin RSO/Riccardo Chailly/Decca 417 093-2DH

SYMPHONY NO4 IN E FLAT (ROMANTIC)
Vienna Philharmonic Orchestra
Conductor: Karl Böhm
Decca 411 581-2DH
ADD Running time: 67.56
Performance: ★ ★ ★   Recording: ★ ★ ★

This 1974 recording, one of the finest to be made of the Fourth Symphony, certainly merits its transfer to Compact Disc, eclipsing all the competition, including Decca's own, and far more recent, digital version with Solti.

Apart from a penetrating performance by Karl Böhm and the Vienna players which is both majestic and monumental, the recording is of vintage quality: wide-ranging, naturally balanced, with a burnished glow to the brass, and suitably atmospheric. What was an LP classic is now a CD one, too.

Other recordings on CD (selection):
BPO/Herbert von Karajan/DG 415 277-2GH

SYMPHONY NO7 IN E MAJOR
Staatskapelle Dresden
Conductor: Herbert Blomstedt
Denon C37-7286
DDD Running time: 67.47
Performance: ★ ★ ★   Recording: ★ ★ ★

The Seventh was the first of Bruckner's symphonies to achieve international recognition. The eminent conductor, Arthur Nikisch, viewed the score as the work of the most remarkable symphonist since Beethoven, and conducted the first performance within a month or two of the work's completion in 1884. Soon it was being heard throughout Europe and the USA, and remained by far the most familiar of his symphonies for several decades.

Herbert Blomstedt uses the Haas edition for this well-shaped and exceptionally well-played account, in which only something of the mystery of the *adagio* seems lacking.

SYMPHONY NO6 IN A MAJOR
Bavarian State Orchestra
Conductor: Wolfgang Sawallisch
Orfeo CO24821A
DDD Running time: 55.06
Performance: ★ ★ ★   Recording: ★ ★ ★

Recorded in the apparently vast acoustic of the Great Hall of the University of Munich, Wolfgang Sawallisch's reading of the Sixth Symphony is compelling in every respect. The big sound-stage naturally gives the music room to expand, but the engineers have succeeded in letting plenty of 'air' into the recording without it suffering the all-too-frequent by-products of blurred detail and confused textures. The very clear, but wholly natural, result is indeed impressive.

SYMPHONY NO8 IN C MINOR
(c/w **Wagner: Siegfried Idyll***)
Concertgebouw Orchestra, Amsterdam
Conductor: Bernard Haitink
Philips 412 465-2PH2 (2 discs)
ADD*/DDD Running time: 103.50
Performance: ★ ★ ★   Recording: ★ ★ ★

Even though Bruckner believed the Eighth to be his best work, he still lacked the confidence to deflect criticism and when the conductor, Hermann Levi, whom the composer respected very highly, declared the symphony incomprehensible, Bruckner embarked on a revision that was to occupy him six years, until 1890, and cost him his health.

Of the four versions of the Eighth currently available on CD, Haitink's takes the palm. Carlos Paita on Lodia is very good, and Giulini's reading is deeply felt but at times slow to the point of becoming static.

Haitink is no less spacious or serene, but does maintain vital momentum through Bruckner's rolling symphonic acres. It is a performance of both poetry and power.

Other recordings on CD:
VPO/Carlo Maria Giulini/DG 415 124-2GH2
Philharmonic SO/Carlos Paita/Lodia 1LO-CD783/4
(1887 Version)
Frankfurt RSO/Eliahu Inbal/TelDec ZK8.48218

SYMPHONY NO9 IN D MINOR
Concertgebouw Orchestra, Amsterdam
Conductor: Bernard Haitink
Philips 410 039-2PH
DDD Running time: 62.38
Performance: ★ ★ (★)
Recording: ★ ★ (★)

When it seemed likely that death would prevent the completion of the Ninth Symphony, Bruckner suggested that his choral *Te Deum* would make a suitable ending but, as with Schubert's Eighth, the 'last' movement completed actually proves to be a wholly satisfying conclusion. In so many ways, this deeply reflective *adagio* comes over as the last stretch of an epic spiritual pilgrimage.

Haitink certainly conveys this mood in his measured but well-contrasted approach. It is cogently argued throughout, with both strength and commitment, and the Concertgebouw acoustic seems ideal.

FRÉDÉRIC CHOPIN
(b. Zelazowa Wola, Poland, 1 March 1810; d. Paris 17 October 1849)

Daguerrotype of Chopin: his genius was mainly distilled in exquisite miniatures.

Chopin was one of a trilogy of composers for whom the piano was the prime means of expression. Whatever the virtues of Schumann's symphonies and the 'programme symphonies' and symphonic poems of Liszt, their appeal has never matched that of their greatest solo piano compositions (and in the former's case, his output of songs).

Chopin, however, never even attempted a symphonic composition, and in his two piano concertos, the orchestra plays a wholly supportive rôle. He will remain the first, and perhaps the finest poet of the piano, by turns dramatic, lyric, heroic, joyful, melancholy, and despairingly pessimistic.

He was half-French, half-Polish by birth, and seemed to inherit the elegance of the former and the fiery nationalism of the latter. His gifts were soon apparent and he was just nine when he made his concert debut. Yet, although he had lessons in Warsaw, the young Chopin was largely self-taught.

He enjoyed socialising, and rapidly became the darling of the Parisian 'salon set' upon settling there in 1831. Six years later he encountered Madame Aurore Dudevant, better known now as the novelist George Sand, and their subsequent affair lasted ten years, including a sojourn in Majorca intended to help Chopin recover health and strength (he had a frail constitution). It did him little good and, moreover, he and George Sand parted after a quarrel.

His last concerts were given in England during 1848, but the tour was cut short by illness and he returned to Paris, dying there the following year. As he requested, he was buried in Père Lachaise cemetery, and at the internment a box full of Polish earth, which had been given him some twenty years earlier, was opened and sprinkled over his coffin.

Recordings principally by Vladimir Ashkenazy and Maurizio Pollini, and now joined by RCA's remastered Artur Rubinstein collection, give excellent coverage of Chopin on Compact Disc. First choice in the piano concertos should be resolved by the promised appearance of both Krystian Zimerman's recordings on a single CD.

CHOPIN

PIANO CONCERTO NO1 IN E MINOR OP11
(c/w Liszt: Piano Concerto No1 in E Flat Major S124)
Martha Argerich: Piano
London Symphony Orchestra
Conductor: Claudio Abbado
Deutsche Grammophon 415 061-2GH
ADD Running time: 55.07
Performance: ★ ★ (★) Recording: ★ ★

This imaginative coupling of two of the great virtuoso concertos dates from 1967 but comes up bright as a new pin in this transfer. The recorded balance favours the solo instrument, but not to an unacceptable degree, given the spacious acoustic that surrounds both piano and orchestra. The latter does sound, however, rather confined compared to the full sound-stage found in the best of today's concerto recordings, but given the largely secondary role allotted it in both works, perhaps that can be forgiven.

Argerich's is a fluent performance, but a well-structured one, thanks to the firm orchestral base laid down by Abbado. The slow movement is indeed poetic.

The main competition to this performance is likely to come from Zimerman's coupling of the two Chopin concertos.

Argerich adds an urbane, cultured rendering of the Liszt concerto, one that approaches, but does not quite match, Richter's classic account on Philips.

Other recordings on CD:
(Chopin Piano Concerto No1)
Emanuel Ax/Philadelphia O/Eugene Ormandy/RCA RD85317
Krystian Zimerman/LAPO/Carlo Maria Giulini/DG 415 970-2GH

PIANO CONCERTO NO2 IN F MINOR OP21/KRAKOWIAK: CONCERT RONDO FOR PIANO AND ORCHESTRA OP14
Bella Davidovich: Piano
London Symphony Orchestra
Conductor: Neville Marriner
Philips 410 042-2PH
ADD Running time: 47.35
Performance: ★ ★ Recording: ★ ★

This elegant and sensitive performance of the F minor concerto just lacks that degree of vitality which distinguishes, say, Zimerman's sparkling recording for DG (as mentioned above, now scheduled for Compact Disc issue). The 'feminine' approach, though, has much to commend it, not least the subtle shading and sonorous tone Bella Davidovich is able to bring to the score. The orchestral accompaniment is good, if not outstanding, although the LSO's contribution is hardly enhanced by a recording which projects a close, unnecessarily wide piano image. Otherwise the sound, full with an agreeable ambience, is most acceptable. The fill-up, the *Krakowiak*, is well-played.

Other recordings on CD:
Ivo Pogorelich/CSO/Claudio Abbado/DG 410 507-2GH
Andras Schiff/Concertgebouw O/Antal Dorati/Decca 411 942-2DH
Emanuel Ax/Philadelphia O/Eugene Ormandy/RCA RD85317
Krystian Zimerman/LAPO/Carlo Maria Giulini/DG 415 970-2GH

BALLADES: NO1 IN G MINOR OP23/NO2 IN F MAJOR OP38/NO3 IN A FLAT OP47/NO4 IN F MINOR OP52/IMPROMPTUS: NO1 IN A FLAT MAJOR OP29/NO2 IN F SHARP OP36/NO3 IN G FLAT MAJOR OP51/NO4 IN C SHARP MINOR OP66 (FANTAISIE IMPROMPTU)
Bella Davidovich: Piano
Philips 411 427-2PH
DDD Running time: 58.26
Performance: ★ ★ ★
Recording: ★ ★ (★)

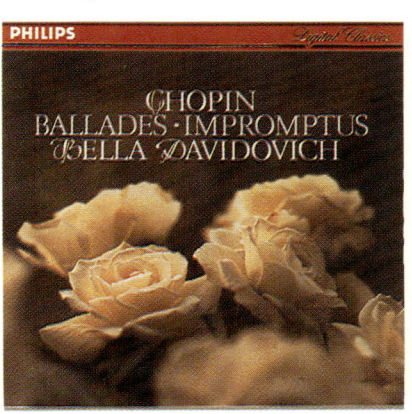

It was good programming to couple these two sets of freely expressive pieces, the more introspective *Ballades*, written over an eleven-year span between 1831 and 1842, and the *Impromptus* of 1837–42, including the well-known *Fantaisie Impromptu*. It is interesting to recall that, if Chopin's instructions for the fate of his music after his death had been followed, the score of the latter would have been destroyed.

These sensitive performances by Bella Davidovich were recorded in venues in London and Switzerland, but with negligible difference in sound quality. Detail and tonal quality are very good.

Other recordings on CD(selection):
(Ballades 1-4)
François-René Duchable/Erato ECD88023
(Impromptus 1-4)
Murray Perahia/CBS MK39708

IMPROMPTUS: NO1 IN A FLAT MAJOR OP29/NO2 IN F SHARP MAJOR OP36/NO3 IN G FLAT MAJOR OP51/NO4 IN C SHARP MINOR OP66 (FANTAISIE IMPROMPTU)/BARCAROLLE IN F SHARP MAJOR OP60/BERCEUSE IN D FLAT MAJOR OP57/FANTAISIE IN F MINOR OP49
Murray Perahia: Piano
CBS MK39708
DDD Running time: 48.09
Performance: ★ ★ ★
Recording: ★ ★ (★)

As befits someone described as 'the poet of the piano', these are eloquent readings, lovingly and beautifully played. The charms of the *Berceuse* can rarely have been so gracefully conveyed, or the lyrical flights of the *Barcarolle*. Only the *Fantaisie* Op49, a work of great depth and nobility, one of Chopin's most substantial conceptions, seems wanting in drama; otherwise these are immaculately-judged performances, well-recorded.

CHOPIN

There is a certain softness to the sound, but it is discreetly distanced, and the 'empty hall' ambience seems altogether appropriate for this music.

Other recordings on CD:
(*Impromptus* 1–4)
Bella Davidovich/Philips 411 427-2PH
(*Barcarolle*)
Vladimir Ashkenazy/Decca 410 180-2DH

MAZURKAS: OP30 NOS1—4/OP33 NOS1—4/NOCTURNES: OP32 NOS1 AND 2/NOCTURNE IN C MINOR OP. POSTH./ SCHERSO NO2 OP31/WALTZ OP34 NO3/ VARIATION NO6 (FROM HEXAMERON)/ IMPROMPTU NO1 OP29/LARGO IN E FLAT MAJOR OP POSTH
Vladimir Ashkenazy: Piano
Decca 410 122-2DH
DDD Running time: 51.13
Performance: ★ ★ ★
Recording: ★ ★(★)

Apart from the *Favourite Chopin* compilation, Ashkenazy's recitals have all been based on chronology rather than genre, each disc featuring a variety of works from one period in the composer's career. In the case of this recording, it is the years 1836–38, which yield a diverse collection of compositions including the unrelievedly gloomy *Largo* in E flat. The rest, however, are in somewhat brighter mood, although Ashkenazy perfectly captures the dark, impassioned side to the mazurkas.

There are many examples of his intuitive judgement among these finely-honed performances: the *Scherzo* is but one, while the unaffected quality of both the *Nocturnes* and the *Impromptu* is a pleasure to hear.

The recording, made in the Kingsway Hall, London, has an imposing power and presence, although not at the expense of inner clarity. The result, however, does project the upper register of the piano rather more than the rest.

Other recordings on CD:
(*Mazurkas* – selection)
Arturo Benedetti Michelangeli/DG 413 449-2GH

FAVOURITE CHOPIN: BALLADE NO3 OP47/PRELUDE NO25 OP45/WALTZES OP64 NO1 AND NO2/BARCAROLLE OP60/ETUDES OP10 NO3 (TRISTESSE) NO5 (BLACK KEY) NO12 (REVOLUTIONARY)/ETUDE OP25 NO11 (WINTER WIND)/NOCTURNE OP55 NO1/POLONAISE OP40 NO1 SCHERZO NO3 OP39/PRELUDE OP28 NO5 (RAINDROP)
Vladimir Ashkenazy: Piano
Decca 410 180-2DH
ADD Running time: 60.28
Performance: ★ ★ ★   Recording: ★ ★

The disc's title is wholly accurate: this is indeed a collection of the best-known (if not always the best) Chopin, the only drawback of which is that the unremitting succession of familiar melodies can become a little indigestible. However, the disc is also a tribute to Vladimir Ashkenazy's art and as a 'Chopin primer' could hardly be bettered.

As you would expect from recordings spanning seven years (1975–82), quality varies. Some of the more elderly show their age through tape hiss and a slightly metallic tone, but none are less than acceptable. The more technically minded will be able to compare a wide range of acoustics and recording techniques, too!

MAZURKAS: NOS19, 20 OP30 NOS2 AND 3/NO22 OP33 NO1/NO25 OP33 NO4/ NO34 OP56 NO2/NO43 OP67 NO2/NO45 OP67 NO4/NOS46, 47 OP68 NOS1 AND 2/NO49 OP68 NO4/PRELUDE NO25 OP45/BALLADE NO1 OP23/SCHERZO NO2 OP31
Arturo Benedetti Michelangeli: Piano
Deutsche Grammophon 413 449-2GH
ADD Running time: 53.19
Performance: ★ ★ (★)
Recording: ★ ★ (★)

While there is much to admire in Michelangeli's recital, not least its diamond-like clarity and brilliance, there is a certain clinical aloofness to some of the readings which is less attractive. There is no denying, though, the magic he brings to the *Ballade* and the *Scherzo*, which are spellbinding.

The 1972 recording was always one of DG's best piano sounds, and its realistic presence and timbre can be appreciated the more on Compact Disc. In contrast to some keyboard recordings from that period, the lack of any aggressive edge to the sound and the firm, controlled lower registers, are worthy of note.

Other recordings on CD:
(*Mazurkas* – selections)
Vladimir Ashkenazy/Decca 410 122-2DH
(*Mazurkas* – complete)
Artur Rubinstein/RCA RD85171 (2 discs)

ÉTUDES OP10 NOS1-12/OP25 NOS1-12
Vladimir Ashkenazy: Piano
Decca 414 127-2DH
AAD Running time: 65.34
Performance: ★ ★ ★
Recording: ★ ★ (★)

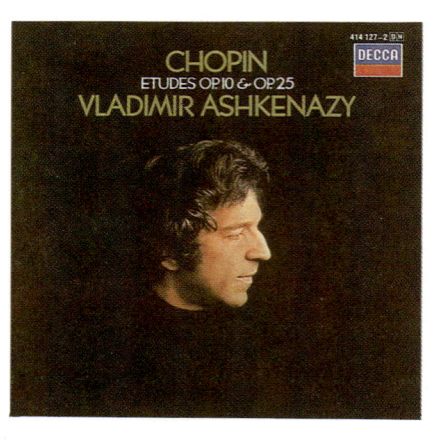

Ashkenazy's imaginative and well-conceived performance of the *Études*, recorded in 1974, emerges well from this immaculate Compact Disc transfer. The sound is full and well-defined, with good extension. Some edginess is detectable when the going gets loud, and the image is stretched a little, but these are minor distractions.

These incomparable miniatures, with their astonishing fertility of ideas, were composed over a ten-year span from 1829 to 1839. The first set, Op10, was dedicated to Liszt, the second to Liszt's mistress, the Countess d'Agoult!

It should be added that Maurizio Pollini runs Ashkenazy very close, in terms of performance, but the recording is not of the same quality.

Other recordings on CD (complete):
Maurizio Pollini/DG 413 794-2GH
Francois-René Duchable/Erato ECD88001

NOCTURNES: NO3, OP9 NO3/NOS4, 5, 6 OP15 NOS1, 2 AND 3/NOS7, 8 OP27 NOS1 AND 2/NOS13, 14 OP48 NOS1 AND 2/NO16 OP55 NO2/NO17 OP62 NO1
Vlado Perlemuter: Piano
Nimbus NIM5012
DDD Running time: 50.07
Performance: ★ ★ ★
Recording: ★ ★ (★)

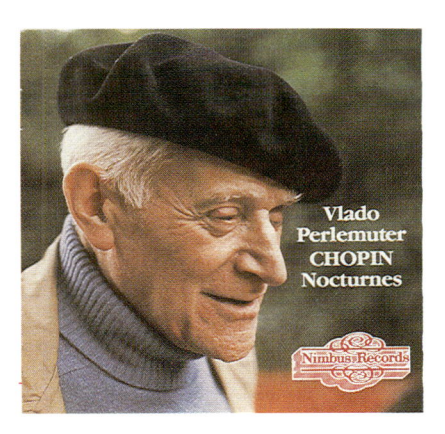

For those wanting only a selection from the *Nocturnes*, rather than Arrau's complete survey, these performances by another octogenarian, Vlado Perlemuter, can be recommended. Like Arrau, advancing years do not seem to have impaired the control or the strength of Perlemuter's playing, and there is a clarity and impetus to his performances which is refreshingly different from the limpid lingerings some younger pianists feel Chopin warrants. No doubt the Nimbus 'single-take' recording philosophy assists this feeling of spontaneity, and Perlemuter has obviously relished the challenge such recording presents.

The firmly-focussed piano certainly excites the ambience of the venue, and the 'empty ballroom' effect may not be to all tastes, especially those accustomed to a closer, more sterile sound. However, it is certainly an exact replica of the performance, and puts nothing between player and listener.

Other recordings on CD:
(complete)
Claudio Arrau/Philips 416 440-2PH2
(selections)
Daniel Barenboim/DG 415 117-2GH

NOCTURNES NOS1—21: OP9 NOS1—3/ OP15 NOS1—3/OP27 NOS1 AND 2/OP32 NOS1 AND 2/OP37 NOS1 AND 2/OP48 NOS1 AND 2/OP55 NOS1 AND 2/OP62 NOS1 AND 2/OP72/NO20 OP POSTH/ NO21 OP POSTH.
Claudio Arrau: Piano
Philips 416 440-2PH2 (2 discs)
DDD Running time: 121.49
Performance: ★ ★ ★   Recording: ★ ★ ★

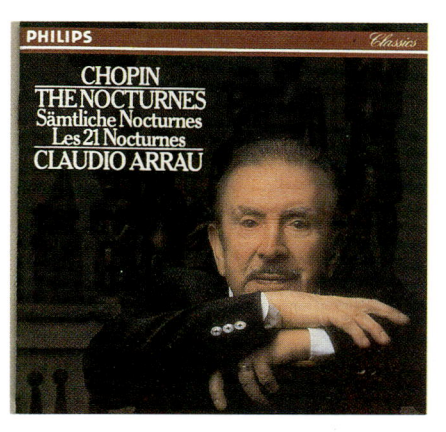

It was the Irish composer, John Field, who developed the nocturne as a keyboard composition, but Chopin who, over a span of twenty years, invested the form with a depth and range of expression undreamed of by Field or his contemporaries. Chopin's twenty-one examples, including two published posthumously, contain some of his most evocative and imaginative writing, with the two Op62 *Nocturnes* standing at the apex of his achievement in their daring treatment of melody and harmony.

It requires playing of the highest order to meet the widely-contrasted demands of these compositions, but that is what Claudio Arrau possesses in abundance. The touch is unerring, with remarkable clarity and care. The recording is correspondingly refined, rich-toned and detailed.

Other recordings on CD (selections only):
Daniel Barenboim/DG 415 117-2GH
Vlado Perlemuter/Nimbus NIM5012

PIANO SONATA NO2 IN B FLAT MINOR OP35/PIANO SONATA NO3 IN B MINOR OP58
Maurizio Pollini: Piano
Deutsche Grammophon 415 346-2GH
DDD Running time: 51.51
Performance: ★ ★ ★   Recording: ★ ★ ★

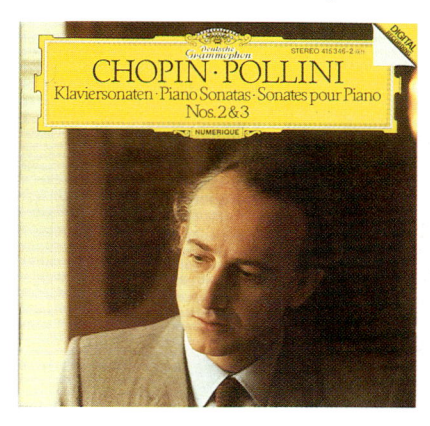

In the opinion of Schumann, the movements of the B flat minor sonata, including the celebrated *Marche funèbre*, constitute four of Chopin's *'most bizarre creations'*. It is an extraordinary work, not least in the tersely demonic *presto* finale, which lasts barely a minute-and-a-half and offers no respite from the resigned pessimism which pervades the whole sonata.

The notoriety of the Second Sonata has tended to overshadow the Third of 1844 (as

CHOPIN

is evident in the paucity of recordings), yet it is no less imaginative than its predecessor, if not quite as radical in conception.

These are gripping performances from Pollini, in every way a match for his previous Chopin recordings, with sound that is both truthful and transparent. Duchable's readings on Erato are also very good, but in most respects Pollini's have the edge.

Other recordings on CD:
(Piano Sonata No2)
Josef Bulva/Orfeo C111841A
John Bingham/Meridian/ECD84070
Ivo Pogorelich/DG 415 123-2GH
(Piano Sonatas Nos2 and 3)
François-René Duchable/Erato ECD88083

PRELUDES OP28 NOS1—24
Maurizio Pollini: Piano
Deutsche Grammophon 413 796-2GH
ADD Running time: 36.18
Performance: ★ ★ ★
Recording: ★ ★ (★)

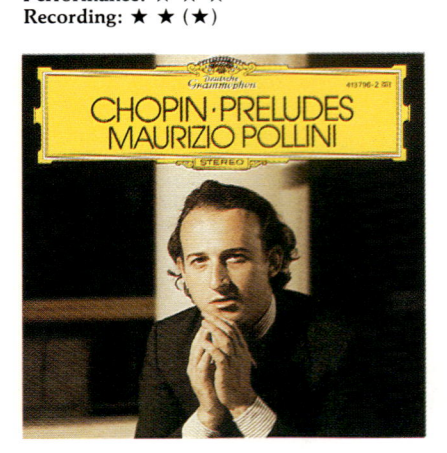

As a distillation of Chopin's genius, the Op28 *Preludes* are unsurpassed: they are tautly and economically constructed, spanning a profoundly wide range of mood and feeling, yet wholly unified. Although some were written before 1836, most date from a less-than-idyllic spell in Majorca, between 1838-9, this perhaps reflected in the extremes of light and dark depicted in them.

Pollini's performance reaches those extremes without losing the essential unity of the design, and his individual response to even the most familiar of the *Preludes* never fails to excite. This is playing of the highest order, well captured by the mid-seventies recording: fairly forward, but clean and unclangorous, and with tape hiss unobtrusive.

Other recordings on CD:
(complete)
Deszo Ranki/Hungaroton HCD12316-2

POLONAISES: NO1 IN C SHARP MINOR OP26 NO1/NO2 IN E FLAT MAJOR OP26 NO2/NO3 IN A MAJOR OP40 NO1/NO4 IN C MINOR OP40 NO2/NO5 IN F SHARP MINOR OP44/NO6 IN A FLAT MAJOR OP53/NO7 IN A FLAT MAJOR OP61 (POLONAISE FANTAISIE)
Maurizio Pollini: Piano
Deutsche Grammophon 413 795-2GH
AAD Running time: 61.03
Performance: ★ ★ ★
Recording: ★ ★ (★)

Although Chopin utilised two of the musical forms indigenous to his native Poland, the notion of composer as fervent patriot does not stand up to close scrutiny. Reluctant as he may have been to leave at the outset, he made little attempt to return once accustomed to the pleasures of life in Paris.

Despite that, the *Mazurkas* and the *Polonaises* have come to symbolise the spirit of Polish nationalism, and although the composer intended to make no political gesture of any kind through them, their powerful, impassioned content surely indicates the depth of feeling he retained for his homeland.

Certainly, that is what comes across in Maurizio Pollini's fiery yet sensitive interpretations. The playing is outstanding in every respect, and makes its full impact through a fairly close and immediate recording. Analogue origins are no drawback; the slightly bright edge to the sound could just as easily occur on the most recent of digital recordings! Tape hiss presents no problems.

WALTZES: NO1 OP18/NOS2, 3, 4 OP34 NOS 1, 2 AND 3/NO5 OP42/NOS6 (MINUTE WALTZ) 7, 8 OP64 NOS1,2 AND 3/NOS9, 10 OP69 NOS1 AND 2/ NOS11, 12, 13 OP70 NOS1, 2 AND 3/ NO14 OP POSTH
Claudio Arrau: Piano
Philips 400 025-2PH
ADD Running time: 60.40
Performance: ★ ★ ★   Recording: ★ ★ ★

It was the *Waltzes* and the *Nocturnes* which first brought Chopin to the attention of audiences in his adopted city, Paris, and the range of expression he was able to find within the confines of what, to them, must have seemed a quite innocuous dance form, must have been startling. No ballroom music, this; the waltz here provides a frame inside which Chopin exercises his imagination to the full.

None of that invention passes by unnoted, or unnoticed, in Claudio Arrau's majestic performance. Perhaps he does invest some of the detail with more gravity than it warrants, but this is surely preferable to skimming over it. This is playing which reveals something new at each listening, and is perfectly caught in Philips' lustrous recording.

Other recordings on CD:
Maria João Pires/Erato ECD88067
Cyprien Katsaris/TelDec ZK8.43056

AARON COPLAND
(b. Brooklyn, New York, USA, 14 Nov 1900)

One of the most exciting, and approachable, of 'modern' composers, Aaron Copland was the son of an immigrant Jewish family originally named Kaplan.

Copland spent the first twenty years of his life in Brooklyn living, as he once said, *'on a street that can only be described as drab'*. Early piano lessons, followed by schooling in harmony, fostered his desire to become a composer and at twenty-one came the opportunity of three years' productive study in Paris with Nadia Boulanger and Paul Vidal. Back in the United States, in 1925, he composed an organ concerto for Boulanger to play on her American tour (it was later reworked – without the solo instrument – as his first symphony). This, and the acceptance by the American League of Composers of two piano works, brought his name to the attention of a wide audience. Copland was awarded the first scholarship from the Guggenheim Memorial Foundation, which gave him the freedom to embark on a wide range of composing activities, and to explore a fascinating variety of styles.

The five-movement suite *Music for the Theater* and the Piano Concerto demonstrate the influence of jazz during the 'twenties. The *Dance Symphony* and the *Short Symphony* of 1933 are outstanding works, and no less so the *Piano Variations* and *Statements for Orchestra* which show the composer at his most austere and terse, vigorously exploring the potential of dissonance.

In sharp contrast, in the late 'thirties, Copland adopted a more overtly popular style – he called it *'imposed simplicity'* – and the result was some of the works for which he is now best-known: *Rodeo, Billy the Kid, El Salón Mèxico*. An equally famous work, the ballet score *Appalachian Spring*, won him a Pullitzer Prize in 1945.

EL SALÓN MÈXICO/DANCE SYMPHONY/FANFARE FOR THE COMMON MAN/FOUR DANCE EPISODES FROM RODEO
Detroit Symphony Orchestra
Conductor: Antal Dorati
Decca 414 273-2DH
DDD Running time: 51.17
Performance: ★ ★ ★   Recording: ★ ★ ★

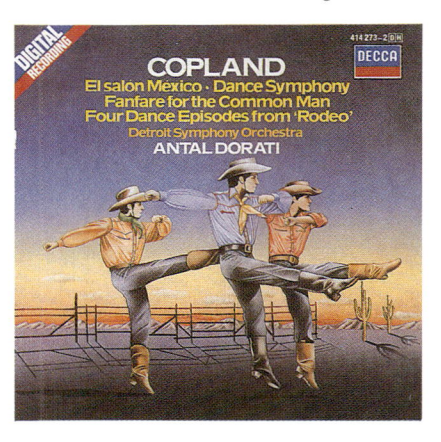

Like Stravinsky, Copland had an innate flair for dance music and it is well demonstrated in this group of four popular works from the period 1929–42. The earliest is the Dance Symphony, a reworking of material from a few years before; the latest, *Rodeo*, and the short but effective *Fanfare for the Common Man*. All represent Copland at his most colourful and accessible, and there is no attempt by Dorati to disguise their extrovert nature. With superlative playing from the Detroit orchestra and a brilliant Decca recording, this disc is sheer delight.

Other recordings on CD:
Atlanta SO/Louis Lane/Telarc CD80078
Milwaukee SO/Lukas Foss/Pro Arte CDD102

APPALACHIAN SPRING: BALLET FOR MARTHA (1945 SUITE)
(c/w Barber: Adagio for Strings/Bernstein: Overture to Candide/Schuman: American Festival Overture)
Los Angeles Philharmonic Orchestra
Conductor: Leonard Bernstein
Deutsche Grammophon 413 324-2GH
DDD Running time: 50.17
Performance: ★ ★ ★
Recording: ★ ★ (★)

Predictably, both conductor and orchestra put everything into this all-American programme, recorded at live concerts as is invariably Bernstein's practice these days. The results here certainly argue the case well: exuberant in Bernstein's own *Candide* Overture, and William Schuman's enjoyably brash *American Festival Overture*; intense in Samuel Barber's haunting, noble *Adagio*. Bernstein is at his best in the Copland, and if the couplings appeal, then this version of *Appalachian Spring* can be recommended.

The recording is fairly bright, but acceptably balanced and richly-textured. The Los Angeles orchestra can rarely have sounded quite so splendid.

Other recordings on CD:
(*Appalachian Spring*)
Atlanta SO/Louis Lane/Telarc CD80078
Detroit SO/Antal Dorati/Decca 414 457-2DH)

CLAUDE DEBUSSY
(b. St Germain-en-Laye, France, 22 August 1862; d. Paris, 25 March 1918)

Claude Debussy is usually accredited with founding the 'impressionist' school of music, emphasis being put on tonal contrasts in sound in the same way that painters such as Monet emphasised the behaviour of light.

In reality, Debussy never entirely threw off the basic traditional principles as the painters felt able to do: thematic content may sometimes be elusive, even amorphous, but is usually there; similarly structure which is discernible despite the veiled and softened outlines. If anything, Debussy brought refinement to Romanticism, with an absolute mastery of orchestral balance and clarity. His influence has been enormous, despite a comparatively small output of major works.

A student at the Paris Conservatoire since the age of twelve, Debussy won the Prix de Rome at twenty-two with the cantata, *L'enfant prodigue*, entitling him to three-years' free study in Italy. Wagner had little lasting influence on him; more can be attributed to Russian composers such as Musorgsky whose music he encountered while working in Moscow as travelling piano tutor to the children of Nadezhda von Meck, sometime patron of Tchaikovsky.

In Paris, his personal life was something of a scandal. For ten years he had lived with one Gabrielle Dupont, but in 1899 he suddenly married dressmaker's assistant Rosalie Texier. A relationship was formed with Emma Bardac, wife of a rich banker, and the hapless Rosalie attempted suicide. Emma, meanwhile, became pregnant as a result of the liaison.

Debussy left all behind him by crossing the English Channel and spending the summer of 1905 in the seaside town of Eastbourne. He returned to an illegitimate daughter, and the indifferent reaction to the first performance of one of his finest works, *La Mer*. This followed the controversial debut (but eventual acceptance) of his solitary opera, *Pelléas et Mélisande* in 1902.

Throughout his career, he continued to produce a host of freely imaginative, often experimental, piano works and wonderfully sensitive song-settings, many using the verse of the 'symbolist' poets to whom he was closely attuned: Mallarmé, Verlaine and Baudelaire.

The divorce of both parties allowed him to marry Emma Bardac. His final years saw the composition of the orchestral *Images*, the highly original ballet, *Jeux*, and many no less innovative piano pieces, but he developed cancer, leaving unfinished on his death a second

Revolutionary both in musical technique and in what he aimed to express in his compositions, Debussy has proved widely and lastingly influential among twentieth century composers.

opera, based on Edgar Allan Poe's macabre tale *The Fall of the House of Usher*. The final twist in his tortured personal life had come with the death aged just fourteen, of his daughter – his beloved Chou-Chou.

Lovers of Debussy's music are lucky in having at least one recommendable version of most of his major compositions – chamber and instrumental, as well as orchestral – on CD. It's a privilege few other composers yet enjoy.

LA MER: TROIS EQUISSES SYMPHONIQUES
TROIS NOCTURNES*
Ambrosian Singers*
London Symphony Orchestra
Conductor: André Previn
EMI CDC 7 47028-2
DDD Running time: 50.47
Performance: ★ ★ ★   Recording: ★ ★ ★

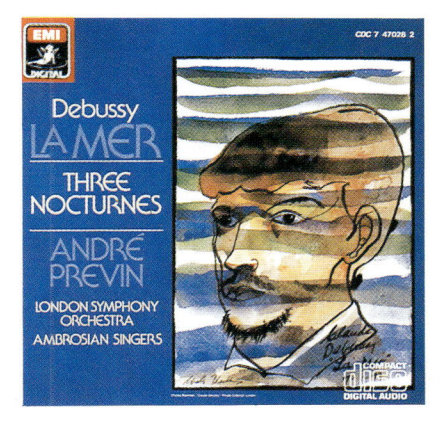

The sea always held a fascination for Debussy, and recollections from childhood holidays spent by the Mediterranean, as well as the more dramatic impressions left by crossings of the English Channel, contributed to his most ambitious orchestral composition, the triptych of symphonic tableaux entitled *La Mer*. At its first performance in 1905, the work elicited praise and criticism in about equal measure, some critics complaining that they could not 'hear' the sea in it at all. But it was never intended to be that literal a composition, more an evocation of mood and a reflection of the sense of awe and mystery that the oceans can inspire.

With Previn, that ocean would appear to be the crystal-clear Mediterranean: vivid, sharply-defined, with the usual keen observation of rhythm. A warm, well-lit performance altogether different from that of Colin Davis who seems to conjure darker, more forbidding waters. There is no doubt that the latter is the more atmospheric of the two performances, a feeling sustained by the comparatively opaque recording. Previn's, by contrast is luminous and crisply-detailed, if with a slightly edgy quality to the strings.

However, he manages to secure first preference here with a marvellous performance of the *Nocturnes*, where the sea once again plays a part: the song of the *Sirènes* floating across moonlit waters.

Other recordings on CD:
(*La Mer/Nocturnes*)
BSO/Colin Davis/Philips 411 433-2PH
SRO/Ernest Ansermet/Decca 414 040-2DH
(*La Mer*)

St Louis SO/Leonard Slatkin/Telarc CD80071
(*Nocturnes*)
Concertgebouw O/Bernard Haitink/Philips 400 023-2PH

TROIS NOCTURNES
JEUX – POEME DANSE
Collegium Musicum Amstelodamense
Concertgebouw Orchestra, Amsterdam
Conductor: Bernard Haitink
Philips 400 023-2PH
AAD Running time: 42.55
Performance: ★ ★ ★   Recording: ★ ★ ★

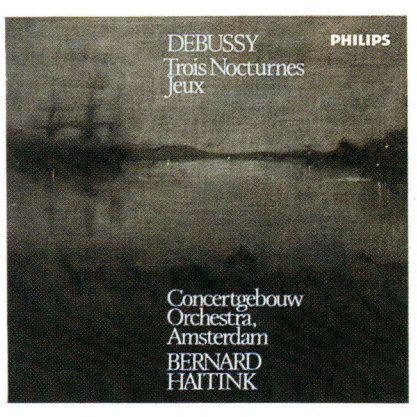

This was one of the first Compact Discs (Stravinsky's *Firebird*, also on Philips, was another) to demonstrate how much the new medium could do for good analogue masters, as well as digital ones. Indeed, when released among the launch batch of CDs in 1983, it was only too obvious how much *better* this sounded compared with most of its wholly digital counterparts!

But, then, Philips analogue recordings with the Concertgebouw have always been among the very best anyway, and coupled with Haitink's incomparable interpretations of Debussy, they were always going to be outstanding in any medium.

The *Trois Nocturnes* were first performed together in 1901, although the genesis of their composition began some eight years earlier. The very different, more complex and far-reaching score of *Jeux* was finished in 1912, to a commission from Diaghilev. Belonging more to the world inhabited by Debussy's solo piano music, *Jeux* has never shared the same popularity as the vividly pictorial *Nocturnes*, but a performance such as Haitink's is a most eloquent advocate.

On the evidence here, Haitink's other analogue recordings for Philips with the Concertgebouw would fully merit CD transfer.

Other recordings on CD:
(*Nocturnes* only)
SRO/Ernest Ansermet/Decca 414 040-2DH
LSO/Andre Previn/EMI CDC 7 47028-2
Boston SO/Colin Davis/Philips 411 433-2PH

DEBUSSY

IMAGES: GIGUES/IBERIA/RONDES DE PRINTEMPS
PRELUDE A L'APRES-MIDI D'UN FAUNE*
Peter Lloyd: Flute*
London Symphony Orchestra
Conductor: André Previn
EMI CDC 7 47001-2
DDD Running time: 47.59
Performance: ★ ★   Recording: ★ ★ (★)

This was EMI's first digital recording to be issued, and was launched with much ballyhoo a few years ago. The LP version was widely praised, and overall the CD is similarly praiseworthy, although the new medium reveals a few extraneous noises which were masked by the vinyl. There is no change, however, to the natural balance, luminous clarity and perspectives which were achieved in the simply-made recording. The digital recorder (which precluded the use of multi-tracking) was one EMI had developed themselves, but were later forced to abandon for a more economic, bought-in alternative. One can only speculate, listening to Previn's Debussy, what results might now have been achieved had they continued to refine their own hardware.

Musically, Previn has tended to emphasise the rhythmic side of Debussy's music, and eschewed the 'impressionistic veil' some interpreters like to drape over it. There is an obvious benefit in the lucidity of detail and overall texture, but also a possible trade-off in atmosphere and mystery, something most keenly felt here in the dreamy, sensuous *Prélude*: surely if a 'haze' was desirable, it is that of a hot afternoon! It is, however, beautifully played.

The *Images* (not to be confused with those for solo piano) are impressions of France, England and Spain, although only the latter is specifically titled, *Iberia*; the others are *Rondes de Printemps* and *Gigues* respectively. Vivid and colourful, *Iberia* is the most successful of the three, an astonishing achievement considering Debussy only once ventured across the border into Spain.

Previn is at his vibrant, exciting best in the *Images*, and earns a recommendation, although if Philips were considering remastering the fabulous Haitink recording for CD. . .

Other versions on CD:
(*Prélude à l'Après-midi d'un faune*)
St Louis SO/Leonard Slatkin/Telarc CD80071
SRO/Ernest Ansermet/Decca 414 040-2DH
ASMF/Neville Marriner/Philips 412 131-2PH
LAPO/Erich Leinsdorf/Sheffield Lab CD LAB24

PRELUDES: BOOK I
Arturo Benedetti Michelangeli: Piano
Deutsche Grammophon 413 450-2GH
AAD Running time: 42.38
Performance: ★ ★ ★   Recording: ★ ★

Given the paucity of recordings by this unique artist (almost as rare as his appearances on the concert platform), it is no surprise that DG have remastered this 1978 recital for CD. After all, few performers can approach Michelangeli in his interpretations of Debussy: meticulous in conveying every detail, each nuance and fine degree of shading, and so jewel-like in tone. There is a certain cool aloofness to it all: perhaps it is *too* calculated, but the result is undeniably spellbinding.

Debussy himself simply described the *Préludes* as *'colours and rhythmicised time'*, but each is a minor musical adventure. Several from Book I are well-known individually – *The Girl with Flaxen Hair*; *The Engulfed Cathedral*; *Puck's Dance*; and *Minstrels* – yet generally the titles were appended after the pieces were composed.

The analogue recording has come up well, with the necessary detail, weight and tonal quality. However, Jacques Rouvier's performance on Denon (see below) has even finer, more atmospheric sound, and his interpretations compare very favourably. This may well be preferable to some.

Other recordings on CD (complete):
Jacques Rouvier/Denon C-37 7121

PRELUDES: BOOK II
Jacques Rouvier: Piano
Denon C37-7043
DDD Running time: 39.03
Performance: ★ ★ ★   Recording: ★ ★ ★

In the second set of *Preludes*, the effect of improvisation is heightened still further, as much depending on the playing technique as on the notes themselves. The composer did, after all, request that the piano be made to sound like an instrument *without* hammers.

Once again, the inspirations are diverse in the extreme: dead leaves, mists, an illustration from J.M. Barrie's *Peter Pan*, an American comic juggler, one General Lavine, an Egyptian funerary urn, Dickens' Mr Pickwick, and most impressionistic of all, *Feux d'Artifice* (Fireworks).

Jacques Rouvier responds with characteristic flair and imagination, in a recording that combines a lively presence with a smooth, limpid piano tone. There is not a trace of clatter or excessive brilliance.

CHILDRENS' CORNER SUITE/REVERIE/ D'UN CAHIER D'ESQUISSES/BERCEUSE HEROIQUE/DANSE/MAZURKA/ NOCTURNE/LE PETIT NEGRE/ MORCEAU DE CONCOURS/LA PLUS QUE LENTE
Jacques Rouvier: Piano
Denon C37-7372
DDD Running time: 48.47
Performance: ★ ★ (★)
Recording: ★ ★ ★

The piano sound that Denon obtains here is outstanding – every bit as good as that Philips provides for Zoltan Kocsis' Debussy recital. Here, the immediacy and the realism of timbre, range and image are quite startling, and Rouvier's playing is of a comparable standard. Some of the nuances of this varied selection elude him however (although not the irony of *La Plus que Lente*.) Most importantly, his performance of the *Childrens' Corner Suite*, the central work, is exceptional: enchanting in *The Snowflakes are Dancing*, suitably exuberant in *Golliwog's Cakewalk*. Did Chou-Chou, Debussy's daughter, for whom he wrote the suite between 1906 and 1908, fully appreciate its qualities one wonders? There is no doubting them with Rouvier's playing.

STRING QUARTET IN G MINOR OP10
(c/w Ravel: String Quartet in F Major)
Quatuor Enesco
Forlane UCD16521
DDD Running time: 59.45
Performance: ★ ★ ★
Recording: ★ ★

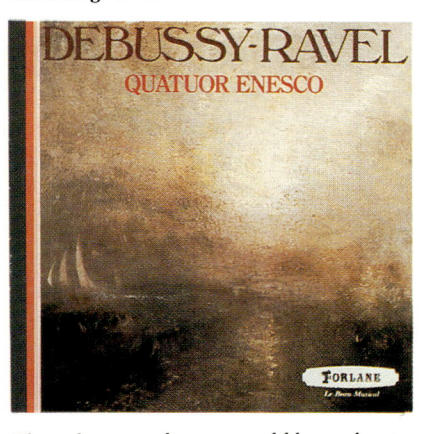

The only regret that one could have about these two quartets is that the composers did not write more for the medium. Despite both adopting – surprisingly perhaps – a strict classical four-movement framework, there is considerable contrast between the two.

The Debussy of 1893 ingeniously adapts a single motif to all four movements, while the Ravel is a richly melodic work.

These are well-conceived performances from this Paris-based Rumanian quartet, with excellent intonation and ensemble set in a warm, slightly opaque acoustic.

Other recordings on CD (selection):
Orlando Quartet/Philips 411 050-2PH

SONATA FOR FLUTE, VIOLA AND HARP/SYRINX (FOR SOLO FLUTE)/ PREMIERE RAPSODIE FOR CLARINET AND PIANO/PETITE PIECE/SONATA FOR VIOLIN AND PIANO/SONATA FOR 'CELLO AND PIANO
Athena Ensemble
Chandos CHAN8385
AAD Running time: 54.56
Performance: ★ ★ ★ Recording: ★ ★ ★

Debussy planned to write six *sonates pour divers instruments*, but in the event only finished three in the period 1915–1917 before illness took its toll of his powers (the Violin Sonata was the last work he completed). All are contained on this well-filled disc, along with the lovely clarinet rhapsody and that quintessentially sensuous French flute piece, *Syrinx*. Originally part of the incidental score to the play *Psyche*, *Syrinx* is music that, more than most, benefits from the utterly silent background CD can offer. Equally ethereal and arcadian in its content and gossamer-like textures is the Sonata for flute, viola and harp, a magical piece that comes off beautifully here. Indeed, all the performances are highly pleasurable, and the transparent recording sees to it that each instrument has a reasonable amount of 'air' around it, as is essential if this often evanescent music is to achieve the desired effect.

Other recordings on CD:
('Cello Sonata)
Mari Fujiwara/Jacques Rouvier/Denon C37-7563

SUITE BERGAMASQUE/IMAGES (OUBLIEES)/POUR LE PIANO/ESTAMPES
Zoltan Kocsis: Piano
Philips 412 118-2PH
DDD Running time: 55.52
Performance: ★ ★ ★ Recording: ★ ★ ★

A recording which amply demonstrates the benefits that CD can bring to the solo piano: no wow or flutter to cause pitch variations; clarity and definition throughout the full range of the instrument; the softest touch clearly audible. Moreover, it has an exceptionally truthful balance and 'presence', not to mention a fine tonal quality.

This excellent sound enhances a well-thought-out recital of the familiar, and the not-so-familiar Debussy: the *Images (Oubliées)* really were 'forgotten images'. The composer discarded them (apart from re-working one piece for the suite *Pour le Piano*, which is also featured here, and thus makes for an interesting comparison). As a result, this set of *Images*, which, it must be said, is not top-drawer Debussy, was not published until 1977.

No such reservations exist about the rest of the programme, where Kocsis produces thoughtful and idiomatic accounts of the popular *Estampes* and the *Suite Bergamasque*, even investing the much-abused *Clair de Lune* with a rare freshness and fantasy. Indeed, his playing throughout manages to be both technically immaculate but nonetheless imaginative.

It is to be hoped that Kocsis will tackle more of corpus of Debussy's piano music, and Ravel, too. He is certainly one of the best of young pianists.

FREDERICK DELIUS
(b. Bradford, Yorkshire, 29 January 1862; d. Grez-sur-Loing, France, 10 June 1934)

The music of Frederick Delius stands or falls according to the quality of its interpretation. Badly performed, the comparative lack of *fortissimos* and its generally lyrical nature can make for dull listening indeed. (*'A sense of flow is the main thing'* remarked the composer, once.) But sympathetically played and conducted, the effect can be quite magical and enchanting. Delius' music needs to be in loving hands, like those of his greatest champion, Sir Thomas Beecham, or one-time amanuensis, Eric Fenby.

His family, wool merchants of Dutch/German extraction, had Delius earmarked for a career in the same trade, despite the talent for music he displayed. They decided to send him to Florida to manage an orange grove in order to nurture his business acumen; instead it merely broadened his musical horizons and ambitions. He handed over the estate to his brother, preferring to offer his services as a violin and piano teacher.

With the help of Edvard Grieg, whom he had come to know from a visit to Norway, Delius gained a place at the Leipzig Conservatoire, and it was there that his *Florida Suite* was first performed in 1889 based on what he had heard and seen in America, especially negro music. A concert of works in London came the following year, but English audiences were less receptive than those of Germany – at least until 1907 when the conductor Thomas Beecham heard *Appalachia* for the first time and began a crusade on behalf of Delius' music which was to continue for the rest of his performing career.

In 1897, Delius married Jelka Rosen and they moved to a house near Fontainebleau in France that was to be home for the rest of their lives. There he continued to compose his utterly individual brand of music, a kind of post-impressionist Romanticism. He scorned the German 'classics' (indeed, there was very little music other than his own that he did care for) and followed his own instincts totally.

Sadly, by the early 1920s, he was in the grip of syphilis, and it was a blind, half-paralysed creature that Eric Fenby came to assist in 1928. He patiently collaborated with Delius on his last, and some of his finest, compositions. Beecham and others organised a 'Delius Festival' in 1929 which forced many in Britain to revise their assessment of the composer. For a while Delius enjoyed unprecedented success in his native land, but it did nothing to alter his contempt for English

The blind Delius is read to by his loyal and devoted wife of nigh-on forty years, Jelka.

DELIUS

conventions and morality, which persisted until his death in 1934.

Compact Disc has done little for Delius thus far, with a great many compositions conspicuous by their absence: *Paris, Sea Drift, Appalachia, Brigg Fair*, among others. However, the specialist Unicorn-Kanchana label is making a commendable effort to change the situation. It is to be hoped that their splendid two-record set, *The Fenby Legacy*, may enjoy CD release soon.

VIOLIN CONCERTO/SUITE FOR VIOLIN AND ORCHESTRA/LÉGENDE FOR VIOLIN AND ORCHESTRA
Ralph Holmes: Violin
Royal Philharmonic Orchestra
Conductor: Vernon Handley
Unicorn-Kanchana DKP(CD)9040
DDD Running time: 53.57
Performance: ★ ★ ★   Recording: ★ ★ ★

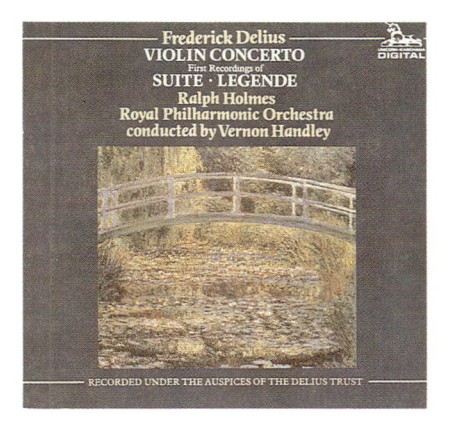

As well as giving the lie to the idea that Delius could not compose above *pianissimo*, the Violin Concerto also disproves the notion that he had no grasp of musical logic: analysis will uncover a wholly coherent structure to this under-rated work, the surprisingly brutal third episode does sound – as Eric Fenby puts it – '*as if the whole orchestra is shaking its angry fist at you.*'

Much rarer Delius completes this disc, which also stands as a sad but fitting epitaph to the soloist, Ralph Holmes, who died tragically young in 1984. He plays with remarkable perception and beauty of tone, perfectly caught in the refined, well-integrated recording.

ON HEARING THE FIRST CUCKOO IN SPRING/SUMMER NIGHT ON THE RIVER/A SONG BEFORE SUNRISE/TWO AQUARELLES (arr Fenby)/INTERMEZZO AND SERENADE FROM HASSAN (arr Beecham)/PRELUDE FROM IRMELIN/LATE SWALLOWS (arr Fenby)/INTERMEZZO FROM FENNIMORE AND GERDA (arr Beecham)
Bournemouth Sinfonietta
Conductor: Norman del Mar
Chandos CHAN8372
ADD Running time: 49.22
Performance: ★ ★ (★)   Recording: ★ ★

As an introduction to Delius' shorter orchestral works, this could hardly be bettered. As well as a number of the more popular pieces, Norman del Mar has included the Two Aquarelles and *Late Swallows*, each of which may prove a pleasant discovery for many listeners.

Apart from a slightly opaque quality, the mid-seventies recording has worn well; Chandos have made an excellent job of the transfer to Compact Disc. The performances are more than acceptable, given the paucity of Delius' representation on CD: some, indeed, are very good, even if missing some of the magic Beecham could bring.

Other recordings on CD:
(On hearing the first cuckoo in Spring)
LPO/Vernon Handley/Chandos CHAN8330

THE SONG OF THE HIGH HILLS ORCHESTRAL SONGS
Felicity Lott: Soprano/Sarah Walker: Mezzo-soprano/Anthony Rolfe-Johnson: Tenor
Ambrosian Singers
Royal Philharmonic Orchestra
Conductor: Eric Fenby
Unicorn-Kanchana DKP(CD)9029
DDD Running time: 58.50
Performance: ★ ★ ★   Recording: ★ ★ ★

If ever a work exploited the potential of CD, it is *The Song of the High Hills*, with its vast range of sonorities, from the softest, most ethereal choral writing to blazing climaxes for full orchestra. It is Delius, the nature-mystic, at his most visionary, yet for many years after its completion in 1912 it remained his least-known orchestral work. The forces used are large and, as always with Delius, sensitive interpretation is vital. No one is better equipped to offer that than Eric Fenby.

He is equally successful with the orchestral songs, in what is their first recording. Here, too, a team of first-class solo voices adds considerably to the appeal of compositions which are invariably on the gently lyrical side, and which in lesser hands could veer towards the monotonous. Instead the result is spellbinding, aided by an exceptionally transparent, naturally- and clearly-balanced recording, which is also perfectly distanced for these works. Unicorn-Kanchana are doing as proudly by Delius on CD as they have on LP.

ANTONIN DVOŘÁK
(b. Nelahozeves, near Prague, Czechoslovakia, 8 Sept 1841; d. Prague, 1 May 1904)

Throughout his career, Dvořák's gift for beautiful, memorable melody never failed him.

Today we would describe Antonín Dvořák as a 'natural': as his great friend and supporter, Brahms wrote: *'I am in a frenzy of envy over the ideas that come quite naturally to this fellow.'* Certainly, few composers have ever been endowed with such a gift for conjuring captivating and memorable melodies. Works such as the *New World* Symphony may have come in for critical disparagement on purely musical grounds, but have never lost their place in the public affection, nor seem likely to.

However, this master tunesmith began life as a butcher's boy, working for his father (who was also the village publican and a keen exponent of that peculiarly Slav instrument, the zither). The young Dvořák took to singing and the violin, and in 1857 went to Prague for piano and organ lessons. When a resident orchestra was being established for the National Theatre in the city, he was employed as a viola player, and also began composing around this time. Soon his orchestral works and operas were getting a hearing, but to earn a decent living (he had just married) he took up an offer to become a church organist.

It was the generosity of the Austrian Ministry of Fine Arts in granting him a pension for life that enabled Dvořák to devote most of his time to composition, and international recognition came with the first set of lively Slavonic Dances, Op46, and the beautiful *Stabat Mater*, which became a particular favourite in Britain.

In 1891 he was offered the directorship of the National Conservatory of Music in New York. Dvořák pondered long and hard, asking for – and getting – better terms before deciding to leave his beloved homeland. Although he enjoyed considerable success in America, homesickness eventually overtook him and he returned to Europe, later becoming head of the Prague Conservatory.

DVOŘÁK

SYMPHONY NO7 IN D MINOR OP70
The Philharmonic Symphony Orchestra
Conductor: Carlos Paita
Lodia LO-CD782
DDD Running time: 37.03
Performance: ★ ★ ★   Recording: ★ ★

Only five of Dvořák's nine symphonies were published in his lifetime, of which this was the second. With the subsequent appearance of the remaining four, it took its true place in the order of composition as the Seventh, being completed in March 1885 and given its premiere in London (to whose Philharmonic Society it was dedicated) the following month, with the composer conducting.

The most 'classical' of the nine in its formal, symmetrical structure, the 'Slavonic' element so characteristic of Dvořák's music is nevertheless discernible, most especially in the graceful theme of the scherzo.

As with so much of Dvořák's output, the Seventh benefits from a performance that, above all, brings out its warmth and lyricism, something that the rather stern Czech recording on Supraphon surprisingly fails to do. Carlos Paita, however, does have the right response: a glowing performance with rich, full-bodied sound. While not as finely detailed as the best CDs, it is pleasantly free of artificial brilliance.

Other recordings on CD (selection):
VPO/Lorin Maazel/DG 410 997-2GH
Czech PO/Vaclav Neumann/Supraphon C37 7073

SYMPHONY NO8 IN G MAJOR OP88
SCHERZO CAPRICCIOSO OP66
Cleveland Orchestra
Conductor: Christoph von Dohnanyi
Decca 414 422-2DH
DDD Running time: 49.12
Performance: ★ ★ ★   Recording: ★ ★ ★

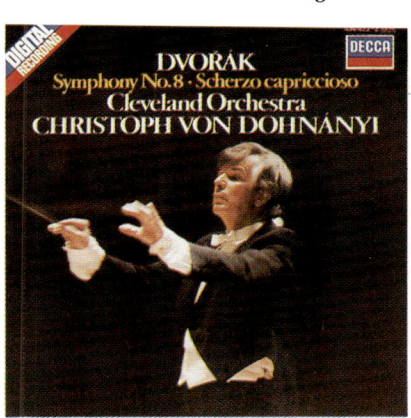

This augurs well if Dohnanyi is planning further Dvorak with his new orchestra. He avoids any temptation to over-sugar this affable and highly tuneful score, preferring to let the music express itself within well-judged tempi. Dynamics and phrasing also benefit from a similar attention to detail, and the whole recording – well-balanced, detailed, and comfortably distanced – is entirely successful.

Other recordings on CD (selection):
LPO/Vernon Handley/Chandos CHAN8323
Minnesota O/Neville Marriner/Philips 412 542-2PH2

SYMPHONY NO9 IN E MINOR OP95
'FROM THE NEW WORLD'
Vienna Philharmonic Orchestra
Conductor: Kyril Kondrashin
Decca 400 047-2DH
DDD Running time: 42.39
Performance: ★ ★ ★   Recording: ★ ★ ★

A restrained – almost understated – reading of not only Dvořák's most famous work, but one of the most perenially popular of all symphonies. But restraint is no bad thing here, especially when the performance is such an affectionate and well-prepared one; and the recording, too, is pleasantly mellow and spacious, enhanced by a warm, rounded tonal quality.

Dvořák accepted a certain American influence in the work (although only adding its nickname at the last moment) but dismissed suggestions that he had used Negro or Indian folk melodies. There is no denying, however, that the famous *largo* bears a passing resemblance to the old spiritual, *Swing low, sweet chariot*, an eternally lovely movement which has survived numerous abuses as background music and the like.

He completed the work in 1893, two years after taking up a teaching post in the United States, and if the slow movement has a distinctive American quality, then the *scherzo* and final *allegro con fuoco* are unmistakeably rooted in the Slavonic folk tradition, a tradition which never lost its appeal for Dvořák, even at three thousand miles distance.

Needless to say, there is no shortage of alternative recordings of the *New World*, but excellence of both performance and recording gives Kondrashin's the edge.

Other recordings on CD:
CSO/James Levine/RCA RCD14552
VPO/Lorin Maazel/DG 410 032-2GH
CSO/Georg Solti/Decca 410 116-2DH
LPO/James Conlon/Erato ECD88036
BPO/Klaus Tennstedt/EMI CDC 7 47071-2
Czech PO/Vaclav Neumann/Supraphon C37-7002
Minnesota O/Neville Marriner/Philips 412 542-2PH2

'CELLO CONCERTO IN B MINOR OP104
(c/w Tchaikovsky: Variations on a Rococo Theme for 'Cello and Orchestra Op33)
Mstislav Rostropovich: 'Cello
Berlin Philharmonic Orchestra
Conductor: Herbert von Karajan
Deutsche Grammophon 413 819-2GH
ADD Running time: 60.03
Performance: ★ ★ ★
Recording: ★ ★ (★)

Rostropovich's unashamedly romantic view of the 'Cello Concerto is difficult to resist. The expressive warmth of his playing and the rich, eloquent timbre of the instrument seduce the ear as few others do.

Karajan proves the ideal partner, keeping a tight but flexible rein on proceedings, and eliciting a response from the Berliners every bit as committed as that of the soloist. From the very nature of his playing, Rostropovich is bound to dominate the proceedings, but the recorded balance is by no means lopsided. This 1969 recording had always looked a worthy candidate for remastering, and the clarity and freshness of the Compact

DVOŘÁK

Disc does not disappoint. As with the LP, Tchaikovsky's magnificent set of variations makes for a generous filler.

Other recordings on CD:
Frans Helmerson/Gothenburg SO/Neeme Järvi/BIS CD245
Lynn Harrell/Philharmonia O/Vladimir Ashkenazy/Decca 410 144-2DH

SERENADE IN E MAJOR OP22
SERENADE IN D MINOR OP44
Academy of St Martin-in-the-Fields
Conductor: Neville Marriner
Philips 400 020-2PH
DDD Running time: 51.03
Performance: ★ ★ ★
Recording: ★ ★ (★)

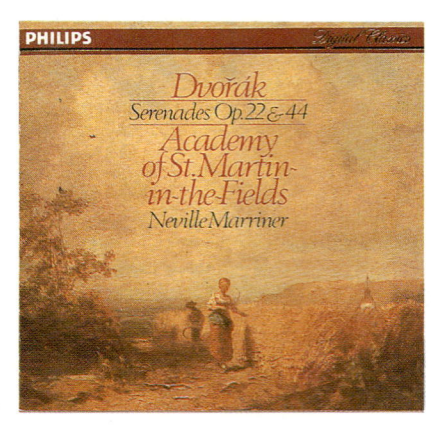

Dvořák's melodic gift is nowhere better heard than in the relaxed and undemanding Op22 serenade, as felicitous a work as any ever written. The Op44, for wind ensemble with just 'cello and double bass accompaniment, is no less charming, and makes for a very satisfying coupling here, a change from the Tchaikovsky string serenade with which the Op22 is most often paired.

The composition of three serenades was Dvořák's original intention: the Op22 was completed in 1875, the Op44 in 1878, but the proposed third eventually became the *Czech Suite* Op39. The *Serenade for Strings* is interesting in that it was probably one of the works Dvořák submitted to 'a judging panel who were empowered to allocate state grants to *'young, poor, talented painters, sculptors and musicians in the Austrian half of the Empire'*. The composer was certainly eligible for a grant on all counts, but more importantly, contact with the judging panel introduced him to Brahms, who was to become the most distinguished champion of his music.

These are most agreeable performances of both works, but in recording terms, the wind serenade comes off best, with better imaging and a greater sense of depth. By contrast, the sound for the Op22 is, if anything, over-full, tending to thicken the texture. There is a pleasant sense of space, however, and the ensembles in both works are well-distanced.

Other recordings on CD (selection):
(*Serenade for Strings* Op22 only)
BPO/Herbert von Karajan/DG 400 038-2GH
English String O/William Boughton/Nimbus NIM5016
(Op22 and Op44)
Orpheus CO/DG 415 364-2GH

SLAVONIC DANCES SERIES 1 OP46/ SERIES 2 OP72
Scottish National Orchestra
Conductor: Neeme Järvi
Chandos CHAN8406
DDD Running time: 70.19
Performance: ★ ★ ★
Recording: ★ ★ (★)

Unlike Brahms, who in the main utilised existing folk melodies for his *Hungarian Dances*, Dvořák merely drew on the rhythm and spirit of the music of his native land: the rest came from his own inexhaustible melodic inspiration. It was the Op46 set which made his name internationally.

Järvi's performances are generally brisk and infectiously lively. He is reluctant to dally in the slower sections, and some may feel the end result lacks a little charm. It is, however, infinitely preferable to the self-indulgent approach encountered elsewhere: they are, after all, dances, and a measure of exuberance is hardly out-of-place.

The recording dips slightly below Chandos' usual high standard, not as crisply-defined as most from this source, but that said, it still has a presence and excitingly natural quality that few others attain.

Other recordings on CD:
RPO/Antal Dorati/Decca 735-2DH
Czech PO/Vaclav Neumann/Supraphon

PIANO TRIO NO4 IN E MINOR OP90 (DUMKY)
(c/w Suk: Elegie Op23)
Suk Trio
Supraphon C37S-7057
DDD Running time: 37.21
Performance: ★ ★ ★
Recording: ★ ★ (★)

The best-known of Dvořák's four piano trios was first performed in 1891 at a concert to accompany the award of an honorary degree to the composer by Prague University. Dvořák took the piano part.

The nickname comes from the plural form of a Slavic ballad called the *dumka* the distinguishing feature of which is the combination of a slow, melancholy rhythm and a hectic one, a pattern which Dvořák duly employs here, juxtaposing passages of contemplation and vehemence.

Both the trio, and the short *Elegie* by Josef Suk, are sensitively performed in a well-balanced recording, with excellent imaging and tonal quality. A pity, therefore, that the playing time hardly represents good value.

EDWARD ELGAR
(b. 1857, Broadheath, near Worcester, England, 2 June 1857; d. 1934, Worcester, 23 February 1934)

Elgar was born within sight of the Malvern Hills and it became a landscape ever close to his heart; inset: Elgar in 1915, then England's most celebrated composer.

Although now accepted as the first composer of stature to have emerged in England since the 17th century and Henry Purcell, recognition was a long time coming for Edward Elgar.

Born into a lower-middle class family (his father was a piano tuner who ran a music shop in Worcester), Elgar was almost entirely self-taught, principally organ and violin. He wrote his first music for the church where he was organist, and for the brass band of a local asylum, but his composing career only took off after marriage to Caroline Alice Roberts, the daughter of a major-general and as strong-willed a character as that parentage would suggest. Putting Elgar firmly on the musical map became her mission.

Initial optimism, however, was dashed as, one-by-one, scores were returned from publishers. Disillusioned and despondent, the couple returned to Worcester, where Elgar returned to teaching and to local music-making. His background was against him, as was his lack of social connections and his Catholicism, yet success did finally come: the *Imperial March* of 1897 is now largely forgotten, but it caught the festive, nationalistic mood of Queen Victoria's Diamond Jubilee celebrations of that year.

Then came the *Enigma Variations*, an immediate and resounding success which, along with the *Pomp and Circumstance* marches, remains his most popular composition. Other masterpieces followed, including *The Dream of Gerontius*, so well-received in Germany and establishing Elgar's name through Europe.

Now came the honours and the accolades, including a knighthood in 1904. Even his arch-rival, Sir Hubert Parry was forced to remark: 'In his music, he has reached the hearts of the people'.

But if the music was outgoing, its composer began to withdraw from the world. Troubled by illness, he despaired when inspiration did not readily come. The First World War had a profound effect on him and he put all the sadness he felt into one last, great orchestral work, the 'Cello Concerto of 1919.

Following the death of his beloved Alice in 1920, the greatest blow of all, Elgar composed little. In 1924 he quitted London to live out the rest of his days as a country gentleman in Worcester, and he died, as he was born, within sight of its cathedral and the sound of its bells.

Elgar's representation on Compact Disc has improved significantly of late, with alternatives soon available in the symphonies, as there are in the concertos, and a *Gerontius* due from CRD. However, a recommendable version of *Enigma* has yet to appear: Charles Mackerras' new version, coupled with a superlative *Falstaff* should be a CD priority for EMI.

SYMPHONY NO2 IN FLAT MAJOR OP63
Philharmonia Orchestra
Conductor: Bernard Haitink
EMI CDC 7 47299-2
DDD Running time: 58.51
Performance: ★ ★ ★
Recording: ★ ★ (★)

Although sketches exist from 1903 and 1904, Elgar began serious work on this symphony only in 1909. He laid it aside again for over a year, finally completing the composition in February 1911 after working furiously for several weeks.

The Second is dedicated to the memory of Edward VII, who had died the previous year, but the elegiac mood surely extends beyond that, especially in the profound emotion of the noble second movement. Despite its outward opulence and grandeur, the work is not without its disturbing elements, evidenced by Elgar's description of it as, '*a passionate pilgrimage in which sorrow and extravagance finally lead to a haven of rest*'.

With Haitink, the interpretation is cool, measured, yet wholly compelling throughout, made all the more moving by the dignified restraint he exerts: one of the greatest performances of the Second Symphony in any medium.

The sound is leaner, perhaps colder than EMI usually afford to Elgar, and not quite as well-defined as some of their CDs. But the unobtrusive recording balance, natural weight and impact are much in its favour.

VIOLIN CONCERTO IN B MINOR OP61
Nigel Kennedy: Violin
London Philharmonic Orchestra
Conductor: Vernon Handley
EMI CDC 7 47210-2
DDD Running time: 53.45
Performance: ★ ★ ★   Recording: ★ ★ ★

In stature, the Violin Concerto easily stands comparison with the greatest in the repertoire, including the Beethoven and Brahms, which in its conception and mood it most apparently echoes. Lengthy for a concerto, it asks much of the soloist both in terms of technique and expression, such is the intensity of feeling in the writing.

Dedicated to, and first performed in November 1910, by the legendary Fritz Kreisler, the most famous recording of the work remains that made in 1932 by the sixteen-year-old Yehudi Menuhin with the composer conducting. Much of the feeling of that performance is recaptured by a not-so-very-much-older Nigel Kennedy. He succeeds in being assured in technique and commanding in expression, without being at all 'showy'. His affinity with the Concerto is evident throughout, as is Vernon Handley's accompaniment, which has the mark of a great Elgarian. Together they come closer to the heart of this work than any other contemporary version.

The sound complements the character of the recording, integrating soloist and orchestra and resisting any temptation to 'spotlight' the violin, so that the end result has natural distancing and a refined atmosphere.

Other recordings on CD:
Itzhak Perlman/CSO/Daniel Barenboim/DG 413 312-2GH

CONCERTO FOR 'CELLO AND ORCHESTRA IN E MINOR OP85
(c/w Walton: 'Cello Concerto)
Yo-Yo Ma: 'Cello
London Symphony Orchestra
Conductor: André Previn
CBS Masterworks MK39541
DDD Running time: 59.21
Performance: ★ ★ ★
Recording: ★ ★ (★)

This was to prove Elgar's last orchestral masterpiece, composed in the traumatic aftermath of the First World War. The autumnal mood, and certainly the elegiac, poignant first movement, surely reflect

Elgar's feelings at the time. Indeed, the main theme of that movement, the embodiment of a dignified yet unrequited sadness, is one of the most moving in all music.

Like the Violin Concerto, the work makes great demands of the soloist, both technically and emotionally, and, similarly, there is a 'classic' recording by which all others are inevitably judged, in this case that featuring Jacqueline du Pré as soloist.

But Yo-Yo Ma has nothing to fear from such comparisons; while du Pré's version remains irreplaceable, both the coupling and the more modern sound quality may sway the vote in his favour. He copes effortlessly with the demands of the piece, and shows great sensitivity and depth of feeling, especially in the slower passages and the wistfully reflective *adagio*. The LSO, under Andre Previn – proving yet again what a fine Elgar conductor he can be – provide a sympathetic accompaniment.

Yo-Yo Ma – and Previn – are no less successful in the Walton, which dates from the late 'fifties and, while enjoyable enough, can perhaps be criticised as being a little thin on thematic material and not up to the standard of his earlier Violin and Viola Concertos.

The recording is interesting in being made for CBS in London by Decca engineers using their own digital system, and not unexpectedly, it has all the qualities of openness, refinement and natural perspectives usually associated with that combination. There is a slightly close focus on the soloist which, while allowing appreciation of the rich timbre he produces, does emphasise the odd sniffle, which can be distracting.

Other recordings on CD:
(Elgar concerto only)
Jacqueline du Pré/LSO/John Barbirolli/EMI CDC 7 47329-2
Heinrich Schiff/Staatskapelle Dresden/ Neville Marriner/Philips 412 880-2PH

'CELLO CONCERTO IN E MINOR OP85*
SEA PICTURES OP87 OP37†
Jacqueline du Pré: 'Cello*
London Symphony Orchestra
Janet Baker: Mezzo-soprano†
Conductor: John Barbirolli
EMI CDC 7 47329-2
AAD Running time: 54.02
Performance: ★ ★ ★   Recording: ★ ★

The innate poignancy of this concerto here encompasses the performer as well, for Jacqueline du Pré, who came as close as any soloist to the heart of this work, was to succumb to a wasting disease which eventually prevented her from playing the 'cello again. This recording is as much a lasting reminder of the warmth and humanity that characterized her playing, as a realisation of Elgar's marvellous score.

It was made in 1965, under the baton of Sir John Barbirolli, himself an accomplished 'cellist, and who significantly played the solo part in the Concerto's second-ever performance. No surprise, therefore, that the rapport between soloist and conductor here is quite magical.

The same epithet applies to Janet Baker's *Sea Pictures*. Elgar was no great songwriter, but some of the undoubted skill as a composer of oratorio is apparent in this set of songs and the result is his finest effort in the genre.

The purity and clarity of the solo voice is most marked in this CD transfer, although the recording of the concerto was never quite up to the highest standards of EMI's mid-'sixties productions. CD improves transparency, brings greater weight to the basses and tightens up the timpani, but can do little about the harshness in orchestral *tutti*. *Sea Pictures* shows the greater gains. But this is not a disc to be judged simply on its technical quality: in its eloquent, rhapsodic interpretation of the 'Cello Concerto it remains unique.

Other recordings on CD:
('Cello Concerto only – see above)

INTRODUCTION AND ALLEGRO FOR STRING QUARTET AND STRING ORCHESTRA OP47/ELEGY OP58/ SOSPIRI OP70/SERENADE IN E MINOR OP20/CHANSON DE MATIN OP15 NO1/ CHANSON DE NUIT OP15 NO2/ SPANISH LADY SUITE OP89
English String Orchestra
Conductor: William Boughton
Nimbus NIM5008
DDD Running time: 46.21
Performance: ★ ★ (★)
Recording: ★ ★ (★)

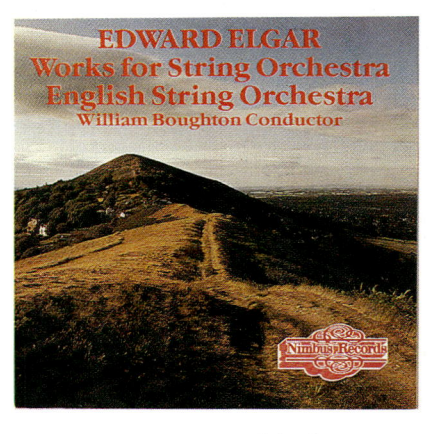

This attractive collection of the shorter works nevertheless contains two undisputed masterpieces: the exuberant *Introduction and Allegro* of 1905 and the lovely E minor *Serenade*, which Elgar wrote as a third wedding anniversary present for Alice in 1892. Equally melodic are the two *Chansons*, salon pieces, but very skilful ones nevertheless. Of the other pieces here,

ELGAR

Sospiri (*Sighs*) is deceptively simple, but proves hauntingly memorable.

The recording displays all the usual Nimbus qualities of natural balance and spacious acoustic, with lively reverberation, which suits these works admirably, although the resonance robs the *Introduction and Allegro* of some of its crisp rhythmic incisiveness. However, the spontaneous performances allow this recording to be recommended as a very enjoyable and representative selection of the 'lighter' Elgar.

Other recordings on CD:
(*Chanson de Matin/Chanson de Nuit*)
Bournemouth Sinfonietta/Norman del Mar/ Chandos CHAN8371
(*Serenade for Strings*)
ASMF/Neville Marriner/ASV CD DCA518
Bournemouth Sinfonietta/George Hurst/ Chandos CHAN8375
(*Sospiri*: version for violin and piano)
Nigel Kennedy/Peter Pettinger/Chandos CHAN8380

CONCERT OVERTURES: FROISSART OP19/COCKAIGNE (IN LONDON TOWN) OP40/IN THE SOUTH (ALASSIO) OP50/OVERTURE IN D MINOR (Handel orchestrated Elgar)
Scottish National Orchestra
Conductor: Alexander Gibson
Chandos CHAN8309
DDD Running time: 54.14
Performance: ★ ★ ★   Recording: ★ ★ ★

Here we have Elgar at his most flamboyant and extrovert: three brilliant overtures of his own, and a reworking of one by Handel (from Chandos Anthem No2, to be exact). *Froissart* of 1890 was his first orchestral composition of significance and, despite its showy character, it already bears an unmistakably Elgarian stamp. There is no doubting, however, the mastery of *Cockaigne*, an affectionate and captivating portrait of London in its diverse moods. *In the South* owes its origins to a very different location and an obviously pleasurable stay at Alassio in Italy.

The sound on this recording is appropriately full-blooded and wide-ranging, with impressive height, depth, and altogether credible scale, while Gibson obtains performances of exuberant vitality and virtuosity from the Scottish orchestra. The whole effort has enormous élan, and comes over as a recording that all involved enjoyed making; it is just as easy and pleasurable to listen to.

THE WAND OF YOUTH — SUITES NOS 1 AND 2, OP1A and 1B/NURSERY SUITE
Ulster Orchestra
Conductor: Bryden Thomson
Chandos CHAN8318
DDD Running time: 63.29
Performance: ★ ★ ★   Recording: ★ ★ ★

During the summer of 1907, after re-examining sketches dating from up to thirty years earlier and re-working a number of them, Elgar produced two suites based on nursery tales, no doubt with nostalgic recollections of his own childhood woven into them. Whatever its youthful origins, this is as fine a sample of the 'lighter' Elgar as any, deftly and evocatively scored, and well served by this impressive Chandos recording.

Completing a generous programme, the *Nursery Suite* was written while Elgar was Master of the King's Music for the monarch's grand-daughters, now Queen Elizabeth and Princess Margaret. It was first performed in 1931.

With enjoyable performances and a well-balanced recording, this is an unexpected but welcome addition to the Elgar discography.

STRING QUARTET IN E MINOR OP83 PIANO QUINTET IN A MINOR OP84
John Bingham: Piano
The Medici Quartet
Meridian ECD84082
AAD Running time: 67.46
Performance: ★ ★ ★   Recording: ★ ★ ★

As the First World War drew to its close, Elgar, revitalised both by the end of the conflict and by his move from London to a more congenial Sussex cottage, worked simultaneously on three major chamber works: the two recorded here, and a violin sonata. All three emerged as major compositions. Although characteristic of their creator, there was much about them that was very different from the pre-war music: his wife imaginatively described their reflective, wistful nature as '*wood magic*'.

Many years later, during the composer's final illness, his friend, Troyte Griffith, listening with Elgar to the String Quartet, said to him after hearing the slow movement: '*Surely that is as fine a movement by Beethoven?*'

'Yes it is,' replied Elgar, 'and there is something in it that has never been done before.'

When Griffith asked what that was, Elgar simply replied, '*Nothing you would understand, merely an arrangement of notes.*'

There is no denying the profound quality of that movement, or of both Quartet and Quintet in their entireity, and they are done full justice in these performances.

Almost uniquely for recordings made in the past few years, these have been produced on analogue rather than digital equipment – and with just one stereo microphone. The result is wholly convincing, with Elgar's often elaborate scoring cleanly defined, and the piano in the quintet well-balanced (always a difficult combination to record, since so much depends on the judgement of the pianist as well as the engineer). The result is honest, unfussy sound that simply and effectively does its job.

MANUEL DE FALLA
(b. Cadiz, Spain, 23 November 1876; D. Alta Gracia, Argentina, 14 November 1946)

Along with Isaac Albéniz and Enrique Granados, Falla was one of the outstanding composers of the modern Spanish national school, whose founding father, Felipe Pedrell taught all three. Falla received his first music lessons from his mother, and became keenly interested in both folk music (he later organised folk festivals) and the music of the church.

From 1907 until the outbreak of war in 1914 Falla resided in Paris, composing little but absorbing much from his association with Ravel, Debussy and Dukas, and coming to compose *El Amor Brujo*, followed in 1919 by his most perennially popular work, the ballet, *The Three-Cornered Hat*.

A very self-critical composer, Falla allowed few of his works to be published: the atmospheric *Nights in the Garden of Spain* was one, and the 'marionette opera', *Master Peter's Puppet Show* another.

On his return to Spain in 1914, he settled first in Madrid, then divided his time between Granada and Majorca. During the Spanish Civil War, his loyalties were with Franco, but disillusion set in soon afterwards and in 1940 he left to spend the rest of his life in Argentina.

The little of Falla's music that currently exists on CD is very fine (see reviews below), but there is much worth adding.

THE THREE-CORNERED HAT: BALLET*†
EL AMOR BRUJO: BALLET**
Colette Boky: Soprano*/Huguett
Tourangeau: Mezzo-soprano**/Richard
Hoenich: Bassoon†
Montreal Symphony Orchestra
Conductor: Charles Dutoit
Decca 410 008-2DH
DDD Running time: 62.10
Performance: ★ ★ ★   Recording: ★ ★ ★

Has there ever been a finer combination of performance and recording than these two dazzling pieces? From the opening drum beats and commanding rattle of the castanets, the feeling of 'being in the best seat in the house' is complete, such is the sense of presence established by the St Eustache acoustic in Montreal. Thereafter, it is sheer pleasure, both in terms of the captivating and beautifully-played performances (it certainly sounds as though all involved had fun making this!), and in Falla's vivid, colourful and exciting scores.

While in Paris between 1907 and 1914, he had seen the fascination that his homeland exerted on the likes of Debussy and Ravel, and on returning to Spain at the outbreak of war he completed his own 'homage to Andalusia', the ballet *El Amor Brujo* (*Love, the Magician*), following this with the *Sombrero dos tre picos* (*The three-cornered hat*) in which the influence of the *cante jondo*, the Moorish folk music of Andalusia, was again much in evidence. He was persuaded by Diaghilev to make a fully-fledged ballet from the tale, and the first production occurred in London in 1919, with sets – appropriately enough – by Picasso.

Other recordings on CD:
(*The three-cornered hat*)
Mexico State SO/Enrique Batiz/That's Entertainment CDACD85704
Pittsburgh SO/Andre Previn/Philips 411 046-2PH
SRO/Ernest Ansermet/Decca 414 039-2DH
(*El Amor Brujo*)
Pittsburgh SO/Andre Previn/Philips 411 046-2PH

NIGHTS IN THE GARDENS OF SPAIN
(c/w Albeniz: Rapsodia Espanola and Turina: Rapsodia Sinfonica)
Alicia de Larrocha: Piano
London Philharmonic Orchestra
Conductor: Rafael Frühbeck de Burgos
Decca 410 289-2DH
DDD Running time: 52.05
Performance: ★ ★ ★
Recording: ★ ★ (★)

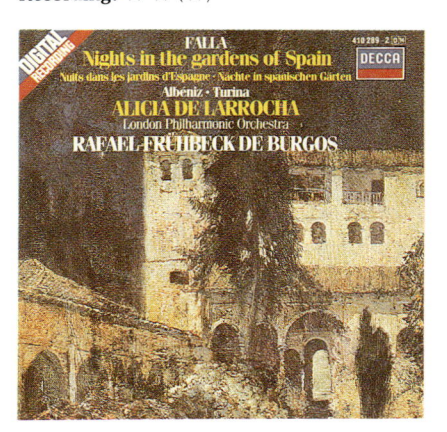

More subtle in its 'Spanishness' than the two great ballets, *Nights in the Gardens of Spain* remains a sensuous, impressionistic evocation of sights, smells, and sounds. Some of the writing, for strings and horns especially, is quite magical, although it is the solo piano part which takes the limelight: indeed, the score, completed in Paris in 1914, was originally for piano alone. Here, the forward placing of the instrument gives the work more of a concerto feel, but thankfully the orchestra is not reduced to 'peeping over the soloist's shoulders', so to speak. Rather, the whole sound is well-projected in a generous ambience which suits the broad, sweeping nature of the piece. A ravishing and spontaneous performance.

Other recordings on CD:
Mexico State SO/Enrique Batiz/That's Entertainment CDACD85704

GABRIEL FAURÉ
(b. Pamiers, Ariége, France, 12 May 1845; d. Paris, 4 Nov 1924)

It is curious that a composer who, for thirty years held a series of posts connected with music for the Catholic church, should write but one religious composition, albeit an exceptional one: the ever-popular *Requiem*. Along with the gentle, wistful *Pavane*, it is his best-known composition, yet Fauré's importance lies more in his songs and his chamber music, amongst which the two Piano Quartets (see below) are outstanding.

His talents were first discovered by Louis Niedermeyer, then heading the school for church music which he had revived and which henceforth bore his name. Niedermeyer lighted upon Fauré while touring France looking for young talent. He was sufficiently impressed with the nine-year-old to offer free board, lodging and tuition at the school, which later boasted Saint-Saëns as one of its tutors. He and Fauré got on well.

Fauré left the École Niedermeyer in 1865 and in the years which followed he held posts such as choirmaster of the Madeleine church in Paris and professorship of composition at the city's Conservatoire, where he taught, among others, Ravel. He was also appointed to the post of Inspector of Music throughout the schools of France.

Sadly, he suffered increasing deafness from around 1905 and, after the First World War, spent his last years in semi-retirement. It was only after his death that his true stature as a composer, especially of songs, was truly recognised. A classicist in intellect, but romantic at heart, he had a natural lyrical gift. Beneath its generally restrained, civilised gentility, it is music capable of wide expression, and certainly vocal masterpieces such as *La Bonne Chanson* are worthy of a place in the CD catalogue.

SUITE: PELLÉAS ET MÉLISANDE OP80/ FANTASIE POUR FLUTE (orch. Aubert) OP79/PAVANE OP50/SUITE: MASQUES ET BERGAMASQUES OP112
William Bennett: Flute
Academy of St Martin-in-the-Fields
Conductor: Neville Marriner
Argo 410 552-2ZH
DDD Running time: 42.14
Performance: ★ ★ (★)
Recording: ★ ★ ★

This enjoyable selection of Fauré's most popular orchestral works is most beautifully played and recorded, and of course scores such as the delicately-scored *Fantasie* for flute are tailor-made for the background silence Compact Disc can offer. Written as a test piece in 1898, it presents no problems, however, for William Bennett. The dreamily wistful *Pavane* dates from twelve years earlier and is performed here with the chorus part added a year later.

By contrast, it is the *galant* style of the 17th Century which pervades the delicious *Masques et Bergmasques*, while, in composing incidental music to Maeterlinck's symbolist drama, *Pelléas et Mélisande*, Fauré was but the first of several composers to be attracted to this work.

Other recordings on CD:
(*Pavane* Op50)
St Louis SO/Leonard Slatkin/Telarc CD80059
Europe CO/James Judd/IMP Red Label PCD805

PIANO QUARTET NO1 IN C MINOR OP15/PIANO QUARTET NO2 IN G MINOR OP45
The Nash Ensemble
CRD Records CRD3403
ADD Running time: 65.38
Performance: ★ ★ ★   Recording: ★ ★ ★

It would be wrong to assume these works represent the Fauré of the engaging, but lightweight salon music. Their outward geniality is deceptive, for they contain some of the toughest and most impassioned music he produced. This is nowhere better demonstrated than in the highly-charged emotions of the *adagio* of the second quartet: most definitely not the voice of a composer of trifles, and displaying a consummate mastery of scoring for four instruments, especially the viola.

CRD are to be commended on transferring these rewarding performances to Compact Disc, particularly as the recording quality is of an equally high standard, well-balanced, sharply-defined and with a lively, almost tangible presence.

CÉSAR FRANCK
(b. Liège, Belgium, 10 December 1822; d. Paris, 8 November 1890)

If Debussy led the modern 'impressionist' school of French music, then Franck must be regarded as the leader of the opposite camp, where classicism still reigned, albeit infused with a certain romantic mysticism.

César proved to be a gifted pupil, collecting several prizes with compositions, the level of invention of which often left the judges perplexed. It was hardly surprising, therefore, that during his 40-year tenure as organist of the Church of St Clotilde Franck became famous for his improvisations. His original compositions, however, attracted little attention: he was more revered as a teacher, becoming professor of organ at the Conservatoire at the age of fifty.

However, such was his self-critical attitude that it was not until he was sixty-eight that he felt he had written something truly worthwhile: a string quartet. Ironically, just a month later, he was struck a blow on the head by the pole of a horse bus and died from the injury a few months later.

His music is very personal in style: if he was affected at all by the all-prevailing influence of Wagner, it was by the Wagner of *Tannhäuser* or *Lohengrin* rather than *Tristan*. A consummate mastery is displayed in the Symphony in D minor, the Violin Sonata (see under Ravel for a recommended version of this), the Prelude, Chorale and Fugue of 1884, and the Symphonic Poem *Les Éolides* of 1876. His reverence for Bach is nowhere better heard than in the magnificent Chorale No2.

The Unicorn-Kanchana label must be congratulated on adding a good measure of Franck's organ compositions to the CD catalogue (see below), but in the orchestral field, the Symphonic Variations, for one, deserves better representation.

CHORAL NO2 IN B MINOR/FANTAISIE IN A MAJOR OP35 (FROM TROIS PIÈCES)/GRAND PIÈCE SYMPHONIQUE OP17 (FROM SIX PIÈCES)
Jennifer Bate: Organ
Unicorn-Kanchana DKP(CD)9014
DDD Running time: 52.11
Performance: ★ ★ ★   Recording: ★ ★ ★

Although neither the instrument (a Cavaillé-Coll organ would obviously have been preferable), nor the acoustic (the vastness of Beauvais Cathedral) are entirely appropriate for Franck's organ music, there is no doubt that Jennifer Bate's performances of these marvellous works, including the majestic *Choral*, confound criticism. As she proved in her recordings of Olivier Messaien, she has an unerring feel for latter-day French organ music, and if this disc appeals, then her other Franck recital on DKP(CD)9030 can be just as warmly recommended.

The recording is excellent, and notable for being Ambisonic/UHJ-encoded. Therefore, utilising a suitable decoder and four (or more) loudspeakers will considerably enhance the illusion of space and ambience.

Other recordings on CD:
(*Choral* No2)
Peter Hurford/Argo 411 710-2ZH and Decca 411 929-2DH
Charley Olsen/Denon C37-7015
(*Fantaisie*)
Michael Murray/Telarc CD80096

SYMPHONY IN D MINOR
(c/w Saint-Saëns: Le Rouet d'Omphale – Symphonic Poem Op31)
Orchestre National de France
Conductor: Leonard Bernstein
Deutsche Grammophon 400 070-2GH
DDD Running time: 51.53
Performance: ★ ★ (★)
Recording: ★ ★ (★)

The D minor is that very rare animal – a French symphony in the style of Beethoven. Of all Gallic composers, only Saint-Saëns and Lalo attempted anything comparable to César Franck's lonely masterpiece. It occupied him between 1886 and 1888 and was first played in Paris in 1889, which is where Leonard Bernstein recorded this performance, at a concert in 1981. And a very eloquent and warmly affectionate reading it is, too, although not entirely without moments of self-indulgence.

The playing is first-rate, and the recording well-balanced, if a little congested in the tuttis. The brass can become fierce. However, in the absence of any competition, and the inclusion of an enjoyable 'filler', it earns a recommendation.

GEORGE GERSHWIN
(b. Brooklyn, New York, 26 September, 1898; d. Hollywood, California, 11 July, 1937)

Gershwin composes at the piano: he made a name as a dazzling jazz pianist before applying his keyboard skills to the classical form of the concerto, although the jazz influence remained.

To George Gershwin, musical divides were there to be crossed, as perhaps befitted a Jewish-American born in the great melting-pot of New York. His teenage studies in classical piano and theory did not prevent him from getting to know how things were done in the popular sphere – he did 'song plugging' (what we would now term 'hypeing') and took jobs as rehearsal pianist in music halls.

In 1919, he not only wrote the evergreen *Swanee*, but composed a string quartet, while his *Scandals of 1922*, managed to embrace both *Stairway to Paradise* and the one-act opera, *Blue Monday*.

During the 1920s, both his song-writing gifts and his formidable abilities as a jazz pianist were fully recognised, and he enjoyed wide acclaim, along with his hardly less talented lyricist brother, Ira Gershwin.

Then, in 1924, came the commission which was to establish Gershwin's name with a wholly different audience. The 'jazz concerto' requested by bandleader, Paul Whiteman, became *Rhapsody in Blue*, one of the most enduringly popular compositions of this century. He continued this successful synthesis of styles and traditions with both the Piano Concerto in F and *An American in Paris*.

It was on his second visit to that city in 1928, as part of a tour intended to bring himself up-to-date with what was happening in modern European music, that he encountered Ravel, Stravinsky and Prokofiev, and also equipped himself with a full set of Debussy's scores. Gershwin was not only wholly receptive to new ideas, but very self-critical, and one can only speculate on the directions his music would have taken if a brain tumour had not caused his untimely death at the age of thirty-nine.

Gershwin's greatest vocal composition, the 'folk opera' *Porgy and Bess* is discussed in our companion volume. Overall he must be considered adequately represented on Compact Disc.

GERSHWIN

PORGY AND BESS: SYMPHONIC PICTURE/SECOND RHAPSODY*/ CUBAN OVERTURE
Christina Ortiz: Piano*
London Symphony Orchestra
Conductor: André Previn
EMI CDC7 47021-2
DDD Running time: 43.22
Performance: ★ ★ ★
Recording: ★ ★ (★)

These are sparkling performances from Previn, even if the Second Rhapsody cannot compare with its predecessor – The *Rhapsody in Blue* – for imagination and melodic appeal. However, the main work, Robert Russell Bennett's suite of themes from *Porgy and Bess*, is successful in every respect.

The spacious and expansive recording, in the main, is naturally balanced, with delicious detail. A little edginess to the sound, and a slightly-too-prominent piano do not detract from the pleasure.

Other recordings on CD:
(*Porgy and Bess: Symphonic Picture*)
Dallas SO/Eduardo Mata/RCA RD14551
(*Second Rhapsody*)
Michael Tilson Thomas/LAPO/CBS MK 39699
(*Cuban Overture*)
Dallas SO/Eduardo Mata/RCA RD14551

PORGY AND BESS: SYMPHONIC PICTURE (arranged Robert Russell Bennett) (c/w Grofé: Grand Canyon Suite)
Detroit Symphony Orchestra
Conductor: Antal Dorati
Decca 410 110-2DH
DDD Running time: 60.08
Performance: ★ ★ ★   Recording: ★ ★ ★

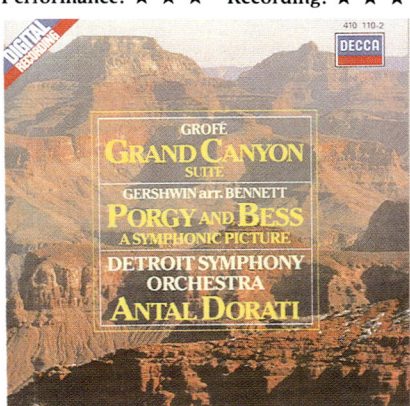

These are beautiful performances, the Gershwin especially captivating – these famous melodies can rarely have been as seductive, yet Dorati is never indulgent in his treatment of them. The Detroit orchestra's playing is very fine indeed, as it is in the *Grand Canyon Suite*, by Ferde Grofé.

Grofé's depiction of the United States' most famous natural feature is suitably vivid and colourful, and is similarly well-performed here, with a detailed and naturally-balanced sound offering great depth and weight, especially to the basses. This is an exciting recording.

Other recordings on CD:
(*Porgy and Bess: symphonic picture* – see above)

RHAPSODY IN BLUE/AN AMERICAN IN PARIS
Eugene List: Piano
Cincinatti Symphony Orchestra
Conductor: Erich Kunzel
Telarc CD80058
DDD Running time: 33.36
Performance: ★ ★ (★)   Recording: ★ ★

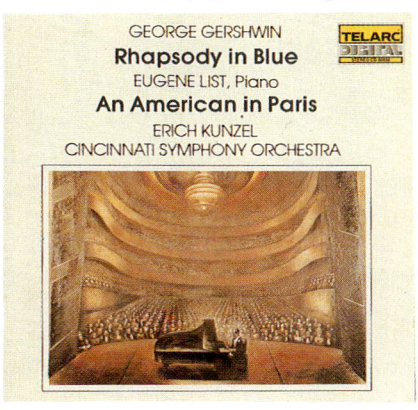

Now, if Telarc had added the Piano Concerto in F to this programme, it would have become – with merely a couple of reservations – a desirable disc indeed. As it is, any recommendation must be tempered by the poor playing time of just over thirty-three minutes.

That said, the performances are good, *American in Paris* perhaps coming off the better of the two, milking the melodies for all their worth and possessing an effervescent swagger. The *Rhapsody* lacks some rhythmic bite, but the piano part is well played by Eugene List.

The otherwise open and rich-toned recording is marred by the overpowering bass drum, so typical of early Telarc digital productions. More than on some of those other records, it can be annoyingly prominent here.

Of the alternatives in *Rhapsody in Blue*, Tilson Thomas on CBS is good, although his accompanying programme of the rarer Gershwin will not appeal to all. Bernstein on DG inflates both the lyrical and the jazz elements, and not entirely in the work's favour; his 1959 recording (LP only) was much better and CBS could do worse than remaster it.

Curiously, for a musician who cut his teeth on jazz, both Previn's versions are disappointing, the Philips from 1985, and the earlier EMI which has just been remastered for CD. However, to return to the opening comment, both of these *do* offer good value by including the piano concerto. In truth, the ideal CD Gershwin compilation has yet to appear.

Other recordings on CD (selection):
(*An American in Paris*)
Dallas SO/Eduardo Mata/RCA RD14551
Katia and Marielle Labeque (original two-piano version)/EMI CDC7 47044-2
Pittsburgh SO/André Previn/Philips 412 611-2PH
(*Rhapsody in Blue-selection*)
LAPO/Leonard Bernstein/DG 410 025-2GH
LAPO/Michael Tilson Thomas/CBS MK39699
Pittsburgh SO/André Previn/Philips 412 611-2PH

EDVARD GRIEG
(b. Bergen, Norway, 15 June 1843; d. Bergen, 4 September 1907)

Norway's voice in music's 19th Century 'nationalist' movement was Edvard Grieg, although his paternal roots were in Scotland (the original family name was Greig). He became easily the most famous of Scandinavian composers (before Sibelius), although that description would have raised his hackles: he regarded his music as specifically Norwegian in character and pedigree, and quite distinct from that of Sweden, Denmark and Finland. Curiously, although he remains best known for an unashamedly romantic piano concerto and the brilliant incidental music to Ibsen's *Peer Gynt*, Grieg was essentially a minaturist, most at home with songs (his best settings are, again, of Ibsen, and his compatriot, Björnsen) and short piano pieces. There are also some fine, but rarely performed, chamber works, and throughout his music, he seems most at home in a lyrical rather than dramatic mood.

It was inevitable that the piano should become his instrument: his mother was one of Norway's finest players and his first teacher. In his mid-teens, after periods of study in Leipzig and Copenhagen, he returned to Norway to found a music society in Christiania (now Oslo) and remained its principal conductor for thirteen years.

An important moment was his 'discovery', through the enthusiasm of a friend, of traditional Norwegian folk music. Grieg joined wholeheartedly in exploring its every aspect and, inevitably, it came to colour and flavour his original compositions.

Although he travelled greatly between 1874 and 1894, Grieg spent his final years first in Norway, latterly in a villa near his home town of Bergen where he died. Appropriately, his body is buried high in a cliff wall which looks out on a breathtaking view of a fjord, and within sight of his old home.

Let us hope that Compact Disc will eventually come round to exploring the full riches of Grieg's piano and chamber music.

PEER GYNT: INCIDENTAL MUSIC – SUITE NO1 OP46/SUITE NO2 OP55
(c/w Sibelius: Pelléas and Mélisande: Suite Op46)
Berlin Philharmonic Orchestra
Conductor: Herbert von Karajan
Deutsche Grammophon 410 026-2GH
DDD Running time: 64.31
Performance: ★ ★ ★   Recording: ★ ★ ★

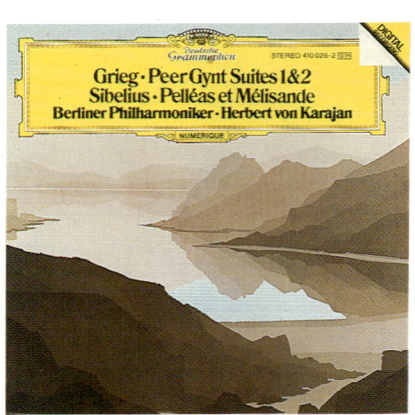

The '*few fragments*' that Grieg composed as incidental music for the first performance of Ibsen's play have now become infinitely better-known than the play itself. Indeed, the two concert suites are so familiar, it takes quite a recording to have you listening afresh, but Karajan succeeds in doing just that. The Berlin Philharmonic's fabulous playing is a prime reason, but so is Karajan's unerring touch with this score: mysterious, romantic, magically expressive – absolutely spine-tingling in *Hall of the Mountain King*.

Sibelius' 1905 score for Maeterlinck's drama is no less atmospheric, despite its economical scoring. Its poetry is fully realised here in a richly sonorous and majestic recording.

Other recordings on CD:
(*Peer Gynt* suites – part)
RPO/Walter Weller/Decca 411 933-2DH
St Louis SO/Leonard Slatkin/Telarc CD80048
(*Pelléas and Mélisande*)
Gothenburg SO/Neeme Järvi/BIS CD-263

PIANO CONCERTO IN A MINOR OP16
(c/w Schumann: Piano Concerto in A Minor Op54)
Radu Lupu: Piano
London Symphony Orchestra
Conductor: André Previn
Decca 414 432-2DH
AAD Running time: 61.19
Performance: (Grieg) ★ ★ ★
(Schumann) ★ ★   Recording: ★ ★ (★)

This 1973 recording, full and rich, and convincingly natural in the best Decca tradition, justifies its selection for Compact Disc re-mastering. It emerges with a firmer bass and more sharply defined detail; the piano tone is most impressive.

Lupu is at his best in the Grieg, lyrical without slipping into an excess of romanticism, and bringing a surprising freshness to this familiar warhorse of a concerto. He is less happy in the Schumann, and if this is the principal interest, then another version – Brendel on Philips, for example – would have to be suggested.

Other recordings on CD (selection):
(Grieg Piano Concerto)
Krystian Zimerman/BPO/Herbert von Karajan/DG 410 021-2GH
(Schumann Concerto – see Schumann)

FROM HOLBERG'S TIME: SUITE IN THE OLDEN STYLE
(c/w Mozart: Serenade in G Major K525 Eine Kleine Nachtmusik/Prokofiev: Symphony No1 in D Major Op25 Classical)
Berlin Philharmonic Orchestra
Conductor: Herbert von Karajan
Deutsche Grammophon 400 034-2GH
DDD Running time: 52.00
Performance: ★ ★ ★   Recording: ★ ★

These are superb performances. Karajan takes nothing for granted in what, at least in the case of the Mozart and Prokofiev, are much-performed pieces, and the playing of the Berlin orchestra is similarly fresh and predictably opulent. The pointing and phrasing in *Eine Kleine Nachtmusik* is a delight to hear and, most relevant here, Grieg's Renaissance pastiche receives a splendid interpretation.

The well-defined and generally agreeable recording suffers somewhat from a surfeit of microphones, sections of the orchestra, although discreetly distanced, tending to sound isolated from one another. Once accustomed to this, however, the disc offers nothing but sheer enjoyment.

Other recordings on CD:
(Holberg Suite)
National PO/Willi Boskovsky/Decca 411 933-2DH
ASMF/Neville Marriner/Philips 412 727-2PH
(Prokofiev Symphony No1)
Los Angeles CO/Gerard Schwarz/Delos D/CD3021
CSO/Georg Solti/Decca 410 200-2DH
SNO/Neeme Järvi/Chandos CHAN8400
(Eine Kleine Nachtmusik – see under Mozart)

LYRIC PIECES (selection)/MORNING MOOD (from Peer Gynt)/'FROM HOLBERG'S TIME': SUITE IN THE OLD STYLE/NORWEGIAN DANCE NO2
Cyprien Katsaris: Piano
Teldec ZK8.42925
DDD Running time: 64.59
Performance: ★ ★ ★   Recording: ★ ★ ★

His ten books of *Lyric Pieces* for piano occupied a span of thirty-five years in Grieg's career, from 1866 to 1901. These short, uncomplicated, but appealing studies shared no common links of theme or subject, other than an affectionate, often elegaic feel for nature, Norway, and Northern latitudes in general.

Cyprien Katsaris plays a well-contrasted, representative selection ranging from the earliest, Op12 No1, to *Es war einmal* and *Efterklang* from the very last book, Op71. He completes an attractive and generous recital with two short pieces, *Morning* from *Peer Gynt*, the delightful *Norwegian Dance No2*, plus the piano version of the *Holberg Suite*, a work not dissimilar to Ravel's *Le Tombeau de Couperin* in style, feel and intention.

All are captured in an exceptionally vivid, well-projected and lifelike sound, with pure, rounded piano tone and left- and right-hand fingerwork clearly distinguished. It is fairly closely observed, but not to the degree of becoming brittle or edgy. A desirable addition to the rather thin Grieg on CD.

PEER GYNT: INCIDENTAL MUSIC OPP46 AND 55 NOS1—12
Lucia Popp: Soprano
Ambrosian Singers
Academy of St-Martin-in-the-Fields
Conductor: Neville Marriner
EMI CDC7 47003-2
DDD Running time: 33.38
Performance: ★ ★ ★
Recording: ★ ★ (★)

As well as the usual eight instrumental items from *Peer Gynt*, this version includes four others from Grieg's wonderful score, including the beautiful *Cradle Song*, here sung quite magically by Lucia Popp. The order of the items is also of note, being that intended for theatre rather than concert use, and vocal contributions now enhance several of them (although the recorded balance is not always satisfactory).

Overall, the performances are all that could be wanted, and apart from a few oddities of balance between voices and orchestra, so is the recording. Instrumental imaging and perspective is especially noteworthy – as are the timpani thwacks! There are excellent contributions from all concerned, sympathetically directed by Neville Marriner.

Other recordings on CD (complete):
Elly Ameling/San Francisco SO/Edo de Waart/Philips 411 038-2PH

GEORGE FRIDERIC HANDEL
(b. Halle, Saxony, Germany, 23 February 1685; d. London, 14 April 1759)

Although born the same year, and of the same protestant stock, as his compatriot J S Bach, Handel's career took a very different course. Where Bach's career was confined to the towns of north Germany, Handel travelled widely, ending up not only a naturalised British citizen, but being buried in the hallowed ground of Westminster Abbey.

Neither his father, a barber-surgeon, nor his mother, the daughter of a cleric, particularly wanted their son to take up music, despite his obvious talents. A university course in law was begun, but by 1703 Handel was installed as a violinist with the Hamburg Opera orchestra, and was composing his first operas. When he travelled to Italy in 1706, it was with a considerable reputation as an organist and harpsichordist, and the impression left by what he heard there was to influence him for the rest of his career.

On his return to Germany, Handel was appointed director of music to the Elector of Hanover, but the tenure was short for, while visiting London to produce his opera *Rinaldo*, Handel was attracted by the commercial opportunities for music-making apparent in the British capital. Soon after, he set off to make his fortune there, much to the annoyance of his employer. This was somewhat unfortunate as the Elector of Hanover was later to succeed to the British throne, but it was an embarrassment Handel managed to survive.

The production of his own operas at the King's Theatre was his main occupation, although the whim of public taste being what it is, he enjoyed both success and failure in these ventures. He supplemented the expensive opera productions with somewhat cheaper-to-stage oratorios, yet ironically it was to be the latter upon which his reputation rested for neary two centuries after his death, along with the popular instrumental compositions – *Musick for the Royal Fireworks* and the *Water Music* suites. The revival of Handel's operas is mainly a recent phenomenon.

In 1741, facing bankruptcy, he abandoned opera altogether. By 1745, his health was failing and, at the age of 68, blindness set in. Bach, of course, suffered similarly, and one theory is that both composers' blindness was the result of unsuccessful operations by the same itinerant surgeon.

Vauxhall Gardens, where crowds flocked to hear rehearsals in 1749 of the Fireworks Music, *and in the south walk of which a statue of Handel was placed (to the right in this engraving).*

HANDEL

Handel died aged 74, a week after a performance of *Messiah* where, despite his poor health, he had played the organ. It is the best-loved aria from that oratorio, 'I know that my redeemer liveth', which is inscribed on the scroll he carries in the rather grandiose statue in Westminster Abbey, a memorial for which he made provision in his own will.

Handel has been described as *'a magnificent opportunist'* and there can be no doubt that profit was the motive for much of what he did, although that alone is no reason to think any the less of his music. He wrote rapidly, was not afraid to exploit the convention of the time that 'borrowing' from other composers' work was quite permissible, and as a result turned out a measure of the tedious and the trivial. But he also produced sufficient music of indisputable greatness to guarantee his place among the immortals, and, on a practical level, his contribution to the musical life of England should not be under-estimated.

Handel's tercentenary, like Bach's, has ensured his adequate representation on Compact Disc in both the orchestral and chamber fields, but less so in the instrumental.

CONCERTO GROSSO IN C MAJOR HWV318 (ALEXANDER'S FEAST)/ SONATA A 5 IN B FLAT MAJOR HWV288/OBOE CONCERTOS: NO1 IN B FLAT MAJOR HWV301/NO2A IN B FLAT MAJOR HWV302A/NO3 IN G MINOR HWV287
David Reichenberg: Oboe
Simon Standage: Violin
The English Concert
Director (from the harpsichord): Trevor Pinnock
Archiv 415 291-2AH
DDD Running time: 47.29
Performance: ★ ★ ★   Recording: ★ ★ ★

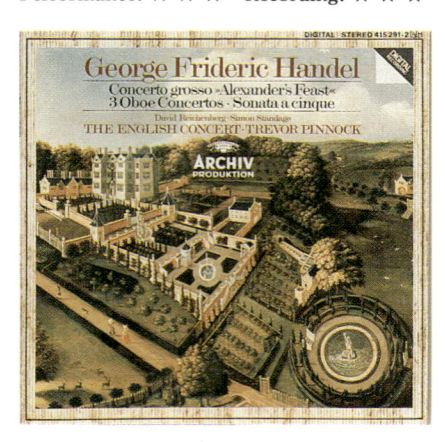

The C Major concerto earns its subtitle from being employed as an *entr'acte* in the oratorio of the same name. Completed in 1736, it is in many ways a forerunner of the far-reaching Op6 concertos, while the Sonata a 5 – to all intents and purposes a small-scale violin concerto – was Handel's first attempt at concerto writing. It dates from 1707; the influence of Corelli is apparent.

There is much of interest on this well-recorded disc and, although there are doubts about the authenticity of two of the oboe concertos, the B flat and the G minor, it matters little with solo (and ensemble) playing of this calibre, which is on a par with the rest of The English Concert's Handel series.

Other recordings on CD:
(Oboe Concertos 1-3)
The St James' Baroque Players/Ivor Bolton/ Meridian ECD84106

CONCERTI GROSSI OP3 NOS1-6 HWV312-317
The English Concert
Director (from the harpsichord): Trevor Pinnock
Archiv 413 727-2AH
DDD Running time: 54.54
Performance: ★ ★ ★   Recording: ★ ★ ★

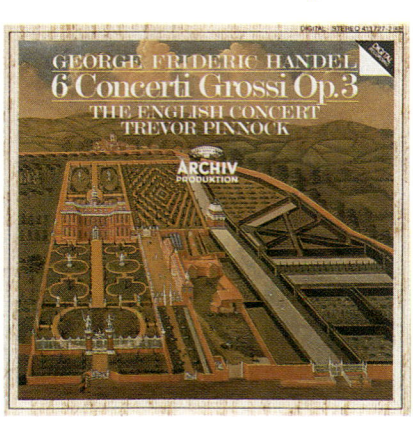

It is difficult to imagine that this splendid music was originally written as either curtain-raisers or interval background music for Handel's operas, oratorios and anthems. Or perhaps that is the effect of listening to the English Concert's performances which do make the most persuasive argument for all the collections of Concerti Grossi.

The Op3 set was finally collated and published in 1734, and it can rarely have been played in the intervening centuries with such verve and commitment as here. Tempi and dynamics are perfectly judged, as is the excellent recording.

Other recordings on CD:
ASMF/Neville Marriner/Philips 411 482-2PH
VCM/Nikolaus Harnoncourt/TelDec ZA8.35545

HANDEL

CONCERTI GROSSI OP6 NOS1-4/5-8/9-12 HWV319-330
The English Concert
Director (from the harpsichord): Trevor Pinnock
Archiv 410 897-2AH/410 898-2AH/410 899-2AH (3 discs, available separately)
DDD Running time: 159.34 (3 discs)
Performance: ★ ★ ★   Recording: ★ ★ ★

Unlike their predecessors, the Op3 concertos, those of Op6 were always intended to be more than just incidental music. In every respect – length, variety of composition, scope of expression, development of thematic material – they are far more ambitious works and obviously intended to succeed or fail in their own right. In so many ways, these concertos are the precursors of the classical era.
  Once again, the English Concert's stylish and well-conceived performances are enhanced by an extremely good recorded sound, the balance retaining unity of ensemble without sacrificing inner clarity.

Other recordings on CD (selection):
ASMF/Iona Brown/Philips 410 048-2PH3

ORGAN CONCERTOS, OP4: NO1 IN G MINOR HWV289/NO2 IN B FLAT MAJOR HWV290/NO3 IN G MINOR HWV291/NO4 IN F MAJOR HWV292/NO5 IN F MAJOR HWV293/NO6 IN B FLAT MAJOR HWV294*/CONCERTO IN A MAJOR WoO HWV296
Simon Preston: Organ
Ursula Holliger: Harp*
The English Concert
Director (from the harpsichord): Trevor Pinnock
Archiv 413 465-2AH2 (2 discs)
DDD Running time: 90.02
Performance: ★ ★ ★   Recording: ★ ★ ★

Faced with stiff competition to his Covent Garden Theatre from the new company at the King's, the self-styled *Opera of the nobility*, Handel decided to make his productions the more attractive by introducing both ballet music (in the operas), and some freshly-composed organ concertos in the *entr'actes* of his oratorios.
  However, when the collection was published in 1738 as his Op4, the harpsichord was specified as an alternative. Moreover, the Sixth Concerto was written for harp (although the organ could be substituted), hence the lightness of its orchestration. The soloist in a fine performance here is Ursula Holliger.
  Simon Preston is in excellent form in the remaining concertos and, as with their recording of the Op7 set (also on Archiv – 413 468-2AH2), these performances by the English Concert can be thoroughly recommended.
  The recording is less atmospheric than that of the competing set from Ton Koopman on Erato (reviewed elsewhere), but neither is it quite so bright.

Other recordings on CD:
(1-12)
Herbert Tachezi/VCM/Nikolaus Harnoncourt/TelDec ZB8.35282
(1-6)
Leopold Hager/Luxembourg Rad & TV SO/Forlane UCD16534
(1-6, 13-16)
Edgar Krapp/Stuttgart RSO/Eurodisc 610 260

ORGAN CONCERTOS: OP4 NOS1-6/OP7 NOS1-6/SECOND SET NOS1 (CUCKOO AND THE NIGHTINGALE) AND 2/ARNOLD EDITION NOS1 AND 2
Amsterdam Baroque Orchestra
Director (from the organ): Ton Koopman
Erato ECD88136 (3 discs)
DDD Running time: 206.53
Performance: ★ ★ ★
Recording: ★ ★ (★)

Handel was a great keyboard improviser and, not anticipating performing needs two hundred years on, simply wrote *ad libitum* for many passages in the scores for these concertos. They therefore present a rare opportunity for the present-day soloist to exercise imagination as well as technique; Ton Koopman rises splendidly to the challenge.
  This set brings together all Handel's sixteen surviving works for organ and orchestra, including the well-known *Cuckoo and the Nightingale*, and the Op7 set.
  These well-conceived performances are given a pleasantly bright, crisp recording by Erato. Blower and action noise from the organ is evident, but not distracting, and the whole is 'wrapped' in a lively acoustic. Although there is little to choose between the Erato and Archiv versions in terms of performance and recording, it is worth noting that the former succeeds in containing everything on three discs rather than four.

Other recordings on CD (complete):
Simon Preston/English Concert/Trevor Pinnock/Archiv 413 465-2AH2 and 413 468-2AH2

HANDEL

THE WATER MUSIC: HORN SUITE IN F MAJOR/MUSICK FOR THE ROYAL FIREWORKS
Acadamy of Ancient Music
Director: Christopher Hogwood
L'Oiseau-Lyre 400 059-2OH
ADD Running time: 58.45
Performance: ★ ★ ★
Recording: ★ ★ (★)

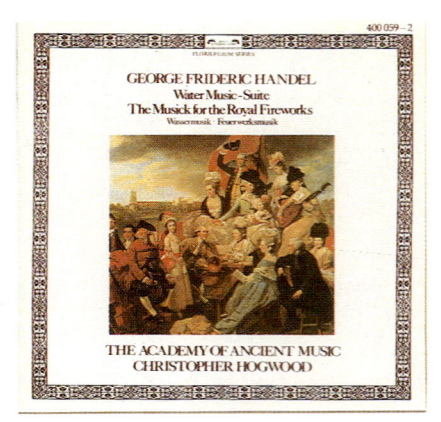

The Water Music, composed around 1717 for what must have been extremely noisy royal riverboat parties, consists of three suites, of which the above is just the first – an important point to bear in mind when selecting a recording.

However, the Fireworks Music presents no such complications, apart from being available in a 'drums-and-wind' outdoor version and a slightly more subdued 'indoor' one. Most performances seek an equable compromise here, although Christopher Hogwood employs what his researches have suggested were the original forces, with a wind instrument group doubled by the normal complement of strings.

Authenticity apart, these are lively performances, well, if not outstandingly recorded.

For a complete *Water Music*, Pinnock's exhilarating Archiv disc must be a first recommendation all-round.

MUSICK FOR THE ROYAL FIREWORKS/ CONCERTI A DUE CORI: NO2 IN F MAJOR/NO3 IN F MAJOR
The English Concert
Director (from the harpsichord): Trevor Pinnock
Archiv 415 129-2AH
DDD Running time: 53.28
Performance: ★ ★ ★   Recording: ★ ★ ★

The end of the War of Austrian Succession called for some public celebration, so a firework display, to be attended by the King, was duly arranged for 27 April 1749, in London's Green Park. Handel was asked for some suitably joyful music to accompany the pyrotechnics, and obliged with a suite which, along with the Water Music, has become his most widely-known instrumental composition.

Needless to say, it has also proved popular on record, with plenty of choice among Compact Disc versions. Pinnock offers a good mix between the 'indoor' version with strings and the more rousing 'outdoor' one, and couples this fine performance of the *Fireworks* with two equally enjoyable ones of concertos for horns. The recording is also good.

Mention must also be made of the lively Telarc/Cleveland *Fireworks*, which is brilliantly played and recorded.

Other recordings on CD (selection):
(Fireworks Music)
AAM/Christopher Hogwood/L'Oiseau-Lyre 400 059-2OH
Cleveland Winds/Frederick Fennell/Telarc CD80038
(coupled as above)
English Baroque Soloists/John Eliot Gardiner/Philips 411 122-2PH

WATER MUSIC: HORN SUITE IN F MAJOR HWV348/TRUMPET SUITE IN D MAJOR HWV349/FLUTE SUITE IN G MAJOR HWV350
The English Concert
Director (from the harpsichord): Trevor Pinnock
Archiv 415 525-2AH
DDD Running time: 54.61
Performance: ★ ★ ★   Recording: ★ ★ ★

Despite the competing claims of other versions, notably John Eliot Gardiner's on Erato, there can be little doubt that Pinnock's is the finest version of the complete *Water Music* currently available – on LP as well as Compact Disc. The combination of lithe, exhilarating performances and a lively acoustic which shows the period-instrument sound to best advantage is unbeatable. Indeed, this is one of the very best recordings the Archiv engineers have afforded the English Concert: it is unalloyed pleasure throughout.

Other recordings on CD (complete):
English Baroque Soloists/John Eliot Gardiner/Erato ECD88005
VCM/Nikolaus Harnoncourt/TelDec ZK8.42368
Los Angeles CO/Gerard Schwaz/Delos D/CD3010
BPO/Riccardo Muti/EMI CDC7 47145-2
Scottish CO/Alexander Gibson/Chandos CHAN8382

TRIO SONATAS OP5 NOS1-7 HWV396-402/SONATAS FOR TWO VIOLINS AND CONTINUO HWV394*/ HWV403
Academy of St Martin-in-the-Fields Chamber Ensemble
Philips 412 599-2PH2 (2 discs)
DDD/ADD* Running time: 98.46
Performance: ★ ★ (★)
Recording: ★ ★ ★

Two sets of trio sonatas in the *sonate da camera* (chamber sonatas) style were published during Handel's lifetime, a set of six as Op2, and seven as Op5. Three more, discovered in 1879, were given a nickname from the town where they were unearthed, Dresden. It is enjoyable music, mostly derived from existing works as was invariably Handel's practice, but with at least four of the sonatas containing fresh material.

Philips have engineered a fairly closely-focussed, but impressively-defined recording for the Academy ensemble's spirited, if occasionally stylistically inconsistent, performances.

Incidentally, the Academy's companion set of Handel's chamber music, on Philips 412 598-2PH2 can be equally recommended.

OBOE CONCERTOS: NO1 IN B FLAT MAJOR HWV301/NO2A IN B FLAT MAJOR HWV302A/NO3 IN G MINOR HWV287/CONCERTO GROSSO IN G MAJOR OP3 NO3 HWV314/SONATAS FOR OBOE AND CONTINUO: IN F MAJOR OP1 NO5 HWV363A/IN C MINOR OP1 NO8 HWV366/IN B FLAT MAJOR HWV357
Paul Goodwin: Oboe
St James' Baroque Players
Director: Ivor Bolton
Meridian ECD84106
AAD Running time: 56.11
Performance: ★ ★ ★
Recording: ★ ★ (★)

Usefully bringing together all Handel's known concertos and sonatas for oboe, these are stylish performances from Paul Goodwin and the St James' ensemble. The string sound is particularly fine, mercifully free from those tonal 'bulges' which sometimes afflict 'authentic' Baroque playing. The oboe sound is similarly attractive, although it is balanced close enough for key clicks to be audible.

That apart, balance and ambience are all that could be wanted, and a particular pleasure here is the finale of the B flat sonata, where the bassoon, part of the continuo along with harpsichord and archlute, engages in a lively duet with the soloist.

Oddly – and annoyingly – playing this disc reveals the inclusion of no less than twenty-eight index points, yet the accompanying booklet fails to detail them in any way.

Other recordings on CD:
(Oboe Concertos Nos1–3)
David Reichenberg/English Concert/Trevor Pinnock/Archiv 415 291-2AH
(Oboe Sonatas HWV357, HWV363a)
ASMF Chamber Ensemble/Philips 412 598-2PH

RECORDER SONATAS: NO1 IN G MINOR OP1 NO2 HWV360/NO2 IN A MINOR OP1 NO4 HWV362/NO3 IN C MAJOR OP1 NO7 HWV365/NO4 IN F MAJOR OP1 NO11 HWV369/NO5 IN B FLAT MAJOR HWV367A/NO6 IN D MINOR HWV377
L'Ecole d'Orphée
CRD Records CRD3412
ADD Running time: 57.25
Performance: ★ ★ ★   Recording: ★ ★ ★

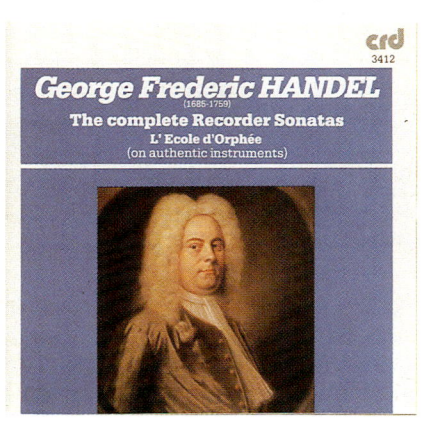

These recordings have been culled from a complete survey of Handel's chamber music by the authentic-instrument group, L'Ecole d'Orphée. The first reaction after hearing this issue is to earnestly hope that CRD will be transferring more from the series to Compact Disc in the near future.

The performances are enhanced by a clean, firmly-focussed recording, outstandingly truthful in both balance and presence. The lovely sound of the treble recorder is beautifully caught.

The first four sonatas, written in the *sonata da chiesa* style derived from Corelli, date from 1725/6, though for the fifth, the score fails to specify a solo instrument. However, the range of the solo part entirely suggests the treble recorder was the intention.

Other recordings on CD:
(Recorder Sonatas HWV367a/HWV377)
ASMF Chamber Ensemble/Philips 412 602-2PH

FRANZ JOSEPH HAYDN
(b. Rohrau, Austria, 31 March 1732; d. Vienna, 31 May 1809)

Haydn enjoyed a long and mostly successful career: when he was born, Bach was only in his forty-eighth year, and when he died, Beethoven, whom he had briefly taught, was just thirty-nine. Between times, he had witnessed the flowering, and enjoyed the friendship of perhaps the greatest musical genius of all, Mozart.

There is a tendency to regard Haydn as a rather conservative composer and, at the opposite extreme, to credit him with rather more innovatory skill than he truly deserves: he did not 'invent' the symphony nor the string quartet, but he did develop the potential of the forms as no one else at the time and, in so doing, cleared the way for Mozart and Beethoven.

Although he did not tear up the classical rule book (neither did Mozart), he was no conservative. At its best, which was often, his music is as intense and as powerfully expressive as any. Yet he also recognised the importance of humour, and it should be remembered that Haydn, throughout that long career, was employed to write music that entertained. If it also enlightened, then all well and good.

He was one of two musically gifted brothers (the other, Michael, made his mark, too) and at six joined a local choir school, soon graduating to the choir of St Stephen's Cathedral in Vienna. He gained a reputation as a bit of a prankster, which will come as no surprise to those who know his music, and first exercised his composing skills with keyboard sonatas.

Vienna, pictured during the early years of the 18th Century when Haydn (inset left), the first of the four great composers of the Viennese Classical school, was enjoying a well-earned retirement. Beethoven was at the peak of his confident 'middle period', but it was with Mozart, who had died in 1791, that Haydn had the greatest rapport. Inset right: Conductor, Sir Colin Davis, who has recorded the series of Haydn's London symphonies for Philips, with several now issued on Compact Disc.

At twenty-eight, he made perhaps the worst decision of his life by marrying one of his pupils, something of a harridan who was of little assistance to him either in his music-making or his life.

After a period in the service of the Morzin family where he composed his first symphonies, Haydn became the musical director for the Hungarian Esterházys, with an orchestra, choir and singers under his control. It was a post he held for some thirty years and the relative isolation of life on the family estate allowed him to develop his talents almost unhindered. By the time his patron, Prince Nicolas, died in 1790, Haydn had furnished him with copious quantities of symphonies, quartets and keyboard sonatas, and had also retained the constant respect and affection of all who worked under him.

Suddenly finding himself without ties, Haydn accepted an offer from the impresario, Salomon, to go to London. He was seen off by his friend Mozart who later confided he thought the journey would be too much for the fifty-eight-year-old and feared he would not see him return. He did not, but it was because of his own untimely death, not Haydn's.

This visit, and a second yielded the greatest sequence of Haydn's symphonies – and his last – those numbered from 93 to 104. Such was his stature now that the Esterházy family re-employed him to write just one religious work for them each year, and Haydn responded as magnificently as ever with the series of settings of the mass which set the seal on his illustrious career.

Although the best of the symphonies are reasonably well represented on Compact Disc, there is still a long way to go before the string quartets are given their due. The issue of the Salomon Quartet's Hyperion recordings on CD would be make an excellent beginning.

SYMPHONIES: NO6 IN D MAJOR HOB 1:6 (LE MATIN)/NO7 IN C MAJOR HOB 1:7 (LE MIDI)/NO8 IN G MAJOR HOB 1:8 (LE SOIR)
Academy of St-Martin-in-the-Fields
Conductor: Neville Marriner
Philips 411 441-2PH
DDD Running time: 58.37
Performance: ★ ★ ★   Recording: ★ ★

A notable feature of all three of these early symphonies is the inclusion of prominent solo parts, almost along the lines of the Baroque concerto grosso. Haydn produced all three shortly after entering the service of the Esterházy family and, as well as being fine music, they were no doubt intended, through the solo writing, to show off to his new employers the capabilities of his orchestra. The Esterházys could hardly have failed to be impressed. Although the symphonies do complement each other well, only the title of No7 can be authenticated: the notion of the 'morning-noon-evening' triptych, appealing as it is, was a later invention.

This is one of the best Haydn recordings to have come from Marriner and the Academy: lithe, stylish performances, glowingly recorded if lacking in detail.

SYMPHONY NO44 IN E MINOR (TRAUERSINFONIE)/SYMPHONY NO77 IN B FLAT MAJOR
Orpheus Chamber Orchestra
Deutsche Grammophon 415 365-2GH
DDD Running time: 43.38
Performance: ★ ★ ★   Recording: ★ ★ ★

While the darkly impassioned E minor symphony is well enough known (the nickname means *Mourning Symphony* and its *adagio* was played at Haydn's funeral according to his own wish), the B flat, No77, is something of a neglected masterpiece.

The New York-based Orpheus Chamber Orchestra plays without a conductor, the necessary interpretative decisions being made between the principals of each section of the ensemble. The technique generally yields excellent results here (apart from the trio of No77); the performances are well-judged (apart from several damagingly omitted repeats) and well-played.

SYMPHONY NO45 IN F SHARP MINOR HOB 1:45 (FAREWELL)/SYMPHONY NO49 IN F MINOR HOB 1:49 (LA PASSIONE)
Franz Liszt Chamber Orchestra, Budapest
Director: Janos Rolla
Hungaroton HCD12468-2
DDD Running time: 44.15
Performance: ★ ★ (★)
Recording: ★ ★ (★)

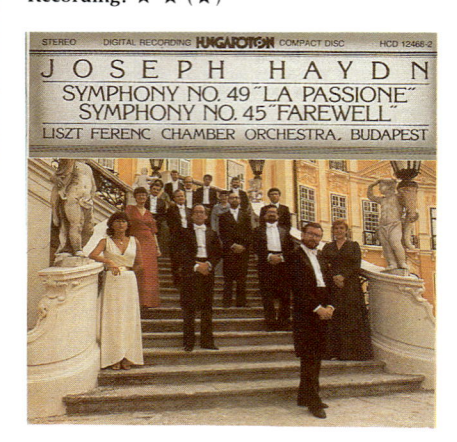

Despite the numbering, No49 is the earlier of these two symphonies, dating from 1768 during a period when Haydn wrote few symphonies, concentrating for various reasons on chamber music. Its dramatic nature merits the later nickname, while that of No45 (1772) stems from the last movement where, in the closing bars, the instruments fall silent one-by-one, ending with just the first and second violins playing. In Haydn's time the musicians would also have snuffed out the candles used to illuminate their music stands. And the purpose of this curious musical gesture? Simply to indicate to the orchestra's princely patron that it was time for a holiday!

Janos Rolla and his players bring off the 'farewell' most effectively, as they do the rest of the work, although the opening movement lacks some sparkle. The recording, warm and full, positions the orchestra at just the right distance and with the field currently to itself, this Hungarian production can be recommended.

SYMPHONY NO91 IN E FLAT MAJOR HOB 1:91/SYMPHONY NO92 IN G MAJOR HOB 1:92 (OXFORD)
Concertgebouw Orchestra, Amsterdam
Conductor: Colin Davis
Philips 410 390-2PH
DDD Running time: 53.07
Performance: ★ (★)   Recording: ★ ★ ★

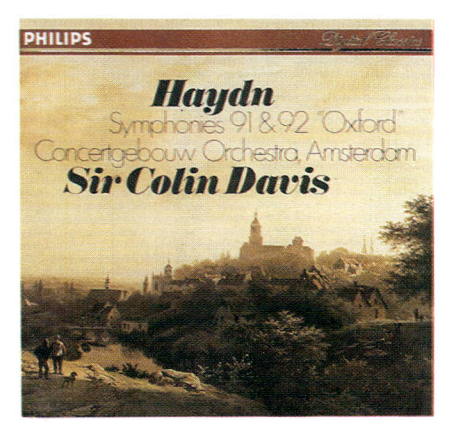

This is one of the less attractive issues from Colin Davis' series of the London symphonies. Overall the performances are enjoyable enough, but in No91 Davis sadly turns the *Trio* into a soft-centred, sentimental, unstylish *ländler*, and is also inconsistent regarding the quaver gracenotes in the first movement, taking them long on weak beats, and short on the strong ones.

He also misses important repeats, and his own vocal contribution is often all too audible. It is a pity because the coupling is an interesting one.

Other recordings on CD:
(Symphony No92)
VPO/Leonard Bernstein/DG 413 777-2GH

SYMPHONIES: NO93 IN D MAJOR HOB 1:93/NO94 IN G MAJOR HOB 1:94 (SURPRISE)/NO96 IN D MAJOR HOB 1:96 (MIRACLE)
Concertgebouw Orchestra, Amsterdam
Conductor: Colin Davis
Philips 412 871-2PH
DDD Running time: 67.47
Performance: ★ ★ ★   Recording: ★ ★ ★

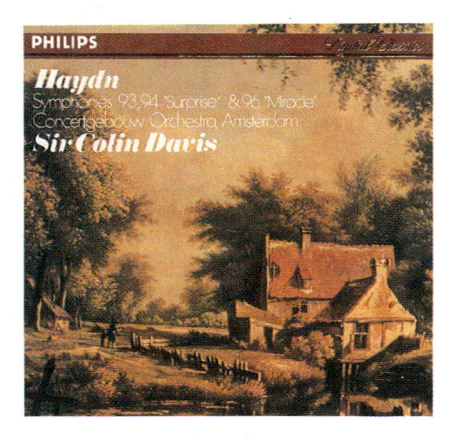

Three very fine performances make for an exceptionally good-value programme here. The playing is of the highest order – the interruption to the tranquility of its third movement that constitutes the 'surprise' of No94 is brought off superbly – and the recording is weighty and detailed, although not quite as well-defined as others made in the Concertgebouw. Once again, Colin Davis' fresh and lively approach to Haydn brings copious rewards.

Other recordings on CD:
(Symphony No94)
BPO/Herbert von Karajan/DG 410 869-2GH
LPO/Georg Solti/Decca 411 897-2DH
AAM/Christopher Hogwood/L'Oiseau-Lyre 414 330-2OH
(Symphony No96)
BPO/Herbert von Karajan/DG 410 975-2GH
AAM/Christopher Hogwood/L'Oiseau-Lyre 414 330-2OH

SYMPHONY NO94 IN G MAJOR HOB 1:94/(SURPRISE)/SYMPHONY NO96 IN D MAJOR HOB 1:96/(MIRACLE)
The Academy of Ancient Music
Director (from the fortepiano): Christopher Hogwood
L'Oiseau-Lyre 414 330-2OH
DDD Running time: 49.20
Performance: ★ ★ ★   Recording: ★ ★ ★

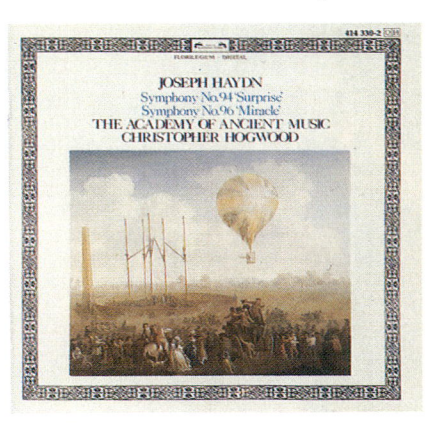

Although not representing such good value as Colin Davis' Philips disc, which also includes Symphony No93, this coupling of the *Miracle* and the *Surprise*, is worthy of consideration for two lively, well-characterised performances recorded in a bright, open acoustic. The overall sound is very transparent, with the orchestra well-integrated, and if anything, the end result is better-defined and marginally preferable.

In terms of performance, though, there is little in it. All departments of the Academy are on top form, with the woodwind, trumpets and (obviously enthusiastic!) drums worthy of special mention. It is a question of whether you prefer late Haydn in big- or small-band formats as here, and whether you appreciate Hogwood's greater generosity over repeats. There is no doubt that, in movements such as the *vivace* finale of the *Miracle* and the minuet of the *Surprise*, the Academy are extremely persuasive!

SYMPHONY NO100 IN G MAJOR HOB 1:100/(MILITARY)/SYMPHONY NO104 IN D MAJOR HOB 1:104/(LONDON)
The Academy of Ancient Music
Director (from the harpsichord): Christopher Hogwood
L'Oiseau-Lyre 411 833-2OH
DDD Running time: 51.09
Performance: ★ ★ ★   Recording: ★ ★ ★

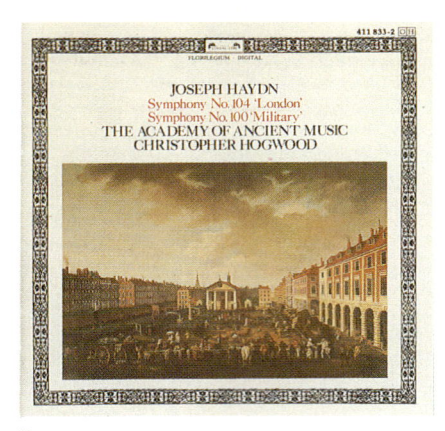

HAYDN

It is difficult to imagine better Haydn performances (and recordings) than these. Anyone who believes Haydn's music to be on the dull side compared with that of his Viennese compatriots, would have any such belief pleasantly disproved here. It is also dramatic proof of the effect good performances can have on our musical appreciation, or the lack of it, and by implication, the disservice poor interpretation can do the best of music.

There is an irresistible vitality and freshness here, and the care taken over the readings is wholly evident. The march-like *allegretto* of Symphony No100, the *'military movement'* which gives the work its nickname, is brought off with great *élan*.

However, exactly why Symphony No104 should have become the *London* when any of its eleven immediate predecessors was equally entitled to take that name, is not known. What is certain, is that this is among the most recommendable of Haydn recordings.

Other recordings on CD (selection):
(coupled as above)
Concertgebouw O/Colin Davis/Philips 411 449-2PH

SYMPHONY NO101 IN D MAJOR HOB 1:101/(CLOCK)/SYMPHONY NO104 IN D MAJOR HOB 1:104/(LONDON)
Scottish Chamber Orchestra
Conductor: Raymond Leppard
Erato ECD88079
DDD Running time: 58.48
Performance: ★ ★ (★)
Recording: ★ ★ (★)

The second six of the twelve *London* (or *Salomon*) symphonies, Nos 99–104, were a result of Haydn's second visit to the city in 1794/5, and were destined to be the last symphonies he was to write, as well as being among the very finest. Four of the six have nicknames, that of No101 deriving from the second movement, *andante*, where a gentle stream of lovely music flows over a pendulum-like, 'tick-tock' pulse.

Its playing is one of the highspots of these mainly excellent readings from Raymond Leppard and the Scottish orchestra.

The Erato sound is impressively expansive, both in width and height, and richly reverberant. The orchestra is forwardly-balanced, but well-integrated with the acoustic, and very cleanly-recorded.

Leppard's version of *The Clock* is preferable to Karajan's (currently the only rival), and if that symphony especially is wanted, the coupling can be recommended. However, competition in No104 is stiffer.

Other recordings on CD:
(Symphony No101)
BPO/Herbert von Karajan/DG 410 869-2GH
(Symphony No104 – see above)

'CELLO CONCERTO IN C MAJOR HOB VIIb:1/'CELLO CONCERTO IN D MAJOR HOB VIIb:2
Christophe Coin: 'Cello
The Academy of Ancient Music
Director (from the harpsichord): Christopher Hogwood
L'Oiseau-Lyre 414 615-2OH
DDD Running time: 52.56
Performance: ★ ★ (★)
Recording: ★ ★ (★)

Although it was known that Haydn wrote a 'cello concerto around 1765, some eighteen years before the popular D major work, the manuscript had always been presumed lost until, in 1961, a set of parts was discovered in Prague, and subsequently authenticated. And a valuable discovery it proved to be, for this C Major concerto is, if anything, more arresting than its partner.

Christophe Coin's is a committed, virtuoso performance of the C Major, although his intonation lets him down on a couple of occasions. He is no less interesting in the D major, even if his cadenza to the opening *allegro* is over-long. With equally vital accompaniments, and a natural balance, there is no better way to discover these concertos, which demonstrate just how imaginatively Haydn could compose for solo instruments.

Other recordings on CD:
(coupled as above)
Julian Lloyd Webber/ECO/Philips 412 793-2PH
('Cello Concerto in D major only - selection)
Mari Fujiwara/Netherlands CO/Michi Inoue/Denon C37-7023 and C37-7060 (alternative couplings)
Yo Yo Ma/ECO/Jose-Luis Garcia/CBS MK39310

TRUMPET CONCERTO IN E FLAT MAJOR HOB VIIe:1 (c/w Hummel: Trumpet Concerto in E Major)
New York 'Y' Chamber Symphony
Soloist and conductor: Gerard Schwarz
Delos D/CD3001
DDD Running time: 33.01
Performance: ★ ★ (★)
Recording: ★ ★ (★)

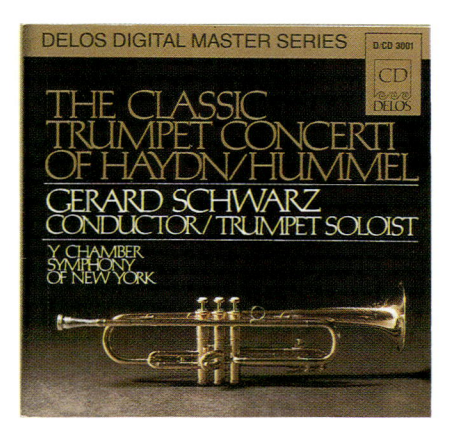

The Trumpet Concerto, composed when he was sixty-four for that prime mover in the development of the keyed trumpet, Anton Weidinger, was Haydn's last symphonic work. Johann Nepomuk Hummel's no less distinguished concerto makes an apt partner – it, too, was written for Weidinger, in 1803, but unpublished during the composer's lifetime, mainly because Hummel despaired of an instrument being manufactured that could do it justice.

These are strongly-projected performances from Gerard Schwarz, the demanding finales presenting no fears for him, and his ripe tone is finely captured by the atmospheric recording.

Playing time, however, is poor, and if the Haydn is the principal attraction, then an alternative version such as that by John Wallace on Nimbus is worth considering, despite its heavily-reverberant acoustic. That offers some fifty-seven minutes of music.

Other recordings on CD (selection):
(Haydn *Trumpet Concerto*)
John Wallace/Philharmonia O/Christopher Warren-Green/Nimbus NM5010
Wynton Marsalis/National PO/Raymond Leppard/CBS MK37846 and MK39310
Maurice André/Philharmonia O/Riccardo Muti/EMI CDC7 47311-2

STRING QUARTETS: NO76 IN D MINOR OP76 NO2 HOB III:76 (FIFTHS)/NO77 IN C MAJOR OP76 NO3 HOB III:77 (EMPEROR)/NO78 IN B FLAT MAJOR OP76 NO4 HOB III: 78 (SUNRISE)
Eder Quartet
TelDec ZK8.43110
DDD Running time: 63.26
Performance: ★ ★ (★)
Recording: ★ ★ (★)

The Op76 set of quartets, to which these works belong, have long been the best-known and most popular that Haydn wrote. It is a well-merited popularity, too, given their mastery of quartet style, and thematic invention. All three, played here by the Hungarian Eder Quartet, have nicknames; the first from the musical intervals that follow one another at the opening of the first movement. The third, No78, also takes its name from the ascending opening bars, while the slow movement of No77, consisting of a set of variations on Haydn's patriotic song, *Gott erhalte Franz der Kaiser*, inevitably became known as the *Emperor*. Its theme will now be instantly recognisable as the national anthem of West Germany.

The Eder players do not wholly resolve all the tempo problems posed, especially in the *presto* of the *Emperor*, but overall these are immensely satisfying performances. The excellent tonal quality is nicely captured by the full, broad, but well-integrated recording; the firm, rich sound of the 'cello a particular delight.

It would be exciting to think that the Eder, and other quartets, will be exploring Haydn's quartets further on CD.
Other recordings on CD:
(*String Quartets Nos76 and 77*)
Berlin Philharmonic Quartet/Denon C37-7094
(*String Quartet No77*)
Amadeus Quartet/DG 410 866-2GH
(*String Quartet No78*)
Orlando Quartet/Philips 410 053-2PH

STRING QUARTET NO78 IN B FLAT MAJOR OP76 NO4 HOB III:78 (SUNRISE)/ STRING QUARTET NO80 IN E FLAT MAJOR OP76 NO6 HOB III:80
Orlando Quartet
Philips 410 053-2PH
DDD Running time: 47.27
Performance: ★ ★ ★   Recording: ★ ★ ★

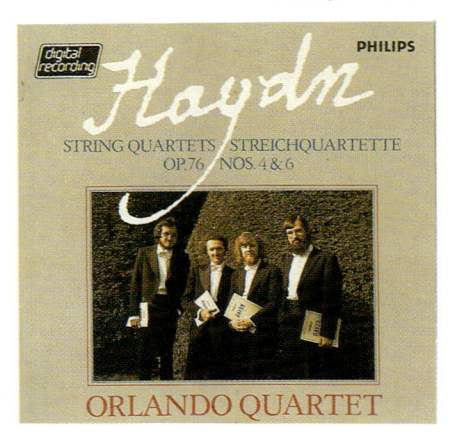

With slightly close, but outstandingly natural recording, set in precisely the right acoustic, this is one of the very best chamber music issues to have appeared on Compact Disc. The playing, too, compels attention, warmly and eloquently responsive to these magnificent scores.

Although the Eder Quartet on TelDec offer the better playing-time value in their three selections from Op76, there is no doubt the Orlando have the edge artistically and technically. If only one was to be included in a collection, it would have to be this wholly rewarding Philips disc.

GUSTAV HOLST
(b. Cheltenham, England, 21 September 1874; d. London, 25 May 1934)

By curious coincidence, the year 1934 witnessed the deaths of three prominent English composers: Elgar, Delius and Holst. In the main, the first two had completed their life's work, but not so Gustav Holst who had just entered a new phase of creativity, having at last purified and clarified his style of composition according to principles he had striven to fulfil all his life.

The trombone was Holst's instrument, but his living came from various teaching posts, the most successful at St Paul's Girl School in West London. Teaching gave him a valuable understanding of both the orchestra and the voice, and this he put to good effect in a number of compositions in the ensuing years, such as the revolutionary *Hymn of Jesus*, the *Choral Symphony* and the remarkable opera, *Savitri*.

Holst never achieved the financial success that would allow him to concentrate exclusively on composition and had to work as a music teacher all his life. An accident in 1924 weakened him for the final ten years of his life; he died leaving a promising symphony incomplete.

Many of the works listed above, and other fine compositions, including his most sublime orchestral piece, the Hardy-inspired, *Egdon Heath*, have yet to appear on CD. One hopes that situation will be remedied with issues from, say, EMI, Unicorn or Hyperion.

THE PLANETS – SUITE OP32
Ambrosian Singers
London Symphony Orchestra
Conductor: André Previn
EMI CDC 7 47160-2
ADD Running time: 50.56
Performance: ★ ★ ★   Recording: ★ ★

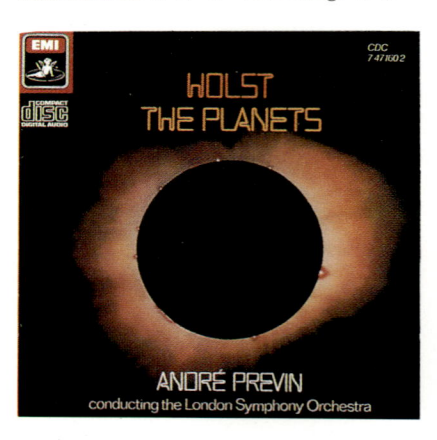

A favourite 'hi-fi demonstration' record since its appearance in 1974, it is not surprising that EMI have chosen to remaster what is also a superlative performance of Holst's most popular work, despite the duplication with Simon Rattle's digital recording in their CD catalogue. Ironically, Previn's version outshines its more recent companion, as it does rivals from other labels: better recorded than Solti, Karajan, or Maazel and better performed than Gibson. The fresh, unmannered, well-shaped reading is matched by a vivid, well-detailed, if slightly dry sound that comes up well in the new medium.

EMI may well, of course, decide to add one of their two Boult versions on CD, too, in which case the competition will be greater, but for the moment Previn is a wholly satisfactory first choice.

Other recordings on CD (selection):
LPO/Georg Solti/Decca 414 567-2DH
BPO/Herbert von Karajan/DG 400 028-2GH
SNO/Alexander Gibson/Chandos CHAN8302

ST PAUL'S SUITE OP29 H118
(c/w Elgar: Serenade in E minor Op20/ Warlock: Capriol Suite/Ireland: Concertino Pastorale)
Bournemouth Sinfonietta
Conductor: George Hurst
Chandos CHAN8375
ADD Running time: 54.10
Performance: ★ ★   Recording: ★ ★

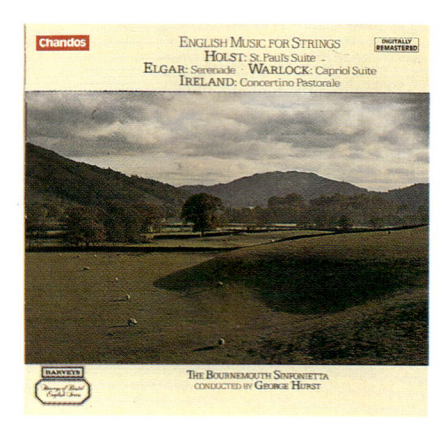

One of several mid-seventies recordings of English music remastered by Chandos for Compact Disc, this offers a sparkling performance of one of the two suites Holst wrote especially for the orchestra of St Paul's Girls School where he taught. Light as it is, however, it would have taxed the young players in many respects.

The Suite is appropriately coupled here, with Elgar's charming serenade, Peter Warlock's *echt*-Elizabethan *Capriol Suite*; and, the most substantial piece, John Ireland's lyrical *Concertino Pastorale* which, despite some *longeurs*, is a memorable work.

The recording is good, but shows its age compared to Chandos' more recent efforts. However, an appealing 'English sampler'.

LEOŠ JANÁČEK
(b. Hukvaldy, Moravia, 3 July 1854; d. Ostrau, Czechoslovakia, 12 August 1928)

Leoš Janáček was not so much a late developer, as a *very* late developer! His most remarkable works – four operas, a Slavonic mass, two string quartets among them – were all products of the last ten years of his life, written between the ages of sixty-four and seventy-four.

He was the son of an impoverished village schoolmaster, becoming a choirboy at the Queen's Monastery in Brno at the age of eleven. There he came under the influence of the monk-cum-composer, Krizkovsky, who also imbued the boy with the strong sense of Czech nationalism that was to be important to him throughout his life.

At just sixteen, Janáček became choirmaster himself, moving on to study at the Prague Organ School (and establishing a friendship with Dvorák) and then, in 1879, at Leipzig. Returning home, he settled in Brno, becoming director of the Beseda Choral Society and thereafter the town was the focal point of all his musical activities, including researches into the characteristics of natural sounds: animal cries, birdsong, and human speech and dialect.

SINFONIETTA
TARAS BULBA: RHAPSODY FOR ORCHESTRA
Czech Philharmonic Orchestra
Conductor: Vaclav Neumann
Supraphon C37-7056
DDD Running time: 46.01
Performance: ★ ★ ★   Recording: ★ ★ ★

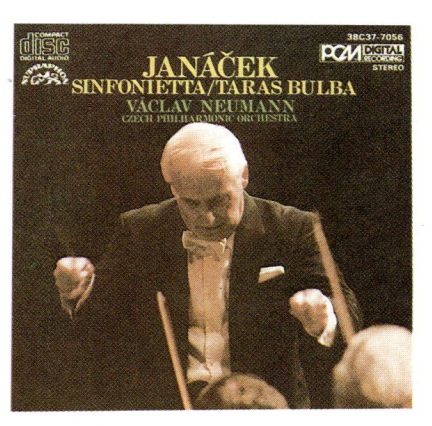

'A very nice sinfonietta with fanfares,' was Janacek's modest assessment of this original and colourful piece, apparently inspired by a military band concert and, upon its completion in 1926, dedicated to the Czech army (its published title was *Military Sinfonietta*). The fanfares of the first movement are a veritable blaze of brass, requiring nine trumpets, two bass trumpets and two tenor tubas. One need hardly comment that these provide an arresting opening, and the remainder of the work is no less appealing.

Taras Bulba, a work of the First World War period, derives its inspiration from Gogol's tale of a Ukranian partisan leader who leads a campaign to free his nation from Polish dominance. The parallels with Janacek's own Czechoslovakia are evident, and musically, this is the more dramatic of the two compositions here.

They make an obvious and popular coupling and the choice on CD rests between Mackerras' powerful and exciting Decca recording, which is scrupulous to the letter of the original score in the *Sinfonietta*, and Vaclav Neumann on Supraphon: no less splendid and thrilling, and getting the vote over the Decca with a greater ambience and atmosphere. Mackerras' brass can seem oppressively as well as impressively close, and the fanfare, especially, benefits from being able to expand and soar into the space the Supraphon venue places around it.

Both versions are excellent – the final choice must be left to personal preference.

Other recordings on CD:
(coupled as above)
VPO/Charles Mackerras/Decca 410 138-2DH
PO/Simon Rattle/EMI CDC 7 47048-2

STRING QUARTET NO1 'KREUTZER SONATA'
STRING QUARTET NO2 'INTIMATE PAGES'
Smetana Quartet
Supraphon C37S-7545
DDD Running time: 40.34
Performance: ★ ★ ★   Recording: ★ ★

Janacek's two string quartets are both products of his astonishingly prolific later years, when his inspiration was fired by the love he felt for Kamila Stosslova, a woman thirty-eight years his junior and the subject of the 'intimate pages' from which the second quartet derives its sub-title. This vividly pictorial and emotional work, far removed from the abstract musical expression usually associated with the string quartet genre, was completed in 1928.

Five years earlier, his first quartet sprang from altogether different passions: Tolstoy's story of the adultress murdered by her husband, the *Kreutzer Sonata*, deeply affected Janacek. The quartet that he produced as a result again deals in realities, the harsh sonorities of tension, anger, jealousy and rage.

Both are marvellous works, worthy of a wider audience.

By digital standards, this 1976 taping almost qualifies for vintage status, but it proves to be very good indeed: little ambience to speak of, but firm imaging and good tonal quality. The players are set at a reasonable distance, too, which helps in setting an optimum listening level. This is a rewarding issue.

FRANZ LISZT
(b. Dobr'jan (Raiding), Hungary, 22 October 1811; d. Bayreuth, Bavaria, Germany, 31 July 1886)

The 'holy' Liszt is mercilessly caricatured in this 19th Century cartoon as a six-handed note-monger.

Few composers have scaled the artistic heights, and plunged to the depths of banality in quite the same way as Franz Liszt. Opinions about the stature and worth of his music are unlikely ever to be reconciled. What is certain is that all the evidence points to his being the greatest piano virtuoso of his age, and conceivably of all time.

His father, a good amateur musician employed as a bailiff by Haydn's patrons, the Esterházy family, gave him his first lessons, but such were the prodigious gifts of the young Ferenc (to give him his Hungarian name), he was soon studying in Vienna too.

At the age of twelve, he began his long, full, and widely-travelled career as a concert pianist, being based in Paris between 1823 and 1837. There he mixed with others of a Romantic vein, Berlioz and Chopin among them. Rome became his home after 1837, and it was in the period between 1834 and 1844 that he had the first of his celebrated love affairs, with Countess Marie d'Agoult, who bore him three children. Between 1847 and 1863, Princess Caroline Sayn-Wittgenstein was the object of his affections, encompassing the period of his employment as Director of the Weimar Court Opera (1848-1861).

The year after that second tempestuous affair ended, Liszt became devoutly religious, steeping himself in Christian mysticism which had a profound effect on his music. Even without the spiritual message of their titles, many of these pieces would be recognisable as expressions of the most sublime faith and vision. Liszt even went so far as to take lay orders and the title, the Abbé Liszt.

He left a legacy of some 1,300 works, of which some 400 were original. The rest were transcriptions of others for piano solo, most successfully the songs of Schubert, most presumptuously, the symphonies of Beethoven.

Certainly he was a restless, and ultimately important, innovator, even if his enthusiasm at times got the better of his taste. To the end, he encouraged progressive ideas: it was no accident the term *'music of the future'* was coined in his house.

Jorge Bolet's series of recitals for Decca have considerably enhanced the Liszt discography in every medium, not solely Compact Disc. These, added to discs by Alfred Brendel and Claudio Arrau offer good coverage of the major solo piano compositions, but so far there is little choice among the orchestral works.

LISZT

PIANO CONCERTO NO1 IN E FLAT MAJOR S124/PIANO CONCERTO NO2 IN A MAJOR S125
Sviatoslav Richter: Piano
London Symphony Orchestra
Conductor: Kirill Kondrashin
Philips 412 006-2PH
ADD Running time: 41.12
Performance: ★ ★ ★   Recording: ★ (★)

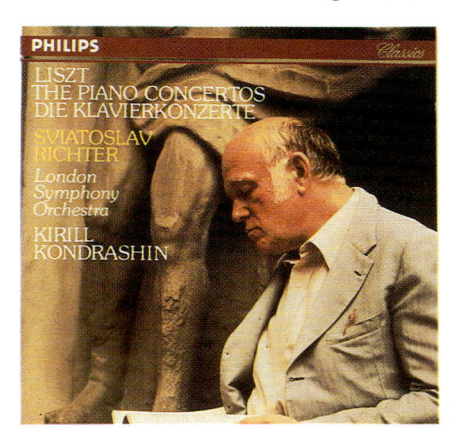

Philips' engineers have done their best to refurbish the sound quality of these 1961 recordings, but there are obviously aspects such as the over-sized yet lightweight piano, blurred tonal balance and inevitable tape hiss, about which they could do nothing. So why the inclusion here? Simply that Richter's interpretations of the Liszt concertos remain unsurpassed and, despite the recording drawbacks, are just as compelling as they ever were. This is one of the great recordings, artistically if not technically, and merits a place in any collection.

Other recordings on CD:
(Piano Concertos Nos1 and 2)
François-René Duchable/LPO/James
  Conlon/Erato ECD88035
Michele Campanella/LPO/Herbert
  Soudant/PRT CDPCN7
(Piano Concerto No1)
Martha Argerich/LSO/Claudio Abbado/DG
  415 061-2GH

TOTENTANZ (DANCE OF DEATH) FOR PIANO AND ORCHESTRA S126/ MALÉDICTION FOR PIANO AND ORCHESTRA S121/FANTASIA ON HUNGARIAN FOLK THEMES FOR PIANO AND ORCHESTRA S123
Jorge Bolet: Piano
London Symphony Orchestra
Conductor: Ivan Fischer
Decca 410 079-2DH
DDD Running time: 46.53
Performance: ★ ★ ★
Recording: ★ ★ (★)

The ancient *Dies Irae* theme is the basis for the set of variations which constitute the *Totentanz*, as bizarre a work as any written in the mid-19th Century. Not that the highly imaginative harmonic progressions of *Malédiction* are any less so, a work from around Liszt's thirtieth year. The *Fantasia* is the lightest music here, and it is satisfying to have all three complementary compositions on one disc.
  Bolet gives perceptive performances, admirably accompanied by the LSO under Ivan Fischer. They do not play down the dramatic nature of the music, and Bolet's highlighting of its many contrasts consistently commands attention, as does the vivid recording.

Other recordings on CD:
(*Totentanz*)
France Clidat/RTL SO/Jean-Claude
  Casadeus/Forlane UCD16516
(*Fantasia on Hungarian Folk Themes*)
François-René Duchable/LPO/James
  Conlon/Erato ECD88035
France Clidat/RTL SO/Jean-Claude
  Casadeus/Forlane UCD16516

A FAUST SYMPHONY G108
John Aler: Tenor
Rotterdam Philharmonic Orchestra and Chorus
Conductor: James Conlon
Erato ECD88060
DDD Running time: 73.40
Performance: ★ ★ ★
Recording: ★ ★ (★)

Liszt's most substantial and cogently-argued orchestral work, dating from 1857, takes as its inspiration the principal protagonists in Goethe's *Faust*: Gretchen, Mephistopheles, and Faust himself. Here, his command of descriptive composition attained new heights, and the results are immensely effective.
  Conlon conducts the symphony with conviction and understanding, nicely pointing the contrasts. The Rotterdam orchestra is with him all the way. With well-upholstered, richly-textured, but clear, coherent and open sound, this Erato issue currently has the field to itself, but any future competition would have to be very good indeed to overtake it.

SYMPHONIC POEMS: LES PRÉLUDES S97/ORPHEUS S98/TASSO, LAMENTO E TRIONFO S96
Hungarian State Orchestra
Conductor: János Ferencsik
Hungaroton HCD12446-2
DDD Running time: 47.43
Performance: ★ ★ ★   Recording: ★ ★

During his period at the Weimar court opera, from 1848 to 1861, Liszt produced twelve symphonic poems on a rich variety of subjects. These are three of the better-known and, if *Les Préludes* is the most popular, there is no doubt the best music is to be found in the lyrical, Italian-flavoured, *Orpheus*. In their finely-judged performances, the Hungarians manage to play down the more vulgar and inflated aspects of *Les Préludes*, and the work sounds all the better for it.
  The very undemonstrative recording is set back to the point of reticence, but has a lovely warmth and bloom. For once in a recording, a violin solo needs more presence: considering that it carries the main melodic line, the solo in *Orpheus* could be more prominent.

Other recordings on CD:
(*Les Préludes* – selection)
Philadelphia O/Riccardo Muti/EMI CDC7
  47022-2
BPO/Herbert von Karajan/DG 413 587-2GH

LISZT

ANNÉES DE PÈLERINAGE – DEUXIÈME ANNÉE: ITALIE G161
Jorge Bolet: Piano
Decca 410 161-2DH
DDD Running time: 50.47
Performance: ★ ★ ★
Recording: ★ ★ (★)

Although in some respects the recording is not quite up to the highest standards of this series, it remains a splendid sound with startling range. Some of the crystalline clarity of other issues is, however, missing.
  Not that this detracts from Bolet's spellbinding, grandly-conceived performances. He is the master of the music's many moods and the playing, for example, of the great Petrarch sonnets is quite ravishing.

PIANO SONATA IN B MINOR S178/ LÉGENDES S175: ST FRANCIS OF ASSISI PREACHING TO THE BIRDS: ST FRANCIS OF PAOLA WALKING ON THE WATER/LA LUGUBRE GONDOLA NOS 1, 2 S200/1, S200/2
Alfred Brendel: Piano
Philips 410 040-2PH
DDD Running time: 62.08
Performance: ★ ★ ★
Recording: ★ ★ (★)

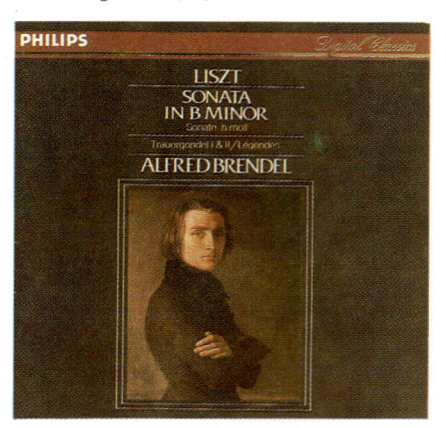

In the aftermath of Beethoven and Schubert, few composers imbued in the world of Romantic 'programme' music, felt equipped to tackle the 'pure' music of the classical sonata, and even fewer did so successfully. Liszt's solitary sonata, a taut, concentrated, one-movement work of half-an-hour's duration, was unquestionably the most significant contribution to the genre for several decades. He completed it in 1853 and dedicated it to Schumann.
  There have been many fine recordings of the sonata, but on Compact Disc, the choice narrows to Jorge Bolet on Decca and, reviewed here, Alfred Brendel on Philips. Although contrasting, there is no doubting the validity of both performances.
  Brendel's is a coolly intellectual approach, with a total grasp of structure, and full of arresting subtleties of tone and dynamics. Bolet is no less convincing or interesting, and the final choice here must be a personal one. Brendel's more appropriate couplings may well decide it: the simple beauty of the *Légendes*, and the cold, grey waters of Venice so effectively evoked in the *Gondolas*. His recording is good, too, although the piano image is over-wide and a

little 'steely' in mid-register. The power and precision in the lower registers, however, is remarkable.

Other recordings on CD:
(Piano Sonata in B minor)
Jorge Bolet/Decca 410 115-2DH
John Browning/Delos D/CD3022
Deszo Ránki/Denon C37-7547
François-René Duchable/Erato ECD88091
(*Légendes*)
François-René Duchable/Erato ECD88091

ANNÉES DE PÈLERINAGE – PREMIÈRE ANNÉE: SUISSE
Jorge Bolet: Piano
Decca 410 160-2DH
DDD Running time: 50.15
Performance: ★ ★ ★   Recording: ★ ★ ★

Some of Liszt's finest compositions are contained within this Swiss-inspired collection, begun around 1835–6 during his Alpine sojourn with the Countess d'Agoult. Indeed, a mountain storm is depicted in *Orage*, and conveyed equally vividly are the sonorous peals of *Les Cloches de Genève*. Perhaps the most concentrated examples of Liszt's genius among this group of nine pieces are the three exquisite miniatures, *Au lac de Wallenstadt*; *Pastorale*; and *Au bord d'une source*, but none could want for a more persuasive advocate than Jorge Bolet.
  Graced with the usual glittering and startlingly lifelike recording quality Decca have produced throughout, this is one of the finest recitals in Bolet's Liszt cycle – not that any are less than highly desirable.

HARMONIES POÉTIQUES ET RELIGIEUSES: FUNÉRAILLES S173/7/ HUNGARIAN RHAPSODY IN C SHARP MINOR S244/12/ÉTUDES D'EXÉCUTION TRANSCENDANTE D'APRÈS PAGANINI: LA CAMPANELLA S140/3/ LIEBESTRÄUME S541/3/MEPHISTO WALTZ NO1 S514/PARAPHRASE DE CONCERT FROM VERDI'S RIGOLETTO S434
Jorge Bolet: Piano
Decca 410 257-2DH
DDD Running time: 50.28
Performance: ★ ★ ★   Recording: ★ ★ ★

Usefully, this disc doubles both as an excellent introduction to the many qualities of Jorge Bolet's Liszt interpretations, and as representative of most facets of Liszt's art: the nationalist, the transcriber, the tunesmith, the virtuoso, and the deeply expressive, masterly piano composer.
  It is an excellent selection by Bolet, and certainly displays his extraordinary virtuosity to the full. The recording has startling presence and truthful timbre, with notable clarity and precision in the upper register. It is also enhanced by a lively halo of ambience, and the sum total is simply one of the finest CDs of piano music to grace the catalogue.

Other recordings on CD (selection):
(*Funérailles* – see below)
(*La Campanella*)
Jean-Yves Thibaudet/Denon C37-7050
(*Liebesträum* No. 3)
Jean-Yves Thibaudet/Denon C37-7050
Daniel Barenboim/DG 415 188-2GH

LISZT

ANNÉES DE PÈLERINAGE – ITALIE: APRÈS UNE LECTURE DU DANTE S161/7/ SIX CHANTS POLONAIS DE FRÉDERIC CHOPIN S480/HARMONIES POÉTIQUES ET RELIGIEUSES: FUNÉRAILLES S173/7
Claudio Arrau: Piano
Philips 411 055-2PH
DDD Running time: 50.07
Performance: ★ ★ ★   Recording: ★ ★

Liszt's principal literary influences were Goethe and Dante and the quasi-sonata inspired by the latter was completed in 1849 and included in the Italian volume of *Années de Pelèrinage*. The transcriptions from Chopin's sixteen Polish songs occupied him for some thirteen years from 1847, and are affectionately done, while *Funérailles*, a lament for – among others – Chopin, is one of the most potent of the *Harmonies*.

Together they make for a well-balanced recital from Arrau, superlatively played. The *Dante lecture* is especially successful as, in the main, is the recording, which is fairly close and bright, with a wide image.

Other recordings on CD (selection):
(*Après une lecture du Dante*)
Jorge Bolet/Decca 410 161-2DH
(*Funérailles*)
Jorge Bolet/Decca 410 257-2DH
Shura Cherkassky/Nimbus NIM5021

VENEZIA E NAPOLI S162/LES JEUX D'EAU À LA VILLA D'ESTE/ BÉNÉDICTION DE DIEU DANS LA SOLITUDE/BALLADE NO2 IN B MINOR S171
Jorge Bolet: Piano
Decca 411 803-2DH
DDD Running time: 58.24
Performance: ★ ★ ★   Recording: ★ ★ ★

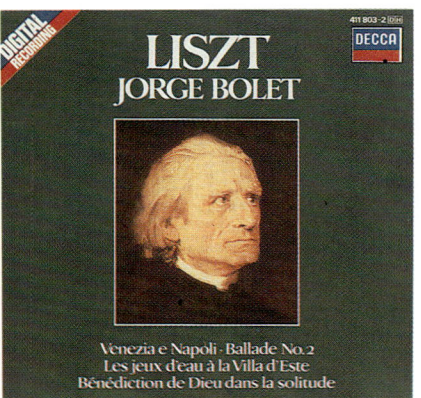

Appealing as Liszt's synthesis of popular Italian tunes is, likewise his sublime 'musical fountains', fourth of his *Années de Pèlerinage, troisième année*, pride of place here must go to the *Bénédiction*, third of the ten *Harmonies poétiques at religieuses* of 1845–52. Liszt took the title for this set, which contains at least three of his greatest piano compositions (including the *Bénédiction*) from a collection of poems by Lamartine.

The 'benediction' proper is the central section of the piece, music of hypnotic simplicity and serenity, which leads to the noble radiance of the concluding episode.

In contrast, the B minor *Ballade* rounds off Jorge Bolet's recital in extrovert vein. Once again, his playing is revelatory, always deeply considered and meticulously conveyed, with a recording possessing comparable qualities.

Other recordings on CD (selection):
(*Les jeux d'eau à la Villa d'Este*)
Carol Rosenberger/Delos D/CD3006
(*Bénédiction de Dieu dans la solitude*)
François-René Duchable/Erato ECD88091
(*Ballade No2*)
Jean-Yves Thibaudet/Denon C37-7050
Vladimir Horowitz/RCA RD14585

ÉTUDES D'EXÉCUTION TRANSCENDANTE NOS1–12
Claudio Arrau: Piano
Philips 416 458-2PH
ADD Running time: 66.32
Performance: ★ ★ ★
Recording: ★ ★ (★)

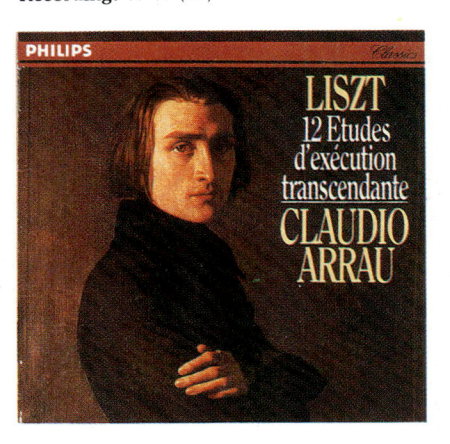

Liszt's first *Études* were written around 1826, twelve of a planned forty-eight. In 1837, he composed another set, based on these 1826 studies, but now the most complex and fantastic virtuoso pieces. They were purely for himself: it is doubtful any other pianist could have played them.

They were again revised in 1851, and by now all but two bore descriptive titles. It is astonishingly varied music, and by no means a constant barrage of notes: *Feux follets* (*Will o'the wisp*), for example, is the most delicate of pieces, rarely rising above *piano*.

Arrau's Concertgebouw recordings of the *Études* date from 1974–6, and are both meticulous and imaginative. There is great panache to the playing, with a feel for the music that is born out of a lifetime's association with the composer. The big-boned, glittering piano sound is impressive without being overwhelming.

GUSTAV MAHLER
(b. Kaliště, Bohemia 7 July 1860; d. Vienna, 18 May 1911)

If there is one composer whose popularity has blossomed in the age of the LP record, it is Gustav Mahler. Recordings have enabled music lovers to discover and absorb his vast symphonic canvasses in a way that would never have been possible through the concert hall alone. It is also true, of course, that Mahler's music is now in the repertoires of many more conductors and orchestras than it was three decades ago, although that, too, reflects its wider appreciation.

Above all, it does seem his time has come. His extraordinary synthesis of the sublime, the grotesque, the sentimental, the exotic and even the banal enjoys an acceptance and affection today greater than at any other time since the composer's death. Perhaps it is simply that this unique mixture has more relevance for present generations than any previous ones.

Mahler spent his childhood in the town of Jilhava in Bohemia, where his father owned a brewery. In 1878, he graduated in composition, but decided to pursue conducting as his main occupation for the eminently sensible reason that it paid better. And he became an exceptionally fine conductor, feared and revered in equal measure for his intolerance of anything less than the highest standards.

There were very few people that he had any time for, least of all opera house managements, and he parted company with a number after angry disputes. By 1886, Mahler was conducting Wagner in Leipzig, and establishing beyond doubt his greatness as a conductor.

But his life was far from contented. There was a hopeless love affair; the deaths in quick succession of his father, mother and sister; there was the failure of his First Symphony; and, after a promising start, his resignation from the Royal Opera, Budapest, after another irreconcilable clash of wills.

From 1891, he enjoyed a successful tenure at Hamburg, yet even that was soured by the suicide of his younger brother. When a senior post in Vienna became vacant, Mahler, anticipating that being a Jew would count against him, converted to Catholicism. He got the job and, despite all the inevitable controversies, held on to it for ten years, composing during the summer months when the opera house was closed.

Conducting was his profession (and he was a very good one); composing could only be a holiday activity

A measure of happiness came with marriage in 1901 to Alma Schindler, who continued to champion her husband's music through all its years of neglect, up to her death in 1964, when she would have seen the first signs of that long-awaited revival.

But fate had not finished dealing its hammer blows to Gustav Mahler, the blows that with grim premonition he had scored into the last movement of his Sixth Symphony. The death of his daughter was followed by the diagnosis of his own heart disease, and he died in Vienna in May 1911, leaving a legacy of song-cycles and symphonies. Since both are closely inter-related, they are discussed together here rather than divided between this volume and its companion one.

Mahler's current popularity is evident from the alternatives now available in all the symphonies, even the Seventh, the most difficult to bring off convincingly. Given that, it seems churlish to point out that a complete *Das Knaben Wunderhorn* has yet to appear on CD.

SYMPHONY NO1 IN D MINOR (TITAN)
Frankfurt Radio Symphony Orchestra
Conductor: Eliahu Inbal
Denon C37-7537
DDD Running time: 54.55
Performance: ★ ★ ★
Recording: ★ ★ ★

The poor reception given the First Symphony after its première in November 1889, prompted Mahler to write an explanatory programme for the work's next performances some four years later, and to give the work its subtitle. Unfortunately, the programme proved as bewildering to audience and critics as had the music; both it and the title were dropped by the fourth performance, in Berlin in 1896. Also deleted was the second movement, an andante originally called *Blumine* (*Flowers*), although many subsequent performances have reinstated it.

Eliahu Inbal, however, adheres to Mahler's final thoughts in what proves a most auspicious start to his Mahler cycle with the Frankfurt orchestra. It is a finely-judged, unmannered performance given a warm, well-balanced recording. The 'terracing' of the orchestra is particularly noteworthy, offering utterly natural perspectives, while the range, especially at the bass end, is hugely impressive.

Other recordings on CD:
CSO/Claudio Abbado/DG 400 033-2GH
NYPO/Zubin Mehta/CBS MK37273
Philadelphia O/Riccardo Muti/EMI CDC7 47032-2
CSO/Georg Solti/Decca 411 731-2DH

SYMPHONY NO2 IN C MINOR
(RESURRECTION)
Kathleen Battle: Soprano
Maureen Forrester: Contralto
St Louis Symphony Chorus and Orchestra
Conductor: Leonard Slatkin
Telarc CD80081/2 (2 discs)
DDD Running time: 81.24
Performance: ★ ★ ★
Recording: ★ ★ (★)

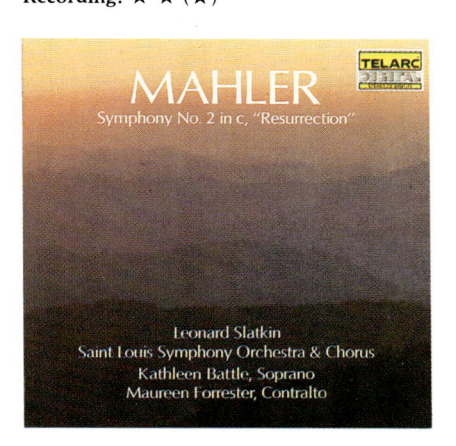

This is an extremely well-conceived performance of Mahler's vast apocalyptic vision, scrupulous to the score markings and showing throughout the care that has gone into moulding the interpretation. How essential that is in the long build-up to the overwhelming climax of the symphony, music that is as taxing to record as it is to perform. Here it is brought off extremely well, thanks to the spacious acoustic and finely-judged dynamics.

There are many other good points to the recording: the natural layering of the orchestra the placing of the solo voices, and the overall ambience (although the 'off-stage' effects could have been more atmospheric). Some transparency may be lacking but Slatkin's *Resurrection* remains preferable to any other currently available – although Sinopoli's new DG recording, listed for release as we went to press, is bound to spark interest.

Other recordings on CD:
LPO/Klaus Tennstedt/EMI CDS7 47041-8
Philharmonia O/Giuseppe Sinopoli/DG 415 959-2GH2

MAHLER

SYMPHONY NO3 IN D MINOR
Christa Ludwig: Mezzo-soprano
Prague Philharmonic Chorus
Kuhn Children's Chorus
Czech Philharmonic Orchestra
Conductor: Vaclav Neumann
Supraphon C37-7288/9 (2 discs)
DDD Running time: 90.34
Performance: ★ ★ ★   Recording: ★ ★ ★

Recommending a recording of the Third Symphony, Mahler's hymn to the miracles and mysteries of God and nature, is by no means easy with five eligible versions on Compact Disc. Adding up both the technical and artistic pros and cons, however, narrows the choice to Vaclav Neumann on Supraphon and Claudio Abbado on DG.

Both are well-recorded, with sound of impressive range, and good, natural acoustics. In the Supraphon issue, the distant brass effects are well-managed and Christa Ludwig, as well as being in fine voice, has the better balance of the two soloists. However, Jessye Norman is no less radiant, and the Vienna boys' voices have a slight edge over their Czech counterparts. The intense, benedictory sixth movement, originally sub-titled by Mahler, *What love tells me*, is beautifully played by both orchestras, with the VPO at its most sumptuous.

If Abbado's is the more finely-crafted of the two performances, it is difficult not to be swept along by the sheer spontaneity of Neumann's reading: the choice is yours.

Other recordings on CD:
VPO/Claudio Abbado/Deutsche Grammophon 410 715-2GH2
CSO/Georg Solti/Decca 414 268-2DH2
Frankfurt RSO/Eliahu Inbal/Denon C37-7828/9
CSO/James Levine/RCA RD81757

SYMPHONY NO4 IN G MAJOR
Kathleen Battle: Soprano
Vienna Philharmonic Orchestra
Conductor: Lorin Maazel
CBS MK39072
DDD Running time: 60.58
Performance: ★ ★ ★   Recording: ★ ★ ★

As a glance at the list below shows, competition between versions of this symphony on CD is formidable, with at least three thoroughly recommendable recordings. But it is Maazel who seems to come closest to Mahler's original conception with a combination of charm and poetry that conveys the disarming innocence, lightness, and even naivity of the work. If anything, he errs on the side of understatement!

The recording is refined, open and uncannily transparent, and the Viennese orchestra play like angels. Similarly angelic is the voice of Kathleen Battle, which proves ideal in the *Wunderhorn* song which concludes this radiant and joyful symphony with its childlike, fairytale vision of *The Heavenly Life*. The vision was also Mahler's, and the Fourth was to be his happiest utterance in music. Such blissful existence is ended abruptly by the fanfare that announces the Fifth Symphony.

Other recordings on CD:
CSO/Georg Solti/Decca 410 188-2DH
LPO/Klaus Tennstedt/EMI CDC 7 47024-2
VPO/Claudio Abbado/DG 413 454-2GH
Concertgebouw O/Bernard Haitink/Philips 412 119-2PH
CSO/James Levine/RCA RD80895

SYMPHONY NO5 IN C SHARP MINOR/ SYMPHONY NO10 IN F SHARP MINOR: ADAGIO
London Philharmonic Orchestra
Conductor: Klaus Tennstedt
EMI CDS7 47104 8 (2 discs)
ADD Running time: 103.25
Performance: ★ ★ (★)
Recording: ★ ★ (★)

This first of the central trilogy of purely instrumental symphonies was premiered in Cologne in 1904, and has since become best-known for its fourth movement, the *adagietto* for harp and strings, one of Mahler's most beguiling creations.

All round, Klaus Tennstedt offers the most satisfying performance currently on Compact Disc, although James Levine runs him close. Sinopoli's version begins promisingly, but disappoints with a rather stern approach to both the *adagietto* and concluding *rondo*.

Tennstedt, too, is a little severe in the finale, while the unnecessary close-miking of the harp in the *adagietto* is annoying. Otherwise, he is given a recording of great depth, with a startling bass extension, although not as lucid a sound as others in this series.

In the final analysis, none of the CD versions of the Fifth supersedes Barbirolli's great recording from the 1960s, coincidentally – like Tennstedt's – on EMI. One would hope that it is high on their list for remastering.'

Other recordings on CD:
BPO/Herbert von Karajan/DG 415 096-2GH2
Philadelphia O/James Levine/RCA RD82905
Philharmonia O/Giuseppe Sinopoli/DG 415 476-2GH
CSO/Solti/Decca 414 321-2DH

SYMPHONY NO6 IN A MINOR FIVE RÜCKERT LIEDER*
Christa Ludwig: Contralto*
Berlin Philharmonic Orchestra
Conductor: Herbert von Karajan
Deutsche Grammophon 415 099-2GH2 (2 discs)
ADD Running time: 102.04
Performance: ★ ★ ★   Recording: ★ ★ ★

The Sixth is Mahler's bleakest utterance – not here the salvation-through-faith of the Second, or the redemption-through-love of the Eighth, or the transcendence to spiritual peace of the Ninth or *Das Lied von der Erde*. There is no relief to be found even in the symphony's lyrical *andante* which is steeped in the most painful nostalgic yearnings. The hopelessness and pessimism of the last movement are compounded by three mighty 'blows of fate', which came to have such grim and personal significance for the composer himself.

The three current versions of the Sixth present an interesting contrast. Solti's is tough and relentless, while Tennstedt, with a magnificent and weighty EMI recording, manages to find a glimmer of hope in the prevading blackness. But should there be any such relief? Karajan, in the best all-round performance, appears to think not. His is a powerful, controlled reading, with plenty of bite but not at all over-driven as is Solti's. The recommendation is reinforced by a wonderfully clear and well-balanced mid-seventies recording, digitally transferred from the analogue original and revealing so much more than the LP pressings. A further bonus is Christa Ludwig's sensitive performance of the five settings of poems by Friedrich Rückert.

Other recordings on CD (selection):
LPO/Klaus Tennstedt/EMI CDS7 47050-8

SYMPHONY NO7 IN E MINOR
Chicago Symphony Orchestra
Conductor: Claudio Abbado
Deutsche Grammophon 413 773-2GH2 (2 discs)
DDD Running time: 78.39
Performance: ★ ★ ★   Recording: ★ ★ ★

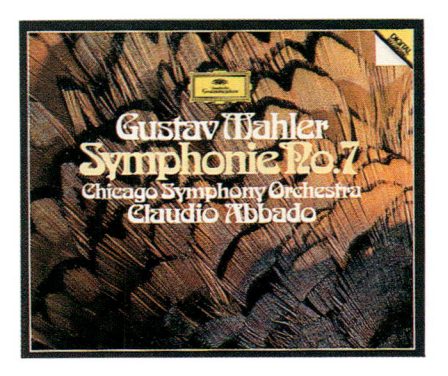

Abbado's grasp of the structure of this strangest and most elusive of Mahler's symphonies, and his understanding of its bizarre character, make for an immensely convincing performance. There is an admirable lucidity to this very refined recording, partly stemming from Abbado's direction and the dedicated playing of the Chicago Orchestra, and partly from some very well-judged recording.

Within the natural, spacious, 'concert hall' presentation, the all-important detail of the score is subtly illuminated (despite the large orchestra, much of the music is for small, chamber-like groups of instruments). Moreover, the many vehement climaxes are smoothly and comfortably contained.

Other recordings on CD:
Concertgebouw O/Bernard Haitink/Philips 410 398-2PH2
CSO/James Levine/RCA RD84581(2)
CSO/Georg Solti/Decca 414 675-2DH2

SYMPHONY NO8 IN E FLAT MAJOR
Heather Harper, Lucia Popp, Arleen Auger: Sopranos; Yvonne Minton, Helen Watts: Altos; Rene Kollo: Tenor; John Shirley-Quirk: Baritone; Martti Talvela: Bass
Vienna State Opera Choir
Vienna Singverein
The Vienna Boys' Choir
Chicago Symphony Orchestra
Conductor: Georg Solti
Decca 414 493-2DH2 (2 disc set)
ADD Running time: 79.36
Performance: ★ ★ ★   Recording: ★ ★

Mahler's oratorio symphony, the first entirely choral symphony in music, was completed in 1906, but not performed until 1910 – the occasion proved to be the last time Mahler would conduct in Europe. Although the composer disliked the description, the concert programme that day subtitled the work *Symphony of a thousand* (an accurate assessment of the numbers involved) and the nickname has stuck, despite the use of considerably smaller forces in today's performances.

In two unequal parts, the symphony first features a setting of the words of the early Christian hymn, *Veni Creator Spiritus*, and then the closing scene from part two of Goethe's *Faust*: the power of the Christian spirit, and the redeeming power of love. No wonder that, of all his works, this was the one Mahler chose to dedicate to his wife, Alma, to whom he was devoted.

It is a tribute to Mahler's skill as an orchestrator that, despite the apparently overwhelming musical forces in play, the result never seems cloying or congested. The symphony nevertheless presents formidable problems to the recording engineer. Despite this, the Decca team manage a pretty good

MAHLER

result here. It is not a natural balance – the voices are too close for one thing – but it is an undeniably impressive and effective one, which comes up cleanly in this analogue-digital transfer.

No question about the performance, though, which is one of Solti's most memorable achievements: electrifying, exhilarating, edge-of-the-seat stuff!

Other recordings on CD:
Boston SO/Seiji Ozawa/Philips 410 607-2PH2
Czech PO/Vaclav Neumann/Supraphon C37-7307/8

DAS LIED VON DER ERDE (THE SONG OF THE EARTH)
Brigitte Fassbaender: Contralto
Francisco Araiza: Tenor
Berlin Philharmonic Orchestra
Conductor: Carlo Maria Giulini
Deutsche Grammophon 413 459-2GH
DDD Running time: 64.19
Performance: ★ ★ ★   Recording: ★ ★ ★

In Hans Bethge's translations of ancient Chinese poetry, Mahler found words which mirrored his own feelings in the period following the death of his elder daughter and the diagnosis of his own heart disease: the transience of human life, its pleasures and miseries, all seeming inconsequential in the face of the inevitable. Nature can die and be reborn with each passing year, but is ours to enjoy only briefly.

He began setting the poems in the summer of 1907, and within twelve months a large-scale 'song-symphony' had taken shape; *'the most personal thing I have ever written,'* he told Bruno Walter.

Although a large orchestra is used, the scoring is frequently for small groups of instruments, which, in recording, calls for the greatest possible textural clarity. That is certainly achieved here, with the Berlin sound at its best.

Surprisingly, this was the Berlin Philharmonic's first encounter with Giulini, and the partnership works wonderfully well. Of the soloists, Fassbaender is the better of the two, compelling in *Der Abschied*. The tendency is to compare all the tenor soloists in this work with the great Fritz Wunderlich, who sings for Klemperer, but it is hardly fair. Araiza is more than acceptable, although a slightly lighter treatment of *Von der Jugend* (*Youth*) would have been preferable.

All considered, this is currently the finest stereo Compact Disc version of one of the greatest of orchestral song cycles.

Other recordings on CD:
Kathleen Ferrier/Julius/Patzak/VPO/Bruno Walter/Decca 414 194-2DH
Jessye Norman/Jon Vickers/LSO/Colin Davis/Philips 411 474-2PH
Christa Ludwig/Fritz Wunderlich/New PO/Otto Klemperer/EMI CDC7 47231-2
Yvonne Minton/Rene Kollo/CSO/Georg Solti/Decca 414 066-2DH

DAS LIED VON DER ERDE (THE SONG OF THE EARTH)
Kathleen Ferrier: Contralto
Julius Patzak: Tenor
Vienna Philharmonia Orchestra
Conductor: Bruno Walter
Decca 414 194-2DH
ADD Running time: 60.32
Performance: ★ ★ ★   Recording: ★ ★
(MONO)

Kathleen Ferrier's career was tragically short. By the time she came to make this recording in 1952, the cancer which was to prove fatal the following year had been diagnosed, and the final song of the cycle, *Der Abschied* (*The Farewell*) could never have been sung with such profound feeling or poignancy. She is not in altogether perfect voice, but that hardly matters in the face of singing of such radiance and perception.

No less remarkable are the contributions of Julius Patzak and, one-time close friend of Mahler himself, the conductor, Bruno Walter. This has always been a classic recording, and one for which there remains a special affection. But the remastered sound requires no sentimental concessions; it reveals a surprisingly wide, transparent image, with good height, and the kind of detail and tonal quality that would enhance many a more recent effort. If there is one mono recording worth its place in any stereo CD collection, this is surely it.

Other recordings on CD:
(see listing under Giulini/Deutsche Grammophon review)

SYMPHONY NO9 IN D MINOR
Berlin Philharmonic Orchestra
Conductor: Herbert von Karajan
Deutsche Grammophon 410 726-2GH2
(2 discs)
DDD Running time: 84.37
Performance: ★ ★ ★
Recording: ★ ★ (★)

Karajan came late in his career to Mahler, and even now has recorded only four of the symphonies and three of the song cycles. Yet he has tackled the Ninth twice, the second of the two performances recorded live at the Berlin Festival in September 1982. When issued, it had the distinction of being the first recording from any of the major labels to appear on Compact Disc only and almost sufficient reason in itself to buy a player.

It is a performance of almost unbearable intensity and drama, Karajan somehow penetrating deeper into the heart of this work than, perhaps, anyone before, and the response of the Berlin orchestra is quite phenomenal. Not an experience for every day (and no everyday experience), and hardly something to be dipped into, even if the discs are extremely well-indexed.

The recording is on the close side, but clear and atmospheric, and the audience is utterly unobtrusive.

Another notable Ninth is that by Bruno Walter on CBS, well-controlled and strongly projected, and, despite its early stereo origins, sounding very well indeed transferred to Compact Disc.

Other recordings on CD (selection):
LPO/Klaus Tennstedt/EMI CDS7 47113-8
Columbia SO/Bruno Walter/CBS MK42033

DAS KLAGENDE LIED
Helena Döse: Soprano, Alfreda Hodgson: Mezzo-soprano, Robert Tear: Tenor, Sean Rae: Baritone
City of Birmingham Symphony Orchestra Chorus
City of Birmingham Symphony Orchestra
Conductor: Simon Rattle
EMI CDC7 47089-2
DDD Running time: 65.11
Performance: ★ ★ (★)
Recording: ★ ★ (★)

This *'fairy tale for the concert hall'*, for which Mahler provided his own words, was completed in 1880, but revised on two occasions over the ensuing twenty years. One of the 'revisions' was the deletion of the entire first movement, entitled *Waldmarchen* (*Forest Legend*), but it is marvellous music and well worthy of reinstatement as Rattle does here.

The performance is lively and spontaneous; not without the occasional rough patch, but benefitting from Simon Rattle's obvious affection for the score. Although the problem of balancing the contribution of the off-stage band is not wholly resolved, the bright, crisply-detailed sound is satisfying in the main.

LIEDER EINES FAHRENDEN GESELLEN*/ KINDERTOTENLIEDER/RÜCKERT LIEDER: NOS1/3-5
Dietrich Fischer-Dieskau: Baritone
Bavarian Radio Symphony Orchestra*
Berlin Philharmonic Orchestra
Conductor: Rafael Kubelik*/Karl Böhm
Deutsche Grammophon 415 191-2GH
ADD Running time: 59.30
Performance: ★ ★ (★)
Recording: ★ ★ (★)

One of the CD-only compilations issued to mark the sixtieth birthday of this most remarkable of lieder singers, this disc couples Fischer-Dieskau's 1970 performance of the *Lieder eines fahrenden Gesellen (Songs of a Wayfarer)*, deeply felt and beautifully sung, with two 1964 recordings accompanied by Karl Böhm: four of the five *Rückert Lieder*, and – also settings of Friedrich Rückert – *Kindertotenlieder (Songs on the death of children)*.

Balances are satisfactory, the earlier ones very natural and unforced, and apart from an occasional tendency to over-dramatisation, so are the performances.

Other recordings on CD:
(*Lieder eines fahrenden Gesellen*)
Yvonne Minton/CSO/Georg Solti/Decca
  414 674-2DH2
Kirsten Flagstad/VPO/Adrian Boult/Decca
  414 624-2DH
(*Kindertotenlieder*)
Christa Ludwig/BPO/Herbert von Karajan/
  DG 415 096-2GH2
Kirsten Flagstad/VPO/Adrian Boult/Decca
  414 624-2DH
(*Five Rückert Lieder*)
Christa Ludwig/BPO/Herbert von Karajan/
  DG 415 099-2GH2

FELIX MENDELSSOHN
(b. Hamburg, Germany, 3 February 1809; d. Leipzig, 4 November 1847)

There can have been few artists who have shared the kind of advantages with which Felix Mendelssohn was born. Not only did he possess a great talent, there was nothing to hinder its development. His father, a banker, was able to provide everything his son could want (except a more robust constitution) including putting a private orchestra at his disposal. He was taught in Berlin by one of the very finest teachers, Carl Friedrich Zelter, and it was to be expected that, by fifteen, he had a number of symphonies and an opera to his credit (all later discarded). However, at seventeen, he proved wholly worthy of his privileged status by writing a brilliant overture inspired by Shakespeare's *A Midsummer Night's Dream*.

Jewish by birth, but Protestant by religion (the family name was changed from Mendelssohn to Bartholdy when his father renounced Jewry, hence the latter's appearance in some references to the composer), Felix also excelled in other areas of the arts: he was a classical scholar, a painter, and a linguist. That must have stood him in good stead on the many travels he undertook, including ten visits to Britain, which came to love him as much as he loved it.

His oratorio, *St Paul*, was first produced while he was director of music at Düsseldorf, and in 1845 he came to Leipzig as conductor of its famous Gewandhaus Orchestra, and to found, and become the first director of, the conservatory there. Fulsome praise greeted the first performance of another oratorio, *Elijah*, at its première in Birmingham in 1846, and for eighty years it vied with Handel's *Messiah* for pre-eminence among British choral societies.

Easy success, it must be said, did not spoil him as a personality, but his output beautifully-crafted as much of it is, is also facile and lacking in substance at times. Although one of the 'Romantics' in style, his music mostly has a detached, 'classical' quality, rarely exploring emotional depths or personal *angst*. That said, is there a more effective piece of impressionism than the wonderful *Hebrides* overture?

Mendelssohn was the first composer to write independent concert overtures such as this, although it will probably be counted as his only innovation, unless one includes the jewels of varying lustre he entitled *Songs Without Words*, which are worthy of better representation on

Mendelssohn became a favourite of Queen Victoria and Prince Albert, here at the organ.

Claudio Abbado, the conductor responsible for an outstanding cycle of the five symphonies.

Compact Disc.

Those, and the E minor string quartet and the Octet apart, there is a reasonable choice in the major symphonies and the elegant and tender Violin Concerto. A single disc of the popular overtures would be welcome however. Previn's newly-remastered version of the *Midsummer Night's Dream* music will challenge Marriner's excellent version, but look out for a *truly* complete version of this score, on two CDs and complete with dialogue, now available from Nimbus.

SYMPHONIES: NO1 IN C MINOR OP11/
NO2 IN B FLAT MAJOR OP52 (HYMN OF PRAISE)*/SYMPHONY NO3 IN A MINOR OP56 (SCOTTISH)/SYMPHONY NO4 IN A MAJOR OP90 (ITALIAN)/SYMPHONY NO5 IN D MAJOR OP107 (REFORMATION)/OVERTURES: A MIDSUMMER NIGHT'S DREAM OP21/
THE HEBRIDES OP26 (FINGAL'S CAVE)/
THE FAIR MELUSINE OP32/SCHERZO FROM OCTET OP20 (orchestral version)
Elizabeth Connell*, Karita Mattila*: Sopranos/Hans-Peter Blochwitz*: Tenor/
London Symphony Chorus*
London Symphony Orchestra
Conductor: Claudio Abbado
Deutsche Grammophon 415 353-2GH4

(4 discs)
DDD Running time: 245.55
Performance: ★ ★ ★   Recording: ★ ★ ★

On four well-filled discs (an average of over sixty minutes of music on each), Claudio Abbado directs distinguished performances of the five symphonies, plus a selection of overtures, and Mendelssohn's own orchestration of the *scherzo* from the Octet Op20, which offers an alternative to the original minuet and trio in the First Symphony.

Although it unmistakeably displays its classical influences, the First is a work of considerable skill and maturity: he was just nineteen when he wrote it, but had already tackled the symphonic form several years earlier with the String Symphonies of 1821–23.

The Second, the *Hymn of Praise*, that great favourite of Victorian choral societies, contains some ravishing music. Dating from 1840, the Second takes numerical precedence over the *Scottish* and *Italian*, which were begun in the early 1830s, since the former took until 1842 to complete, and the latter were not published at all during the composer's lifetime. It sounds like perfection to us, but Mendelssohn always wanted to revise this most infectiously happy of symphonies.

MENDELSSOHN

The Fifth, the *Reformation* (so-called because it was intended to celebrate the tercentenary of the Diet of Augsburg in 1530) also remained unpublished. Less well-known than its predecessors, but unjustly so given its bubbling *scherzo* and noble slow movement, Abbado's is just the performance to win more friends for this symphony.

Indeed the only question-mark over any of these performances is the very fast speed adopted for the *saltarello* of the *Italian*, which, although quite electrifying, is short on charm. Otherwise, these are outstanding interpretations, with clean, spacious sound. Presentation is excellent in every respect, a match for the performances. This set comes thoroughly recommended.

Other recordings on CD:
(Symphony No3)
ASMF/Neville Marriner/Argo 411 931-2ZH
Bavarian RSO/Colin Davis/Orfeo
 CO89841A
(Symphony No4)
Hungarian State O/Ivan Fischer/
 Hungaroton HCD12414-2
Philharmonia O/Giuseppe Sinopoli/DG 410
 862-2GH
ASMF/Neville Marriner/Argo 411 931-2ZH
(Symphony No5)
Hungarian State O/Ivan Fischer/
 Hungaroton HCD12414-2

SYMPHONY NO3 IN A MINOR OP56 (SCOTTISH)/SMYPHONY NO4 IN A MAJOR OP90 (ITALIAN)
Academy of St Martin-in-the-Fields
Conductor: Neville Marriner
Argo 411 931-2ZH
ADD Running time: 65.41
Performance: ★ ★ (★)
Recording: ★ ★ (★)

Mendelssohn's two most popular symphonies fit perfectly on a single CD, and for those not wanting Abbado's complete survey, this disc should fit the bill. The performances are generally very good, and the recording clean and well-defined.

Marriner adopts a surprisingly slow tempo for the opening of the *Scottish*, but it works, and that much-debated coda in the final movement is brought off with great style (there are those who believe these concluding bars mar an otherwise perfectly-conceived symphony, but Mendelssohn was surely too astute for that – the 'join' may not be perfect, but the effect is wonderful.)

The *Italian* is also a well-shaped, lively performance. It is a pity, though, that (unlike Sinopoli) Marriner fails to make the first movement repeat, and as a consequence has to cut the twenty-or-so bars of fresh music which lead up to it.

Other recordings on CD:
(see listing under Abbado/Deutsche
 Grammophon review)

VIOLIN CONCERTO IN E MINOR OP64 OCTET IN E FLAT OP20 (orchestral version)
St Paul Chamber Orchestra
Soloist and conductor: Pinchas Zukerman
Philips 412 212-2PH
DDD Running time: 61.57
Performance: ★ ★ (★)
Recording: ★ ★ ★

Mendelssohn wrote his best-known chamber work, the Octet, in 1825 when he was just sixteen. He played the viola part himself at its first performance in Leipzig, and the score instruction was notable in asking for the work to be played *'in the style of a symphony orchestra'*. This has since been taken as 'legitimising' its playing, as here, by a string orchestra and, while in no way replacing the original, it makes a wholly acceptable alternative.

Both the Octet and the Concerto receive polished performances with warm, well-balanced recording, and if the coupling appeals, this disc can be recommended.

Other recordings on CD:
(Violin Concerto in E minor Op64 – see
 below)

SYMPHONY NO4 IN A MAJOR OP90 ITALIAN
(c/w Schubert: Symphony No8 in B minor D759 Unfinished)
Philharmonia Orchestra
Conductor: Giuseppe Sinopoli
Deutsche Grammophon 410 862-2GH
DDD Running time: 61.41
Performance: ★ ★ ★ (Schubert)
★ ★ (★) (Mendelssohn)
Recording: ★ ★ (★)

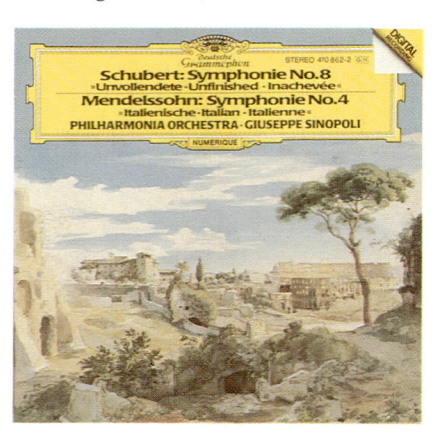

There is no doubting the compelling quality of these performances, such is the freshness Giuseppe Sinopoli brings to these familiar scores. His *Italian* is fast and fiery in the outer movements, but crisp, precise and deliciously pointed. Only in the third movement, *con moto moderato*, does his approach sound a little exaggerated and unduly heavy.

The *Unfinished* comes off better still,

similarly idiomatic, and illuminating the score as few others have done. Overall, these fascinatingly individual readings reward repeated listening.

The Kingsway Hall recording is full and wide-ranging (a little *too* full in the bass, which can sound boomy). Slightly brighter and harder than the results that Decca and EMI usually obtain from this venue, it is nevertheless an extremely clear and atmospheric sound, realistically balanced.

Other recordings on CD:
(Mendelssohn Symphony No4 *Italian* – see above)
(Schubert Symphony No8 – see under Schubert)

VIOLIN CONCERTO IN E MINOR OP64
(c/w Bruch: Violin Concerto in G minor Op26)
Uto Ughi: Violin
London Symphony Orchestra
Conductor: Georges Prêtre
RCA Red Seal RD70111
DDD Running time: 49.26
Performance: ★ ★ (★)
Recording: ★ ★ (★)

Mendelssohn completed his E minor concerto in 1844, some six years after the first ideas had occurred to him. It was promised to Ferdinand David, first violin of the Leipzig Gewandhaus Orchestra, and he duly gave the première in March 1845, since when this most lyrical of works has become one of the five or six great concertos that are part of every virtuoso's repertoire.

The G minor by Max Bruch also belongs to that elite group, and Uto Ughi is one of three soloists to couple it with the Mendelssohn on Compact Disc, another being Anne-Sophie Mutter. However, she is let down by the recording, whereas RCA have opted for a naturally-balanced, reverberant Kingsway Hall sound (if anything a little too reverberant at the expense of inner orchestral clarity). The rich-toned violin is not always as sweet as it might be (the very opening of the Mendelssohn for example) but the performances have a consistent, easy flow to them which is appealing.

Kyung-Wha Chung, on Decca, is not one to linger unnecessarily either, and hers is perhaps the most idiomatic performance of all. The song-like *andante* is beautifully played, and in sharp contrast to the hectic but enthralling finale; moreover, this version comes generously coupled with the Tchaikovsky concerto, and is discussed in more detail under that entry.

Another very fine version of the Mendelssohn comes from Cho-Liang Lin on CBS, although the coupling – Saint-Saëns Third Concerto – is not in quite the same league as Bruch or Tchaikovsky. It is well worth considering, though, if the Mendelssohn is your principal interest.

Uto Ughi, therefore, merits a recommendation, with reservations, and the suggestion to compare these short-listed versions for yourself if at all possible.

Other recordings on CD (selection):
Anne-Sophie Mutter/BPO/Herbert von Karajan/DG 400 031-2GH
Kyung-Wha Chung/Montreal SO/Charles Dutoit/Decca 410 011-2DH
Cho-Liang Lin/Philharmonia O/Michael Tilson-Thomas/CBS MK39007
Itzhak Perlman/CO/Bernard Haitink/EMI CDC7 47074-2
Pinchas Zukerman/St Paul CO/Philips 412 212-2PH
Isaac Stern/BSO/Seiji Ozawa/CBS MK37204

A MIDSUMMER NIGHT'S DREAM: INCIDENTAL MUSIC
Arleen Auger: Soprano
Ann Murray: Mezzo-soprano
Ambrosian Singers
Philharmonia Orchestra
Conductor: Neville Marriner
Philips 411 106-2PH
DDD Running time: 43.44
Performance: ★ ★ ★
Recording: ★ ★ (★)

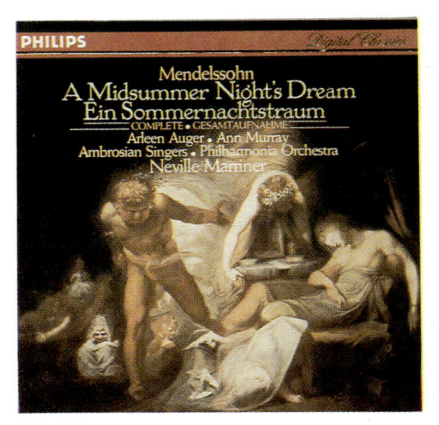

Apart from the rather rushed tempo of the overture, this is a very satisfying version of the affectionate score Mendelssohn wrote to accompany Shakespeare's comedy. The buoyantly cheerful *scherzo* comes off very well, and even the much-abused *Wedding March* reveals an unexpected freshness. With good orchestral playing, especially from the woodwind, and fine contributions from the vocal soloists and choir, Marriner's reading can be enthusiastically recommended, especially as it is enhanced by a pleasantly ambient, uncoloured sound. There is depth, too, and the orchestral perspectives are very natural.

Other recordings on CD (excerpts):
CSO/James Levine/DG 413 137-2GH
Tokyo Metropolitan SO/Peter Maag/Denon C37-7564

WOLFGANG AMADEUS MOZART
(b. Salzburg, Austria, 27 January 1756; d. Vienna, 5 December 1791)

Few would dispute that Mozart was the most musically gifted composer of all time, blessed with the most accurate ear, a phenomenal memory, and innate taste, judgement, and style, not to mention a gift for beautiful melody. As a child prodigy, he was fêted throughout Europe, yet died in near-poverty thirty years later to be buried in an unmarked grave.

His father, Leopold Mozart, himself a musician of some note, soon recognised his son's gifts and proved well able to develop them, not just as his teacher, but as what amounted to his agent and impresario, too.

At five, the young Mozart was composing simple, but hardly childish music, and at six he was touring Europe, playing harpsichord duets with his elder sister, Maria Anna. It has been debated ever since whether Leopold Mozart was a ruthless exploiter of his child prodigy, or was allowing him the kind of broad experience necessary to fully develop his genius.

Of course, the problem with all 'child stars' is that they grow up and with that, interest in them usually declines. Mozart was no exception. He underwent an unhappy period in the service of the Archbishop of Salzburg and, a far cry from being entertained by European nobility, found himself eating with the servants. Things then went from bad to worse. He was infatuated with Aloysia, one of two sisters of the Weber family, a troupe of itinerant musicians whose Bohemian lifestyle did not meet with Leopold Mozart's approval at all.

However, patronage came in the shape of Viennese nobility, including the Emperor himself, and his operas proved a popular success. In 1782, he married the second of the Weber sisters, the undoubtedly devoted but scatterbrained Constanze. Since neither she nor Mozart was particularly good with money, their financial circumstances were rarely healthy, regardless of his success.

In the year prior to his marriage, he had met Haydn for the first time and, despite the twenty-four-year age difference, the two men enjoyed a friendship that was to prove mutually beneficial in many respects. Haydn, ever-generous, told Leopold Mozart: *'I say to you as an honest man, that your son is the greatest composer known to me either personally or by reputation.'*

Haydn's judgement was to be proved abundantly right in the ensuing nine years as Mozart, leading a happy if disorganised life with Constanze, produced a stream of masterpieces, including, during one brief spell of unsurpassed creativity during 1788, his three last and greatest symphonies, Nos 39, 40 and 41; all worthy of consideration for inclusion among the finest symphonies ever written.

In the summer of 1791, despite being engaged on the radiantly optimistic Clarinet Concerto, he began to suffer from morbid depressions. The situation was not helped by the commission for a setting of the Requiem Mass by a 'mysterious stranger' (now known to be somebody's rather poor idea of a joke). Mozart became convinced that the Requiem he was composing was his own and, tragically, so it was to prove.

The circumstances of his death that winter have never been satisfactorily resolved. Was he poisoned by a jealous rival, or by a masonic conspiracy of some sort? It is unlikely we shall ever know.

Mozart is currently better represented than any other composer on Compact Disc, and it is only in the string quartets and quintets that choice is limited (it is a significant deficiency, however). And all without a centenary or the like to celebrate! How the record companies treat the 200th anniversary of his death in five years' time will be interesting to see.

MOZART

A portrait of the young Mozart at the clavichord: his keyboard artistry was prodigious.

SYMPHONY NO29 IN A MAJOR K201
SYMPHONY NO33 IN B FLAT
MAJOR K319
English Baroque Soloists
Conductor: John Eliot Gardiner
Philips 412 736–2PH
DDD Running time: 43.50
Performance: ★ ★ ★   Recording: ★ ★ ★

The A Major is one of three quite remarkable symphonies composed in Salzburg between 1773 and 1774, but undoubtedly surpasses its companions (Nos25 and 28) in craftsmanship, invention and melodic quality. It is, truly, a marvellous little symphony; and is coupled here with the chamber-scaled B flat Major of 1779, in what one hopes will prove to be the first of a Mozart series from Gardiner.

Although, like the Academy of Ancient Music, Gardiner's English Baroque soloists play period instruments, their respective approaches to 'authenticity' differ considerably. Gardiner's way with No29 is to put more emphasis on melodic line. Each movement is elegantly shaped and, on balance, this version is preferable to the Academy's (which has just been issued on Compact Disc, accompanied by Symphony No25).

The performance of No33 is no less satisfying, and with a clean, crisply-defined sound the results portend well for future recordings.

Other recordings on CD:
(Symphony No29 K201)
Concertgebouw O/Nikolaus Harnoncourt/
   TelDec ZK8.43017
VPO/Karl Böhm/DG 413 734–2GH
ASMF/Neville Marriner/Philips 412
   954–2PH6 (set)
AAM/Christopher Hogwood/L'Oiseau-Lyre
   414 631–20H
(Symphony No33 K319)
Concertgebouw O/Nikolaus Harnoncourt/
   TelDec ZK8.42817
ASMF/Neville Marriner/Philips
   412954–2PM6 (set)

SYMPHONY NO31 IN D MAJOR K297/
K300a (PARIS)
SYMPHONY NO40 IN G MINOR K550
(first version)
Academy of Ancient Music
Jaap Schröder: Concert Master
Christopher Hogwood: Continuo
L'Oiseau-Lyre 410 197–20H
DDD Running time: 52.37
Performance: ★ ★ (★)
Recording: ★ ★ (★)

It is the clarinet which attracts the musicological interest here; first, by its use in the D Major of 1778, the first time Mozart had been able to use this instrument (which so fascinated) him in a symphony, and second by its absence from the first edition of the G minor. Clarinets were only added, not altogether satisfactorily, in the second.

The Academy's view of this second of the trilogy of last great symphonies is a brisk and straightforward one, finding little of the usual mystery and melancholy. The approach succeeds in all but the long slow movement which wants for charm, but there are no doubts about the fine performance of the *Paris*. The original (3/4) slow movement of No31, promised in the booklet, is replaced on the record by the later (6/8) Andantino.

The recording offers a well-layered, sharply-defined sound, equably balanced, but with a tendency towards hardness over a certain replay level.

Other recordings on CD (selection):
(Symphony No31 K297/300a)
Concertgebouw O/Nikolaus Harnoncourt/
   TelDec ZK8.42817
ASMF/Neville Marriner/Philips 412
   954–2PH6 (set)
(Symphony No40 in G minor K550)
CSO/James Levine/RCA RCD14413
Concertgebouw O/Nikolaus Harnoncourt/
   TelDec ZK8.42935
VPO/Karl Böhm/DG 413 547–2GH
ECO/Jeffrey Tate/EMI CDC7 47147–2
ASMF/Neville Marriner/Philips 412
   954–2PH6 (set)

MOZART

SYMPHONY NO36 IN C MAJOR K425
(LINZ)
SYMPHONY NO38 IN D MAJOR K504
(PRAGUE)
Columbia Symphony Orchestra
Conductor: Bruno Walter
CBS MK42027
ADD Running time: 51.24
Performance: ★ ★ ★ Recording: ★ ★

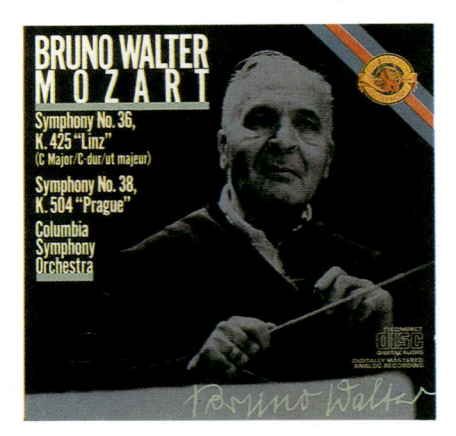

The early sixties sound emerges warm, full, and with a lively ambience which gives almost a 'period' brilliance to the strings. Bass is deep and well-defined, and these are characteristically warm and elegant Mozart performances from Bruno Walter.

Other recordings on CD:(selection)
(Symphony No36 K425)
ASMF/Neville Marriner/Philips 412 954-2PH6 (set)
(Symphony No38 K504)
VPO/Karl Böhm/DG 413735-2GH

SYMPHONY NO38 IN D MAJOR K504
(PRAGUE)
SYMPHONY NO39 IN E FLAT
MAJOR K543
Academy of Ancient Music
Director: Christopher Hogwood
L'Oiseau-Lyre 410 233-20H
DDD Running time: 62.26
Performance: ★ ★ ★
Recording: ★ ★(★)

The music-lovers of Prague well merited the accolade of a 'named' symphony. Their enthusiasm for Mozart and his music never abated during the years when the Viennese became blasé about the achievements of their greatest composer.

Here, along with No39, it receives a lithe, unsentimental, and wholly revealing performance.

Other recordings on CD (selection):
(Symphony No38 K504)
(see above)
(Symphony No39 K543-selection)
VPO/Karl Böhm/DG 413 735-2GH

SYMPHONY NO39 IN E FLAT
MAJOR K543
SYMPHONY NO41 IN C MAJOR K551
(JUPITER)
Dresden Staatskapelle
Conductor: Colin Davis
Philips 410 046-2PH
DDD Running time: 66.27
Performance: ★ ★ ★ Recording: ★ ★ ★

An issue which makes one of Compact Disc's best advertisements! These magnificent performances are not available together on LP (No41 is paired with No28; No39 with No29), and the combined playing time represents good value indeed.

As in his recordings of the late Haydn symphonies, Colin Davis makes perhaps the most persuasive argument of any for 'big-band Mozart'. There is clarity and momentum to these readings, and the playing of the Dresden orchestra is of the highest standard.

Other recordings on CD:
(Symphony No39 K543)
(see above)
(Symphony No41 K551-selection)
CSO/James Levine/RCA RCD14413
AAM/Christopher Hogwood/L'Oiseau-Lyre 411 658-20H
VPO/Karl Böhm/DG 413 547-2GH
ECO/Jeffrey Tate/EMI CDC7 47147-2
VPO/Leonard Bernstein/DG 415 305-2GH
ASMF/Neville Marriner/Philips 412 954-2PH6 (set)

SYMPHONY NO40 IN MINOR K550/
SYMPHONY NO41 IN C MAJOR K551
(JUPITER)
English Chamber Orchestra
Conductor: Jeffrey Tate
EMI CDC7 47147-2
DDD Running time: 63.45
Performance: ★ ★ ★
Recording: ★ ★ (★)

These lithe, stylish performances of Mozart's last, and profoundly contrasting, symphonies only miss full recommendation through the slightly harsh edge which colours the sound during orchestral *tuttis*. However, that should deter no one from investing in some of the most well-conceived and refreshing Mozart playing around.

Apart from the criticisms noted, the sound is generally satisfying, with clear orchestral textures and perspectives. Musically, the ECO's instruments may be modern, but the scale of the sound aims for 'authenticity'.

CLARINET CONCERTO IN
A MAJOR K622
CONCERTO FOR FLUTE, HARP AND
ORCHESTRA IN C MAJOR K299*
Emma Johnson: Clarinet
William Bennett: Flute*
Osian Ellis: Harp*
English Chamber Orchestra
Conductor: Raymond Leppard
ASV CD DCA532
DDD Running time: 55.40
Performance: (K622) ★ ★ (★)/
(K299) ★ ★ ★ Recording: ★ ★ (★)

A popular choice as Britain's 'Young Musician of the Year' in 1984, Emma Johnson gives a polished performance of the Clarinet Concerto, but one that seems to lack a little character and style compared to, say, Anthony Pay on L'Oiseau-Lyre or Thea King on Hyperion, both of whom use the authentic basset clarinet.

There are no doubts, however, about the playing of the effervescent and elegant flute and harp concerto, with the ample opportunities it gives both soloists to shine. The recording here favours the harp, although each instrument is firmly-focussed, and the orchestral sound could have been more expansive.

Criticisms aside, this remains a very enjoyable issue.

Other recordings on CD (selection):
(Concerto for flute and harp K299)
Nicolai Zabaleta/Wolfgang Schulz/VPO/ Karl Böhm/DG 413 552–2GH

CLARINET CONCERTO IN A MAJOR K622*
OBOE CONCERTO IN C MAJOR K314
Antony Pay: Basset clarinet*
Michel Piguet: Oboe
The Academy of Ancient Music
Director: Christopher Hogwood
L'Oiseau-Lyre 414 339–20H
DDD Running time: 47.01
Performance: ★ ★ ★   Recording: ★ ★ ★

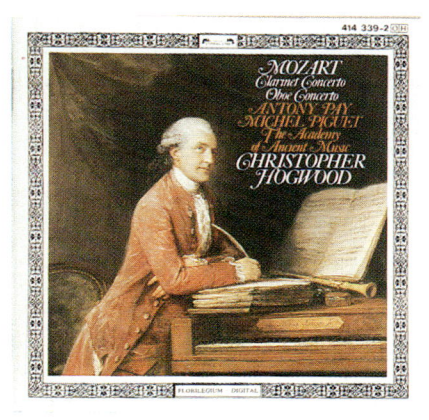

Without taking anything away from Michel Piguet's fine performance of the Oboe Concerto (also reviewed elsewhere in its alternative incarnation for transverse flute), principal interest must lie with the Clarinet Concerto, where a reconstruction of a basset clarinet is used, the instrument for which Mozart wrote the work.

The difference is one of range: the basset clarinet offers three additional semitones below its present-day counterpart, its lowest written note being C (sounding A) as opposed to the modern instrument's E.

However, Antony Pay's and the Academy's performance has much more than academic interest. It is satisfying in every respect.

Other recordings on CD (selection):
(Clarinet Concerto K622)
Alfred Prinz/VPO/Karl Böhm/DG 413 552–2GH
(Oboe Concerto K314)
Heinz Holliger/ASMF/Neville Marriner/ Philips 411 134–2PH

FLUTE CONCERTOS: NO1 IN G MAJOR K313/NO2 IN D MAJOR K314
James Galway: Flute
New Irish Chamber Orchestra
Conductor: André Prieur
Pickwick IMP Red Label PCD807
ADD Running time: 47.38
Performance: ★ ★ ★
Recording: ★ ★ (★)

Written in Mannheim during 1778, these concertos are the result of a commission from a wealthy Dutch amateur who wanted them for the notable flautist of the Mannheim orchestra, Wendling. However, Mozart wrote just one new work, transcribing an existing oboe concerto for the other. No doubt, Wendling and his patron were still well-pleased with what they received. As James Galway's performances amply prove, these are delightful and sparkling works.

This is brilliant playing, the only criticism being that Galway uses too much vibrato, but how these works flow in his hands.

Other recordings on CD (selection):
Peter-Lukas Graf/ECO/Raymond Leppard/ Claves CD50–8505
András Adorján/Munich CO/Hans Stadlmair/Denon C37–7803

HORN CONCERTOS: NO1 IN D MAJOR K412/NO2 IN E FLAT MAJOR K417/NO3 IN E FLAT MAJOR K447/NO4 IN E FLAT MAJOR K495
English Chamber Orchestra
Soloist and conductor: Barry Tuckwell
Decca 410 284–2DH
DDD Running time: 52.12
Performance: ★ ★ ★
Recording: ★ ★ (★)

These are predictably stylish and well-shaped performances from one of the finest horn players not just in Britain, but in the world. These concertos must now be in Barry Tuckwell's blood, and how effortless he makes them sound. Tuckwell makes a strong case for using the modern, valved instrument, as opposed to the natural hand-horn for which the works were written (not numbered in chronological order, incidentally; K412 actually dates from 1791, the rest from 1783–87).

However, Compact Disc offers a fascinating comparison with an 'original instrument' version, that by Hermann Baumann and the Vienna Concentus Musicus on TelDec.

With good, if not outstanding recordings, both versions can be recommended, and it can only be suggested that you listen and compare for yourself.

Other recordings on CD (selection):
Hermann Baumann/VCM/Nikolaus Harnoncourt/TelDec ZK8.41272

PIANO CONCERTO NO8 IN C MAJOR K246
PIANO CONCERTO NO27 IN B FLAT MAJOR K595
Rudolf Serkin: Piano
London Symphony Orchestra
Conductor: Claudio Abbado
Deutsche Grammophon 410 0035–2GH
DDD Running time: 57.05
Performance: ★ ★ ★   Recording: ★ ★ ★

Mozart's last piano concerto, No27, shows him at his most graceful and genial, the music of sunshine and clear blue skies. Here, the veteran pianist, Rudolf Serkin, couples it with a much earlier concerto, K246 of 1776, in one of the very best issues from an otherwise rather variable cycle of the concertos recorded over recent years with Abbado and the LSO.

Ashkenazy's version of K595 is also very

MOZART

good, but Serkin's has the edge, and the better-balanced recording. Surprisingly, these two, along with the recording included in Brendel's ten-disc survey, are the only current Compact Disc issues of this great work, in sharp contrast to the seven of K488 and K456, for example.

Other recordings on CD:
Vladimir Ashkenazy/Philharmonia O/Decca 400 087-2DH (K595 only)
Alfred Brendel/ASMF/Neville Marriner/ Philips 412 856-2PH10 (set)

PIANO CONCERTO NO9 IN E FLAT MAJOR K271 (JEUNEHOMME)
PIANO CONCERTO NO11 IN F MAJOR K413
Malcolm Bilson: Fortepiano
English Baroque Soloists
Director: John Eliot Gardiner
Archiv 410 905-2AH
DDD Running time: 52.53
Performance: ★ ★ ★   Recording: ★ ★

Following the Academy of Ancient Music's very successful 'original instruments' recordings of the Mozart symphonies, Malcolm Bilson's and John Eliot Gardiner's series for Archiv (of which this was the first issue) takes a similarly fresh look at the piano concertos. It was always likely to be a more controversial exercise, since the range and timbre of the fortepiano for which they were written is so radically different from that of the modern concert grand upon which they are most often played.

The instrument used here is an American copy of an Anton Walter fortepiano of the 1780s, now in the Mozart Geburtshaus in Salzburg, which was the composer's own concert instrument. Additionally, the English Baroque Soloists accompany on period instruments, and the opportunity has been taken thoroughly to authenticate the scores used.

Naturally, the results are interesting, but the performances are most enjoyable regardless of musicological considerations: fluent and incisive, with brisk outer movements, and sensitive readings of the haunting *andantino* of K271 and the filigree *larghetto* of K413.

Bilson and Gardiner make an excellent partnership in these two concertos, the first of which was inspired by the visit to Salzburg by a young, French keyboard player, Mademoiselle Jeunehomme. Whatever the effect she had on Mozart, it inspired him to his most mature concerto to date, completing it in 1777.

Recording balance and clarity here are not helped by the acoustic (Walthamstow Town Hall in London), although the overall result is acceptable. However, the change of venue for the second sessions (see below) proved to be worthwhile.

Other recordings on CD:
Rudolf Serkin/LSO/Claudio Abbado/DG 415 206-2GH (K271 only)
Alfred Brendel/ASMF/Neville Marriner/ Philips 412 856-2PH10 (set)

PIANO CONCERTO NO12 IN A MAJOR K414
PIANO CONCERTO NO13 IN C MAJOR K415
Philharmonia Orchestra
Soloist and conductor: Vladimir Ashkenazy
Decca 410 214-2DH
DDD Running time: 55.03
Performance: ★ ★ ★   Recording: ★ ★

These are two of the very best performances from Ashkenazy's Mozart cycle, warmly good-humoured in K414, and no less responsive in K415. The recording has a pleasant ambience, with firm imaging, weight, and a lovely tonal quality, but the forward balance of the piano tends to detract from the orchestral contribution, which is a pity, enjoyable as it is to have Ashkenazy's passage-work set in such sharp relief.

Other recordings on CD:
(Piano Concerto No12 K414)
Rudolf Serkin/LSO/Claudio Abbado/DG 400 068-2GH
Malcolm Bilson/English Baroque Soloists/ John Eliot Gardiner/Archiv 413 363-2AH
Zoltan Kocsis/Ferenc Liszt CO/Janos Rolla/ Hugaroton HCD12472-2
Alfred Brendel/ASMF/Neville Marriner/ Philips 412 856-2PH (set)
(Piano Concerto No13 K415)
Malcolm Bilson/English Baroque Soloists/ John Eliot Gardiner/Archiv 413 416-2AH
Murray Perahia/ECO/CBS MK39223
Alfred Brendel/ASMF/Neville Marriner/ Philips 412 856-2PH10 (set)

PIANO CONCERTO NO13 IN C MAJOR K415
PIANO CONCERTO NO15 IN B FLAT MAJOR K450
Malcolm Bilson: Fortepiano
English Baroque Soloists
Director: John Eliot Gardiner
Archiv 413 464-2AH
DDD Running time: 51.54
Performance: ★ ★ (★)
Recording: ★ ★ (★)

A slight 'enlargement' of the fortepiano image is noticeable here, giving just a little more prominence in the stereo picture, but the generally good balance of these 'authentic' versions of the Mozart concertos is maintained. However, this issue does suffer from some harshness in the orchestral *tuttis*.

It might be something to do with the bold, festive quality of K415, with its sharply incisive drums and trumpets in the outer movements, vividly registered by the recording.

As before, outer movements are on the

brisk side, which loses some of the charm of the opening *allegro* of K450. Otherwise, tempi are well-judged and the performances highly enjoyable.

Other recordings on CD (selection):
Piano Concerto No13 K415)
(see above)
(Piano Concerto No15 K450)
Alfred Brendel/ASMF/Neville Marriner/ Philips 400 018-2PH and 412 856-2PH10 (set)

PIANO CONCERTO NO12 IN A MAJOR K414
PIANO CONCERTO NO 14 IN E FLAT MAJOR K449
Malcolm Bilson: Fortepiano
English Baroque Soloists
Director: John Eliot Gardiner
Archiv 413 463-2AH
DDD Running time: 45.26
Performance: ★ ★ ★   Recording: ★ ★ ★

A switch of recording locations from the vastness of Walthamstow Town Hall (see above) to the more appropriate acoustic of St John's, Smith Square (also in London) pays dividends in sharpening and better-defining the image of the fortepiano which, lacking the projection of the modern piano, needs careful balancing.

This copy of Mozart's own fortepiano is certainly a sweet-toned instrument, and seems wholly free of action noise. With good integration between it and the orchestra, the overall 'period instrument' sound is very agreeable indeed, as are the brisk, stylish performances.

PIANO CONCERTO NO15 IN B FLAT MAJOR K450
PIANO CONCERTO NO21 IN C MAJOR K467
Alfred Brendel: Piano
Academy of St Martin-in-the-Fields
Conductor: Neville Marriner
Philips 400 018-2PH
DDD Running time: 51.56
Performance: ★ ★ ★
Recording: ★ ★ (★)

One of the first Philips CDs to appear, this combines two of the finest performances from Brendel's Mozart cycle; here is considered, elegant, and beautiful playing, though lacking in some spontaneity. It is a minor reservation, though, for both concertos are utterly captivating.

Although the piano dominates a little, the overall balance is lucid and open, with a pleasant transparency and immediacy. Piano tone is excellent.

Other recordings on CD:
(Piano Concerto No 15 K450)
Vladimir Ashkenazy/Philharmonia O/Decca 411 612-2DH
Malcolm Bilson/English Baroque Soloists/ John Eliot Gardiner/Archiv 413 416-2AH
Deszo Ránki/Ferenc Liszt CO/Jánós Rolla/ Hungaroton HCD12316-2
(Piano Concerto No12 K467)
Rudolf Serkin/LSO/Claudio Abbado/ DG410 068-2GH
Vladimir Ashkenazy/Philharmonia O/Decca 411 947-2DH

PIANO CONCERTO NO17 IN G MAJOR K453
PIANO CONCERTO NO18 IN B FLAT MAJOR K456
English Chamber Orchestra
Murray Perahia: Soloist and conductor
CBS MK36686
DDD Running time: 59.00
Performance: ★ ★ ★   Recording: ★ ★ ★

These are towering performances from Perahia of two of the finest of the six great concertos composed during 1784 (something no doubt mirrored in the number of recordings available). The thought put into every aspect of these readings shines through, especially in the subtle shading of the slow movements. The playing is graced by a good recording – the piano is well integrated with the orchestra, as in most of Perahia's Mozart recordings, but the acoustic for once is rather 'closed-in'. Nothing, however, to preclude a recommendation.

Other recordings on CD:
(Piano Concerto No17 K453)
Vladimir Ashkenazy/Philharmonia/Decca 411 947-2DH
Rudolf Serkin/LSO/Claudio Abbado/DG 415 206-2GH
Alfred Brendel/ASMF/Neville Marriner/ Philips 412 856-2PH10 (set)
Andras Schiff/Salzburg Mozarteum O Sandor Végh/Decca 414 289-2DH
(Piano Concerto No18 K456)
Diana Ambacne/Ambache CE/Meridian ECD84086
Emanuel Ax/St Paul CO/Pinchas Zukerman/RCA RD84522
Andras Schiff/Salzburg Mozarteum/Sandor Végh/ Decca 414 289-2DH
Alfred Brendel/ASMF/Neville Marriner/ Philips 412 856-2PH10

PIANO CONCERTO NO19 IN F MAJOR K459
PIANO CONCERTO NO23 IN A MAJOR K488
English Chamber Orchestra
Murray Perahia: Soloist and conductor
CBS MK39064
DDD Running time: 55.59
Performance: ★ ★ ★   Recording: ★ ★ ★

Another of the 1784 concertos, the F Major combines both beauty and brilliance, yet is a comparatively underrated work. That is not the case with the noble A Major Concerto of two years later, an altogether more subtle composition, something reflected in the

MOZART

absence of timpani and trumpets from the score. It contains one of Mozart's most tender and haunting slow movements, played most poetically here by Perahia. Some may think *too* poetically, but the eff is undeniably spellbinding, and makes the sudden appearance of the light, skipping finale all the more delightful.

The recording is very open and spacious, with great depth (if a lack of terracing) to the orchestral sound. The piano could be better-defined, but is tastefully balanced.

Other recordings on CD (selection):
(Piano Concerto No19 K459)
Maurizio Pollini/VPO/Karl Böhm/DG 413 793-2GH
Vladimir Ashkenazy/Philharmonia O/Decca 414 433-2DH
(Piano Concerto No23 K488)
Vladimir Ashkenazy/Philharmonia O/Decca 400 087-2DH
Maurizio Pollini/VPO/Karl Böhm/DG 413 793-2GH
Alfred Brendel/ASMF/Neville Marriner/ Philips 412 856-2PH10 (set)

PIANO CONCERTO NO19 IN F MAJOR K459/PIANO CONCERTO NO24 IN C MINOR K491
Philharmonia Orchestra
Vladimir Ashkenazy: Soloist and Conductor
Decca 414 433-2GH
ADD Running time: 61.23
Performance: ★ ★ ★   Recording: ★ ★ ★

Ashkenazy's is a perceptive reading of the enigmatic C minor concerto, its twilight world so removed in temperament from the concertos which precede and succeed it. He is unfailingly poetic in his playing, but never lapses into self-indulgence. The interpretation of the F Major is just as sensitive, and in both works the orchestral contribution is outstanding. With warm, well-balanced Kingsway Hall recordings, this disc offers two of the plums from what has become a most consistent Mozart cycle, if not as wholly recommendable as Perahia's.

PIANO CONCERTO NO20 IN D MINOR K466
PIANO CONCERTO NO24 IN C MINOR K491
Clara Haskil: Piano
Lamoureux Concerts Orchestra
Conductor: Igor Markevitch
Philips 412 254-2PH
DDD Running time: 58.49
Performance: ★ ★ ★   Recording: ★ (★)

Clara Haskil was an exceptionally fine Mozart player, as these performances, made just before she died, testify. There is no missing the understanding embodied in this playing, so poised and well-contoured, and responsive to every nuance of the score. Perhaps they are a little more romantic than would be the vogue today, but the validity is unquestionable.

With a sympathetic accompaniment by Markevitch and a recording which, although showing its age now, remains acceptable, these are — surprisingly perhaps — the most recommendable compact disc versions of the delightful K466 and the darkly enigmatic, sublime K491, although Ashkenazy is very good in the latter.

Other recordings on CD:
(Piano Concerto No20 K466—selection)
Rudolf Serkin/LSO/Claudio Abbado/DG 400 068-2GH
(Piano Concerto No24 K491-selection)
Vladimir Ashkenazy/Philharmonia O/Decca 414 433-2DH

PIANO CONCERTO NO26 IN D MAJOR K537 (CORONATION)
RONDOS FOR PIANO AND ORCHESTRA: IN D MAJOR K382/IN A MAJOR K386
English Chamber Orchestra
Murray Perahia: Soloist and conductor
CBS MK39224
DDD Running time: 51.32
Performance: ★ ★ ★
Recording: ★ ★(★)

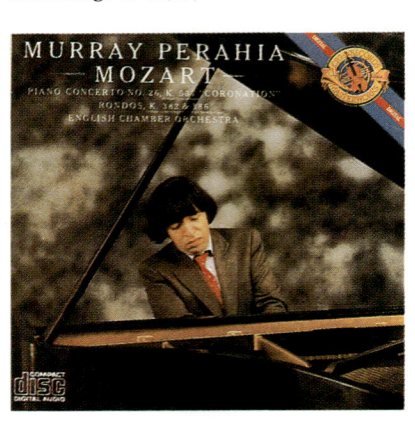

The nickname was appended when Mozart performed the D Major concerto as part of the celebrations for the Coronation of King Leopold II in Frankfurt on 15 October, 1790. It has often been criticised as being lightweight compared with the other late concertos, but Perahia finds unexpected depths in the work and gives a finely-conceived performance.

Of the two Rondos, the A Major was originally attached to the K414 concerto, but discarded, while the D Major was a substitute for the existing finale of the Concerto No5 K175, which is coupled incidentally with the superb C Major Concerto K503 in another outstanding Perahia recording (CBS MK37267).

Although the piano is a little forward, this is a sparkling, transparent recording, well up to the high standard of this series.

Other recordings on CD:
Alfred Brendel/ASMF/Neville Marriner/ Philips 412 856-2PH10 (set)
(Piano Concerto No26 K537 only)
Friedrich Gulda/CO/Nikolaus Harnoncourt/TelDec ZK8.42970
Vladimir Ashkenazy/Philharmonia O/Decca 411 810-2DH

VIOLIN CONCERTO NO2 IN D MAJOR K211
VIOLIN CONCERTO NO4 IN D MAJOR K218
Anne-Sophie Mutter: Violin
Philharmonia Orchestra
Conductor: Riccardo Muti
EMI CDC7 47011-2
DDD Running time: 44.47
Performance: ★ ★ ★   Recording: ★ ★

Anne-Sophie Mutter displays a keen feel for these concertos, and is very sympathetically accompanied by Muti and the Philharmonia. Needless to say, hers is a polished technique, but there is no lack of spontaneity or warmth here, and the result is very satisfying.

The recording, however, is slightly less so. It is not so much that the violin is over-projected, more that the orchestra is too recessed within a fairly spacious acoustic. Attempting to 'retrieve' the orchestra with the volume control inevitably brings up the violin, to an undesirably loud level, especially as the sound already has a fairly sharp edge to it. However, despite these drawbacks, these are performances to enjoy.

Other recordings on CD (selection) :
(Violin Concerto No2 K211)
Iona Brown/ASMF/Argo 411 613–2ZH
(Violin Concerto No4 K218-selection)
Oscar Shumsky/SCO/Yan-Pascal Tortelier/ Nimbus NIM5009

VIOLIN CONCERTO NO4 IN D MAJOR K218
VIOLIN CONCERTO NO5 IN A MAJOR K219
Oscar Shumsky: Violin
Scottish Chamber Orchestra
Conductor: Yan-Pascal Tortelier
Nimbus NIM5009
DDD Running time: 53.01
Performance: ★ ★ ★   Recording: ★ ★ ★

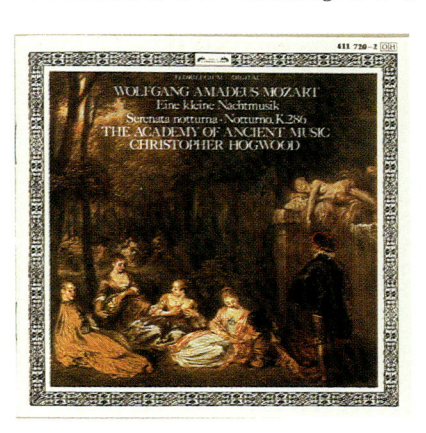

All Mozart's five violin concertos date from 1775, during his tenure with the Archbishop of Salzburg, yet the advance shown by these last two over their predecessors is quite remarkable, both in technical demands and depth of expression.

They receive marvellously spontaneous, lovingly expressive, and fresh performances from Shumsky, who from the outset establishes a lively rapport with Yan-Pascal Tortelier (son of the distinguished cellist). The recording, naturally balanced and truthful in tone, is much more agreeable than that given to Anne-Sophie Mutter on EMI. There, one is conscious of having to actively *listen;* here, the music does not have to 'fight' the sound, with wholly pleasurable results.

Other recordings on CD:
(Violin Concerto No4 K218)
(see above)
(Violin Concerto No5 K219-selection)
Arthur Grumiaux/LSO/Colin Davis/Philips 412 250–2PH

VIOLIN CONCERTO NO2 IN D MAJOR K211
SINFONIA CONCERTANTE IN E FLAT MAJOR FOR VIOLIN, VIOLA AND ORCHESTRA K364*
Iona Brown: Violin and Director
Josef Suk: Viola*
Academy of St Martin-in-the-Fields
Argo 411 613–2ZH
DDD Running time: 49.51
Performance: ★ ★ ★   Recording: ★ ★ ★

The Sinfonia Concertante of 1779 is a masterly work, almost overflowing with ideas, and constantly delighting with its interplay between the two soloists. It receives an extremely fine performance here, thoughtfully shaped and pointed. No less attractive is the performance of the coupling.

Other recordings on CD:
(Sinfonia Concertante K364-selection)
Isaac Stern/Pinchas Zukerman/NYPO/ Zubin Mehta/ CBS MK36692
Itzhak Perlman/Pinchas Zukerman/IPO/ Zubin Mehta/DG 415 486–2GH

SERENADE IN G MAJOR K525 (EINE KLEINE NACHTMUSIK)*
NOTTURNO FOR FOUR ORCHESTRAS IN D MAJOR K286/SERENADE IN D MAJOR K239 (SERENATA NOTTURNA)
Salomon Quartet*
The Academy of Ancient Music
Director: Christopher Hogwood
L'Oiseau-Lyre 411 720–20H
DDD Running time: 55.28
Performance: ★ ★ ★   Recording: ★ ★ ★

Unlikely as it may seem, this is a performance of *Eine Kleine Nachtmusik* which has one sitting up and listening afresh to this most familiar piece of Mozart. It is played with just one string player per part, although the bass line is strengthened by doubling the 'cello with double-bass.

The vigour and élan of the playing certainly sets this performance apart from the rest, and no less interesting is the strange spatial effects obtained in the well-balanced recording of the *Notturno for four orchestras.* This unusual work, not otherwise available on Compact Disc, dates from around 1776, the date of the other popular serenade here, the *Serenata Notturna.* This also benefits from a refreshing performance.

For a more traditional approach to *Eine Kleine Nachtmusik,* Karajan's compilation of Mozart, Prokofiev and Grieg (reviewed under Grieg) can be recommended.

Other recordings on CD:
(*Eine Kleine Nachtmusik* – selection)
BPO/Herbert von Karajan/DG 400 034–2GH
VPO/James Levine/DG 410 085–2GH
I Musici/Philips 410 606–2PH
SCO/Raymond Leppard/Erato ECD88014
ASMF Chamber Ensemble/Philips 412 269–2PH
Prague CO/Charles Mackerras/Telarc CD80108
(*Serenata Notturna)*
BPO/Herbert von Karajan/DG 413 309–2GH
I Musici/Philips 412 120–2PH

MOZART

SERENADE NO10 IN B FLAT MAJOR FOR WIND INSTRUMENTS K361
Members of the Collegium Aureum
Deutsche Harmonia-Mundi 1C 567 199919-2
DDD Running time: 50.02
Performance: ★ ★ ★
Recording: ★ ★ (★)

One feels Mozart must have thoroughly enjoyed himself, exploring the full range of tone colours obtainable from this ensemble of twelve wind instruments and double bass. The result, almost a wind symphony in scale and style, is certainly enjoyable to listen to, every movement superbly crafted; the whole rounded off with one of Mozart's most infectiously happy rondos.

This lively, genial performance is recorded in an expansive, equally lively acoustic, with excellent definition between the instruments, although the clarinets and *corni di basetti* are difficult to distinguish apart.

The alternative version from Harnoncourt is scrupulous to the score, but the performance is nothing like so agreeable.

Other recordings on CD:
Vienna Mozart Wind Ensemble/Nikolaus Harnoncourt/TelDec ZK8.42981

SERENADE IN C MINOR K388
SERENADE IN E FLAT MAJOR K375
The Albion Ensemble
Meridian CDE84107
ADD Running time: 49.39
Performance: ★ ★ ★   Recording: ★ ★ ★

If 'serenade' suggests easy-going music purely for entertainment, there is little of that to be found in these two compositions for eight wind instruments. The 'darkness' of the C minor key makes itself felt in K388 of 1782, a sombre work in many respects, and with a highly-developed contrapuntal minuet which owes much to Mozart's 'discovery' of J. S. Bach.

In the same year, he added two oboes to an earlier E flat wind sextet of clarinets, horns and bassoons, a work of only marginally less intensity.

The nature of both compositions comes over well in these performances by the Albion Ensemble, with excellent playing throughout. The recording, open, airy and with good integration between players and acoustic, wisely resists any temptation to 'go in close' on the ensemble, and the result is no less impressive.

It is with issues such as this that the smaller, independent labels such as Meridian can so enjoyably and usefully enhance the CD catalogue.

Other recordings on CD:
Berlin Philharmonic Wind Ensemble/Orfeo C134851A

OVERTURES: LE NOZZE DI FIGARO K492/DIE ZAUBERFLÖTE K620/LA CLEMENZA DI TITO K621/LUCIO SILLA K135/DIE ENTFÜHRUNG AUS DEM SERAIL K384/DON GIOVANNI K527/IDOMENEO K366/COSI FAN TUTTE K588/DER SCHAUSPIELDIREKTOR K486
Academy of St-Martin-in-the-Fields
Conductor: Neville Marriner
EMI CDC7 47014-2
DDD Running time: 49.46
Performance: ★ ★ ★   Recording: ★ ★ ★

Nine curtain-raisers to Mozart's operas and *singspiele*, including the rarely-heard *Schauspieldirektor*, receive vigorous and energetic performances from Marriner and the Academy, with full, spacious, and generally well-balanced recording. The occasional over-emphasis on the woodwind can perhaps be forgiven when it plays and sounds as beautifully as this.

CLARINET QUINTET IN A MAJOR K581/CLARINET QUINTET (FRAGMENT) IN B FLAT MAJOR K516c/QUINTET FRAGMENT IN F MAJOR FOR CLARINET, BASSET HORN AND STRING TRIO K580b
Alan Hacker: Clarinet
Lesley Schatzberger: Basset horn
Salomon String Quartet
Amon Ra CD-SAR17
DDD Running time: 60.35
Performance: ★ ★ ★   Recording: ★ ★ ★

The disc sleeve catches the eye by promising clarinet quintets by Mozart, and justifies that with the inclusion of two 'fragments' from lost or uncompleted works, both most convincingly and competently 'finished' by Duncan Druce. They are engaging discoveries, if not exciting ones.

Original instruments are used by all concerned here, Alan Hacker employing a variety of 19th century clarinets, two with basset extensions to increase their range. The result is delightful indeed in the main work, Mozart's only completed Clarinet Quintet, K581. Hacker's lovely, ripe tonal quality is a special pleasure, as is the arrestingly clear and natural recording. It has an almost tangible 'drawing room' intimacy and atmosphere wholly appropriate to the music-making.

CLARINET QUINTET IN A MAJOR K581
(c/w Küffner (attrib Weber) Introduction theme and variations in B flat major for clarinet and string quartet)
Sabine Meyer: Clarinet
Philharmonia Quartet, Berlin
Denon C37-7038
DDD Running time: 43.06
Performance: ★ ★ ★
Recording: ★ ★ (★)

It was Sabine Meyer whose introduction into the ranks of the Berlin Philharmonic during 1983 almost resulted in a parting of the ways between the orchestra and their eminent chief conductor, Herbert von Karajan.

However, no such controversy surrounds

her performance of Mozart's best-loved chamber work. Hers is a full, warm tone, and the whole reading is beautifully shaped, especially in the treatment of the broad clarinet line of the opening movements. With good accompaniment from the quartet and a naturally-balanced, if 'front-row' recording, this is most enjoyable.

A pity, therefore, that the coupling is not especially attractive: a work mistakenly attributed to Weber is, in fact, the Clarinet Quintet Op32 by the clarinettist, Josef Küffner. It is an engaging work, but hardly in the same league as the Mozart. A more substantial 'filler' would have greatly increased the appeal of this disc.

Other recordings on CD:
(Mozart: Clarinet Quintet K581)
Michel Portal/Les Musiciens/Harmonia-Mundi HMC90.1118
Keith Puddy/Gabrieli Quartet/Pickwick IMP Red Label PCD810
Alan Hacker/Salomon String Quartet/Amon-Ra CD-SAR17

STRING QUINTETS: NO1 IN B FLAT MAJOR K174/NO2 IN C MAJOR K515/NO3 IN G MINOR K516/NO4 IN C MINOR K406/NO5 IN D MAJOR K593/NO6 IN E FLAT MAJOR K614
Grumiaux Trio (Arthur Grumiaux: Violin, Georges Janzer: Viola, Eva Czako: 'Cello)
Arpad Gérecz: Second violin
Max Lesueur: Second viola
Philips 416 486-2PH3 (3 discs)
ADD Running time: 169.57
Performance: ★ ★ ★
Recording: ★ ★ (★)

On LP, these performances have long been front-runners, and it is all the more so now that they have been transferred to Compact Disc. The recording clearly defines each contribution, without losing the coherence of the whole within a discreetly lively acoustic. Instrumental timbre is excellent, and only a little crowding in the climaxes of the faster movements precludes a full recommendation on sonic grounds.

There are no reservations, however, about the performances of these works, four of which rank among Mozart's greatest chamber works (and, arguably, among the finest chamber music ever written). They are K515 and K516, which in key and in temperament are a mirror image of the last two symphonies, and K593 and K614, which date from Mozart's last year.

The B flat Quintet K174 of 1773 is an early and variable attempt at the genre, while K406 is an arrangement – for purely commercial reasons – of the Wind Serenade K388 (the latter remains the preferable format). Nevertheless, this set is worth aquiring for the four great quintets alone.

Other recordings on CD (selection):
(String Quintets Nos1 and 5, K174/K593)
Smetana Quartet/Josef Suk/Supraphon C37S-7075
(String Quintet No4 K406 – arr. for oboe)
Hansjorg Schellenberger/Berlin Philharmonic Quartet/Denon C37-7034
(String Quintets Nos 2 and 3, K515/K516)
Tackács Quartet/Dénes Koromzay/Hungaroton HCD 12656-2

PIANO QUARTET IN G MINOR K478
PIANO QUARTET IN E FLAT MAJOR K493
Beaux Arts Trio
Bruno Giuranna: Viola
Philips 410 391-2PH
DDD Running time: 61.07
Performance: ★ ★ ★
Recording: ★ ★ (★)

The intensity and complexity of the G minor, the first piano quartet of substance to be composed anywhere, dismayed both publisher and public, who had expected something altogether lighter. The E flat of the following year, 1786, did little to appease them, although it did not share the underlying tension of its predecessor.

These two chamber masterpieces are outstandingly well-performed here, spirited and committed, but with a classical poise (sample the finely-balanced playing of the rondo of the G minor). It is compelling music-making throughout, and the recording, although close (and inevitably emphasising the piano) is clear, smooth and detailed. This is an excellent means to discovering this great music

STRING QUARTET NO14 IN G MAJOR K387
STRING QUARTET NO23 IN F MAJOR K590
Brandis Quartet
Orfeo CO41831A
DDD Running time: 59.07
Performance: ★ ★ ★
Recording: ★ ★ (★)

Usefully coupling the first of the six quartets dedicated to Haydn, and the last of the 'Prussian' set, these well-played performances are recorded fairly closely, but in a spacious acoustic which knits the sound together without losing individual imaging.

It is an expansive sound, and replay level would need to be set carefully to get a realistic presence to the ensemble, without sharpening the edge on the violins. All round, these are noteworthy performances.

STRING QUARTET NO14 IN G MAJOR K387
STRING QUARTET NO15 IN D MINOR K421
Kocian Quartet
Denon C37-7228
DDD Running time: 60.26
Performance: ★ ★ (★)
Recording: ★ ★

MOZART

Denon's collaborations between Japanese recording teams and Czech chamber ensembles produce varying results: some are outstanding, while in others the recording balance seems ill-considered. Here, a fairly close view is taken of the quartet, although mercifully free of that razor-edge which close-miking can impart, especially to violins. It is, however, a dry sound, almost wholly lacking a sense of ambience and the end result is blandly unatmospheric – if anything, *too* smooth (string quartets *do* sound 'sour' at times).

The performances are well-conceived, enjoyable enough, without being distinctive.

More Compact Disc choice in the Mozart quartets is undoubtedly required, but this disc should satisfy those wanting the coupling.

Other recordings on CD (selection):
(String Quartet No14 K387)
Brandis Quartet/Orfeo CO41831
(String Quartet No15 K421)
Smetana Quartet/Denon C37-7003

STRING QUARTET NO17 IN B FLAT MAJOR K458 (HUNTING)
STRING QUARTET NO19 IN C MAJOR K465 (DISSONANCE)
Alban Berg Quartet, Vienna
TelDec ZK8.43055
ADD Running time: 57.14
Performance: ★ ★ ★
Recording: ★ ★ (★)

These two quartets come from the set published in the autumn of 1785 and dedicated to Haydn, *'my six children'* as Mozart called them. The former gets its nickname from the galloping 6/8 rhythm of its first movement, while the latter's is based entirely on the strange and surprising *adagio* passage which introduces the work and seems to belong to a sound world of forty years on, that of Beethoven's late quartets.

These well-crafted performances have been recorded in a lively acoustic which, although imparting a bright, clear presence to the sound, does colour the tonal quality a little – the occasionally 'nasal'-sounding 'cello, for example. Overall balance and integration are good.

Other recordings on CD:
(String Quartet No17 K458)
Smetana Quartet/Denon C37-7003
Amadeus Quartet/DG 410 866-2GH
Kocian Quartet/Denon C37-7538

STRING QUARTET NO21 IN D MAJOR K575
STRING QUARTET NO22 IN B FLAT MAJOR K589
Orlando Quartet
Philips 412 121-2PH
DDD Running time: 50.14
Performance: ★ ★ ★   **Recording:** ★ ★ ★

These are eloquent and beautifully-shaped performances of two of the so-called *'Prussian'* quartets of 1789-90. The playing is consistently interesting (even when Mozart's inspiration very occasionally lets him down), and the B flat Major with its delightful outer movements is especially enjoyable.

The recorded balance is well up to the usual standard Philips obtained with this quartet, with crisp definition and absolute equality between the four players. The overall presentation, with a subtle spaciousness, is exactly right for an uninterrupted view of the performances.

TRIO (DIVERTIMENTO) IN E FLAT MAJOR FOR VIOLIN, VIOLA AND 'CELLO K563
Jean-Jacques Kantorow: Violin
Vladimir Mendelssohn: Viola
Mari Fujiwara: 'Cello
Denon C37-7199
DDD Running time: 45.21
Performance: ★ ★ ★
Recording: ★ ★ (★)

This substantial chamber work, Mozart's only completed string trio but an enormously influential one, especially for Beethoven, was composed in 1788, around the time of the last three symphonies. The dedicatee was Michael Puchberg, a freemason who had given Mozart considerable financial help – he was richly rewarded. No other string trio of the period compares in depth of expression or quality of invention.

It receives an excellent performance here, fairly closely recorded but in a bright, reverberant acoustic, and with firm delineation of each instrument's contribution across a wide sound stage. Denon are to be congratulated in ensuring this work is represented on Compact Disc.

PIANO SONATAS: NO1 IN C MAJOR K279/NO2 IN F MAJOR K280/NO3 IN B FLAT MAJOR K281/NO4 IN E FLAT MAJOR K282/NO5 in G MAJOR K283
Maria-João Pires: Piano
Denon C37-7386
DDD Running time: 59.41
Performance: ★ ★ ★
Recording: ★ ★ (★)

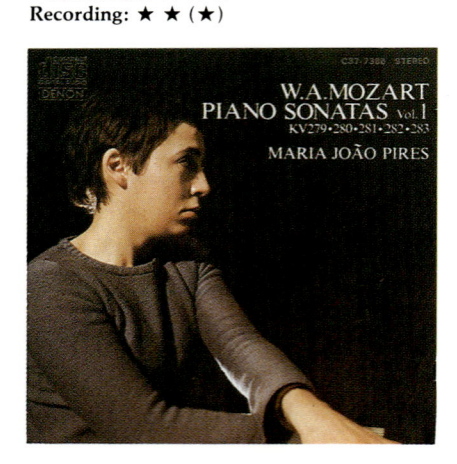

These first five piano sonatas date from between late 1774 and early 1775, when Mozart was nineteen. They come from a set of six (the other is K284), most likely intended for publication as a series to judge by the sequence of related keys in which they are written, and are fascinating works, especially the first, K279, in the imaginative treatment of its ideas. The Italian Rococo influence is discernible, but so is that of Haydn and, through him, C. P. E. Bach and J. C. Bach. But there is also much that is wholly and individually Mozart.

With good, if slightly dry recording, these

are persuasive performances from the Portuguese pianist, Maria-João Pires. A disc that is undemanding, yet very rewarding.

Other recordings on CD:
(Piano sonata No1 K279)
Mitsuko Uchida/Philips 412 617-2PH
(Piano Sonata No5 K283)
Maria-João Pires/Erato ECD88082

PIANO SONATAS: NO11 IN A MAJOR K331/NO12 IN F MAJOR K332/FANTASIA IN D MINOR K397
Mitsuko Uchida: Piano
Philips 412 123-2PH
DDD Running time: 50.10
Performance: ★ ★ ★   Recording: ★ ★ ★

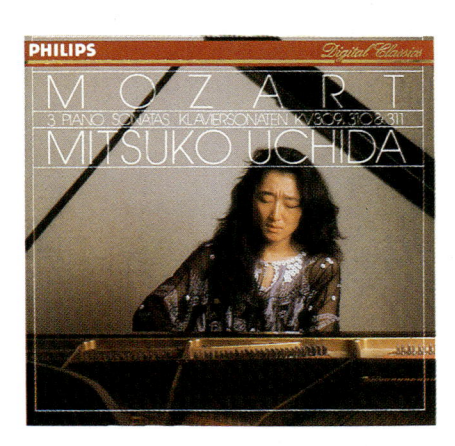

This, the introductory issue in Uchida's outstanding survey of the solo piano sonatas (and selected other compositions), includes the best-known of the sonatas, K331, the one with the *Rondo à la Turque* as its rousing conclusion. Ultimately more rewarding, however, is the opening movement, a delightfully inventive *Theme and variations* of classical elegance.

Uchida's is a magical performance, as is that of the romantic *Fantasia*. The understanding and commitment is typical of the whole series, with equanimity between left and right hand, textural clarity and a disarmingly simple beauty of style.

The recording quality is fairly consistent throughout, and never less than first-rate: a natural and unhampered view of the performances.

Those who come to enjoy Mitsuko Uchida's Mozart through these recommendations can be referred to two other recitals of which space precludes a full review: on Philips 412 616-2PH she tackles the great B flat sonata K333, the C Major K330, the Gigue K574, and the beautiful Adagio in B minor K540, while 412 122-2PH (also Philips) offers another of the most important sonatas, the C Major K545, and Mozart's nineteenth and numerically last sonata, the F Major K533. The Rondo in A minor K511 provides a sparkling 'dessert' for these main courses.

PIANO SONATAS: NO1 IN C MAJOR K279/NO14 IN C MINOR K457/NO17 IN D MAJOR K576/FANTASIA IN C MINOR K475
Mitsuko Uchida: Piano
Philips 412 617-2PH
DDD Running time: 59.43
Performance: ★ ★ ★   Recording: ★ ★ ★

Highlights in this recording from Uchida's complete Mozart cycle are undoubtedly the two C minor compositions, the Sonata K457, and the Fantasia K475, both remarkable works prophetic of the later Beethoven sonatas. They share that almost improvisatory freedom and elevated expression, but most of all it is the humanity of the music which reaches out to touch heart and mind.

In addition, this disc offers us the opportunity to compare Mozart's first and last sonatas. The differences between them are by no means as great as you might imagine, since the early C Major is closely allied to the sonorities of the Baroque harpsichord, while the D Major was a product of the composer's fascination in his later years with counterpoint, especially that of Bach.

Both performance and recording continue the exceptional standards of this series.

Other recordings on CD:
(Piano Sonata No1 K279)
Maria João Pires/Denon C37-7386
(Piano Sonata No14 K457)
Maria João Pires/Denon C37-7389
Maria João Pires/Erato ECD88082
Alfred Brendel/Philips 412 525-2PH
(Piano sonata No17 K576)
Claudio Arrau/Philips 411 136-2PH
Maria João Pires/Denon C37-7390
(Fantasia K475)
Maria João Pires/Erato ECD88082
Maria João Pires/Denon C37-7389

PIANO SONATAS: NO7 IN C MAJOR K309/NO8 IN A MINOR K310/NO9 IN D MAJOR K311
Mitsuko Uchida: Piano
Philips 412 741-2PH
DDD Running time: 53.08
Performance: ★ ★ ★   Recording: ★ ★ ★

While at Mannheim during the tour of 1777-78, Mozart made the acquantance of the daughter of the kappellmeister there, Rose Cannabich, whom, the composer reported *'plays the clavier quite nicely'*. His interest may have extended beyond the mere musical, for the *andante* of the sonata in C Major K309 is nothing less than a portrait in sound of the lady. She seems to have had an effervescent personality: in no other keyboard movement does Mozart use as many dynamic markings as here.

The D Major is an equally lively work, but the A minor K310 has an underlying tragic mien. It was written during the Paris section of the journey, where Mozart's mother was to die.

With recording of great tonal purity and transparency (but wanting just a touch in atmosphere), Mitsuko Uchida's playing is an endless pleasure. The performances, as ever, are most sensitively conceived.

Other recordings on CD:
(Piano Sonata No7 K309)
Maria-João Pires/Denon C37-7387
(Piano Sonata No8 K310)
Maria-João Pires/Denon C37-7387
Alfred Brendel/Philips 412 525-2PH
(Piano Sonata No9 K311)
Maria-João Pires/Denon C37-7388

MODEST MUSSORGSKY
(b. Karevo, Pskov, Russia, 21 March 1839; d. St Petersburg, 23 March 1881)

Mussorgsky was born before his time. In his music, he was an uncompromising, unsentimental, starkly truthful realist in an age populated by romantics, and it was fifty years before anyone listened to what he had to say.

The folk music and stories of childhood were an early influence, before the family moved to St Petersburg which was to be Mussorgsky's home for the rest of his life. Indeed, he never left Russia, which probably explains the fervent nationalism he expounded. Although he learned to play the piano well, the family army tradition ensnared him at seventeen; he became an officer in a crack guards regiment. But music finally exerted the greater pull and he resigned his commission to start lessons with the composer, Balakirev. At first he could rely on an allowance from his family, but when fortunes dwindled, he was forced to take a post in the civil service. One aspect of the army life remained, however – hard drinking.

He composed some eighty songs, among which the cycle *Songs and Dances of Death* is quite remarkable, and two great operas, *Boris Godunov* and *Khovanshchina* (the latter unfinished). His piano composition, *Pictures at an Exhibition* was destined to become his best-known work (albeit in another's orchestrated guise) along with that vividly spine-chilling depiction of a witches sabbath, *Night on Bald Mountain*.

PICTURES AT AN EXHIBITION
(orchestrated Ravel)
NIGHT ON BALD MOUNTAIN
(orchestrated Rimsky-Korsakov)
Cleveland Orchestra
Conductor: Lorin Maazel
Telarc CD80042
DDD Running time: 40.40
Performance: ★ ★ ★
Recording: ★ ★ (★)

When death cut short the promising career of his painter friend, Victor Hartmann, Mussorgsky paid homage by translating ten of Hartmann's drawings into piano pieces, linking them with a 'promenade' theme which took the 'viewer' from one 'picture' to the next. The subjects were diverse, often bizarre: a gnome; an ox-cart; a rich Jew in conversation with his poor compatriot; catacombs; the great gate of Kiev. However, it was five years after the composer's death that the piano score was published, in 1886, and thirty-six years after that when the conductor, Serge Koussevitzky, asked Ravel to produce an orchestrated version.

Lorin Maazel's recording of this work still holds its own even after seven years in the catalogue and much increased competition. It is superbly played, dramatic without seeking exaggerated effects. In general, the sound is open, smooth, and well-imaged if lacking a little depth. The competition is strong, but Maazel's is a realisation of this vivid score that rewards repeated listening.

The coupling is Rimsky-Korsakov's orchestration of Mussorgsky's menacing evocation of a witches' sabbath.

Other recordings on CD (selection):
(*Pictures at an Exhibition*)
LSO/Claudio Abbado/DG 410 033-2GH
Philadelphia O/Riccardo Muti/EMI CDC 7 47099-2
SRO/Ernest Ansermet/Decca 414 139-2DH2
(*Night on Bald Mountain* – selection)
Dallas SO/Eduardo Mata/RCA RCD14439
Concertgebouw/Colin Davis/Philips 411 473-2PH
Moscow RSO/Vladimir Fedoseyeu/Melodiya 880 006
SRO/Ernest Ansermet/Decca 414 139-2DH
LSO/Yuri Aronovich/IMP PCD 804

PICTURES AT AN EXHIBITION (original piano version)
SIX PIANO PIECES
Jacques Rouvier: Piano
Denon C37-7177
DDD Running time: 53.33
Performance: ★ ★ ★   Recording: ★ ★ ★

It would be misguided to assume the original piano version of *Pictures* is a poor relation of Ravel's orchestrated score. In some ways, without the orchestral palette to seduce the ear, it is more revealing of Mussorgsky's inventiveness, especially when the recording is as outstanding as this.

Made in Tokyo, using a Bosendorfer Imperial Grand, the weight, diamond-sharp clarity, and tonal purity of the instrument are reproduced with astonishing accuracy and power. For solidity of image, and precision during the most complex fingerwork, this has few equals. And Jacques Rouvier's performance is equally stunning.

Other recordings on CD:
Geoffrey Saba/IMP-Pickwick PCD818

CARL NIELSEN
(b. Funen Island, Denmark, 9 June 1865; d. Copenhagen, 3 October 1931)

14 March, 1894, and a Copenhagen audience rises to applaud the first performance of a new Danish symphony. From one of the violin desks of the Royal Danish Orchestra, a young man of twenty-eight stands to take a bow. He is Carl Nielsen, and it is his First Symphony.

The path that had brought him there had not been an easy one. Nielsen started life as a farm boy and, when he showed a musical inclination, was packed off to become a bugler in the army. His first lessons in composition came from a tavern bandleader, but they were sufficient to enable him to write some chamber pieces. It was these that persuaded the foremost Danish composer of the period, Niels Gade, to bring the boy to Copenhagen for musical education.

Nielsen's reputation as a composer grew rapidly, although he had to rely on conducting opera and the directorship of the Copenhagen Musical Society for a living. He wrote some outstanding vocal works, including the operas, *Saul and David* and *Maskarade*, but his finest instrumental compositions are undoubtedly the six symphonies which span his entire composing career like giant stepping stones (very much as those of his contemporary, Jean Sibelius).

Certainly the symphonies – and of the shorter orchestral works, *Pan and Syrinx* – deserve to be on CD. EMI have a superb Simon Rattle recording of the latter, coupled with the Fourth Symphony.

SYMPHONY NO2 OP16 'THE FOUR TEMPERAMENTS'
ALADDIN: SUITE FOR ORCHESTRA OP34
Gothenburg Symphony Orchestra
Conductor: Myung-Whun Chung
BIS CD-247
DDD Running time: 56.05
Performance: ★ ★ ★   Recording: ★ ★

The idea for his Second Symphony occurred to Nielsen while enjoying a painting which – intentionally or not – presented a comic depiction of the four distinct natures of mankind. Each of these was to evolve into a symphonic movement: the impetuous, the indolent, the melancholy and the cheerful (or possibly naive). The score is most effective at conveying these 'temperaments', even to the point of recognising that each shares something of the others, too – apart from the 'indolent' who struggles to find any contrast in his brief episode.

In 1918, sixteen years after the Second received its first performance, with some reluctance, Nielsen accepted a commission to provide music for a revival of *Aladdin* by the 19th century Danish playwright, Adam Oehlenschlager. Although he eventually disassociated himself from the production, he was persuaded to make a concert suite from seven items in the colourful, Oriental-style score.

It is lightweight stuff, but pleasurably played here by the Gothenburg orchestra, who also acquit themselves well in the symphony, where the young Korean conductor, Myung-Whun Chung, brother of the great violinist, Kyung-Wha Chung, produces a volatile, full-blooded and wholly sympathetic reading. The success of his very broad approach to the third movement might be questioned, but the overall result is most convincing. Hopefully, he will go on to complete a much-needed Cycle of Nielsen's symphonies.

SYMPHONY NO4 OP29 'THE INEXTINGUISHABLE'
Berlin Philharmonic Orchestra
Conductor: Herbert von Karajan
Deutsche Grammophon 413 313-2GH
DDD Running time: 38.26
Performance: ★ ★ ★   Recording: ★

Given that it was composed during the early years of the First World War (1914-16), it is hardly surprising that Nielsen should have annotated this symphony '*the elementary will to live*', adding: '*Music is life, and like life inextinguishable*'. This was the subtitle he gave the work. It is not difficult to hear in the Fourth a struggle against obstacles, both within and without, in its alternate moods of turbulence, disquiet and even pathos before the final apotheosis when faith and optimism are finally vindicated.

Commitment, too, is the description that comes to mind for this intense and magnificently-played performance. The over-close, often congested recording, however, does not do it full justice and it may be worth waiting to see if EMI issue Rattle's 1985 version on CD. Not only is it more spaciously and naturally recorded, it eschews the vast and unauthentic gap Karajan perpetrates in the Finale (at Fig. 61), and it offers a decent bonus in the shape of the delightful *Pan and Syrinx*.

JACQUES OFFENBACH
(b. Cologne, Germany 20 June 1819; d. Paris, 5 October 1880)

It took an emigré German Jew to make the most telling musical comment on the Paris of *la belle époque*, that frivolous and glittering period. Yet Jacques Offenbach (an assumed name) died having failed in his true ambition of being recognised as a composer of serious operas as well as the popular *opéra-bouffe* for which he is remembered. The nearest he came to that ambition, the tragic-fantastic *Contes de Hoffman (Tales of Hoffman)*, only received its true acclaim after his death.

He was the son of a Jewish cantor and came to Paris to study at the Conservatoire under Cherubini. He decided to remain in the city after those studies, and became a notable 'cellist with the Opéra Comique, which gave him entry into Parisian musical society.

He had already begun composing, but his main occupation for five years was as conductor at the Theâtre Français, a post he left to become an impresario himself, first with his Bouffes-Parisiens, in 1855, and later the Theâtre de la Gaité. It was at these venues he staged his *opéra bouffe*, the brilliantly farcical operetta which had Parisians intoxicated by its music and laughing at themselves and the lives they led, although they were probably blissfully unaware of it.

There are good recordings to choose from in both the famous overtures and Rosenthal's pot-pourri of Offenbach, *Gaité Parisienne*.

OVERTURES: LA BELLE HÉLÈNE/LA FILLE DU TAMBOUR-MAJEUR/ORPHÉE AUX ENFERS/LA GRANDE-DUCHESSE DE GEROLSTEIN/LA PÉRICHOLE/LES DEUX AVEUGLES/BARBE-BLEUE/LA VIE PARISIENNE
Philharmonia Orchestra
Conductor: Neville Marriner
Philips 411 476-2PH
DDD Running time: 43.47
Performance: ★ ★ ★ **Recording:** ★ ★ ★

It sounds as though all concerned had a highly enjoyable time recording these colourful confections. There is a real swagger to the playing of the Philharmonia, and Marriner, rightly, views these overtures as belonging to the world of lightweight operetta, with no grander pretensions than that. It is their lively wit which shines through here, in a recording which is both spacious and dazzling in its impact. Although by no means Offenbach pure-and-simple (others have had a hand in their composition) these overtures are always engaging on the ear.

Other recordings on CD:
(Overtures – selection)
BPO/Herbert von Karajan/DG 400 044-2GH

GAÎTÉ PARISIENNE: BALLET (arranged Manuel Rosenthal)
Pittsburgh Symphony Orchestra
Conductor: André Previn
Philips 411 039-2PH
DDD Running time: 41.03
Performance: ★ ★ ★
Recording: ★ ★ (★)

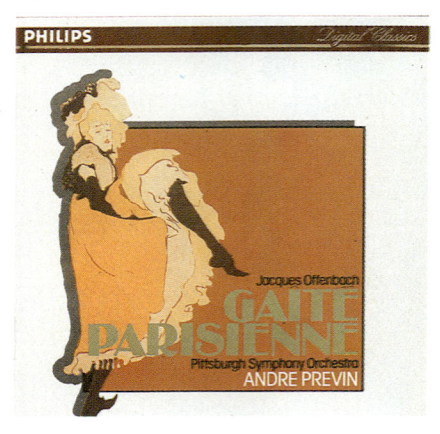

Manuel Rosenthal's 1938 ballet, assembled from seven of Offenbach's operettas, including *La Belle Hélène*, *Orphée aux enfers*, and *Les Contes de Hoffman*, is extremely successful in conveying the spirit of these *'musiquettes'*, as they became known. The range is wide, from the notorious *Can-Can* to the exquisite *Barcarolle*, and can seldom have been better conveyed than here.

Previn's feel for this music is just right; without forcing the pace, and losing the essential elegance of the music, he still brings out its exuberance, and nicely points the fine detail of the score. The well-indexed recording is appropriately bold and brilliant – if anything a little too bold at the bass end with some emphatic brass and percussion.

Other recordings on CD:
Montreal SO/Dutoit/Decca 411 708-2DH

SERGE PROKOFIEV
(b. Krasnoye, Ekaterinoslav, Russia, 23 April 1891; d. Moscow, USSR, 3 March 1953)

He wrote some revolutionary music, but finally returned to Russia and respectability.

From his first year at the St Petersburg Conservatory, Prokofiev was one of music's rebels, effortlessly poking fun at the old order, while proving himself eminently equipped to search – if not always entirely successfully – for a new.

His teachers were Liadov and Rimsky-Korsakov, but his early admiration was for Richard Strauss and the Russian composer-mystic, Alexander Scriabin. He first gained recognition as a pianist, becoming a dazzling performer, and collecting the prestigious Rubinstein prize at the age of twenty-three for his First Piano Concerto (still sounding remarkably original today).

Prompted by the events of 1917, Prokofiev left Russia for self-imposed exile in Paris, not venturing back, even to visit, for ten years.

Despite his absence, Prokofiev's works had continued to be performed in the Soviet Union. Therefore, when he became disillusioned by life in the West and by the course Western music was taking, there was a ready welcome for him on his return to his homeland.

Whether it was a natural development of his career as a composer, or whether the prevailing artistic climate persuaded him a change of style might be wise, his music took on a consciously lyrical and gentler mien after his return in 1932.
Then, like his compatriot, Dmitri Shostakovich, Prokofiev's honeymoon with authority came to an end and he, too, faced its crass criticisms culminating in the official censures of 1948.

His Fifth Symphony succeeded in fulfilling the requirement that music 'should be understandable to all', without compromising its artistic standards in any way.

Without Neeme Järvi's excellent symphony cycle on Chandos, Prokofiev's representation on CD would be poor indeed. Short shrift to date for the Piano Concertos and piano pieces, and a complete *Romeo* would nicely complement Ashkenazy's *Cinderella*.

PROKOFIEV

SYMPHONY NO2 IN D MINOR OP40
ROMEO AND JULIET: SUITE NO1 OP64a
NOs1–7
Scottish National Orchestra
Conductor: Neeme Järvi
Chandos CHAN8368
DDD Running time: 61.06
Performance: ★ ★ ★   Recording: ★ ★ ★

After the unfair neglect of all but the first of Prokofiev's symphonies on record in recent years, Jarvi's consistently fine series with the SNO is most welcome (and what a good orchestra it has become under his baton, too). The Second Symphony, however, has enjoyed little popularity throughout its sixty-year existence.

In many ways, it is a symphony for the machine age, *'made of iron and steel'* was the composer's description, and is a taxing work to listen to. Not so the richly-melodic score for the ballet *Romeo and Juliet*, the first suite from which completes the programme here.

The Chandos recording is most impressive at coping with the close-knit scoring of the symphony, and is as full-bodied and atmospheric as we have come to expect from this source.

SYMPHONY NO3 IN C MINOR OP44/
SYMPHONY NO4 IN C MAJOR OP47
(original 1930 version)
Scottish National Orchestra
Conductor: Neeme Järvi
Chandos CHAN8401
DDD Running time: 59.08
Performance: ★ ★ ★   Recording: ★ ★ ★

A common bond between these two symphonies is Prokofiev's use, in part, of material from his operas: in the case of the demonic, often savage Third, *The Fiery Angel*, and for the more lyrical Fourth, *L'Enfant Prodigue*. Both are tough, uncompromising works from the 1928–30 period, although the Fourth was considerably revised in 1947 (Prokofiev's later thoughts on the work can be heard on another Chandos CD – see below – where it is coupled with a fine performance of the First Symphony).

These are authoritative performances by Järvi, making a convincing case for two works which have never endeared themselves in the manner of the First or Fifth Symphonies. Certainly, Prokofiev's dense scores have not previously been so lucidly and richly recorded.

Other recordings on CD:
(Symphony No4: 1947 version)
SNO/Järvi/Chandos CHAN8400

SYMPHONY NO5 IN B FLAT MAJOR
OP100/THREE WALTZES OP110
Scottish National Orchestra
Conductor Neeme Järvi
Chandos CHAN8450
DDD Running time: 57.10
Performance: ★ ★ ★   Recording: ★ ★ ★

This noble work, along with the First the most popular of the seven symphonies, was first performed in January 1945. As well as embodying the *'grandeur of the human spirit'*, as was Prokofiev's intention, the sense of release from struggle and of a new optimism is only too evident. (How things were to change with the Sixth Symphony.)

Undoubtedly, the Fifth was the right symphony for Järvi to complete his magnificent cycle, one of the truly valuable recording achievements of recent times. Once again, playing and interpretation display meticulous care without losing spontaneity, and in every way this is a match for the rest of the series.

Other recordings on CD:
Israel PO/Leonard Bernstein/CBS MK35877
St Louis SO/Leonard Slatkin/RCA RD85035

VIOLIN CONCERTO NO1 IN D MAJOR
OP19
VIOLIN CONCERTO NO2 IN G MINOR
OP63
Shlomo Mintz: Violin
Chicago Symphony Orchestra
Conductor: Claudio Abbado
Deutsche Grammophon 410 524-2GH
DDD Running time: 49.15
Performance: ★ ★ ★   Recording: ★ ★ ★

The contemplative, even nostalgic mood of the outer movements of the First Concerto is in sharp contrast to the spiky austerity of much else Prokofiev composed around this period, the summer of 1917. Other events that year, and in subsequent years, precluded a performance until 1923, in Paris, whither Prokofiev had been permitted to retreat into temporary exile. French influence also contributed to the Second Concerto: it was commissioned by friends of the violinist, Robert Soetans, who duly gave the premiere in 1935.

Both works receive outstanding performances here, Mintz' playing being at once eloquent, sensitive and beautifully phrased. His partnership with Abbado and the Chicago orchestra produces readings that perfectly evoke the elusive, twilight mood of No1, and the lyrical world of No2. The atmospheric and nicely-distanced recording places the soloist firmly in the same acoustic plane as the orchestra and tellingly demonstrates how superfluous 'spotlighting' is to an effective balance.

Other recordings on CD:
Itzhak Perlman/BBC SO/Gennadi Rozhdestvensky/EMI CDC 7 47025-2

SYMPHONY NO6 IN E FLAT MINOR OP111/WALTZ SUITE OP110
Scottish National Orchestra
Conductor: Neeme Järvi
Chandos CHAN8359
DDD Running time: 56.30
Performance: ★ ★ ★   Recording: ★ ★ ★

The Sixth has strong claims to be regarded as the greatest of Prokofiev's seven symphonies. Written in the aftermath of the Second World War, it contains some of his most penetrating, direct, and darkly emotive writing, shorn of the irony and ambivalence that characterise much of his pre-war music. It is a fierce, often shrill work (do not blame the recording: it is what the score demands), as Prokofiev eschews all refinements of style with the sole purpose of expressing a stark, often brutal reality. It is nowhere better heard than in the metamorphosis of the dance-like theme of the finale, which becomes a hideously grotesque march.

Järvi's is a shattering performance, and the response he obtains from the SNO is total. In a work which is far from easy listening, the strength of this reading is compelling. The attractive and equally well-played Waltz Suite provides a light, and welcome contrast.

This is first-rate in every respect.

LIEUTENANT KIJÉ: SUITE
(c/w Kodály: Háry János: Suite)
London Philharmonic Orchestra
Conductor: Klaus Tennstedt
EMI CDC7 47109-2
DDD Running time: 45.42·
Performance: ★ ★ (★)
Recording: ★ ★ (★)

It was a perfect idea to combine these two good-humoured portraits of military prowess, or rather the lack of it – the 'clerical error' Kijé, and Háry János, the patriotic peasant who convinces all, including himself, that he was single-handedly responsible for the defeat of Napoleon!

The latter remains Kodály's best-loved work, not least because of its colourful blend of orchestral colours and prominent use of percussion, especially that native Hungarian instrument, the cimbalom – which certainly makes its presence felt in this recording. Indeed, detail is its strong point, although overall the sound is more agreeable on CD than on LP.

Tennstedt seems to find more wit in Prokofiev's clever film score than in the Kodály, but both are played with considerable panache.

It is certainly an interesting extension of Tennstedt's repertoire with the London Orchestra with whom he has established such a productive rapport.

Other recordings on CD:
(*Lieutenant Kijé*)
Dallas SO/Eduardo Mata/RCA RD85168
(*Háry János*)
Budapest PO/János Ferencsik/Hungaroton HCD12190

PETER AND THE WOLF OP67
(c/w Saint Saëns: Carnival of the Animals*)
Hermione Gingold: Narrator
Alfons and Aloys Kontarsky: Pianos*
Vienna Philharmonic Orchestra
Conductor: Karl Böhm
Deutsche Grammophon 415 351-2GH
ADD Running time: 53.51
Performance: ★ ★ (★)
Recording: ★ ★ (★)

Karl Böhm, best known for his interpretations of Wagner and the Viennese classics, would not have been the first name to spring to mind as a conductor of Prokofiev's justly popular children's musical fable. In fact, he produces what is probably the best all-round choice currently on Compact Disc, not least thanks to the matchless narration by Hermione Gingold.

PROKOFIEV

She is, admittedly, less successful in relating the storyline to Saint-Saëns *Carnival of the Animals*, but that is as much the fault of Ogden Nash's ill-fitting verses as anything.

For those wanting a narrative accompanying both these scores, this well-recorded version can be recommended (a close focus on the voice is understandable here). For a purely musical version of *Carnival*, opt for Previn's version on Philips coupled with a delightful performance of Ravel's *Mother Goose* suite.

Other recordings on CD:
(*Peter and the Wolf*)
David Bowie/Philadelphia O/Eugene Ormandy/RCA RD82743
Itzhak Perlman/Israel PO/Zubin Mehta/EMI CDC7 47067-2
Terry Wogan/Boston Pops O/John T Williams/Philips 412 559-2PH
(*Carnival of the Animals*)
Pittsburgh SO/André Previn/Philips 400 016-2PH
Israel PO/Zubin Mehta/EMI CDC7 47067-2

PIANO SONATA NO6 IN A MAJOR OP82
(c/w Ravel: Gaspard de la Nuit: Trois Poèmes pour Piano
Ivo Pogorelich: Piano
Deutsche Grammophon 413 363-2GH
DDD Running time: 52.09
Performance: (Prokofiev) ★ ★ ★
(Ravel) ★ ★   Recording: ★ ★ ★

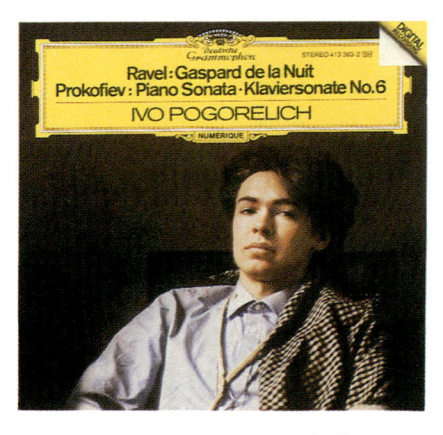

After a gap of sixteen years, Prokofiev returned to the piano sonata in 1939, and working simultaneously on all three, fired off his Sixth, Seventh and Eighth in rapid succession. The idiom was very much akin to their predecessors – the dramatic breaks with tradition and convention; the same driving rhythms and brutal power. At one point in the Sixth, the score asks the performer to play *con pugno* (*with the fist*), a gesture, according to the composer, 'designed to frighten the grandmothers'!

Pogorelich's performance would probably have the desired result. Both playing and recording are stunning, and at times the effect is almost nerve-shattering in its intensity.

For all its similar qualities, the Ravel is less satisfactory, mainly through Pogorelich's unnecessarily exaggerated account of *Le Gibet*. In *Scarbo*, however, he is undeniably riveting.

Other recordings on CD:
(*Gaspard de la Nuit* – see under Ravel)

ROMEO AND JULIET – BALLET: SUITES NOS 1 AND 2 OP64a – selections
Cleveland Orchestra
Conductor: Yoel Levi
Telarc CD80089
DDD Running time: 50.03
Performance: ★ ★ ★
Recording: ★ ★ (★)

The most obvious virtue here is the way Yoel Levi lets the music speak for itself in an articulate and unmannered performance. He is not so generous as, for example, Muti or Rostropovich in the selection he makes (eleven, compared to twelve and fourteen respectively) but most of the popular items are included. He also has the advantage of a typically full-blooded Telarc recording, and superlative playing from the Cleveland Orchestra: every department is on top form here, with bite and sparkle to the phrasing and a delightful rhythmic spring.

It is true that some élan is missing from the performance, but the benefits more than outweigh this.

The sound complements the playing, with a rich 'hall' atmosphere, good depth and weight a wholly convincing presentation.

Other recordings on CD:
Philadelphia O/Riccardo Muti/EMI CDC 7 47004-2
Washington NSO/Mstislav Rostropovich/DG 410 519-2GH
SNO/Neeme Järvi/Chandos CHAN8368
CSO/Georg Solti/Decca 410 200-2DH

CINDERELLA: BALLET OP87
Cleveland Orchestra
Conductor: Vladimir Ashkenazy
Decca 410 162-2DH2 (2 discs)
DDD Running time: 107.36
Performance: ★ ★ ★
Recording: ★ ★ (★)

Ashkenazy proves himself as sympathetic an interpreter of Prokofiev as he is of those other Russian masters, Rachmaninov and Tchaikovsky, with an illuminating account of this magical score. A product of the war years, it was first produced in 1945 and, in common with *Romeo and Juliet*, has an aloof beauty and textural economy that are far from typically Russian.

The superb playing of the Cleveland Orchestra can be fully appreciated in the transparent and finely-detailed recording, although a certain edginess to the sound and lack of warmth preclude an unqualified recommendation.

SERGEI RACHMANINOV
(b. Oneg, Novgorod, Russia, 1 April 1873; d. Beverly Hills, California, USA, 28 March 1943)

In a sense, Rachmaninov was something of a musical dinosaur. While his Russian contemporaries, Stravinsky and Prokofiev, were breaking barriers, he stuck firmly to the ground rules laid down, in the main, by Tchaikovsky. For Rachmaninov, the *Rite of Spring* never happened, which made it ironic that his music should have been banned in the Soviet Union, albeit for just three years between 1931 and 1934 (nonetheless they did lament his death in 1943). He also received his fair share of adverse comment in the West, mainly for the 'heart-on-sleeve' romanticism of the Second Piano Concerto and Second Symphony. But the effect of all this on the composer was nothing compared with that of the disastrous première of his First Symphony.

After showing great promise as a child, Rachmaninov studied at both the St Petersburg (now Leningrad) and Moscow Conservatories, making a considerable name for himself as a virtuoso pianist while still a student. Upon completing his education at twenty, and collecting numerous distinctions, he composed what was to become one of the most famous piano pieces in all music: the Prelude in C sharp minor. All seemed set fair for him but, sadly, Rachmaninov proved to be only at his best when things were going well. The shambles that was the debut of that First Symphony shattered his confidence. The hypnosis treatment he subsequently underwent was partially successful and he did resume composition, but remained prone to depression and morbid melancholia throughout the rest of his life, as some of his music demonstrates only too well.

In 1902 he married his first cousin, Natalia, and the following year became Musical Director of the Moscow Imperial Theatre. However, status alone was insufficient to prevent two of his operas failing there and, more out of pique than anything else, he took his family to Italy and Germany, finally settling in Dresden.

He returned to Russia in 1910, as Conductor of the Moscow Philharmonic, but left in haste once again in 1917, now to escape the revolution. This time he put down roots in the United States, which

In his youth, Rachmaninov, by nature depressive, was deeply affected by the initial failure of his First Symphony.

RACHMANINOV

Vladimir Ashkenazy, not only a superlative interpreter of Rachmaninov at the keyboard, witness the Preludes and piano concertos, but a great interpreter of the symphonies.

had acclaimed him enthusiastically on a concert tour a few years earlier and proved only too pleased to welcome him into exile. He combined concert tours with composition, publishing a third symphony, a fourth piano concerto, and the popular *Rhapsody on a theme of Paganini*. His final, and arguably greatest, orchestral composition was the *Symphonic Dances*, which like so many of his compositions demonstrated that it was still possible to introduce fresh, innovative ideas within traditional forms.

Rachmaninov's is a cosmopolitan music, his sole work with an unmistakably Russian stamp being the setting of the Vespers of the Orthodox Church, dating from 1915. Unfortunately, the only CD version of this fascinating piece uses an unacceptably edited score. Otherwise, Rachmaninov is reasonably well served by the new medium, although his notable contribution to the repertoire of song is barely represented, and a wholly recommendable version of the Third Piano Concerto has yet to appear.

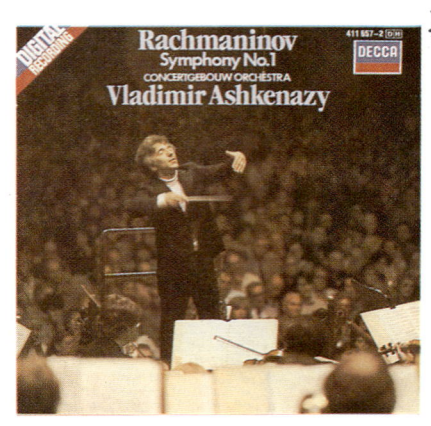

SYMPHONY NO1 IN D MINOR OP13
Concertgebouw Orchestra, Amsterdam
Conductor: Vladimir Ashkenazy
Decca 411 657-2DH
DDD Running time: 42.19
Performance: ★ ★ ★   Recording: ★ ★ ★

There have been few more disastrous first performances than that of the D minor symphony, which took place in 1897, two years after its composition, in St Petersburg (now Leningrad). The unfavourable response caused Rachmaninov, already plagued by depression and self-doubt, to lose his confidence completely – and it all but destroyed him as a composer. It took a three-year course of hypnotherapy before his creative urge was restored.

The original score has never been found, and today conductors rely on a set of orchestral parts unearthed at the Leningrad conservatoire during the Second World War. Hearing the work now, dramatic, exciting, and as richly melodic as anything by Tchaikovsky, it is difficult to see what that first audience could have found so unacceptable, and Rachmaninov may have been right in pointing the finger at Glazunov, who conducted the première.

Ashkenazy came to this symphony last of the three, and it is undoubtedly his finest interpretation in every way. The playing is exhilarating, and the coupling of the Concertgebouw acoustic with sound of spectacular weight and detail, puts this recording in the demonstration class.

SYMPHONY NO2 IN E MINOR OP27
Royal Philharmonic Orchestra
Conductor: André Previn
Telarc CD80113
DDD Running time: 62.45
Performance: ★ ★ ★   Recording: ★ ★ ★

It is only in recent years that this longest and most richly melodic of Rachmaninov's orchestral works has been played without crude cuts being made to the score. Nor is it so many years ago that the composer's orchestral works as a whole were being dismissed as insignificant by many music critics. The main object of the criticism seems to have been that Rachmaninov incorporated such lyrical and extremely 'catchy' melodies into his compositions, especially the symphonies.

Music-lovers, however, generally disagreed, and came to love works like the Second Symphony, not least through persuasive performances and recordings by the likes of the young Andre Previn, whose name has since become synonymous with the work.

In this, his latest version, the interpretation is more daringly expansive and slower to evolve than ever before – he takes nearly eight minutes longer than the more urgent Ashkenazy on Decca – but ultimately the conviction of the performance wins through. The playing is a delight – sample the clarinet solo in the long *adagio*, surely one of the loveliest tunes ever written, critics notwithstanding! With a generous ambience, natural balance, and 'bloom' so characteristic of Telarc productions, the recording perfectly complements the performance.

Other recordings on CD (selection):
Concertgebouw O/Vladimir Ashkenazy/ Decca 400 081-2DH
Los Angeles PO/Simon Rattle/EMI CDC 7 47062-2

SYMPHONY NO3 IN A MINOR OP44
SYMPHONY IN D MINOR ('YOUTH SYMPHONY')
Concertgebouw Orchestra, Amsterdam
Conductor: Vladimir Ashkenazy
Decca 410 231-2DH
DDD Running time: 52.23
Performance: ★ ★   Recording: ★ ★ (★)

This is perhaps the most controversial of Ashkenazy's Rachmaninov series, with widely contrasted tempos – both daringly fast and verging on the lugubrious. However, there is no denying the intensity of this performance of what was to prove the composer's last symphony, written between 1935 and 1936, after he had settled in the United States. The Concertgebouw orchestra, to its credit, stays with Ashkenazy all the way, even through the helter-skelter pace of the finale. Fiery, animated, this is a very Slavic view of Rachmaninov, and one that views him as the natural successor to Tchaikovsky.

As if to prove the point, the interesting 'fill-up', just a fragment of a symphony that Rachmaninov began writing in 1892 at the age of nineteen, clearly displays its debt to Tchaikovsky's Fourth.

The recording is rich and warm, with a smooth, burnished string sound, and notable clarity despite Rachmaninov's frequently complex orchestral textures.

PIANO CONCERTO NO2 IN C MINOR OP18
PIANO CONCERTO NO4 IN G MINOR OP40
Vladimir Ashkenazy: Piano
Concertgebouw Orchestra, Amsterdam
Conductor: Bernard Haitink
Decca 414 475-2DH
DDD Running time: 62.20
Performance: ★ ★ ★   Recording: ★ ★ ★

Ashkenazy's is a performance to win new friends for the much-disparaged C minor concerto. He finds an emotional depth and tragic honesty to the work which generally eludes pianists content only to sugar its superficial sentiment and indulge their expressive whims, and for once the true stature of the concerto emerges. Indeed, it is evident from the start, with Ashkenazy's

RACHMANINOV

scrupulous attention to the *moderato* marking of the score, and he could want for no finer collaborator in this restrained but no less moving approach than Bernard Haitink.

With refined playing from the Amsterdam orchestra, and glorious sound (including a sensible balance between soloist and accompanists), this is an outstanding recording, the more so for the imaginative and generous coupling of the Fourth Concerto (another admirable performance).

Among those pianists offering the more popular combination of the Second and the *Paganini Variations*, that by the young Filipino, Cécile Licad, can be fully recommended if this coupling is preferred.

Other recordings on CD:
(Piano Concerto No2 Op18)
Cécile Licad/CSO/Claudio Abbado/CBS MK38672
Artur Rubinstein/Chicago SO/Fritz Reiner/ RCA RD84934
Sviatoslav Richter/Warsaw National PO/ Stanislaw Wislocki/DG 415 119-2GH
(Piano Concerto No4 Op40)
Zoltan Kocsis/San Francisco SO/Edo de Waart/Philips 411 475-2PH

PRELUDES NOS1-24/PIANO SONATA NO2 IN B FLAT MINOR OP36
Vladimir Ashkenazy: Piano
Decca 414 417-2DH2 (2 discs)
ADD Running time: 106.14
Performance: ★ ★ ★   Recording: ★ ★ ★

Like Chopin, Rachmaninov produced twenty-four preludes encompassing all the major and minor keys, beginning with the most famous, the C sharp minor of 1892 which effectively made his name. More followed in 1903, and the remainder in 1910. In capturing the intrinsic 'mood' of each key, the range of expression is wide indeed, from the gently melancholic to the aggressively dramatic, but Ashkenazy, in these 1976 sessions, proved able to respond to all of them with equal sensitivity and produced one of his most treasurable recordings.

Here the preludes are coupled with a comparably fine interpretation of the Second Piano Sonata (in its original version), which also shares the same warm, lustrous piano tone, with its rich resonance. This set was a happy choice for CD remastering.

Other recordings on CD:
(Preludes – selection)
Andrei Gavrilov/EMI CDC7 47124-2

SYMPHONIC DANCES OP45
ISLE OF THE DEAD OP29
Concertgebouw Orchestra, Amsterdam
Conductor: Vladimir Ashkenazy
Decca 410 124-2DH
DDD Running time: 54.13
Performance: ★ ★ ★   Recording: ★ ★ ★

The last major work that Rachmaninov lived to complete was the *Symphonic Dances* of 1945, an innocuous title which disguises what many believe to be his finest orchestral composition. These are no ordinary dances: for one, the usual elements of joy and gaiety associated with dance are little in evidence. What they have in common is the ominous tread of the *Dies Irae* plainchant, a motif that constantly recurs throughout Rachmaninov's music, including the second work on this disc, *The Isle of the Dead*.

Composed in 1909, the inspiration was a mysterious painting by Arnold Bocklin, itself inspired by San Michele, the 'cemetery island' near Venice. The treatment is literal, even to the representation of the lapping waters and the rocking of the boat as it approaches the sinister isle with its white-draped passenger. The influences are firmly Wagnerian; very *Tristan*-esque.

The Isle of the Dead is superbly performed, even by the high standards of Ashkenazy's Rachmaninov series, while the demonic menace he injects into the *Dances* is perhaps closest to what Rachmaninov intended. The performances are never less than polished, and the recording is first-rate in every way, stunning in its range and impact.

Other recordings on CD:
(Symphonic Dances)
BPO/Lorin Maazel/DG 410 894-2GH
Moscow Radio SO/Vladimir Fedoseyev/ JVC/Melodiya VDC523

PRÉLUDES: OP23 NOS1, 2, 5, 6/OP32 NO12/ÉTUDES
TABLEAUX OP39 NOS3, 5/ELÉGIE OP3 NO1/MOMENTS
MUSICAUX OP16 NOS3, 4, 5, 6
Andrei Gavrilov: Piano
EMI CDC7 47124-2
DDD Running time: 50.14
Performance: ★ ★ ★   Recording: ★ ★

Recorded by EMI in Moscow, there is richness and weight to this piano sound – and no want of impact: played at a realistic level, the first notes of Op23 No2 should pin you to your seat! That apart, this is a masterly recital by Gavrilov, not only technically assured, but alternatively fiery and lyrical as the works demand.

The *Études Tableaux* of 1917 were the penultimate of Rachmaninov's major piano works, while he emulated Chopin in the twenty-four *Préludes* in all the major and minor keys, of which Gavrilov offers a well-chosen selection. The *Moments Musicaux* of 1896 owe their inspiration to Schubert.

For those who enjoy Rachmaninov's solo piano music, given the lack of Compact Disc representation, this becomes an essential acquisition.

Other recordings on CD:
(Préludes – complete)
Vladimir Ashkenazy/Decca 414 417-2DH2

MAURICE RAVEL
(b. Ciboure, near St Jean de Luz, France, 7 March 1875; d. Paris, 28 Dec 1937)

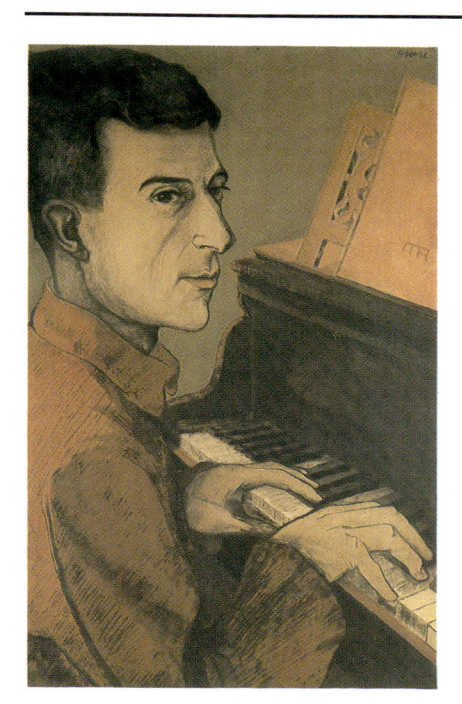

Above: A portrait of Ravel at the piano: many works were originally for the keyboard.

Right: Charles Dutoit who, with the Montreal orchestra, has done Ravel proud.

Surprisingly, the roots of this most urbane of men were in the French Basque country, around the Pyrennean border with Spain. It goes some way to explain the Iberian stimulus in some of his music although, in truth, the peninsula exerted a similar fascination over Debussy who had no blood ties with the area whatsoever.

Ravel inherited his father's love of music. He spent his childhood near Paris and, soon after entering the Conservatoire there, much to his delight became a pupil of Fauré and Chabrier. From the former he learned about the architecture of music; from the latter came the art of melody, rhythm, and that clarity of expression which was to become a hallmark of his work. A less predictable influence was the gifted eccentric, Erik Satie.

Much to the annoyance of Fauré and others, however, Ravel's manifest talents were ignored in consecutive years by the Conservatoire's professors when it came to awarding the prestigious Prix de Rome. Eventually, the affair became a public scandal, and an impassioned newspaper campaign forced the resignation of the director and his replacement by Fauré.

It is difficult to understand now why the eminent academics failed to see the qualities of Ravel's early compositions, which were mainly for solo piano. The *Pavane pour une infante defunte* remains a favourite today, in its orchestrated version, as do the *Miroirs* and his most potent piano work, *Gaspard de la Nuit*.

Many masterly compositions appeared in the period leading up to 1914, most significantly the ballet *Daphnis et Chloé*. By now, Ravel was second only to Debussy in stature among contemporary French composers, but war interrupted his progress: he volunteered for service and, after initial rejection, was drafted as an ambulance driver, only to be discharged as medically unfit after eighteen months.

His first post-war composition of note was the remarkable, evocative, and disturbing *La Valse*: in few other pieces of music does a dream so quickly and uncontrollably become a nightmare. However, it was a far less distinguished piece which was to bring him his greatest fame – *Bolero*: its popularity, much boosted by an American tour in 1927/8, irked the composer somewhat, and anyone believing it representative of Ravel is missing much that is infinitely finer. Examples are the two jazz-influenced piano concertos of the early 1930s.

Tragically, Ravel suffered a motor accident in 1935 from which he never fully recovered. An operation two years later was only partially successful and he died later in hospital.

Ravel is one composer that CD has served well, principally thanks to the work of Charles Dutoit and the Montreal Symphony Orchestra who offer highly recommendable versions of the major orchestral works. One chamber work, however, surely deserves representation soon: the Introduction and Allegro for harp, flute, clarinet and string quartet. This delightful work, in its translucency, classical elegance and charm, is surely the essence of Ravel.

ALBORADA DEL GRACIOSO/BOLERO/ RAPSODIE ESPAGNOLE/LA VALSE
Montreal Symphony Orchestra
Conductor: Charles Dutoit
Decca 410 010-2DH
DDD Running time: 50.36
Performance: ★ ★ ★   Recording: ★ ★ ★

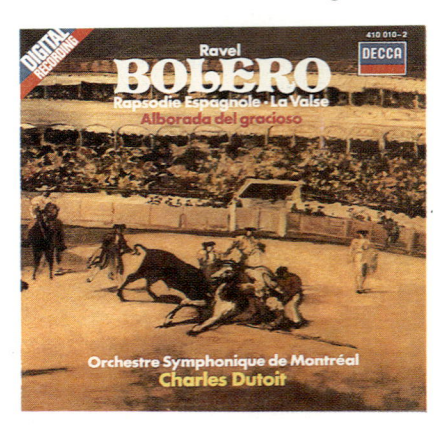

It is difficult to see this collection of four of Ravel's most popular orchestral pieces (including the famous – or infamous! – *Bolero*) being surpassed for a considerable time, either artistically or technically. Here are near ideal performances with ideal sound: weighty, detailed, wide-ranged, yet satisfyingly natural.

Two of the works are products of Ravel's fascination with Spain: the pastiche of *Alborada del Gracioso* (literally, *Jester's Serenade*) and the incandescence and mystery of *Rapsodie Espagnole*. The link between *Bolero* and *La Valse* is that they both undergo a musical metamorphosis, concluding on a note of hysterical frenzy. Certainly the latter, commissioned but then rejected by Diaghilev, begins happily and secure enough in the elegant world of the Viennese waltz, but the dream becomes a whirling, spinning nightmare until the dancers...the answer is left to the imagination.

Other recordings on CD (selection):
(selection, all including *Bolero*)
SRO/Ernest Ansermet/Decca 414 046-2DH
Philadelphia O/Riccardo Muti/EMI CDC 7 47022-2

PIANO CONCERTO IN G MAJOR*
PIANO CONCERTO FOR THE LEFT HAND*
MENUET ANTIQUE/UNE BARQUE SUR L'OCEAN/FANFARE FROM 'L'EVENTAIL DE JEANNE'
Pascal Rogé: Piano
Montreal Symphony Orchestra
Conductor: Charles Dutoit
Decca 410 230-2DH
DDD Running time: 56.51
Performance: ★ ★ (★)
Recording: ★ ★ ★

Ravel wrote the Left-Hand Concerto for his pianist friend, Paul Wittgenstein, who lost an arm in the First World War. Far from being a mere display piece, it is a work of considerable dramatic power and not a little anger. The, at times, searing intensity of the score is remarkable. The G Major, though, is in lighter vein, utilising the three-movement classical form, but taking advantage of the idiom of its era (it was composed in 1929) by including a strong jazz flavour (with a sprinkling of George Gershwin). It is work that truly seduces the ear with its light, open scoring and glittering passage-work, especially in the vivacious finale.

Pascal Rogé has exactly the lightness of touch required here, although he might have treated the outer movements with a little more verve. However, the jazz elements are nicely projected and the overall feel of the performance is very satisfying. The Left-Hand Concerto is similarly well-played, if lacking a little in character and depth of expression.

Ravel's orchestrations of two of his piano pieces, plus the fanfare he contributed to that 'composers' co-operative' effort, *Jeanne's Fan*, make for worthwhile fillers.

The piano, which has a splendid tone to it, is equably balanced within the orchestral canvas, adding to the pleasures of this issue.

MA MERE L'OYE (MOTHER GOOSE): BALLET/PAVANE POUR UNE INFANTE DEFUNTE/LE TOMBEAU DE COUPERIN/ VALSES NOBLES ET SENTIMENTALES
Montreal Symphony Orchestra
Conductor: Charles Dutoit
Decca 410 254-2DH
DDD Running time: 66.51
Performance: ★ ★ ★   Recording: ★ ★ ★

RAVEL

Another well-filled disc from Dutoit and the Montreal orchestra, stylish and fluently played and, once again, immaculately recorded. The combination of natural scale, timbre, imaging and definition coupled with the sumptuous acoustic of St Eustache church, Montreal, is producing some of Compact Disc's finest advertisements!

The principal work here is the delightful orchestral score which Ravel produced for *Ma Mère l'Oye,* originally a work for piano duet. Equally delectable, the bitter-sweet *Valses*; the wistful *Pavane*; and the neo-18th century dance suite which the composer linked to his illustrious predecessor of the French school, Couperin. Again, all three works were originally composed for piano, and amply demonstrate Ravel's incomparable skill as an orchestrator.

Other recordings on CD:
(Le Tombeau de Couperin)
CSO/Georg Solti/Decca 400 051-2DH
ASMF/Neville Marriner/ASV CD DCA517
(Ma Mère l'Oye)
Pittsburgh SO/Andre Previn/Philips 400 016-2PH
Dallas SO/Eduardo Mata/RCA RD84815
(Valses Nobles et Sentimentales)
SRO/Ernest Ansermet/Decca 414 046-2DH
Dallas SO/Eduardo Mata/RCA RD84815
(Pavane pour une infante défunte)
St Louis SO/Leonard Slatkin/Telarc CD80052
ASMF/Marriner/Philips 412 131-2PH

DAPHNIS ET CHLOE: BALLET
Montreal Symphony Choir and Orchestra
Conductor: Charles Dutoit
Decca 400 055-2DH
DDD Running time: 55.57
Performance: ★ ★ ★   Recording: ★ ★ ★

This was one of the first recordings effectively to silence early criticisms of Compact Disc. Few could dispute that Ravel's magical score was being heard with a new translucency and clarity of presentation, and the open, airy acoustic only added to the spellbinding illusion.

The music-making, too, is of a different order, Dutoit managing to sound spontaneous while still adhering scrupulously to the score. The Canadian players are as responsive as he could wish for, seizing the opportunity to show their virtuosity in the breathtakingly fast finale.

The ballet itself, which draws on a romantic fable from Greek poetry, was commissioned from Ravel by Diaghilev in 1909. It was a while in the making, but has justly become one of the composer's most loved compositions.

Other recordings on CD:
LSO/Andre Previn/EMI CDC 7 47123-2
VPO/James Levine/DG 415 360-2GH

PIANO TRIO IN A MINOR
(c/w **Chausson:** Piano Trio in G minor Op31)
Beaux Arts Trio
Philips 411 141-2PH
DDD Running time: 60.21
Performance: ★ ★ ★   Recording: ★ ★ ★

By Ravel's standards, the four-movement Piano Trio of 1914 is a large-scale work, lasting for over twenty-eight minutes. But the endlessly imaginative treatment of its memorable themes ensures it does not outstay its welcome. Particularly memorable are the elegant, poignant melody of the first movement, the stately *passacaglia* of the third, and the fiery tune of the fourth with its distinct echoes of Basque folk music. The delightful second-movement *scherzo* derives its title 'Pantoum' from a verse form in Malaysian poetry, the *pantun*, which Ravel adapts as a musical device.

Ernest Chausson's Trio of 1881 shows very different influences, the strong classical disciplines of his teacher, Franck, and to a lesser extent, Brahms. A noble, imposing work, it succeeds in creating remarkably rich textures from just three instruments, and it is a tribute to the balancing here that the strings are not swamped by the piano. The equilibrium between the players is finely maintained throughout both works in a lucid, firmly-focussed and full-bodied recording (a rich 'cello tone and true weight to the piano are especially noteworthy).

RAVEL

SONATA FOR VIOLIN AND PIANO
(c/w Franck: Violin Sonata in A major)
Jean-Jacques Kantorow: Violin
Jacques Rouvier: Piano
Denon C37-7079
DDD Running time: 43.31
Performance: ★ ★ ★   Recording: ★ ★ ★

This is a beautiful production, which extends even to the Van Gogh painting reproduced on the cover of the inset booklet! There is near perfect balance between the two instruments, each crisply defined in a subtle but influential acoustic. The distancing is ideal – the players sounding perhaps fifteen feet away.

What was to be his last chamber work occupied Ravel for some four years, on-and-off, between 1923 and 1927. In it, he not only plays off the two instruments against each other, but stresses their inherent incompatibility (hence the importance of a well-adjusted recording balance). The exceptionally fluent writing has that arcane, almost ethereal feel to it which is so typical of Ravel, but it additionally reveals the influence of American blues and jazz on the composer.

The inclusion of only two sonatas hardly constitutes good value for money though: the Debussy sonata could easily have been included as well. This is the only disappointment in an otherwise delightful recording.

Other recordings on CD (selection):
(Franck sonata)
Itzhak Perlman/Vladimir Ashkenazy/Decca 414 128-2DH

GASPARD DE LA NUIT/PAVANE POUR UNE INFANTE DEFUNTE/VALSES NOBLES ET SENTIMENTALES
Vladimir Ashkenazy: Piano
Decca 410 255-2DH
DDD Running time: 58.48
Performance: ★ ★ ★
Recording: ★ ★ (★)

For over twenty years Ashkenazy's LP version of *Gaspard*, one of Ravel's most potent and darkest compositions, led the field. Rather than replacing it, this new digital recording effectively complements it. Essentially, Ashkenazy has not changed his view over two decades: perhaps the approach is gentler, more sensuous now, and is combined with an analytical quality enhanced by the well-defined, rich-toned sound. Ashkenazy's observance of the most subtle tempo changes brings nothing but admiration, and *Le Gibet* (the gallows) is as chilling as no doubt Ravel intended.

Rewarding performances of the *Valses* and the ever-popular *Pavane* complete a generous programme.

In respect of *Gaspard* there are strong challenges from Pogorelich on Deutsche Grammophon, although his playing is self-consciously mannered in places, and Perlemuter on Nimbus (who brings the authority of having known the composer well). Good as it is, though, his performance is rather too direct to evoke the true atmosphere of the work.

Other recordings on CD:
(*Gaspard de la Nuit*)
Vlado Perlemuter/Nimbus NIM5055
Ivo Pogorelich/DG 413 363-2GH
Deszo Ranki/Hungaroton HCD12317-2
Carol Rosenberger/Delos D/CD3006

MIROIRS/LE TOMBEAU DE COUPERIN
Yukie Nagai: Piano
BIS CD-246
DDD Running time: 60.10
Performance: ★ ★   Recording: ★ ★ (★)

A disc which usefully combines two of Ravel's greatest contributions to the solo piano repertoire, notwithstanding the fact that *Le Tombeau* and two of the five *Miroirs* were subsequently, and most successfully, transcribed for orchestra. (These were *Alborada del Gracioso* and *Une barque sur l'ocean*, and both appear in their orchestral guise on other discs featured here).

In the *Miroirs* of 1905, Ravel displayed a new sensitivity to the natural sounds he heard around him – birdsong, church bells, the swell of the sea, even the fluttering of moths – with delectable results. However, his mastery of pastiche was never in doubt and is nowhere better heard than in the exquisite suite ostensibly dedicated to the composer, Francois Couperin, but which is more a homage to the whole style of 18th Century French music.

Sensitive, finely detailed playing is evident throughout from Yukie Nagai, whose delicate touch is entirely appropriate: sample the faithfully judged *pianissimos*. This is a good, clean recording.

Other recordings on CD:
(*Miroirs*)
Vlado Perlemuter/Nimbus NIM5005
(*Le Tombeau de Couperin*)
Vlado Perlemuter/Nimbus NIM5011

OTTORINO RESPIGHI
(b. Bologna, Italy, 9 July 1879; d. Rome, 18 April 1936)

Respighi's reputation today rests almost entirely upon a handful of brilliant orchestral showpieces which all too readily display their indebtedness to one of his teachers, Rimsky Korsakov. They belong to what is loosely called his 'Roman' period (the three most popular pieces all depict aspects of life and scenes in the Italian capital) from 1916 to 1926. For three of those years, 1923 to 1925, Respighi also headed the St Cecilia Conservatory in Rome.

As well as his spell with Rimsky-Korsakov in Russia, Respighi also followed up his early tuition in his home town of Bologna, with a series of lessons under Max Bruch in Berlin. The influence of Debussy and Richard Strauss can be felt in his earlier, descriptive, phase, but it was an interest in early Italian music and Gregorian plainchant which led into a second 'Gregorian' period of creativity, and such neglected works as the *Concerto Gregoriano* for violin, the *Concerto in modo misolidico*, and, later, *Metamorphoseon*, are certainly worthy of wider recognition.

A recent Chandos Compact Disc eloquently argues the case for this last work, and additionally offers an impressive performance of the rather facile but undeniably exciting score of *Belkis, Queen of Sheba* (CHAN 8405).

However, the evocative, sumptuously and vividly orchestrated 'Roman' impressions – *Pines of Rome*; *Fountains of Rome*; and *Feste Romane* – will no doubt maintain their pre-eminence in Respighi's output, followed by the less impressive *Church Windows* and *Brazilian Impressions*. All are available in satisfactory CD versions, although it is surprising to see that *Three Botticelli Pictures* has yet to reach the catalogue, especially as part of the triptych, the *Adoration of the Magi*, is one of Respighi's most sublime scores.

PINES OF ROME/FOUNTAINS OF ROME/FESTE ROMANE
Montreal Symphony Orchestra
Conductor: Charles Dutoit
Decca 410 145-2DH
DDD Running time: 60.23
Performance: ★ ★ ★   Recording: ★ ★ ★

The 'Roman trilogy' undoubtedly represents the peak of Respighi's brand of 'romantic impressionism', with a range of melodic invention and orchestral mastery displayed throughout its three colourful scores. And rarely can they have been so well played or recorded, the full richness and weight of the orchestral sound presented with almost tangible width and depth, and pin-point stereo imaging. Clarity is maintained even in the loudest passages, and the discreet highlighting of solo instruments is justifiable in that it allows full appreciation of some exciting, virtuoso playing; brilliant stuff!

Other recordings on CD:
(coupled as above)
Philadelphia O/Riccardo Muti/EMI CDC7 47316-2
(*Pines of Rome/Fountains of Rome* only)
BPO/Herbert von Karajan/DG413 822-2GH
San Francisco SO/Edo de Waart/Philips 411 419-2PH
Atlanta SO/Louis Lane/Telarc CD80085

CHURCH WINDOWS: FOUR SYMPHONIC IMPRESSIONS/BRAZILIAN IMPRESSIONS: SUITE FOR ORCHESTRA
Philharmonia Orchestra
Conductor: Geoffrey Simon
Chandos CHAN8317
DDD Running time: 45.22
Performance: ★ ★ ★   Recording: ★ ★ ★

The title post-dated the composition (it was derived from the *Piano Preludes on Gregorian Themes* of 1922) as did the attribution of individual stained glass images to the pieces. Nevertheless, *Church Windows* is a remarkably effective work despite its rather contrived origins.

Equally vivid in their imagery are the *Brazilian Impressions*: for instance, the second is set in a snake garden and a tambourine played with side-drum sticks chillingly conjures up a rattlesnake. Throughout, Respighi misses no opportunity to indulge his love of orchestral colour, and the samba-derived finale is a delight.

Excellent performances, and a stunning recording: natural, yet glitteringly detailed and exciting.

NICOLAI RIMSKY-KORSAKOV
(b. Tikhvin, Novgorod, Russia, 18 March 1844; d. Lyubensk, near St Petersburg, 21 June 1908)

Of all well-known composers, Rimsky-Korsakov's background is one of the most unlikely. He came from an aristocratic Russian family and, at the age of twelve, became a cadet in the Imperial Navy, with no intention of making a career in anything else. Music was very much an amateur pastime, and while his naval squadron was stationed in St Petersburg he took full advantage of the local concert scene. Then, a meeting with the composer Balakirev led to some lessons in composition and, while on a cruise taking in the North and South Atlantic, Rimsky found sufficient time between his duties as an officer to write a symphony. He completed it in England, while his ship called in at the Thameside port of Gravesend.

The pull of music gradually increased and he completed a number of vocal and orchestral works, yet no one was more surprised than he suddenly to be offered the post of Professor of Composition at the St Petersburg Conservatory, mainly on the strength of that First Symphony and the symphonic poem, *Sadko*. To his credit, though, Rimsky acknowledged his ill-preparedness for the post and plunged into a demanding course of study.

As a result, he became the best technician and theorist of the group of Russian 'nationalist' composers prominent in the second half of the

Rimsky-Korsakov corrects a score: his metamorphosis from Russian naval officer to teacher of composition at the St Petersburg Conservatoire was nothing short of extraordinary.

19th Century (Balakirev, Borodin and Mussorgsky were the others of note) and his treatise on instrumentation, like that of Berlioz, has become a classic work on the subject.

As well as doing much to further the cause of his friends, Borodin and Mussorgsky (not always in the best long-term interests of their music it must be said), Rimsky taught both Prokofiev and Stravinsky and the impact of his incomparable understanding of orchestration was most pronounced on the latter.

Vivid colours and strong melodies characterise Rimsky-Korsakov's work, sometimes it must be said at the expense of substance. In all he composed fifteen operas, three symphonies, choral works and songs, but is best known today for the exquisite *Scheherazade* and the infectiously lively *Capriccio espagnol*, both of which are contained on a Decca CD reviewed below. This, plus Chandos' three-disc set of orchestral works, neatly encompasses the 'essential' Rimsky-Korsakov on Compact Disc.

The latter offers excellent performances of suites from several of the operas (now largely unperformed in their complete state) and, along with many other popular melodies, includes the tune everybody knows – *Flight of the Bumblebee*.

SCHEHERAZADE: SYMPHONIC SUITE OP35*/CAPRICCIO ESPAGNOL OP34
Richard Roberts: Violin*
Montreal Symphony Orchestra
Conductor: Charles Dutoit
Decca 410 253-2DH
DDD Running time: 61.09
Performance: ★ ★ ★   Recording: ★ ★ ★

Dutoit takes a comparatively leisurely view of *Scheherazade*, emphasising the beauty of the score more than its drama. Not that the end result is lacking in impact or excitement, especially with the demonstration-standard sound. The recording is naturally-balanced and allows detail, including the prominent solo violin role, to emerge from within the orchestral texture.

On Philips, Kondrashin's is a more volatile reading, equally well recorded, but the Decca offers a substantial bonus in the shape of an exhilarating performance of Rimsky's 'Iberian impression', the *Capriccio Espagnol*, now as famous on the ice rink as it is in the concert hall!

Other recordings on CD (selection):
Concertgebouw O/Kirill Kondrashin/Philips 400 021-2PH
Philadelphia O/Riccardo Muti/EMI CDC7 47023-2
SRO/Ernest Ansermet/Decca 414 124-2DH

MAY NIGHT: OVERTURE/SUITES: THE SNOW MAIDEN/CHRISTMAS EVE/MLADA/THE INVISIBLE CITY OF KITEZH/THE GOLDEN COCKEREL/THE TALE OF TSAR SULTAN
Scottish National Orchestra
Conductor: Neeme Järvi
Chandos CHAN8327-9 (3 discs)
DDD Running time: 147.37
Performance: ★ ★ ★   Recording: ★ ★ ★

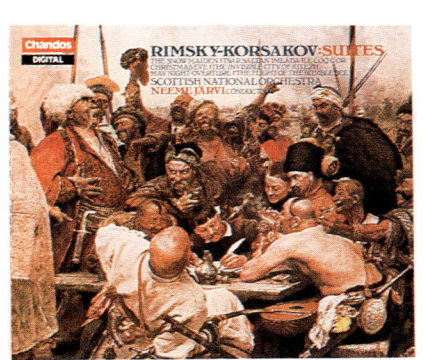

Anyone looking to explore the 'rarer Rimsky' will find plenty to relish in this set of colourful concert suites from his operas. There are some delectable musical confections here, superbly performed, and rounded off with a breathtaking rendering of *The Flight of the Bumblebee*.

The playing is complemented by an equally vivid recording, exciting in its expansive scale and detail, in typical Chandos fashion, but just a touch light and soft in the bass. Järvi's touch proves as sure in the Rimsky as in the very different Prokofiev symphonies, also on Chandos.

Other recordings on CD:
(*The Golden Cockerel/The Tale of Tsar Sultan*)
Rotterdam PO/David Zinman/Philips 411 435-2PH
(*May Night/The Snow Maiden*)
Rotterdam PO/David Zinman/Philips 411 446-2PH

GIOACCHINO ROSSINI
(b. Pesaro, Italy, 29 February 1792; d. Paris, 13 November 1868)

Rossini was unequalled as a composer of comic opera, not only in quality, but in quantity. After twenty-one prolific years in which he completed no less than thirty-nine operas, he virtually retired, age 37, to enjoy the life of luxurious self-indulgence he felt he had earned!

Many of the operas are performed only rarely today, their names known for a few famous arias which constitute the staple fare of recital recordings. However, the popularity of *The Barber of Seville*, *William Tell*, *The Italian Girl in Algiers* and *La Cenerentola* never seems to wane. Additionally, Rossini was also responsible for many attractive piano pieces; two rapturous choral works, the *Stabat Mater* and the *Petite Messe Solenelle* (which is actually far from *petite* in that it occupies four LP sides!); and several deliciously lively String Sonatas.

He had a singer for a mother (a notable leading lady in comic opera) and a town trumpeter for a father (a role he coupled with that of inspector of slaughterhouses). Tuition in the 'cello and composition began at the Bologna Conservatory in 1806, and with it came a love of Mozart (an Austrian) so intense that, with carefree disregard for accuracy, he was nicknamed *'the little German'* by his fellow pupils.

He quickly made his name as an opera composer although *The Barber of Seville* surprisingly was booed at its first performance in 1816, the audience evidently resenting an attempt to usurp Paisiello's popular opera of the same name. Thirteen years later, in 1829, *William Tell* concluded his dazzling career as a composer. The following year, he separated from his wife, a Spanish soprano who had sung many of his heroines, and developed a friendship with one Olympe Pélissier, whom he eventually married in 1846. He divided the rest of his days between Paris and Italy, generally in the enjoyment of good food and wine.

Rossini's operas and choral works are fully discussed in a companion volume, *Opera on Compact Disc*, the reviews below dealing with concerts of overtures and other instrumental music.

ROSSINI, par GILL

OVERTURES: LA SCALA DI SETA/IL BARBIERE DI SIVIGLIA/SEMIRAMIDE/IL VIAGGIO A REIMS/LE SIÈGE DE CORINTHE/GUGLIELMO TELL
Philharmonia Orchestra
Conductor: Riccardo Muti
EMI CDC7 47118-2
ADD Running time: 52.13
Performance: ★ ★ ★   Recording: ★ ★ ★

This alternative selection of popular overtures, if a less generous one, is performed with as much verve and panache as Chailly's Decca recording. The sound is similarly impressive, rich and weighty and in an ample acoustic. Muti's approach is perhaps the more dramatic of the two, Chailly's the wittier, but choice is really a matter of which overtures you want and which you can do without.

Other recordings on CD (miscellaneous overtures):
NPO/Riccardo Chailly/Decca 400 049-2DH
Orpheus CO/DG 415 363-2GH

LA BOUTIQUE FANTASQUE (Rossini arranged Respighi)/SOIRÉES MUSICALES – BALLET SUITE OP9 (Rossini arranged Britten)/MATINÉES MUSICALES – BALLET SUITE OP24 (Rossini arranged Britten)
National Philharmonic Orchestra
Conductor: Richard Bonynge
Decca 410 139-2DH
DDD Running time: 64.11
Performance: ★ ★ ★   Recording: ★ ★ ★

A wealth of miscellaneous compositions which Rossini, with typical wit, dubbed '*Sins of my old age*', provided two modern composers, Ottorino Respighi and Benjamin Britten with the basic material for what proved to be successful and popular ballet scores.

Respighi's *Boutique Fantasque* of 1919 was a commission from Diaghilev, while Britten's equally attractive suites date from 1936 and 1941. All receive lively performances here, elegant, sparkling, and vividly recorded. The sound is forward, but expansive in width as well as depth, and there is no missing any of the inner detail of these scores.

Left: *An 1867 cartoon shows Rossini lighting the touch paper on his 'rocket', the popular name given to the brilliant and exciting climaxes the composer was so adept at writing:* William Tell *and* The Thieving Magpie *offer two examples.*

SONATAS FOR STRINGS: NO1 IN G MAJOR/NO3 IN C MAJOR/NO4 IN B FLAT MAJOR/NO5 IN E FLAT MAJOR
Camerata Bern
Director and concert master: Thomas Furi
Deutsche Grammophon 413 310-2GH
DDD Running time: 55.05
Performance: ★ ★ ★
Recording: ★ ★ (★)

It is astonishing to recall that these *Sonate a quattro*, lightweight but nonetheless technically accomplished, are the work of a twelve-year-old. Rossini composed them around 1804 in a moment of exceptional precocity, and while they may owe their form to the serenade and divertimento, the approach is wholly individual. There are no pretensions to the lofty ideals of the classical sonata – the object is entertainment, pure and simple; exactly the description, too, for these dashing performances.

The sound has suitable piquancy and brilliance within a ripely resonant acoustic, and the only disappointment here is that Camerata Bern included only four of the six sonatas when both CD and LP would have accommodated the full set of six without difficulty, as on Rolla's disc.

Other recordings on CD:
Liszt CO/Janos Rolla/TelDec ZK8.43099

OVERTURES: GUGLIELMO TELL/IL SIGNOR BRUSCHINO/IL VIAGGIO A REIMS/LA SCALA DI SETA/LA GAZZA LADRA/IL TURCO IN ITALIA/L'ITALIANA IN ALGERI
National Philharmonic Orchestra
Conductor: Riccardo Chailly
Decca 400 049-2DH
DDD Running time: 56.37
Performance: ★ ★ ★
Recording: ★ ★ (★)

Given a vivid, full-blooded Kingsway Hall recording, Chailly responds with exuberant performances of a generous selection of opera overtures. Included are the delightful *Gazza Ladra* (the *Thieving Magpie*), *La Scala di Seta* (*The Silken Ladder*), and the much-abused *Guglielmo Tell* (*William Tell*), the popularity of which has tended to obscure the fact that it is a superbly-constructed piece, a symphonic poem of some note.

The wide-ranging recording ruthlessly captures passing underground railway trains and other extraneous noises, but the effect is only slightly detrimental to what is a hugely enjoyable disc.

CAMILLE SAINT-SAËNS
(b. Paris, 9 October France, 1835; d. Algiers, 16 December 1921)

Ironically, he had little regard for his best-known work, Carnival of the Animals.

Saint-Saëns was what would be described today as a 'good professional'. Not a prolific composer, although he enjoyed a long creative career; not one to whom ideas came easily, but remarkably adept at making the most of sometimes unpromising and distinctly thin material; and certainly no revolutionary, although versatile and undeniably skilful in selecting and utilising the less extreme aspects of the classical and romantic styles.

That all tends to suggest his music was rather dull and predictable, which is by no means the case, as anyone familiar with the Third Symphony, the *Carnival of the Animals, Danse Macabre,* the Piano Concertos and the best of the symphonic poems would confirm.

Something of a child prodigy (a concert pianist at age ten) he came from a well-to-do Norman family, gaining an organ scholarship to study at the Paris Conservatoire, and privately with the composer, Charles Gounod. Although he composed a symphony at sixteen, his first successes were as an organist, and for some twenty years he held the renowned position of organist-in-residence at the Madeleine Church in Paris.

Saint-Saëns was an early member of the French National Music Society, and did much to revive interest in earlier composers such as Rameau. He was also a youthful admirer of Wagner, even playing host to the great man when he visited Paris, but the Franco-Prussian war put an end to such adulation and soon Saint-Saëns – an articulate writer – was arguing against the Wagnerian influence on French music. The war also persuaded him to enlist in the French National Guard for a time. Marriage in 1875 to a girl twenty years his junior (they separated after six years) was followed in 1877 by the first performance (ironically in Germany) of his best known vocal work, the opera *Samson et Dalila.*

A complete performance of the latter has yet to appear on CD, and several orchestral works merit a place, too. Saint-Saëns' best-known compositions, the *Carnival* and the Third (*Organ*) Symphony are, however, well represented.

SAINT-SAËNS

PIANO CONCERTO NO2 IN G MINOR OP22
PIANO CONCERTO NO4 IN C MINOR OP44
François-René Duchable: Piano
Strasbourg Philharmonic Orchestra
Conductor: Alain Lombard
Erato ECD88002
AAD Running time: 48.01
Performance: ★ ★ ★   Recording: ★ ★

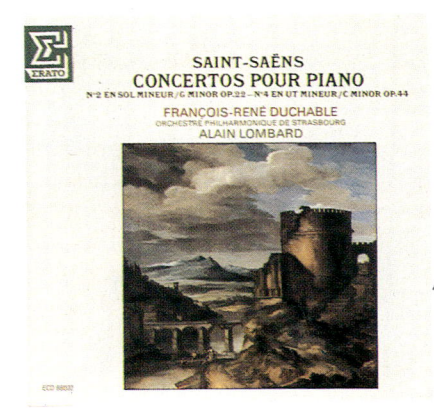

Despite a rather reticent recording, these are two fine performances of probably the best-known of Saint-Saëns five piano concertos. The balance favours the piano to an extent (a Bösendorfer, incidentally, of lovely tone, if lacking some brilliance because of the recording) but the orchestral perspectives are good. The acoustic is also very pleasant.

The analogue master displays some hiss during the softer passages, but not enough to detract from what is a valuable issue given the scant treatment of the Saint-Saëns concertos on Compact Disc.

SYMPHONY NO3 IN C MINOR OP78 (ORGAN SYMPHONY)
Peter Hurford: Organ
Montreal Symphony Orchestra
Conductor: Charles Dutoit
Decca 410 201-2DH
DDD Running time: 34.24
Performance: ★ ★ ★   Recording: ★ ★ ★

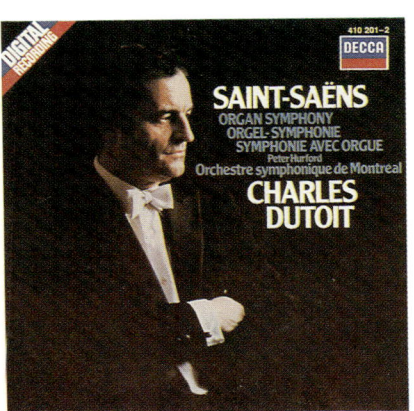

This most famous of French symphonies was actually written to a commission from the Royal Philharmonic Society of London (Saint-Saëns was much revered in Britain) and received its premiere there in May, 1886. Apart from the grandeur of its melodies, and the Lisztian treatment of them, the work is most distinguishable by the roles given to two pianos and organ, and it is the inclusion of the latter in the balance which has been the downfall of many an otherwise good recording.

No black marks, though, for this lyrical and exuberant performance, where everything assumes its rightful place in a truthful and transparent sound-stage. The clarity of the pedal notes is remarkable, and Peter Hurford's tasteful restraint in the 'big' organ entry is admirable.

Less admirable, however – given the generous programming in, say, Dutoit's Ravel series – is the running time. There are sufficient shorter works by Saint-Saëns that would have provided decent fillers.

Other recordings on CD (selection):
Philadelphia O/Eugene Ormandy/Telarc CD80051
LPO/Enrique Batiz/ASV CD DCA524

LE CARNAVAL DES ANIMAUX: GRANDE FANTAISIE ZOOLOGIQUE
(c/w Ravel: Ma Mère L'Oye (Mother Goose): Ballet)
Joseph Villa, Patricia Jennings: Pianos
Pittsburgh Symphony Orchestra
Conductor: André Previn
Philips 400 016-2PH
DDD Running time: 49.15
Performance: ★ ★ ★   Recording: ★ ★ ★

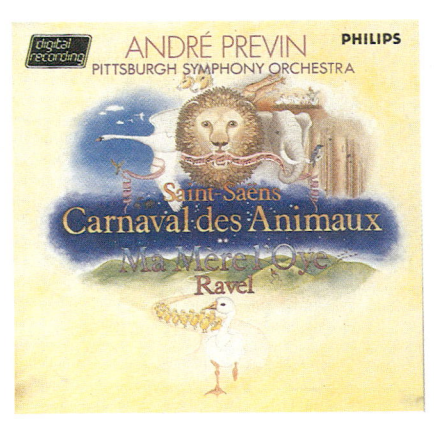

A surprising aspect to what, along with the *Organ Symphony*, is Saint-Saëns' best-loved work, is that the composer himself did not consider it at all representative of his music and forbade further public performances after the première in 1886. Only the famous 'cello solo, *Le Cygne* (The Swan), was permitted to be played.

Both the Saint-Saëns and the Ravel works are beautifully performed here (the Saint-Saëns without narration), with spacious, transparent sound. If the Ravel fares the better technically, it is only because the image of the pianos in the *Carnaval* is a little too wide.

Other recordings on CD:
(*Le Carnaval des Animaux*)
Hermione Gingold/Aloys and Alfons Kontarsky/VPO/Karl Böhm/DG
Itzhak Perlman/Katia and Marielle Labeque/Israel PO/Zubin Mehta/EMI CDC7 47067-2
(*Ma Mère L'Oye*)
Montreal SO/Charles Dutoit/Decca 410 254-2DH
Dallas SO/Eduardo Mata/RCA RD84815

FRANZ SCHUBERT
(b. Vienna, Austria, 31 January 1797; d. Vienna, 19 November 1828)

Schubert's short, rather podgy, bespectacled figure was a familiar sight in Bognor's coffee house on the Singerstrasse. Often he could be seen gazing in awe at the gruff-looking character seated in an opposite corner, but always too shy to approach him. He, after all, was Ludwig van Beethoven.

If anyone had suggested that one day the name of Franz Schubert would be the subject of similar reverence, it would no doubt have provoked disbelief among the motley crew of Bohemians whose company he enjoyed.

First and foremost, of course, Schubert was a songwriter, and an incomparable one. His gift for word-setting and for melody was unique and, moreover, astonishingly consistent. In a period of just eighteen years, he wrote over six hundred songs, and found time for some four hundred other compositions. If in these, his touch was sometimes less secure than in his *lieder*, he nevertheless produced masterpieces worthy of standing alongside those of his idol, Beethoven: the last three piano sonatas; the three great string quartets and the string quintet; the *Wanderer Fantasy*; the *Trout* Quintet and the Octet; the 'Great' C major symphony; and, of course, the *Unfinished*, which on the strength of its two completed movements alone belongs among the greatest symphonies ever composed.

What Schubert achieved in his brief life is remarkable enough; what he might have attained had he been allowed more than just thirty-one years can only be wondered at.

The son of a schoolmaster, he spent all his life in Vienna, attending the choir school of the Royal Chapel at eleven, and becoming an assistant in his father's school at seventeen. But any thoughts of an academic career were soon abandoned to devote himself to music.

As well as possessing a good voice, he played both the violin and piano, and his first compositions, among them quartets for his family to play, date from around 1810/11.

He lived a fairly impoverished existence, keeping body and soul together on meagre earnings from music teaching. Informal concerts of chamber music or songs in his lodgings were a regular feature of his life, and much of his music was never heard outside this environment.

Composition came easily, and he wrote rapidly, seldom indulging in the kind of painstaking quest for perfection that occupied Beethoven. It is true some of his more ambitious efforts are flawed, and much was left incomplete, but considering just *how* quickly he must have composed at times – several songs in one day, for example – there are rarely signs of haste. And always there was the ceaseless flow of disarmingly beautiful melody.

In the winter of 1822/3, he contracted a disease – most probably syphilis – which left him severely ill, and was never wholly cured. In 1827, he finally met Beethoven and in March of that year was one of the torchbearers at the great man's funeral. Eighteen months later he, too, was dead from typhoid. His death shocked his friends and acquaintances: one, Johann Mayrhofer, described Schubert as, *'a mixture of tenderness and coarseness, sensuality and candour',* which reflects something of the character of his music, too.

Improbable as the idea would have seemed to him during his lifetime, Schubert, rightly, was buried alongside Beethoven.

In many respects, Compact Disc has served Schubert's instrumental music poorly, with little choice in the string quartets (other than the *Death and the Maiden,* No14), but one recommendable version of the Octet, and few options in the piano sonatas. The imminent release on CD of Stephen Bishop-Kovacevich's Hyperion recording of the last and most sublime of the sonatas, No21 D960, will be very welcome.

Left: This watercolour of Schubert was done in 1825, three years before his untimely death. He left an incomparable legacy of songs, plus many titanic instrumental compositions.

Below: Vienna, where Schubert was born and lived his entire life, seldom going beyond its walls.

SCHUBERT

SYMPHONY NO4 IN C MINOR D417 (TRAGIC)
SYMPHONY NO5 IN B FLAT MAJOR D485
Academy of St Martin-in-the-Fields
Director: Neville Marriner
Philips 410 045–2PH
DDD Running time: 60.04
Performance: ★ ★(★)
Recording: ★ ★

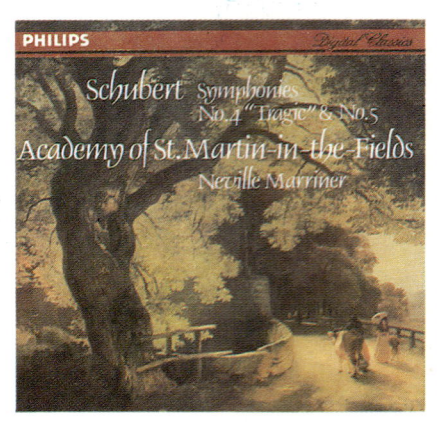

Of these two symphonies completed by the nineteen-year-old Schubert in 1816, the B flat is the lighter work.

Using a small-scale orchestra, which is especially apt in the light-textured Fifth, Marriner gives two fine readings of these youthful works. He loses a little of the charm with a brisk performance of the first movement of No5, but the succeeding *andante* is superbly judged.

It is this work which fares the better in the recording which is on the weighty side and rather thickly textured, although the woodwind are prominent enough.

SYMPHONY NO5 IN B FLAT MAJOR D485/SYMPHONY NO8 IN B MINOR D759 (UNFINISHED)
Vienna Philharmonic Orchestra
Conductor: Georg Solti
Decca 414 371–2DH
DDD Running time: 49.14
Performance: ★ ★ ★ **Recording:** ★ ★ ★

For a conductor who can often seem severe and unrelenting in his interpretations, Solti's approach to Schubert is surprisingly relaxed and genial. The pace is not forced at all, and the end result, with superb playing from the VPO, and warm, well-balanced recording, provides two of the best Schubert performances currently available.

The classical perfection of the Fifth of 1816, arguably the finest of the early symphonies, makes an excellent foil for the bold originality of the *Unfinished*.

Other recordings on CD:
(Symphony No5 D485)
ASMF/Neville Marriner/Philips 410 045–2PH and 412 176-2PH6 (set)
Berlin Staatskapelle/Otmar Suitner/Denon C37-7156
(Symphony No8 D759 – selection)
Philharmonia O/Giuseppe Sinopoli/DG 410 862-2GH
Cleveland O/Christoph von Dohnanyi/Telarc CD80091
BSO/Colin Davis/Philips 410 393-2PH
ASMF/Neville Marriner/Philips 411 439–2PH and 412 176-2PH6 (set)

ROSAMUNDE: Incidental music to the play by Helmina von Chézy D797
Elly Ameling: Soprano
Leipzig Radio Chorus
Leipzig Gewandhaus Orchestra
Conductor: Kurt Masur
Philips 412 432–2PH
DDD Running time: 60.44
Performance: ★ ★ ★ **Recording:** ★ ★ ★

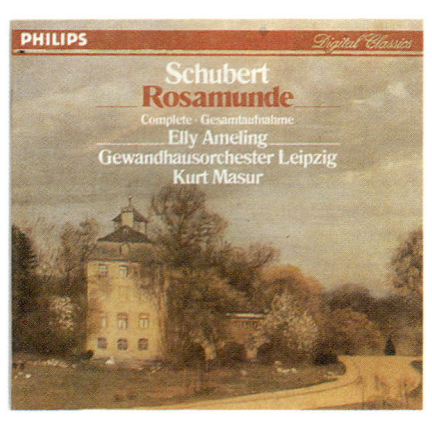

The play for which it was written in 1823 may be long-forgotten, but Schubert's incidental music continues to delight, especially through performances as affectionate as this. Masur brings out the wealth of melody Schubert invested in this score (by his very nature, it was probably beyond him to do anything else). With a warm, clear recording, this issue is warmly welcomed, especially as it is currently the only complete *Rosamunde* on Compact Disc.

Elly Ameling sings beautifully in the vocal items, as does the Leipzig choir.

Other recordings on CD (selections from the complete score):
Boston SO/Colin Davis/Philips 410 393–2PH
Vienna SO/Nikolaus Harnoncourt/TelDec ZK8.43187
CSO/James Levine/DG413 137–2GH

SYMPHONY NO9 IN C MAJOR D944 (THE GREAT C MAJOR)
Vienna Philharmonic Orchestra
Conductor: Georg Solti
Decca 400 082–2DH
DDD Running time: 55.24
Performance: ★ ★ ★ **Recording:** ★ ★ ★

SCHUBERT

Little needs to be said about this outstanding performance: the Vienna Philharmonic at its opulent best, Solti again displaying his sympathy with Schubert, and a beautifully-balanced recording, detailed yet unforced, enhanced by the lovely acoustic of the Sofiensaal in Vienna. It is wholly satisfying in every respect, and without doubt the best-played and recorded of current CD versions.

Other recordings on CD (selection):
Cleveland O/Christoph von Dohnanyi/ Telarc CD80110

PIANO QUINTET IN A MAJOR OP114 D667 (THE TROUT QUINTET)
Andras Schiff: Piano
Members of the Hagen Quartet
Alois Posch: Double bass
Decca 411 975-2DH
DDD Running time: 44.00
Performance: ★ ★ ★
Recording: ★ ★ (★)

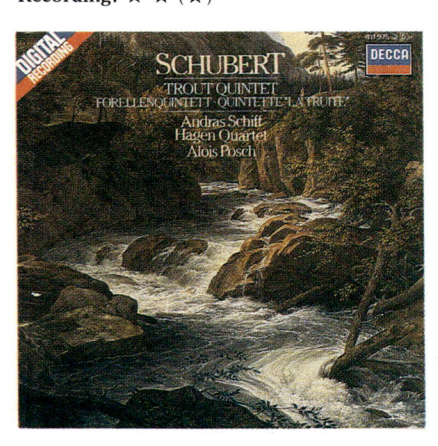

Of all the versions of Schubert's best-loved chamber work, none comes closer than this to the true spirit of the piece, the intimate, almost domestic quality of the music. Unlike, say, Brendel and the Cleveland Quartet who tend to dramatise where it is not called for, Schiff, Posch, and the three members of the Hagen family of Viennese musicians never forget the essentially genial nature of the *Trout*.

Theirs is a warm, mellow performance with just the occasional quirk of tempo to raise an eyebrow, and although the acoustic is too cavernous, the difficult balance between the five instruments has been managed well, with – thankfully – no undue emphasis on the piano, as is so often the case. However, it would have been rewarding to hear more of the viola (which has the main tune) in the second of the variations on the song *'Die Forelle:'* which gives the work its nickname; the 'cello is too dominant here. Such criticisms, though, are minor.

Other recordings on CD:
Ata Arad/Ludwig Streicher/Vienna Haydn Trio/TelDec ZK8.42695
Alfred Brendel/James van Demark/members of the Cleveland Quartet/Philips 400 078-2PH
Emil Gilels/Norbert Brainin/Peter Schidlof/ Martin Lovett/Rainer Zepperitz/DG 413 453-2GH
Sviatoslav Richter/Georg Hörtnagel/ members of the Borodin Quartet/EMI CDC7 47009-2

STRING QUARTET NO12 IN C MINOR D 703 (QUARTETTSATZ)
STRING QUARTET NO14 IN D MINOR D810 (DEATH AND THE MAIDEN)
Vermeer Quartet
TelDec ZK8.42868
DDD Running time: 49.24
Performance: ★ ★ ★
Recording: ★ ★ (★)

The forty bars of the unfinished C minor quartet constitute one of Schubert's most concentrated and ambitious explorations of sonata form, and no less far-reaching is the intensely dramatic D minor quartet, written between 1824 and 1826, and taking its nickname from the variations on Schubert's song of the same name which form the second movement.

Both works are well-played by the American Vermeer Quartet, performances that are fresh and unexaggerated. The readings have both assurance and authority, but the poignancy and sometimes painful sorrow of the D minor does not elude them.

The recording sharply defines each instrument within a pleasing acoustic, but the wide dynamic range between *ppp* and *fff*, coupled to the forward balance, could turn a naturally 'spiky' quartet sound into something too aggressive on some systems, if a 'realistic' replay level is sought.

Other recordings on CD:
(coupled as above)
Amadeus Quartet/DG 410 024-2GH
Tokyo Quartet/MMG MCD10004 (String Quartet No14 D810 only)
Brandis Quartet/Orfeo C007821
Orlando Quartet/Philips 412 127-2PH

SCHUBERT

STRING QUINTET IN C MAJOR D956
Alban Berg Quartet
Heinrich Schiff: 'Cello
EMI CDC7 47018-2
DDD Running time: 47.33
Performance: ★ ★ ★   Recording: ★ ★ ★

The C Major Quintet was one of five great chamber masterpieces composed by Schubert in the year he died, and has strong claims to be regarded as the very finest. Certainly, this must rank as one of the best performances of the work, the character of each movement perfectly caught – nowhere more so than in the lighthearted *scherzo* and its contrastingly elegaic *trio*.
  The recording is fairly forward, but with a good sense of space around the instruments and transparency to the texture.

Other recordings on CD:
Yo Yo Ma/Cleveland Quartet/CBS
   MK39134
Douglas Cummings/Lindsay Quartet/ASV
   CD DCA537

STRING QUARTET NO14 IN D MINOR D810 (DEATH AND THE MAIDEN)
Orlando Quartet
Philips 412 127-2PH
DDD Running time: 40.20
Performance: ★ ★ ★
Recording: ★ ★ (★)

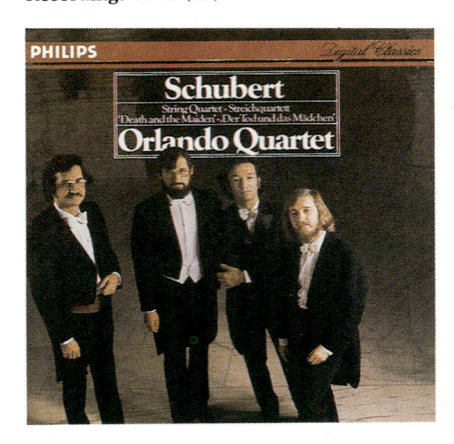

The story goes that a violinist of the quartet who first performed this work took its composer to one side and, no doubt with the best intentions, advised him to stick to songwriting. Sufficient comment for Schubert to put the work to one side (along with numerous others) where it waited seven years for its next performance, by which time the composer was dead.
  This recording attempts to offer something approaching what was heard at that 'première' by using a new critical edition. And a very fine performance it is, well-conceived and skilfully played, and effectively recorded. The only disappointment is the playing time: every competitive CD version offers a 'filler'.

PIANO TRIO IN B FLAT MAJOR OP99 D898
PIANO TRIO NO2 IN E FLAT MAJOR OP100 D929
ADAGIO IN E FLAT MAJOR OP.POSTH.148 D897 (NOTTURNO)
TRIO IN B FLAT MAJOR IN ONE MOVEMENT D28
Beaux Arts Trio
Philips 412 620-2PH2 (2 discs)
DDD Running time: 98.45
Performance: ★ ★ ★
Recording: ★ ★ (★)

Although Schubert's two completed piano trios are close in terms of date of composition (both during 1827), they are very different in temperament, the lyrical, smiling B flat Major contrasting with the more dramatic, darker-hued, but ultimately triumphant E flat Major.
  It is in the latter that the Beaux Arts Trio is at its best; a little of the gaiety of the B flat is missing in this broad, relaxed reading. However, these are performances to complement the classic versions of these works made by this same trio with one change of personnel some twenty years ago.
  The recording is close, well-integrated and very truthful, but tends to project the piano (usually at the expense of the 'cello), although this may be as much a musical effect as a technical one.

Other recordings on CD:
(Piano Trio No1 D898)
Borodin Trio/Chandos CHAN8308
Israel Piano Trio/CRD Records CRD3438
(Piano Trio No2 D929)
Borodin Trio/Chandos CHAN8324
Israel Piano Trio/CRD Records CRD3438
Les Musiciens/Harmonia Mundi/
   HMC90.1047

PIANO TRIO IN E FLAT MAJOR OP100 D929
Les Musiciens
Harmonia Mundi France HMC90.1047
AAD Running time: 47.11
Performance: ★ ★ ★   Recording: ★ ★ ★

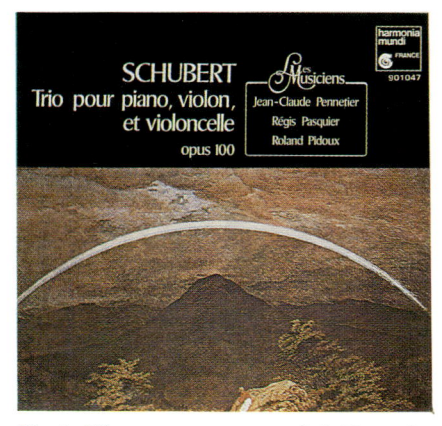

The indifferent response accorded this work at its debut was in sharp contrast to Schumann's enthusiastic description just over a year later, in 1838: he called it *'a phenomenon of inflamed heaven'*.

It is an apt description when the work is performed with the kind of passion and commitment shown by this trio of French musicians. Their playing has both urgency and vitality. and, unlike the Beaux Arts trio (reviewed elsewhere), they are recorded in a lively acoustic, and with the kind of broad image that allows each contribution to be clearly heard without losing the essential homogenity of sound.

This is one of several excitingly natural recordings of chamber and instrumental music, not to mention medieval and Renaissance repertoire, which distinguish the French Harmonica-Mundi label.

PIANO SONATA NO4 IN A MINOR D537/PIANO SONATA NO13 IN A MAJOR D664
Alfred Brendel: Piano
Philips 410 605-2PH
DDD Running time: 47.49
Performance: ★ ★   Recording: ★ ★ ★

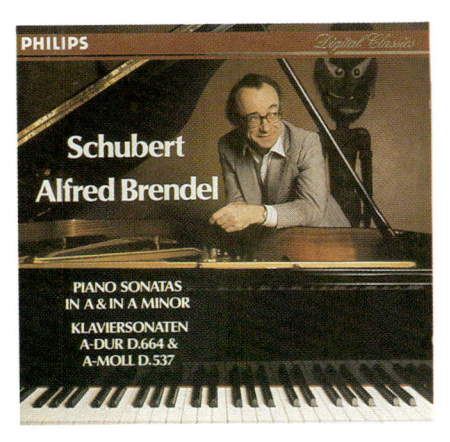

Bringing together the first and the last of Schubert's early completed sonatas makes for interesting listening. Though only some two years separates their composition (1817 and 1819) the greater poise and confidence of the A Major is apparent.

It is that simplicity which seems to be missing from Brendel's performances here. The essential flow is disturbed by the occasional over-emphasis, although there are also many nuances of style to admire. He is certainly accorded an astonishingly truthful sound by the Philips engineers. Equally recommendable is the coupling of D664, with the Sonata No17 D784, by Sviatoslav Richter (see below).

Other recordings on CD:
(Piano Sonata No4 D537)
Arturo Benedetti Michelangeli/DG 400 043-2GH
(Piano Sonata No13 D664)
Sviatoslav Richter/JVC VDC520

PIANO SONATA NO20 IN A MAJOR D959
12 LÄNDLER D790
Alfred Brendel:Piano
Philips 411 777-2PH
ADD Running time: 49.29
Performance: ★ ★ (★)
Recording: ★ ★ ★

As ever, Brendel's performance of Schubert's penultimate sonata is a deeply-considered one, with just a few quirks of tempo that might be questioned. The recording dates from 1971, but always represented Philips' piano sound at its best. Now the natural resonance and bell-like tone can be enjoyed afresh, and with greater transparency and immediacy. Tape hiss is unobtrusive, the performance is compelling.

Other recordings on CD:
Michel Dalberto/Erato ECD88116

IMPROMPTUS OP90 D899: NO1 IN C MINOR/NO2 IN E FLAT MAJOR/NO3 IN G FLAT MAJOR/NO4 IN A FLAT MAJOR IMPROMPTUS OP142 D935: NO1 IN F MINOR/NO2 IN A FLAT MAJOR/NO3 IN B FLAT MAJOR/NO4 IN F MINOR
Radu Lupu: Piano
Decca 411 711-2DH
DDD Running time: 66.33
Performance: ★ ★ ★   Recording: ★ ★ ★

The Compact Disc buyer is spoilt for choice in these most intimately lyrical of Schubert's piano works. There is little to choose in terms of performance between Brendel, Perahia and Lupu. Each in his own way produces a performance of rare sensitivity and stature, and if Lupu takes the palm, it is simply because the Decca recording is marginally the better of the three. Every nuance of his playing is clearly caught, and the sound is convincingly real.

Other recordings on CD:
Alfred Brendel/Philips 411 040-2PH
Murray Perahia/CBS MK37291

ROBERT SCHUMANN
(b. Zwickau, Saxony, Germany, 8 June 1810; d. Endenich, 29 July 1856)

He suffered from acute depression, attempting suicide and dying in an asylum.

The influence of literature on the early German Romantic composers is nowhere more evident than in the music of Robert Schumann. Perhaps it is hardly surprising, given that his father was a bookseller and publisher, with a special affection for English novelists and poets such as Scott and Byron.

The idea was that Schumann should enter the law, but at university he found greater attraction in music and took surreptious lessons. His education at Heidelberg was abruptly terminated by the authorities, ostensibly for a failure to pay his fees, but there can be little doubt that his regular bouts of drunkenness influenced the decision.

It was while taking further music tutorage with the teacher, Friedrick Wieck, that he became charmed by his young daughter, Clara, and so began one of the great love stories in music. Wieck would not allow their marriage until, when Clara reached twenty-one in 1840, he could no longer prevent it. A talented pianist herself, it was to be mainly through Clara's efforts that the world came to know Schumann's music. Schumann himself was a great admirer of Bach, and like Mendelssohn did much to revive interest in his music.

Until his marriage, he had composed only solo piano works – *Carnaval* and the *Etudes Symphoniques* were the first, along with the *Noveletten* and *Fantaisiestücke* – but Clara encouraged him to explore new areas: songs (where he excelled), chamber and orchestral music. The years 1840–44 were the happiest for him.

Sadly, Schumann had always been prone to depression, and in the next six years suffered a series of nervous breakdowns. Between times, he undertook concert tours, he conducting and Clara at the piano. In 1850 they left Dresden, which had been their home for several years, and settled in Düsseldorf, where the surrounding Rhineland inspired the Third Symphony, the *Rhenish*.

He was now, though, severely mentally ill. He attempted suicide, and subsequently asked to be placed in an asylum, and there he died.

SCHUMANN

Bernard Haitink, whose Schumann symphonies fill a vital gap in the CD catalogue.

Schumann was at his best with small-scale compositions: songs and piano works, but did write one of the most justly popular of piano concertos. His symphonies, which often display a deceptive confidence and breezy optimism, contain much fine music and attractive melody. Equally fine is the stirring piano quintet, the brilliant *Konzertstück* for four horns, and the long-neglected *Scenes from Goethe's Faust*. The Violin Concerto has both its admirers and its detractors, however. But perhaps the true spirit of Robert Schumann is still best captured in moments of simple beauty like the opening of *Kinderszenen*.

On CD, there is little choice in the symphonies, save for some strange reason, the *Rhenish*; only the Haitink set currently offers the First and Fourth. The Piano Concerto is well-represented, needless to say, but the Piano Quintet deserves coverage, too, and more alternatives in the major solo piano compositions would be welcome.

SYMPHONIES: NO1 IN B FLAT MAJOR OP38 (SPRING)/NO2 IN C MAJOR OP61/ NO3 IN E FLAT MAJOR OP97 (RHENISH)/ NO4 IN D MINOR OP120
Concertgebouw Orchestra, Amsterdam
Conductor: Bernard Haitink
Philips 416 126–2PH2 (2 discs)
DDD Running time: 130.52
Performance: ★ ★   Recording: ★ ★

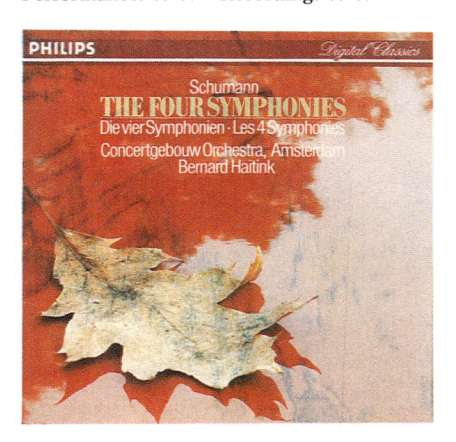

For many, Schumann's symphonies illustrate just how fine a composer he was for the piano and the voice! An extreme reaction, but it is true that the medium proved difficult for someone who was essentially a miniaturist. However, whatever their structural or textural flaws, the four works are full of interest, with many fine themes, satisfying and sometimes strikingly developed.

The first owes its inspiration to Schubert's Ninth, which Schumann had rescued from obscurity, while the Second of 1846 undoubtedly echoes his mental breakdown. The delightful Third reflects the grandeur of the Rhineland.

It is the Fourth which finds Haitink at his most responsive, in a set where he generally does not display the sympathy we might have expected from his interpretations of other composers. The recording, too, falls short of the usual Concertgebouw standard, with a shrill quality to the upper strings, a thin quality to the bass, and some blurring of texture. It is a pity because, on CD at least, the Schumann symphonies need this kind of representation.

Other recordings on CD:
(Symphony No2 Op61)
VPO/Giuseppe Sinopoli/DG 410 863–2GH
(Symphony No3 Op97)
LAPO/Carlo Maria Giulini/DG 400 062–2GH
VPO/Leonard Bernstein/DG 415 358–2GH
Concertgebouw O/Bernard Haitink/Philips 411 04–2PH
(single disc issue from above set)

SCHUMANN

'CELLO CONCERTO IN A MINOR OP129
(c/w Saint-Saëns: 'Cello Concerto No1 in A minor Op33)
Lynn Harrell: 'Cello
Cleveland Orchestra
Conductor: Neville Marriner
Decca 410 019–2DH
DDD Running time: 44.26
Performance: ★ ★ ★   Recording: ★ ★

Schumann composed his solitary 'cello concerto in 1850, since when the rather spartan orchestration has been much criticised. Indeed, the work was re-scored by – of all people – Dmitri Shostakovich. It is a mainly introspective work, drawing upon the emotions of regret and nostalgia that the 'cello can so easily conjure. By contrast, the Saint-Saëns is in the classical mould.

Lynn Harrell is equally at home in both styles, and produces fine performances of both concertos. He looms forward in the sound picture and so gets little assistance from the rather pleasant acoustic, although the 'cello tone is rich and warm. A certain edginess, however, affects both the upper register of the 'cello and the treble overall.

Other recordings on CD:
(Saint-Saëns 'Cello Concerto No1 Op33)
Yo Yo Ma/French National O/Lorin Maazel/CBS MK35848

PIANO CONCERTO IN A MINOR OP54
(c/w Weber: Konzertstück in F minor for piano and orchestra)
Alfred Brendel: Piano
London Symphony Orchestra
Conductor: Claudio Abbado
Philips 412 251–2PH
ADD Running time: 50.11
Performance: ★ ★ ★   Recording: ★ ★

Weber's romantic programme piece based on the tale of a crusader and his loved one, makes a rare and enterprising coupling here. Those looking for a recording of the Schumann concerto with something more adventurous than the Greig A minor Concerto to accompany it, would do well to investigate this issue since it not only offers a very enjoyable performance of the Weber, but an individual and deeply-considered reading of the Schumann.

The sound is full and well-defined, with a forward balance to the piano, but one that is tonally very pleasing.

Other recordings on CD (selection):
(Schumann Piano Concerto Op54 selection)
Krystian Zimerman/BPO/Herbert von Karajan/DG 410 021–2GH
Andras Schiff/Concertgebouw O/Antal Dorati/Decca 411 942–2DH
Radu Lupu/LSO/André Previn/Decca 414 432–2DH

FANTASIESTÜCKE (FANTASY PIECES) OP12
FANTASIA IN C MAJOR OP17
Alfred Brendel: Piano
Philips 411 049–2PH
DDD Running time: 57.58
Performance: ★ ★ ★   Recording: ★ ★ ★

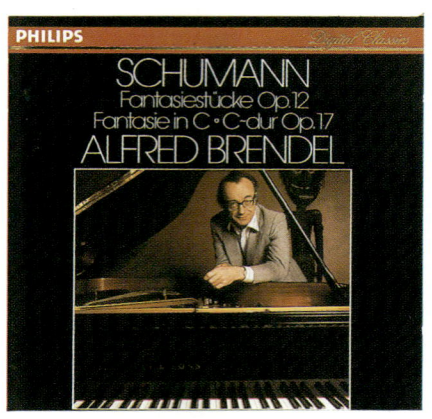

The stories of E. T. A. Hoffman were the inspiration for the *Fantasiestücke* of 1837, a widely- (and wildly-) contrasting mixture of short pieces, while the *Fantasia* Op17, which occupied Schumann between 1836 and 1838, emerged as a very liberal and romantic form of the sonata. It was dedicated, appropriately, to Liszt.

The magic of both works comes across in Brendel's imaginative and revealing performances. He is aided by a well-defined, analytical piano sound, but one that is not so close as to reduce the dynamic contrast available. Without doubt, this is one of the most rewarding recordings of Schumann's music currently on Compact Disc.

Other recordings on CD:
(*Fantasiestücke* Op12)
Friedrich Gulda/Philips 412 113–2PH

KINDERSZENEN (SCENES FROM CHILDHOOD) OP15/KREISLERIANA OP16
Martha Argerich: Piano
Deutsche Grammophon 410 653–2GH
DDD Running time: 52.15
Performance: ★ ★ (★)   Recording: ★

SCHUMANN

While Martha Argerich's affinity for this music can be readily appreciated, as can her keen awareness of the fugitive, fantastic elements in these two scores, the performances are badly let down by the oppressively hard-edged and bright piano sound. Most likely, the excessively close miking is the culprit, and more is the pity, since DG have recently been producing much more pleasing piano balances. Had the change of policy and technique come a little earlier, this could have been a really outstanding and valuable recording. Nevertheless, if the recording proves acceptable, the performances are rewarding, and the disc is noteworthy as the only CD currently available that couples *Kinderszenen* with the equally popular *Kreisleriana*.

Other recordings on CD:
(*Kinderszenen* – complete)
Maria-João Pires/Erato ECD88092
Vladimir Horowitz/RCA RD84572

KINDERSZENEN (SCENES FROM CHILDHOOD) OP15/WALDSZENEN (FOREST SCENES) OP82/BUNTE BLÄTTER (LEAVES OF DIFFERENT COLOURS) OP99 NOS1, 2, 4
Maria João Pires: Piano
Erato ECD88092
DDD Running time: 51.46
Performance: ★ ★ ★   Recording: ★ ★ ★

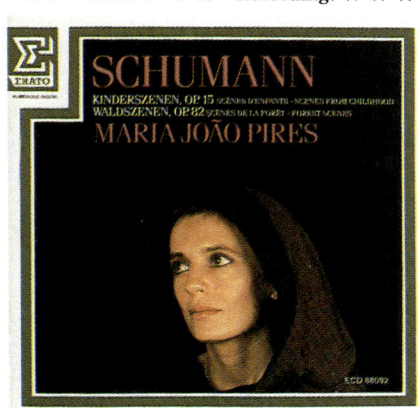

The thirteen delightful pieces that make up *Kinderszenen* are, of course, among Schumann's best-known piano compositions, but the couplings here are of rarer stuff. The *Waldszenen*, written in 1849, sixteen years after *Kinderszenen*, show how the composer's tonal palette had broadened in the period. Items such as *Einsame Blümen* (*Lonely Flowers*) are true gems.

The *Bunte Blätter*, of diverse inspiration, were written over the period 1832–49, and nine of the pieces are included here, among them the best-known, the *Albumblätter*.

Sympathetic and beautifully-judged interpretations from Maria João Pires, are given a close but very rounded and clear recording to match. This is fine Schumann playing. Given the poor CD choice in Schumann's music for solo piano, this issue becomes essential for lovers of the composer and his work.

Other recordings on CD:
(*Kinderszenen*)
Martha Argerich/DG 410 653–2GH
Vladimir Horowitz/RCA RD84572

SYMPHONIC STUDIES IN THE FORM OF VARIATIONS OP13/TOCCATA OP7
(c/w Beethoven: Piano Sonata No32 in C minor Op111)
Ivo Pogorelich: Piano
Deutsche Grammophon 410 520–2GH
DDD Running time: 64.02
Performance: ★ ★
Recording: ★ ★(★)

Both the Toccata and the Etudes date from 1834, the latter one of Schumann's most powerful and complex solo piano compositions – truly symphonic in scale and content. However, Pogorelich's approach to the solemn introduction is not so much imposing as self-indulgent, and it proves to be the prelude to a performance that excites and frustrates in almost equal measure. There is, indeed, much that is revealing about Schumann, but almost as much that speaks volumes about Pogorelich.

The Beethoven is more successful, a finely-wrought reading which, like the Schumann, does have the benefit of a crystal-clear recording.

Other recordings on CD (Schumann Symphonic Studies):
Maurizio Pollini/DG 410 916–2GH

SYMPHONIC STUDIES IN THE FORM OF VARIATIONS OP13/ARABESKE IN C MAJOR OP18
Maurizio Pollini: Piano
Deutsche Grammophon 410 916–2GH
DDD Running time: 38.36
Performance: ★ ★ ★   Recording: ★ ★

In this superb performance of the *Symphonic Studies*, Maurizio Pollini elects to use the first of the two editions of the score, the main difference between it and the more commonly used second edition being the inclusion of a number of variations which Schumann later deleted.

An overall grasp and impulse characterises Pollini's reading, something Pogorelich's controversial performance (also on DG) often lacks. There is a unity and consistency here, and the playing of the attractive *Arabeske* is no less persuasive, although as a 'filler' it hardly compares with Pogorelich's Beethoven in either quality or quantity.

Pollini's recording, although similarly close-focussed, is less tonally agreeable than that given Pogorelich, but if the *Symphonic Studies* are the key work for you, his must be adjudged the most satisfying interpretation.

DMITRI SHOSTAKOVICH
(b. St Petersburg, Russia, 25 September 1906; d. Moscow, USSR, 9 August 1975)

A child of the Bolshevik Revolution – one of his first compositions, written age 11, was a funeral march in memory of its victims – Dmitri Shostakovich weathered for almost six decades a curious, sometimes farcically ambivalent relationship with Soviet authority. Honours arrived in about equal measure with denunciations; for much of the Stalin era he lived in fear, yet after 1941 and the international acclaim accorded the *Leningrad* Symphony, he had 'untouchable' status, eventually acknowledged as not only the finest composer to emerge from the Soviet Union, but one of the great artists of this century.

Yet much of Shostakovich's music, to use a well-worn but nevertheless accurate description, remains ambiguous and enigmatic. With hindsight, it is possible to see much of his 'public' music existing on two levels. For those who sought in it an affirmation of ideology and an effective tool of propaganda, it fulfilled those roles. More perceptive ears heard something very different: marches of triumph were just so much pompous bombast; the smiling, dancing exits from darkness into sunshine were grotesque jokes. Throughout, the paradox that was Shostakovich's life extended into his music.

His father was an engineer of Polish extraction, his mother a fine pianist and his first teacher. By the time he came to attend its Conservatoire, the name of his home town had been changed to Petrograd and was destined to quickly alter once more, to Leningrad.

They were difficult times for all and, when his father died in 1922, Shostakovich was forced to earn money playing accompaniments to silent cinema films. It was around this time that he developed the tuberculosis which was to trouble him for some years, but fortunes changed in 1926 with the immediate popularity of his First Symphony, not only in the Soviet Union but in the West, through performances by a number of eminent conductors. Shostakovich was determined to become an original and individual voice in music. It was a feeling stimulated by exposure to much new European music during the relative cultural freedom of the 'twenties. The 'thirties, however, introduced an era of artistic tyranny, as Stalin resolved to eliminate what he termed the 'anti-people' elements from Soviet art.

Shostakovich first felt the crack of the whip in 1936 when the

Right: Tair Salakhov's portrait of the composer.
Below: The Nevsky Prospekt, one of the main avenues of Leningrad, his home city.

dictator himself stormed out of a performance of the opera, *Lady Macbeth of Mtsensk*, which had enjoyed great popular success up to that point. The next day, *Pravda* poured scorn on the work in a notorious article titled, *Muddle instead of Music*. Fearing the consequences, the composer withdrew his Fourth Symphony, guessing it would come in for similar attack, and began work on a Fifth that would be more overtly appealing to those in power. The premiere was a triumph, Shostakovich was rehabilitated, and the symphony remains his most popular work to this day.

The war years, ironically, proved the least troublesome for Shostakovich. He was allowed to depict tragedy and terror because, it was being inflicted by an external enemy, not, as was the case earlier, by one within.

However, 1946 brought another purge on Soviet art: the nation's leading composers, Shostakovich, Myaskovsky and Prokofiev, were singled out for severe criticism, their music effectively banned from performance.

But Stalin had only four more years to exercise his unpredictable whims. His death in 1953 motivated Shostakovich to his greatest symphonic utterance, the Tenth, and in the ensuing 'thaw', both old and new works were performed throughout the Soviet Union. There was little 'thaw' in his music, however; he was only too aware that, even if the faces in power had changed, the face of power itself had not.

From 1966, he was dogged by ill-health, finally succumbing in 1975, while being treated in the elite Kremlin Hospital. There were effusive tributes from the Soviet leadership, as well as from all round the world, and Shostakovich was buried with full honours in Moscow, sadly not in Leningrad as he had wished.

Thanks mainly to the efforts of Bernard Haitink and Decca, the symphonies are reasonably well represented on CD. It is to be hoped that Decca will continue to re-issue the older recordings in this series. The most serious absentees on CD, though, are the fifteen string quartets, as intimately autobiographical in their way as, say, those of Beethoven and Bartók, and essential to an understanding of Shostakovich's art.

SYMPHONY NO1 IN F MINOR OP10
SYMPHONY NO9 IN E FLAT MAJOR OP70
London Philharmonic Orchestra
Conductor: Bernard Haitink
Decca 414 677-2DH
DDD Running time: 57.23
Performance: ★ ★ ★   Recording: ★ ★ ★

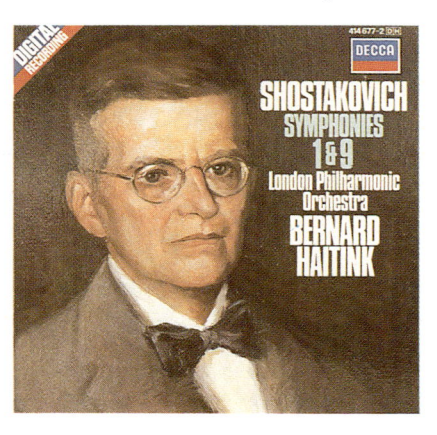

As the Second World War drew to its end, Shostakovich eventually began work on the 'official' celebration of victory that was expected of him. But in his heart he could not come to terms with the prospect and, after struggling to complete the first movement, scrapped the whole idea. Instead, his Ninth Symphony simply expressed joy and relief that the war was over, with no overblown eulogy for the victors, and the work is all the finer for it. Full of charm and wit, it also cleverly makes its point about the empty rhetorical style that those in authority would have preferred him to adopt.

The First Symphony, written twenty years earlier in 1925 as his graduation exercise from the Leningrad Conservatoire, is similarly engaging. It has its youthful flaws, and the diverse influences are detectable, but it is a formidable debut.

Little needs to be said about the performance and recording here, other than observing that in every way it maintains the high standards set by the rest of Haitink's cycle, one of the best advertisements extant for the benefits of digital recording.

Other recordings on CD:
(Symphony No1 only)
SNO/Neeme Järvi/Chandos CHAN8411

SHOSTAKOVICH

SYMPHONY NO5 IN D MINOR OP47
Concertgebouw Orchestra, Amsterdam
Conductor: Bernard Haitink
Decca 410 017-2DH
DDD Running time: 49.55
Performance: ★ ★ ★   Recording: ★ ★ ★

The criticism he incurred in the mid-1930s initially prompted Shostakovich to withdraw his Fourth Symphony before a single performance had been given and then, in 1937, to compose a Fifth. While not the 'anti-people' music he had been earlier accused of writing, the Fifth was only superficially the heroic, pro-Soviet work the authorities accepted it to be.

At its first performance, the composer is said to have described the symphony as *'a Soviet artist's reply to just criticism'*. There has been speculation, however, that the word 'just' was a later addition to the phrase – with altogether different implications for our understanding of the comment.

The triumph is surely a hollow one, the confident posturing an empty gesture: the core of the work is conflict and tragedy. Yet, despite its ambivalent nature, it is one of Shostakovich's most accessible works, and certainly his most popular, as the choice of recordings demonstrates.

First choice must be Haitink, although Maazel is not far behind. Direct, truthful, and unlike Shostakovich's compatriot, Rostropovich, utterly without idiosyncracy, Haitink's reading is also graced by one of the finest, most naturally impressive recordings of recent years. A magnificent achievement by all concerned.

Other recordings on CD:
NYPO/Leonard Bernstein/CBS MK35854
Cleveland O/Lorin Maazel/Telarc CD80067
National SO of Washington/Mstislav
   Rostropovich/DG 410 509-2GH

SYMPHONY NO6 IN B MINOR OP54
SYMPHONY NO11 IN G MINOR OP103
'THE YEAR 1905'
OVERTURE ON RUSSIAN AND KIRGHIZ FOLK THEMES OP115
Concertgebouw Orchestra, Amsterdam
Conductor: Bernard Haitink
Decca 411 939-2DH (2 disc set)
DDD Running time: 102.42
Performance: ★ ★ ★   Recording: ★ ★ ★

Two highly contrasted symphonies: the introspective, very personal, 'pure' music of the Sixth, and the overt propaganda of the Eleventh, written with a mass audience firmly in mind. As the sub-title *1905* implies, it is a programme symphony, commemorating the horrific massacre of unarmed protestors by Czarist guards in that year, one of the events on the road to the revolution of 1917.

Unashamedly exciting, dramatic, even crude, but nevertheless effective, the Eleventh, like its companion, the *Leningrad*, can sound downright banal in the wrong hands. Not with Haitink, however, who invests the work with a musical respectability and dignity without compromising its 'heart-on-the-sleeve' emotional tug or its passages of overwhelming aggression.

The performances of the Sixth, and the attractive overture on folk themes are no less persuasive, and the recording, in the way that has characterized this Haitink cycle, is magnificent – and, at times, quite shattering!

Recommendable versions of two other 'programme' symphonies, Nos7 and 12, have also been reissued in a two-CD set by Decca.

Other recordings on CD:
(Symphony No6 only)
SNO/Neeme Järvi/Chandos CHAN8411
(Symphony No11 only)
USSR SO/Rozhdestvensky/Melodiya 880 019

SYMPHONY NO8 IN C MINOR OP65
Concertgebouw Orchestra, Amsterdam
Conductor: Bernard Haitink
Decca 411 616-2DH
DDD Running time: 61.42
Performance: ★ ★ ★   Recording: ★ ★ ★

The Eighth is the second of the so-called 'War Symphonies', a trilogy which begins with the heroic, if rather shallow, *Leningrad* and ends with the heartfelt relief and light-headed joy of the Ninth. More substantial than both, the Eighth mirrors the grief, suffering and pessimism of the Russian people during the sombre days of 1943.

The epic opening movement is one of Shostakovich's most intensely tragic utterances, (and how CD benefits its moments of still contemplation and near silence), while the message of the two central movements is unmistakeable: the grotesque, pounding third was once described as a *Toccata of Death*. The lighter final movement still fails to dispel the air of tension and disquiet. Little wonder the composer was officially censored for writing such music of *'unrelieved gloom'*.

The Symphony makes its full impact through a recording of staggering power, range and realism, not to mention a performance of greatness.

SYMPHONY NO10 IN E MINOR OP93
Berlin Philharmonic Orchestra
Conductor: Herbert von Karajan
Deutsche Grammophon 413 361-2GH
DDD Running time: 51.20
Performance: ★ ★ ★   Recording: ★ ★

'It's about Stalin, and the Stalin years.' The composer's own description of his Tenth symphony – or perhaps not, if you accept the Soviet view that Shostakovich's memoirs, published after his death, are a fiction. But it is not difficult to see the second movement, especially, as a ferocious picture of unstoppable evil and indiscriminate brutality. Yet the work ends in almost jaunty mood, something that many critics have found irreconcilable with what has gone before. What is indisputable is that the Tenth is among the greatest of Shostakovich's symphonies, arguably the greatest.

Karajan's 1982 digital recording is, in most respects, a worthy successor to his memorable mid-'sixties version. The symphony unfolds with compelling authority, its moods perfectly judged, right through to the inherent ambiguity of the final movement.

SYMPHONY NO15 IN A MAJOR OP141
USSR State Symphony Orchestra
Conductor: Gennady Rozhdestvensky
JVC/Melodia VDC528
DDD Running time: 43.01
Performance: ★ ★ ★   Recording: ★ (★)

After the song-cycle symphonies, Nos13 and 14, it is surprising that Shostakovich returned to the classical four-movement, purely instrumental format for his Fifteenth and – as it was to prove – last symphony. But if the structure was familiar, the content was puzzling in the extreme. As well as quoting from his own works and those of Wagner, the first movement includes an unmistakable references to the main theme from Rossini's *William Tell* overture. What provoked its inclusion we shall never know, although the composer's son, Maxim, who conducted the symphony's first performance in 1972, relates that his father described that movement as a 'toy shop'.

This performance is almost as perplexing, combining as it does the best and worst in recording techniques. On the plus side, there is a lively spaciousness (it appears to have been a concert taping to judge from the sleeve pictures) with excellent timbres and quite the most explosive bass drum on disc. Unfortunately, the engineer insists on bringing forward woodwind and percussion instruments at will, making a nonsense of the imaging and perspectives.

Rozhdestvensky's interpretation is full-blooded and wholly committed. He makes a highly persuasive and involving argument for this symphony, and, while this production may have its faults, lack of excitement most certainly is not one of them.

'CELLO CONCERTO NO1 OP107
'CELLO CONCERTO NO2 OP126
Heinrich Schiff: 'Cello
Bavarian Radio Symphony Orchestra
Conductor: Maxim Shostakovich
Philips 412 526-2PH
DDD Running time: 61.25
Performance: ★ ★ ★   Recording: ★ ★ ★

Two concertos of contrasting character, and contrasting fortunes: the First, premiered in 1959, is now well-established in the 'cello repertoire. Yet the Second, written seven years later, is all but unknown. Its only previous recording, by the dedicatee of both concertos, Mstislav Rostropovich, has been long deleted, so this 1985 issue is especially welcome in demonstrating how unjust that neglect has been.

The CD features compelling performances, both from the masterly soloist and the orchestra, under the direction of the composer's son. The recording is similarly excellent, broadly spacious and with convincing stereo perspectives.

Other recordings on CD:
(Concerto No1 only)
Yo Yo Ma/Philadelphia O/Eugene Ormandy/CBS MK37840
Raphael Wallfisch/ECO/Geoffrey Simon/Chandos CHAN8322

PIANO QUINTET IN G MINOR OP57
PIANO TRIO NO2 IN E MINOR OP67
Mimi Zweig: Violin; Jerry Horner: Viola
The Borodin Trio
Chandos CHAN8342
DDD Running time: 65.27
Performance: ★ ★ ★   Recording: ★ ★

Two of Shostakovich's most important chamber works are coupled on this disc. The earlier, the Quintet, was first performed in Moscow in 1940, with the composer accompanying the Beethoven Quartet, and it found immediate popularity with critics and public alike. The Piano Trio of 1944 can be reckoned as one of the few successful works in that form to have been written this century.

Shostakovich dedicated the Trio to the memory of a friend who died in a Nazi concentration camp and through it he seems to voice his protest, not just at that death but at the millions more brought about by persecution. As with so much of his music, any gaiety is forced, the laughter becomes mockery, and what comes over as banal and shallow is quite intentional, as surely was the Jewish flavour evident in some of the music.

These intense, fluent and authorative performances are a little marred by the recording which rather distractingly emphasises the players' breathing, and which sets the piano a little too far behind the strings. A plausible acoustic, though, and overall a bright, wide-ranging sound.

JEAN SIBELIUS
(b. Hämeenlinna, Finland, 8 December 1865; d. Järvenpää, Finland, 20 September 1957)

The young Sibelius: once the influence of Tchaikovsky had gone, the voice became wholly individual.

The development evident in the music of Sibelius makes for fascinating listening, from the lush romanticism of the first two symphonies to the taut economy of the Sixth and Seventh; from the brusque nationalism of *Finlandia* to those other evocations of his homeland, the haunting *Swan of Tuonela* and dark mystery of *Tapiola*. What he felt for Finland, its landscape and its legends, fired his musical imagination throughout his creative life.

Sibelius' father died when he was just two, but his mother determined that he should receive a good education and, at nineteen, he entered Helsinki University, initially to study law. After a year, he transferred to the Conservatoire and to music. The winning of a travelling scholarship took him to Berlin and Vienna, and later, in 1897, the Finnish government showed both generosity and good judgement in granting him an annual state pension for life.

During these early years, Finland did not exist as an independent nation state; it was under the rule of the Russian Czars, but a strong nationalist movement was developing, and in *Finlandia*, Sibelius wrote its anthem. The work had an impact that extended far beyond Finland, however: it made his name known in Britain and in the years preceding the First World War Sibelius toured Europe and the United States to a warm reception everywhere.

He completed his Third and Fourth Symphonies, the latter marking a distinct change in outlook and temperament, and the attractive Violin Concerto. The heroic Fifth Symphony was a product of the war years.

Latterly, Sibelius left his home at Järvenpää only rarely, and after the completion of his Seventh Symphony, he more-or-less abandoned composition for the last twenty-seven years of his life, although he took a keen interest in contemporary music.

Sibelius' was a wholly individual voice (once he had shaken off the ghost of Tchaikovsky) and his touch was unmistakeable: not so much the statement of themes as their gradual, fragmentary evolution, the broad, yearning character of which readily conjures the sparse expanses and cold sunlight of an Arctic landscape.

Gradually, he became as isolated from the European musical mainstream as his country was isolated geographically, although his popularity in Britain remained fairly constant, not least due to the advocacy of Thomas Beecham.

Sibelius' fascinating legacy is reasonably well-served on CD.

SYMPHONY NO1 IN E MINOR OP39
FINLANDIA OP26:7
Gothenburg Symphony Orchestra
Conductor: Neeme Järvi
BIS CD-221
DDD Running time: 47.23
Performance: ★ ★ ★   Recording: ★ ★ ★

Like Brahms, Sibelius came late to the symphonic medium: his First, richly melodic and characterised by a 'yearning' motif that haunts all four movements (and whose mood was to find expression in much else that he wrote), was completed in 1899 when the composer was thirty-four. Despite its apparently wilful, almost Wagnerian, passions, the First Symphony was also his most coherently conceived writing to date.

It was patriotic fervour, however, that inspired the famous tone poem, *Finlandia* composed in the same year: *'pure inspiration'* was how Sibelius described it.

Both works receive dramatic and spontaneous performances from Järvi and the excellent Swedish orchestra.

Other recordings on CD:
SNO/Alexander Gibson/Chandos
   CHAN8344

SYMPHONY NO2 IN D MAJOR OP43
Philharmonia Orchestra
Conductor: Vladimir Ashkenazy
Decca 410 206-2DH
DDD Running time: 46.09
Performance: ★ ★ ★   Recording: ★ ★ ★

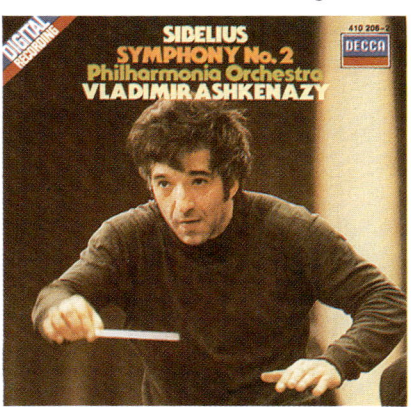

Like its predecessor, the Second Symphony is firmly rooted in the romantic tradition, the influence of Tchaikovsky being readily apparent. But its stirring and memorable themes are uniquely Sibelius.

Ashkenazy's version combines a recording of natural depth and orchestral balance and rich tonal colour – typical, in fact, of recordings made in London's Kingsway Hall – with a vigorously expressive, almost volatile performance that fully points the contrasts of this work. The romance, the passion are paramount, which is surely what Sibelius intended, and the effect is achieved by some splendid playing from the Philharmonia Orchestra. A half-second of totally lost ambience in the *andante* gives a momentary distraction, however.

Other recordings on CD:
SNO/Alexander Gibson/Chandos
   CHAN8303
Gothenburg SO/Neeme Järvi/BIS CD–252
Cleveland O/Yoel Levi/Telarc CD80095

SYMPHONY NO3 IN C MAJOR OP52
SYMPHONY NO6 IN D MINOR OP104
Philharmonia Orchestra
Conductor: Vladimir Ashkenazy
Decca 414 267-2DH
DDD Running time: 58.05
Performance: ★ ★ (★)
Recording: ★ ★ ★

The Third marks a significant change in Sibelius' symphonic style as the romanticism of the first two symphonies, and the influence of Grieg and Tchaikovsky, is replaced by a burgeoning classicism. The search for symphonic unity, which came to dominate his creative thinking, makes itself felt in this majestic work, completed in 1907.

Sixteen years later, out-of-step with mainstream European music, Sibelius expressed his feelings of isolation in the Sixth Symphony. It is a powerful, gripping work, one that mingles cool restraint with the bark of defiance.

Ashkenazy has the measure of both works, especially the Sixth, the first movement of which has a noble breadth to it, and the second a riveting intensity.

Karajan's memorable Sixth, dating from the mid-'sixties, has been remastered for CD and now comes coupled to an equally powerful account of the Fourth Symphony. It is a recommendable alternative.

Other recordings on CD:
(Symphony No3)
SNO/Alexander Gibson/Chandos
   CHAN8389
(Symphony No6)
BPO/Herbert von Karajan/DG 415 107-2GH
SNO/Alexander Gibson/Chandos
   CHAN8389

SYMPHONY NO3 IN C MAJOR OP52
KING CHRISTIAN II: SUITE
Gothenburg Symphony Orchestra
Conductor: Neeme Järvi
BIS CD-228
DDD Running time: 54.50
Performance: ★ ★ ★   Recording: ★ ★ ★

This is an exceptional performance of the Third, most beautifully played by the Swedish orchestra, and naturally but impressively recorded, making the fullest use of the fine acoustic of the Gothenburg Concert Hall. Along with the First and Sixth Symphonies, this is the best of Neeme Järvi's Sibelius cycle.

Additionally, it is good to have a modern recording of the suite from the incidental music Sibelius was persuaded to write for a

SIBELIUS

play by his friend, Adolf Paul: *King Christian II*. The music, dating from 1898, complements what is a powerful drama. It is worthy of greater exposure, including as it does one of the composer's loveliest inspirations: the *Elegie*.

This issue provides a recommendable alternative to Ashkenazy's Third for those preferring Karajan's coupling of the Fourth and Sixth Symphonies.

SYMPHONY NO 4 IN A MINOR OP63
LUONNOTAR OP70*/FINLANDIA OP26
Elisabeth Söderström:Soprano*
Philharmonia Orchestra
Conductor: Vladimir Ashkenazy
Decca 400 056-2DH
DDD Running time: 50.20
Performance: ★ ★ ★
Recording: ★ ★(★)

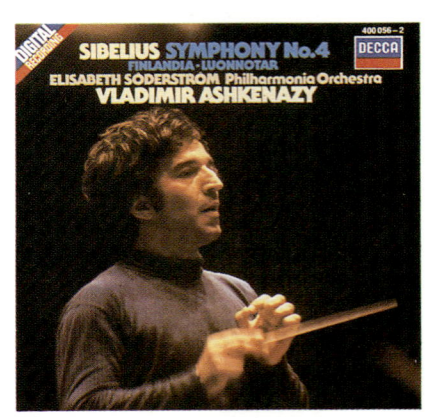

Ashkenazy is wholly in tune with the temperament of this austere, often sombre work which (not entirely surprisingly) has never enjoyed the popularity of the First, Second or Fifth Symphonies. Composed between 1910 and 1911, the Fourth is spare in its colouring, inevitably evoking images of desolate Arctic landscapes. It was another stage in the purifying of Sibelius' musical vocabulary, and it is noteworthy that he asked for the symphony's brooding slow movement to be played at his funeral.

There is no shortage of drama or tension here, but the recording, for once in this series, is somewhat disappointing. Although possessing great immediacy and atmosphere, the close balancing of the woodwind mars the 'voices in the vastness' effect, and the upper strings take on a bright edge in the fortes. Some of the usual Kingsway Hall height and depth seems lacking, too.

That said, however, this remains a superb performance of the Fourth, and the two fillers, including a magical *Luonnotar* from Elisabeth Söderström, are well worth having.

Other recordings on CD:
(Symphony No4)
Gothenburg SO/Neeme Järvi/BIS CD-263
BPO/Herbert von Karajan/DG 415 107-2GH
SNO/Alexander Gibson/Chandos CHAN8388
(*Luonnotar*)
Phyllis Bryn-Julson/SNO/Alexander Gibson/Chandos CHAN8395/6
M A Häggander/Gothenburg SO/Jorma Panula/BIS CD-270

SYMPHONY NO5 IN E FLAT MAJOR OP82
NIGHT-RIDE AND SUNRISE: TONE POEM OP55
Philharmonia Orchestra
Conductor: Simon Rattle
EMI CDC7 47006-2
DDD Running time: 46.11
Performance: ★ ★ ★   Recording: ★ ★ ★

One of Simon Rattle's finest recordings to date, this performance of the heroic, extrovert Fifth of 1915 (so removed in temperament from its predecessor) comes up superbly well in its Compact Disc transfer. With an atmospheric and naturally-balanced sound, spacious, well-layered and detailed, this is undoubtedly the best all-round version currently available on CD, especially with playing of such polish and fluency from the Philharmonia.

The coupling of *Night-Ride and Sunrise* is a rare and valuable bonus, one of Sibelius' most evocative compositions.

Other recordings on CD:
(Symphony No5 Op82)
BPO/Herbert von Karajan/DG 415 108-2GH
Philharmonia O/Vladimir Ashkenazy/Decca 410 016-2DM
Gothenburg SO/Neeme Järvi/BIS CD-222
SNO/Alexander Gibson/Chandos CHAN8388
(*Night-Ride and Sunrise*)
SNO/Alexander Gibson/Chandos CHAN8395/6

SYMPHONY NO7 IN C MAJOR OP105
TAPIOLA: SYMPHONIC POEM OP112
Philharmonia Orchestra
Conductor: Vladimir Ashkenazy
Decca 411 935-2DH
DDD Running time: 40.37
Performance: ★ ★ (★)
Recording: ★ ★ (★)

With the Seventh, Sibelius finally achieved the kind of symphonic unity that had always been his goal. He once said that what he admired about the genre was its *'severity of form and the profound logic that created an inner connection between all the motifs'*. The Seventh certainly achieves that. In a single movement it seamlessly threads together enough ideas to fill any four-movement symphony. The logic of the process is irresistible; the outcome a triumphant resolution.

Completed the year after the Symphony, in 1925, *Tapiola* is the greatest of Sibelius' symphonic poems, an intense, brooding, almost fearsome evocation of Tapio, the Finnish god of the forests. Ashkenazy splendidly captures the disturbing mood of this piece, and offers almost as fine a performance of the Seventh. The recording lacks some depth compared with the best from this source, but there is no denying the power generated in the symphony's overwhelming climax, reproduced with a new clarity on CD.

Other recordings on CD:
(Symphony No7)
BPO/Herbert von Karajan/DG 415 108-2GH
SNO/Alexander Gibson/Chandos CHAN8344

SIBELIUS

TONE POEMS: FINLANDIA OP26/ TAPIOLA OP112/LEGEND: THE SWAN OF TUONELA OP22 NO2/VALSE TRISTE OP44
Berlin Philharmonic Orchestra
Conductor: Herbert von Karajan
Deutsche Grammophon 413 755-2GH
DDD Running time: 43.56
Performance: ★ ★ ★
Recording: ★ ★ (★)

As a representative collection of the 'popular' Sibelius, this could hardly be bettered: only the *Karelia* suite is missing (and could have been included, too!). The performances are all you would expect from a conductor whose empathy with Sibelius has always been quite special. Karajan is able to bring a rare feeling of drama to *Finlandia*, and an equally powerful sense of mystery to *Tapiola*. He can, of course, rely upon the eloquent and sensitive contribution of his orchestra, witness Gerhard Stempnik's lovely cor anglais solo in *The Swan of Tuonela*, second of the *Four Legends*. The *Valse Triste* from the incidental music to *Kuolema* is no less haunting.

Other recordings on CD (selection):
(*Finlandia*)
Philharmonia O/Vladimir Ashkenazy/Decca 400 056-2DH
(*Tapiola*)
Philharmonia O/Vladimir Ashkenazy/Decca 411 935-2DH
SNO/Alexander Gibson/Chandos CHAN8395/6
(*The Swan of Tuonela*)
SNO/Alexander Gibson/Chandos CHAN8394
ASMF/Neville Marriner/Philips 412 727-2PH
(*Valse Triste*)
ASMF/Neville Marriner/Decca 411 933-2DH

VIOLIN CONCERTO IN D MINOR OP47
(c/w **Sinding**: Suite for violin and orchestra Op10)
Itzhak Perlman: Violin
Pittsburgh Symphony Orchestra
Conductor: André Previn
EMI CDC7 47167-2
ADD Running time: 44.57
Performance: ★ ★ (★)
Recording: ★ ★ (★)

Perlman's is a dazzling performance of Sibelius' solitary concerto, one of his early works, wholly romantic in temperament and with the imprint of Tchaikovsky discernible throughout. Yet it was some years after its 1905 première — under the baton of Richard Strauss — before it attained a place in public affection comparable to that given other great romantic concertos, such as Tchaikovsky's.
Here, Perlman and Previn take an essentially broad and eloquent view of the work. The violin is balanced slightly forward, but there is no want of weight or detail from the orchestra. Indeed, it is an exceptionally richly-textured, full-bodied sound, amply resonant and, coupled to the performance, makes for thrilling listening.
The Norwegian composer, Christian August Sinding, was a contemporary of Sibelius and his technically demanding Suite (one of three dating from the 1880s) is played with enormous skill and verve by Perlman. It is a rare and impressive 'fill-up' to the concerto, but those looking for the best value would do well to consider Pierre Amoyal's Erato disc, where both the Sibelius and Tchaikovsky concertos are appropriately coupled. The performances are fine, if not the first choices in either work, but do add up to sixty-seven minutes-plus of music.

Other recordings on CD:
(Sibelius Violin Concerto Op47)
Gidon Kremer/Philharmonia O/Riccardo Muti/EMI CDC7 47110-2
Yuval Yaron/LPO/Herbert Soudant/PRT CDPCN14
Dylana Jenson/Philadelphia O/Eugene Ormandy/RCA RD84548
Pierre Amoyal/Philharmonia O/Charles Dutoit/Erato ECD88109

STRING QUARTET IN A MINOR
STRING QUARTET IN B FLAT MAJOR OP4
Sibelius Academy Quartet
Finlandia FACD345
DDD Running time: 59.40
Performance: ★ ★ ★   Recording: ★ ★ ★

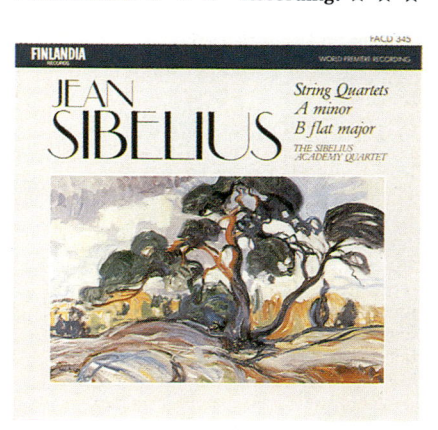

Long before he tackled the symphony, Sibelius was a prodigious composer of chamber music, most of which is now forgotten. While not suggesting that these two quartets dating from 1889 and 1890 are neglected masterpieces, they are far from being mere apprentice works. He wrote the first while studying at the Helsinki Music Institute and, although the structure may owe something to Mozart and Beethoven, the lyrical style undoubtedly shows the influence of Grieg.
The B flat quartet is also classical-cum-romantic in demeanour, with a variation-form second movement based on a Finnish folk-song, and a swirling waltz-like *scherzo*. The finale, after stepping out with a swagger, ends on a note of restful repose.
The Sibelius Academy Quartet, who play with a confident rhythmic flow and great spirit, are recorded in a well-chosen church acoustic which becomes pleasantly lively during the louder passages. With a broad but well-integrated stereo image, detailing is excellent – every strand of sound can be picked out and the 'cello, despite the resonant location, is notably clean and free of 'boom'. Its tonal quality is lovely, as is that of the other three instruments. This is a wholly enjoyable discovery.

JOHANN STRAUSS II
(b. Vienna, Austria, 25 October 1825; d. Vienna, Austria 3 June 1899)

Although it was Johann Strauss II who came to be known as 'The Waltz King', the furnishing of dance music for Viennese society was more a family affair, begun by Johann Strauss I ('The Father of the Waltz'), who had his own touring dance orchestra, and continued by his three sons, Josef and Eduard as well as Johann the younger.

The Strausses provided undemanding, escapist, yet undeniably skilfully-crafted music for the capital of an Empire which, after 1840 was moving into a long, gradual, but inexorable decline. Their music was a vital part of Viennese life, guaranteed to keep spirits high (even after the stock exchange crash of 1873), and its composers were fully aware of their worth. They were not above writing overtly commercial pieces: *Wiener Bon Bons* was composed for the annual manufacturers' ball in 1866, while Josef Strauss' *Feuerfest (Fireproof)* commemorated the making of their 20,000th product by a company of Viennese safemakers.

They were also music-makers 'by royal appointment', commanded to appear at the court ball to celebrate the marriage of the Emperor Franz Josef and Empress Elisabeth, and later, in 1899, to commemorate the fortieth anniversary of the composer's accession, for which Johann Strauss II wrote the *Emperor Waltz (Kaiserwalzer)*, a superbly-wrought composition by any standards. As, of course, is his most famous waltz *The Blue Danube*, an exquisite tone poem.

The Strauss family's music certainly encapsulated the spirit of its time and place, as well as being intensely patriotic. They knew precisely what their public wanted from them, and had the talents to fulfil amply that demand.

Their music is well-represented on Compact Disc, mainly through Deutsche Grammophon's Vienna recordings.

EMPEROR WALTZ OP437/TRITSCH-TRATSCH POLKA OP214/ROSES FROM THE SOUTH OP388/OVERTURE: THE GIPSY BARON/ANNEN-POLKA OP117/WINE, WOMEN and SONG OP333/AT THE HUNT OP373
Berlin Philharmonic Orchestra
Conductor: Herbert von Karajan
Deutsche Grammophon 410 022-2GH
DDD Running time: 45.07
Performance: ★ ★ ★
Recording: ★ ★ (★)

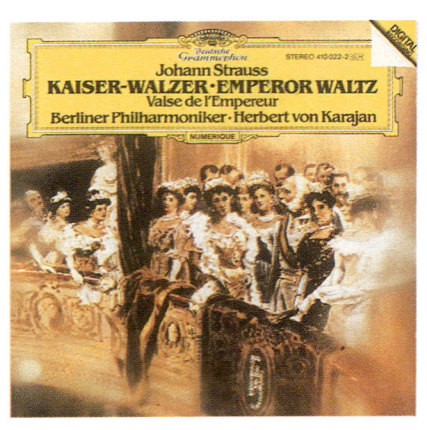

The imperial qualities of the *Emperor Waltz* are fully portrayed in Karajan's performance, one of several Strauss favourites splendidly played here. It is all most opulent and grand, with a suitably impressive recording to match.

Certainly the sound is an improvement on that of the maestro's first Strauss family Compact Disc issue (DG 400 026-2GH). Lovers of the music of the Strausses and Vienna would also enjoy Karajan's other compilation entitled *Radetzky March* on DG 410 027-2GH. Again, superlative performances are enhanced by a recording of good depth and natural balance, and a rich ambience.

Another not to be missed (in fact, if only *one* Strauss CD is wanted, this is probably the best choice) is Willi Boskovsky's Vienna Philharmonic compilation of mid-seventies recordings on Decca. The VPO sound is quite sumptuous, and the generous selection of twelve items is exceptionally well played and recorded. You will find this on Decca 411 932-2DH.

WIENER BONBONS: selections from the 1983 New Year's Day Concert, Vienna
Vienna Philharmonic Orchestra
Conductor: Lorin Maazel
Deutsche Grammophon 410 516-2GH
DDD Running time: 62.09
Performance: ★ ★ ★   Recording: ★ ★ ★

It was Decca who made an historic first digital recording at the 1979 New Year's Day Concert, and comparisons with this 1983 session show how far techniques had developed in the ensuing four years, certainly in dealing with the peculiar demands of taping this event!

This is a refreshing selection of the less-familiar output of the brothers Josef and Johann Strauss, lovingly played, of course. With good perspectives, a warm acoustic, and the beautiful sound of the Vienna Philharmonic to savour, this is one to enjoy.

RICHARD STRAUSS
(b. Munich, Germany, 11 June 1864; d. Garmisch-Partenkirchen, Germany, 8 September 1949)

Few composers can have experienced the critical acclaim and the material success that Richard Strauss was privileged to enjoy. By the age of fifty he was reckoned to be a millionaire. As the natural heir of the Germanic/Wagnerian tradition, his influence was enormous, and despite the excesses of ego that occasionally entered his music, there is no doubt that he was responsible for some of the most original and durable music written in the past one hundred years.

Encouraged by his father, a professional musician, he composed a first piano piece aged six, and a symphony at sixteen. After two years' study in Munich, he took over the directorship of the provincial, but far from amateur, Meiningen Orchestra. A second symphony continued to display the influence of Brahms and Wagner, but with the *Symphonie aus Italien* of 1886, Strauss gave notable voice to his own ideas.

The first of many operas followed in 1893, and in the same period he both embarked on what was to prove a long and happy marriage to one of his leading singers, Pauline de Ahna, and became chief conductor of the Berlin Philharmonic Orchestra.

He was only twenty-four when he wrote the brilliant and hugely admired symphonic poem, *Don Juan*. Five more followed in the same genre. During the 1890s, he composed some of his finest songs, and from 1898–1910 held the post of Director of the Berlin Opera. Home for the rest of his life, however, was to be the splendid house he bought at Garmisch in the Bavarian Alps.

The First World War brought an abrupt end to the opulence, richness and confidence that Strauss' music embodied: his Germany was no more, and worse was to come in the Nazi years.

He came to a kind of compromise with the Nazis: they liked to feel Germany's greatest living composer was supporting them, while Strauss believed that as long as he stayed in his native land, its culture stood a chance of surviving. As a consequence he was left in peace during the war, but afterwards had to face an inquiry into his involvement with the Third Reich. It did exonerate him, but his stock remained tarnished in the eyes of many, and there was nothing that could allay the despair he felt surveying the physical and cultural destruction that surrounded him at his death.

While so many composers enjoyed little financial success, Strauss became a millionaire.

R. STRAUSS

**HORN CONCERTO NO1 IN E FLAT OP11
HORN CONCERTO NO2 IN E FLAT**
(c/w Weber: Concertino for Horn and
Orchestra in E minor OP45
Hermann Baumann: Horn
Leipzig Gewandhaus Orchestra
Conductor: Kurt Masur
Philips 412 237-2PH
DDD Running time: 49.15
Performance: ★ ★ ★   Recording: ★ ★ ★

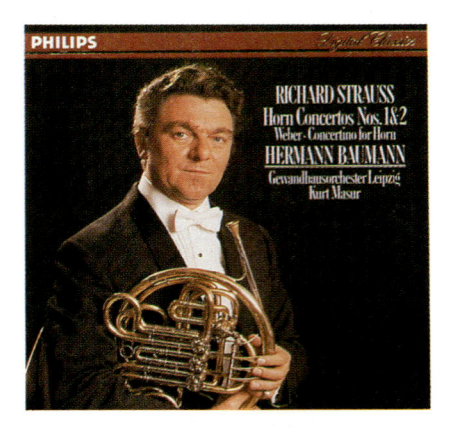

Sixty years separate Strauss' two horn concertos. The first, breezy and high-spirited, was written around 1883 for the composer's father, who was first horn in the Munich Court Opera (unfortunately, the dedicatee found it too difficult). The Second Concerto, this a memorial to Strauss *père*, was first performed in 1943 and is a technically more difficult work, giving full rein to the diverse moods and colours of the instrument, and encouraging the orchestra to take a much more equal role in things.

Hermann Baumann plays both with consummate skill and sensitivity and, for good measure, adds the romantic Weber concertino to the programme. These thoroughly enjoyable performances are well-recorded, with plenty of 'air' in which the horn can take flight – the well-adjusted balance therefore needs to give no undue prominence to the soloist.

TOD UND VERKLÄRUNG (DEATH AND TRANSFIGURATION) OP24/TILL EULENSPIEGELS LUSTIGE STREICHE (TILL EULENSPIEGEL'S MERRY PRANKS) OP28/DON JUAN OP20
Concertgebouw Orchestra, Amsterdam
Conductor: Bernard Haitink
Philips 411 442-2PH
DDD Running time: 59.19
Performance: ★ ★ ★   Recording: ★ ★ ★

These three most popular of Strauss' tone poems are a natural coupling on record and it is no surprise that a number of excellent alternatives are available on Compact Disc. Haitink, though, wins first recommendation with a recording every bit as sharply-defined and revealing as his rivals but benefitting from the warmly spacious acoustic of Amsterdam's Concertgebouw. The playing, too, is first-class.

Other recordings on CD (selection):
(coupled as above)
Detroit SO/Antal Dorati/Decca 400 085-2DH
LSO/Claudio Abbado/DG 410 518-2GH

**SINFONIA DOMESTICA OP53
MACBETH: TONE POEM OP23**
Vienna Philharmonic Orchestra
Conductor: Lorin Maazel
Deutsche Grammophon 413 654-2GH
DDD Running time: 63.26
Performance: ★ ★ ★   Recording: ★ ★

From the outset, Strauss' musical depiction of the evidently blissful home life he led was ripe for critical reproach. Anything that translated such mundanities as bathing the baby into a full-blown orchestral score just had to be. Wisely his father recommended that the composer should find a title which pointed towards *'gaiety of the piece'*, and thus make it seem Strauss was not taking himself *too* seriously. It is that lighter, more humourous aspect that comes through in Maazel's performance, and probably this is all to the good – Karajan, for example (on LP only), makes the 'bath scene' sound like an episode from *The Flying Dutchman*! The recording, made at a live concert, is remarkably 'unmanipulated' by DG's standards, with convincing perspectives and luminous detail.

The inclusion of the early tone poem (but later revised) *Macbeth* makes for good value on this CD, and it, too, is finely judged by Maazel. The playing of the VPO in both works is quite gorgeous.

Other recordings on CD:
(*Macbeth*)
Detroit SO/Antal Dorati/Decca 410 146-2DH

**ALSO SPRACH ZARATHUSTRA (THUS SPAKE ZARATHUSTRA): TONE POEM OP30
DON JUAN: TONE POEM OP20**
Berlin Philharmonic Orchestra
Conductor: Herbert von Karajan
Deutsche Grammophon 410 959-2GH
DDD Running time: 53.57
Performance: ★ ★ ★   Recording: ★ ★ ★

From its unforgettable *Dawn of man* opening to the final apotheosis of the *Night-wanderer's song*, *Zarathustra* is surely the finest of Strauss' tone poems. The present sub-title describes the work as *'freely after Friedrich Nietzsche'*, yet the original was perhaps the more apt: *'symphonic optimism in fin-du-siècle form, dedicated to the 20th Century'*.

The piece was as much a new musical concept as a philosophical one, and probably tells us as much about Richard Strauss as it does about Nietzsche's notion of the 'superman'.

This opulent and sensuous score was first heard in Frankfurt in 1896 and, in the age of 'high fidelity', has proved a 'plum' for recording engineers. Currently leading a substantial CD field is Karajan's newest version, a worthy successor to his famous 1974 record. This is Berlin playing and DG recording at its best (why cannot they always do it this way?). There is real body to the sound, a lustrous string tone, natural perspectives and detailing, and appropriate weight and scale. *Don Juan* makes a highly desirable filler (*Zarathustra* alone is short shrift on LP, let alone CD). This CD is magnificent in every respect.

Other recordings on CD:
(*Also Sprach Zarathustra*)
NYPO/Zubin Mehta/CBS MK35888
Philharmonia O/Georges Pretre/RCA RCD70071
BSO/Seiji Ozawa/Philips 400 072-2PH
Detroit SO/Antal Dorati/Decca 410 146-2DH
CSO/Solti/Decca 414 043-2DH

EIN HELDENLEBEN (A HERO'S LIFE): SYMPHONIC POEM OP40
Peter Mirring: Violin
Staatskapelle Dresden
Conductor: Herbert Blomstedt
Denon C37-7561
DDD Running time: 45.30
Performance: ★ ★ ★   Recording: ★ ★ ★

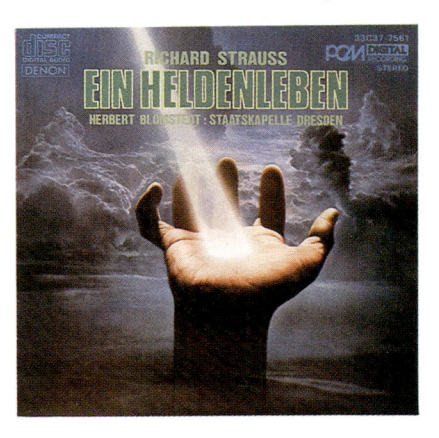

It is perhaps best when listening to this sumptuous and fascinating score to forget the notion of a musical self-portrait: the composer as hero. Assuming he did see himself in the 'title role', Strauss' conceit may be forgiven. He was just thirty-four, he was undeniably and exceptionally talented, and he was quite a celebrity.

There is an artless quality to the programme of *Ein Heldenleben*: the hero's enemies; his companion (exquisitely portrayed by solo violin); his battles; his peaceful deeds; and his final fulfilment and retreat from the world. Strauss may even have seen it as a metaphor for the life of any successful personality, not particularly relating to himself.

However, there is no disputing the mastery of melody, line and orchestration so ably demonstrated in this work. He inserts quotations from his own compositions, *Don Juan* for example, and even includes a cheeky reference to Beethoven's *Eroica*.

Blomstedt presents a convincing interpretation of the piece, much aided by the Dresden orchestra, currently a match for any in Europe. The engineering is good, too, resisting the temptation to indulge Strauss' extravagances with those of its own. The sound is well-presented, in an extremely mellow, natural way, with a rich polish and depth to the strings. All very opulent, but with no lack of impact when required, as in the 'battle scene' which is highly effective.

Although this version leads the field at present, strong competition is likely to come from the new Karajan recording on DG. It has become a work close to the hearts of the Berliners, but perhaps no more than it is in the blood of the Dresdeners.

Other recordings on CD:
Cleveland O/Vladimir Ashkenazy/Decca 414 292-2DH
BSO/Seiji Ozawa/Philips 400 073-2PH
NYPO/Zubin Mehta/CBS MK37756
Cleveland O/Lorin Maazel/CBS MK76676
BPO/Herbert von Karajan/DG 415 508-2GH

TOD UND VERKLÄRUNG (DEATH AND TRANSFIGURATION): TONE POEM OP24 METAMORPHOSEN: STUDY IN C MINOR FOR 23 SOLO STRINGS
Berlin Philharmonic Orchestra
Conductor: Herbert von Karajan
Deutsche Grammophon 410 892-2GH
DDD Running time: 51.34
Performance: ★ ★ ★   Recording: ★

The deathbed recollections and yearnings, and final flight of the soul into eternity in search of the fulfilment it had failed to find on earth, represented Strauss' first detailed programme music when *Tod und Verklärung* was published in 1889. A brilliant score, it contains some of his most evocative and sumptuous writing.

Sixty years later, the composer himself was near death. Around him, the Germany he had loved lay in ruins. In 1945, he took up a theme he had sketched two years earlier, following the destruction of the Munich opera house (the scene of so many of his successes) and produced the finest of his late orchestral works, the study *Metamorphosen*. His mastery of string writing was as great as ever, but the title did not refer to a musical exposition, but to the poetry of Goethe, which Strauss had read at length in his later years. There are also elusive references to Wagner and Beethoven, and over the final quotation from the latter, in the score Strauss wrote '*in memoriam*'.

The performances of both works are outstanding, that of *Metamorphosen* probably as penetrating as we are ever likely to hear. It is a pity, therefore, that the recording does less than justice to either: heavily over-reverberant in *Tod*, with a curious balance which, while refined in the quieter music, assaults the ears with a wholly up-front barrage of sound in the louder passages. It is well-nigh impossible to set a satisfactory volume level. *Metamorphosen* fares better, though those famous Berlin strings surely sound sweeter than this.

Other recordings on CD (selection):
(*Tod und Verklärung*)
Concertgebouw O/Bernard Haitink/Philips 411 442-2PH

IGOR STRAVINSKY
(b. Oranienbaum, nr St Petersburg, Russia, 17 June 1882; d. New York, 6 April 1971)

Only at the very beginning and end of his long composing life could Stravinsky be described as a 'follower': the imprint of his teacher Rimsky-Korsakov is on his earliest scores, in particular the *Firebird* ballet, and at the very end of his career, he belatedly embraced serialism. Between times, with his work undergoing dramatic and unexpected changes, he can be said to have 'led music by the nose', and to have established himself, along with Bartók and Schoenberg, as one of the three most influential composers of this century.

Although the son of an opera singer, Igor Stravinsky was initially destined for a career in the legal profession. Then, in 1902, while travelling in Germany, he encountered Rimsky-Korsakov and from that point, decided that music was to be his life. It was Rimsky who nurtured his obviously abundant talent, and, inevitably, Rimsky's brilliant-colourful Orientalism became a part of Stravinsky's musical make-up. It manifested itself only too clearly in the first two of the ballets commissioned by the impresario Serge Diaghilev for his hugely popular *Ballets Russes*.

However, with his third ballet, Stravinsky depicted another kind of Russia and changed the face of music as few before or since. And he changed it irrevocably. In its free use of tonality and rhythm, by its whole nature, *La Sacre du Printemps (The Rite of Spring)* broke all rules of composition. Yet it was to be as far along that path that Stravinsky was to go (perhaps as far as he could): he exchanged the bold, aggressive colours of *Le Sacre* for the altogether purer and cooler palette of neo-classicism.

Stravinsky left Russia, first for Switzerland, then France, during the First World War; unlike his fellow exile Prokofiev, he never returned there to live. During the twenties and thirties, he developed strong ties with the United States, eventually settling in Hollywood as a naturalized American citizen. He died in the USA in 1971.

It is a pity so much remains ignored by Compact Disc, especially as CBS had the foresight in the late fifties and sixties to record Stravinsky conducting almost his entire output of music, and in stereo.

VIOLIN CONCERTO IN D MAJOR
(c/w Berg: Violin Concerto)
Itzhak Perlman: Violin
Boston Symphony Orchestra
Conductor: Seiji Ozawa
Deutsche Grammophon 413 725-2GH
ADD Running time: 46.59
Performance: ★ ★   Recording: ★ ★

This is an exciting coupling of two of this century's most significant violin concertos, the brilliant, neo-classical Stravinsky of 1931, and the deeply lyrical and poignant concerto of Alban Berg: the most accessible of the composers of the Second Viennese School at his most accessible.

Perlman proves wholly responsive to the very different demands of these two works, with the abundant technique required by the Stravinsky, and the depth of feeling needed in the Berg. The contribution of Ozawa and the Boston players is no less satisfying, but the recording takes little advantage of the excellent acoustic of the Boston Symphony Hall. There is very little depth or perspective especially in the Stravinsky, which is suitably astringent and analytical.

Perlman is well forward of the orchestra, which gives an impressive bite and clarity to his performance, but some of that could easily have been exchanged for a more integrated and natural feel to the whole sound.

Other recordings on CD:
(Berg Violin Concerto)
Kyung-Wha Chung/CSO/Georg Solti/

SYMPHONY IN C
SYMPHONY IN THREE MOVEMENTS
Suisse Romande Orchestra
Conductor: Charles Dutoit
Decca 413 272-2DH
DDD Running time: 49.00
Performance: ★ ★ ★
Recording: ★ ★ (★)

Both Stravinsky's major symphonies date from the 1940s, the Symphony in C was composed for the fiftieth anniversary of the Chicago Symphony Orchestra at the beginning of the decade, and the Symphony in Three Movements occupied him from 1942 to 1945.

Dutoit's versions are currently the best-played of the current options on Compact Disc, although Gibson's are marginally the better recorded. His performances are only available, however, in a two-disc set containing the early Symphony in E flat and the Ode, neither of which are top-drawer Stravinsky.

Other recordings on CD:
SNO/Alexander Gibson/Chandos CHAN8345/6
IPO/Leonard Bernstein/DG 415 128-2GH

L'OISEAU DE FEU (THE FIREBIRD) – BALLET
Concertgebouw Orchestra, Amsterdam
Conductor: Colin Davis
Philips 400 074-2PH
AAD Running time: 46.40
Performance: ★ ★ ★   Recording: ★ ★ ★

The *Firebird* was the first of the three 'Russian' ballets, produced by Diaghilev between 1910 and 1913, and Stravinsky's debt to his teacher Rimsky-Korsakov is nowhere better demonstrated. The brilliant colours contained in that Oriental 'paint-box' devised by Rimsky are put to good effect here in this tale of magic and fantasy.

It is those elements, as well as the strong rhythmic drive, which distinguish Colin Davis's atmospheric performance. The superbly clear and coherent recording (an analogue original) does not have the entirely natural balance Philips usually obtain in the Concertgebouw – some 'spotlighting' is apparent – but has a fullness, depth and tonal lustre which more than compensate. However, even allowing that this was one of the very first CD issues, the complete absence of index points is slightly disappointing. Among the alternatives, Ansermet's is another Vintage performance.

Other recordings on CD (selection):
Detroit SO/Antal Dorati/Decca 410 109-2DH
BSO/Seiji Ozawa/EMI CDC7 47017-2
NPO/Ernest Ansermet/Decca 414 141-2DH

THE FIREBIRD: BALLET SUITE (1919)
(c/w **Borodin: Prince Igor – Overture and Polovtsian Dances**)
Atlanta Symphony Orchestra Chorus
Atlanta Symphony Orchestra
Conductor: Robert Shaw
Telarc CD80039
DDD Running time: 43.05
Performance: ★ ★ (★)
Recording: ★ ★ ★

Both from the musical and technical point of view, there is no shortage of excitement on this recording. What the orchestra and choir lack in polish, they more than make up for in commitment and involvement, with the Borodin the most impressive of the two.

It is a good performance of the *Firebird* suite, though, with Shaw making the most of the deceptive calm of the *round dance* to give the maximum impact to the thunderous entry of Kastchei: always a heart-stopping moment, and nowhere more so than on this typically wide-ranging, spectacular Telarc recording.

PETRUSHKA: BALLET (1947 version)
SCENES DE BALLET
Israel Philharmonic Orchestra
Conductor: Leonard Bernstein
Deutsche Grammophon 410 996-2GH
DDD Running time: 53.10
Performance: ★ ★ ★   Recording: ★ (★)

Bernstein has always excelled at bringing out the vitality, colour, exuberance and sheer fun contained in this score, the second of Stravinsky's compositions for Diaghilev's *Ballets Russes*. Completed in 1911, Nijinsky created the title role in this strange, macabre tale of the puppet show at a Russian shrovetide fair.

The performance has a humanity and an enchantment which overcome the drawbacks of a rather dry, confined acoustic, close orchestral focus (a live recording, incidentally), and an orchestra that does not quite have the polish and precision of its European and American counterparts. But they play as if they love the score as much as their conductor so obviously does.

Other recordings on CD:
LSO/Claudio Abbado/DG 400 042-2GH
Philadelphia O/Riccardo Muti/EMI CDC 7 47015-2
PO/Michael Tilson-Thomas/CBS MK37271

LE SACRE DU PRINTEMPS (THE RITE OF SPRING)
SYMPHONIES OF WIND INSTRUMENTS
Montreal Symphony Orchestra
Conductor: Charles Dutoit
Decca 414 202-2DH
DDD Running time: 44.24
Performance: ★ ★   Recording: ★ ★ ★

Perhaps expectations of this recording ran unfairly high, such has been the standard set by Dutoit and the Montreal orchestra in performing the 20th century repertoire, especially Ravel. This is not the 'ideal' *Rite of Spring* that had been anticipated, but nevertheless it does not fall far short. Certainly, it is by far the best recorded. What the performance lacks is some of the distinct savagery that characterises, above all, Stravinsky's own 1960s version for CBS (surely a prime candidate for CD remastering). If anything, Dutoit is too

STRAVINSKY

respectful, too meticulous; the playing too polished. An element of coarse brutality does not go amiss if this work is still to make something of the impact it did at the first performance in 1913.

Despite the reservations, Dutoit's remains an all-round first choice, artistically and – most emphatically – technically, and unlike any of his rivals, he offers a fill-up: a well-played version of the *Symphonies of Wind Instruments*.

Other recordings on CD:
Israel PO/Leonard Bernstein/DG 410 508-2GH
Cleveland SO/Lorin Maazel/Telarc CD80054
Detroit SO/Antal Dorati/Decca 400 084-2DH
Moscow Radio SO/Vladimir Fedoseyev/JVC/Melodiya 880 003

THE SOLDIER'S TALE
(c/w Prokofiev: Symphony No1 in D Major Op25 (Classical)/Shostakovich: Piano Concerto No1 in C minor Op35*)
Carol Rosenberger: Piano*
Stephen Burns: Trumpet*
Los Angeles Chamber Orchestra
Conductor: Gerard Schwarz
Delos D/CD3021
DDD Running time: 61.20
Performance: ★ ★ (★)
Recording: ★ ★ ★

An old Russian story of a soldier's pact with the devil was the basis of this allegorical work, composed while Stravinsky was in Switzerland during the First World War. It is a work of great inventiveness, especially in the manipulation of rhythm, and is here performed in the version without narration. And a fine performance it is, set in just the right acoustic to ensure the absolute clarity of texture required.

The two larger orchestral works here are given a more atmospheric, more open sound-stage. The Prokofiev comes over well, but Carol Rosenberger misses some of the fun that laces the Shostakovich concerto, although both she and the obligato trumpet are well-recorded.

Other recordings on CD:
(Prokofiev Symphony No1 Op25)
(see under Grieg)
(Shostakovich Piano Concerto No1 Op35)
Dmitri Shostakovich Jr/Montreal I Musici/ Maxim Shostakovich/Chandos CHAN8357

FIREBIRD: BALLET (EXTENDED SUITE)
(c/w Debussy: Prélude à l'après-midi d'un faune)
Los Angeles Philharmonic Orchestra
Conductor: Erich Leinsdorf
Sheffield Lab CD LAB24
ADD Running time: 40.00
Performance: ★ ★ ★   Recording: ★ ★ ★

Technically, there is much of interest here. The tape to produce the CD was made using an analogue recorder, simultaneously with the 'direct-to-disc' cutting of the master for the LP version. That is the process whereby the signal from the microphone is fed directly to the head on the cutting lathe, eliminating the tape stage.

It can be a very effective process, if a demanding one: without tape, the musicians have no scope for editing a performance. Any mistake, and it is right back to the beginning again!

The LAPO certainly rise to the challenge here, and it is also worth noting that the performances were recorded with a single-point stereo microphone, capturing the whole sound from just one location in the hall in exactly the same manner as it would be heard.

And after hearing a recording such as this, subtly impressive and so satisfyingly real to anyone familiar with the sound of an orchestra live, one is forced to conclude that all the extra processing is probably unnecessary in most cases.

The performances – Leinsdorf uses a much more extended score than the usual *Firebird* suite – are very good indeed.

Other recordings on CD:
(Firebird suite)
Philadelphia O/Riccardo Muti/EMI CDC7 47099-2
Atlanta SO/Robert Shaw/Telarc CD80039

APOLLON MUSAGÈTE: BALLET EN DEUX TABLEAUX
(c/w Copland: Appalachian Spring – Ballet for Martha
(1945 suite)
Detroit Symphony Orchestra
Conductor: Antal Dorati
Decca 414 457-2DH
DDD Running time: 53.27
Performance: ★ ★ ★   Recording: ★ ★ ★

It was an inspired idea to couple these two remarkable twentieth century ballets. *Appalachian Spring*, written for Martha Graham's ballet company in 1944, is one of Copland's most evocative scores, a work of enormous nobility and humanity, not without a certain mystical quality. Originally conceived for an ensemble of just thirteen instruments, the composer produced this slightly edited orchestral score soon afterwards.

As well as offering a superlative performance of the Copland, Dorati also gives Stravinsky's no less captivating neo-classical ballet, *Apollon Musagète*, its Compact Disc debut. In both works, the recording is simply outstanding, with impressive depth, scale and detail.

Other recordings on CD:
(Appalachian Spring)
Atlanta SO/Louis Lane/Telarc CD80078
LAPO/Leonard Bernstein/DG 413 324-2GH

PYTOR ILICH TCHAIKOVSKY
(b. Votkinsk, Viatka, Russia, 7 May 1840; d. St Petersburg, Russia, 6 November 1893)

Hyper-sensitive, self-pitying, excitable, his temperament was reflected in his music.

There are many instances in music where the critical assessment of a composer has been at odds with his public popularity, but surely never more so than in the case of Tchaikovsky. He could write ear-catching melodies, though there is nothing inherently wrong in that, but what many find unacceptable is the cloying sentiment and shallowness, and the unashamed appeal to often basic emotions.

In 1863, he resigned his post at the Ministry of Justice to devote himself to music. The pianist and composer Anton Rubinstein became his teacher, but Tchaikovsky owed both he and his brother, Nikolai, a lot more for their encouragement and practical help.

The fantasy, *Romeo and Juliet*, of 1869 marked a significant point in his career, as did the First Piano Concerto of 1875 (although Rubinstein disliked it). Wholly unsuccessful, however, was his marriage to Antonina Milyukova, foolishly undertaken in an effort to silence the gossip Tchaikovsky himself had fuelled by being less than circumspect in his homosexual affairs.

The marriage lasted but eleven weeks and ended almost farcically with Tchaikovsky attempting to drown himself in icy water but succeeding only in catching pneumonia.

Yet there was a woman with whom he did establish a relationship, and for fourteen years. Yet never once during that time, at her express wish, did they meet, although she was often present at concerts when he conducted. Nadezhda von Meck became his benefactress, granting Tchaikovsky a yearly allowance. They communicated only by letter, unless one counts the music from that period (1876–90) which, if only sub-consciously must have been composed with her likes in mind.

For many years, it was assumed that Tchaikovsky died by drinking unboiled water during a cholera epidemic, as potentially successful suicide attempt as any. Now, however, it is thought he sought a far greater certainty of success by simply taking arsenic.

Among his last compositions were the 'autobiographical' Sixth Symphony, and incredibly, the *Casse-Noisette (Nutcracker)* ballet – a greater contrast between abject despair and unmitigated happiness it is difficult to imagine.

TCHAIKOVSKY

SYMPHONY NO1 IN G MINOR OP13 (WINTER DAYDREAMS)
Oslo Philharmonic Orchestra
Conductor: Mariss Jansons
Chandos CHAN8402
DDD Running time: 43.57
Performance: ★ ★ ★   **Recording:** ★ ★ ★

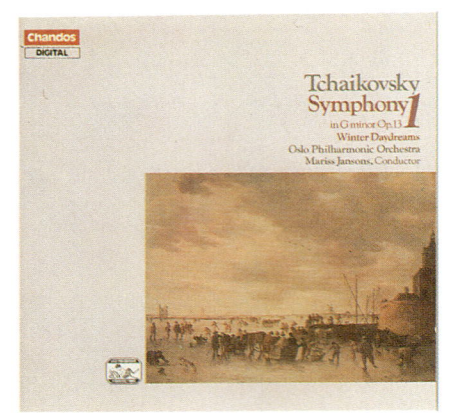

Tchaikovsky sweated blood over this first symphony. It occupied him throughout 1866, working all hours to the point of breakdown, and all the time apparently fearing he might not live to finish it. Several piecemeal performances took place before the premiere of the complete work in February 1868. Still dissatisfied, Tchaikovsky continued his revisions and a final edition did not appear until 1888, complete with the subtitle which was the composer's own very accurate summing up of the work's mood and atmosphere.

While not up to the standard of the last three great symphonies, the First emerges well from a performance as persuasive as this, in every respect up to the other issues in this exciting series.

SYMPHONY NO2 IN C MINOR OP17 (LITTLE RUSSIAN)
London Symphony Orchestra
Conductor: Geoffrey Simon
Chandos CHAN8304
DDD Running time: 39.30
Performance: ★ ★ ★   **Recording:** ★ ★ ★

What distinguishes this recording from any other is its use of the original 1872 score which, although well-received, left Tchaikovsky with doubts about its construction, particularly the first movement (which he re-wrote) and the finale, where he cut some one-hundred and-fifty bars for the final, 1879, version.

The conclusion must be that he was right in both cases, while not overlooking the total conviction of Geoffrey Simon's interpretation – and the splendid playing of the LSO, especially the strings and brass.

Chandos' discreet microphone technique once again produces an outstandingly natural and exciting sound.

Other recordings on CD:
NPO/Claudio Abbado/CBS MK39359

SYMPHONY NO4 IN F MINOR OP36
Oslo Philharmonic Orchestra
Conductor: Mariss Janssons
Chandos CHAN8361
DDD Running time: 41.30
Performance: ★ ★ ★   **Recording:** ★ ★ ★

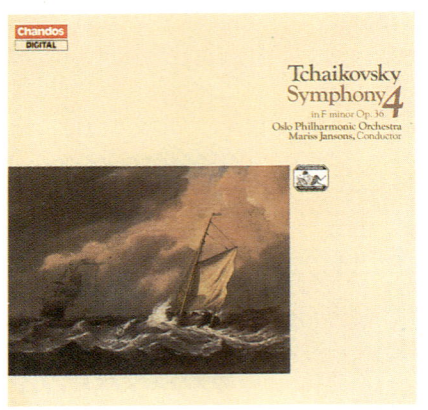

The composer himself detected parallels between his Fourth Symphony and the Fifth of Beethoven: the notion of destiny, the need for struggle and, musically, the use of a darkly pregnant 'fate' motif, commanding attention from the very start of the work.

It may be that his doomed-from-the-start marriage to Antonina Milyukova accounted for the cathartic nature of the Fourth, a crisis resolved in the noisy confidence of the finale, which also bears a strong kinship with the triumphant resolution of Beethoven's Fifth.

Yet the symphony has its lighter side: the dance-like *scherzo*, played *pizzicato* throughout, is one Tchaikovsky's most graceful creations, and there is an undeniably rustic quality to the tempestuous last movement. This duality of temperament comes across strongly in Mariss Jansons' performance, one of the most refreshing and invigorating of this symphony to appear for many a year. It is vital and highly-charged, without being over-driven or lurching between emotional extremes. The recording is as stunning as the playing.

Other recordings on CD:
Pittsburgh SO/André Previn/Philips 400 090-2PH
Cleveland O/Lorin Maazel/Telarc CD80047
CSO/Georg Solti/Decca 414 192-2DH
VPO/Herbert van Karajan/DG 415 348-2GH

SYMPHONY NO5 IN E MINOR OP64
Oslo Philharmonic Orchestra
Conductor: Mariss Jansons
Chandos CHAN8351
DDD Running time: 43.11
Performance: ★ ★ ★   **Recording:** ★ ★ ★

It was with this issue that both Jansons and the magnificent Oslo orchestra made their initial impact. This was not only the best recording for many years of this most heroic of Tchaikovsky's symphonies, but the freshness and spontaneity of the performance demanded attention.

Without resorting to idiosyncracies, Jansons casts new light on the Fifth (as he has done in all the other symphonies recorded to date) and, in the process, enhances its stature. Here, obviously, is someone for whom getting to the heart of these works truly matters: there is nothing superficial about this reading, although it wants for nothing in excitement, and the splendid recording should rouse you from your seat!

Other recordings on CD (selection):
Cleveland O/Lorin Maazel/CBS MK36700
Berlin RSO/Kurt Sanderling/Denon C37-7100
Philadelphia O/Eugene Ormandy/Delos D/CD3015
Moscow RSO/Vladimir Fedoseyev/JVC Melodiya 880005
RPO/André Previn/Telarc CD80107
VPO/Herbert von Karajan/DG 415 095-2GH

SYMPHONY NO6 IN B MINOR OP74 (PATHETIQUE)
Philharmonia Orchestra
Conductor: Vladimir Ashkenazy
Decca 411 615-2DH
ADD Running time: 46.44
Performance: ★ ★ ★   Recording: ★ ★ ★

In every respect, Ashkenazy's is one of the greatest performances of the *Pathétique* ever recorded: volatile, passionately-felt, and exciting, but always stopping short of the emotional excess which has marred so many others. Technically, it is doubtful whether *any* other version of the Sixth has enjoyed such splendid sound, even recent digital versions. If there was an 'Indian summer' for analogue recording at the dawn of the digital age, this was most certainly one of its golden moments.

Compelling listening from first bar to last, this one deserves a place in any Compact Disc collection.

Other recordings on CD:
LAPO/Carlo Maria Giulini/DG 400 029-2GH
Berlin Staatskapelle/Kurt Sanderling/Denon C37-7062
Philadelphia O/Eugene Ormandy/Delos D/CD3016
Moscow RSO/Vladimir Fedoseyev/JVC Melodiya VDC502
National PO/Carlos Paita/Lodia 1LO-CD778
VPO/Herbert von Karajan/DG 415 094-2GH
CSO/James Levine/RCA RD85355

PIANO CONCERTO NO1 IN B FLAT MINOR OP23
(c/w Prokofiev: Piano Concerto No3 in C Major Op26*)
Martha Argerich: Piano
Royal Philharmonic Orchestra
Berlin Philharmonic Orchestra*
Conductor: Charles Dutoit/Claudio Abbado*
Deutsche Grammophon 415 062-2GH
AAD Running time: 62.39
Performance: ★ ★ ★
Recording: ★ ★ (★)

Argerich's 1971 performance of the Tchaikovsky is one to have you listening afresh to this most over-played of concertos. It manages to be exciting, yet controlled, and the rapport between soloist and conductor produces many marvellous moments. Both are content to allow the work to build to its third-movement climax through a measured approach to the first, and a light touch in the second.

The Prokofiev is equally idiomatic and revealing, one of the recordings with which Argerich made her name. The 1967 sound emerges well in this transfer, as does that of the Tchaikovsky from 1971, which always was one of DG's best: wide-ranging, full-bodied and naturally balanced.

This is indisputably the best performance of the Tchaikovsky First currently on Compact Disc, although the new account from Ivo Pogorelich will no doubt come into the reckoning. But, on playing-time certainly, it offers nothing like as good value.

Other recordings on CD:
(Tchaikovsky *Piano Concerto No1*)
Emil Gilels/NYPO/Zubin Mehta/CBS MK36660
Martha Argerich/Bavarian RSO/Kirill Kondrashin/Philips 411 057-2PH
Victoria Postnikova/Vienna SO/Gennadi Rozhdestvensky/Decca 410 112-2DH
Ivo Pogorelich/LSO/Claudio Abbado/DG 415 122-2GH
(Prokofiev *Piano Concerto No3* – see under Prokofiev)

TCHAIKOVSKY

VIOLIN CONCERTO IN D MAJOR OP35
(c/w Mendelssohn: Violin Concerto in E minor Op64)
Kyung-Wha Chung: Violin
Montreal Symphony Orchestra
Conductor: Charles Dutoit
Decca 410 011-2DH
DDD Running time: 70.10
Performance: ★ ★ ★
(Tchaikovsky) ★ ★(★) Mendelssohn
Recording: ★ ★ (★)

Kyung-Wha Chung made a memorable recording of the Tchaikovsky early in her career, and this new issue shows little change of interpretation, apart perhaps from an even faster, more fiery finale. It is a superb performance, with an outstanding orchestral contribution, too.

The recording projects the soloist but not quite as much as in the accompanying Mendelssohn concerto where she is virtually isolated from the proceedings, and the acoustic.

Kyung-Wha Chung's performance of the Mendelssohn eschews any expressive lingering, and emerges an astonishing five minutes faster than Anne-Sophie Mutter on DG. But it does not sound hurried, simply less wistfully romantic than usual, and the approach proves to be one that works.

Other recordings on CD:
Gidon Kremer/BPO/Lorin Maazel/DG 400 027-2GH
Itzhak Perlman/Philadelphia O/Eugene Ormandy/EMI CDC7 47106-2
Yuval Yaron/LPO/Herbert Soudant/PRT CDPCN14
Pierre Amoyal/Philharmonia O/Charles Dutoit/Erato ECD88109

VIOLIN CONCERTO IN D MAJOR OP35
(c/w Sibelius: Violin Concerto Op47)
Pierre Amoyal: Violin
Philharmonia Orchestra
Conductor: Charles Dutoit
Erato ECD88109
DDD Running time: 67.38
Performance: ★ ★ (★)
Recording: ★ ★ ★

Although the performances just miss a full recommendation, those wanting an alternative coupling to Chung's Mendelssohn should consider Pierre Amoyal's fine Erato recording. He takes a lofty and urbane view of both concertos, and generally the approach works well. Unusually in latter-day performances of the Tchaikovsky, he observes the optional cuts in the finale.

Coincidentally, Amoyal's partner, as with Chung, is Charles Dutoit, although the orchestras differ. However, the quality of the accompaniment is every bit as good and Erato's recording is slightly better-balanced than the Decca, too. A good-value CD issue from the French label.

ROMEO AND JULIET:FANTASY OVERTURE
FRANCESCA DA RIMINI: SYMPHONIC FANTASIA AFTER DANTE OP32
Cleveland Orchestra
Conductor: Riccardo Chailly
Decca 414 159-2DH
DDD Running time: 42.00
Performance: ★ ★   Recording: ★ ★(t★)

With the 'Italian' connection between the two works, this is an apt coupling, though hardly a generous one. The recording is warmly ambient and nicely recessed, but also well-detailed. Although the playing is very fine, Chailly's performances – surprisingly for a conductor usually so volatile – are low-voltage ones. *Romeo and Juliet* lacks the essential tension and drama.

The disc is worth considering, however, if *Francesca da Rimini* – a work worthy of greater attention – is a particular favourite.

OVERTURE: 1812 OP49/ROMEO AND JULIET: FANTASY OVERTURE/DANCES FROM EUGENE ONEGIN AND THE OPRICHNIK*
Boston Symphony Orchestra
Tanglewood Festival Chorus
Orchestra of the Royal Opera House, Covent Garden*
Conductor: Colin Davis
Philips 411 448-2PH
ADD Running time: 56.27
Performance: ★ ★ ★
Recording: ★ ★ (★) (Boston)
★ ★ (London)

The *1812* comes off extraordinarily well here, Davis injecting an unexpected freshness into this all-too-familiar piece. He makes a bold departure from the original score by employing a chorus and organ for the Tsarist hymn passages, and it works strikingly well, especially as the voices soar above the tumult at the close. The playing throughout is very good, with no loss of momentum.

In contrast, *Romeo and Juliet* is on the subdued side, but not lacking passion in the tender moments or the swordfight sequences.

The Boston recordings are the better of the two, but the sequence of dances from the operas makes an unusual and attractive filler.

Other recordings on CD (selection):
(*1812 Overture*)
VPO/Lorin Maazel/CBS MK37252
Cincinatti SO/Erich Kunzel/Telarc CD80041
Philadelphia O/Riccardo Muti/EMI CDC7 47022-2
Detroit SO/Antal Dorati/Decca 414 494-2DH
(*Romeo and Juliet*)
LSO/Yuri Aronovich/Pickwick IMP Red Label PCD801
Cleveland O/Lorin Maazel/Telarc CD80068
BPO/Herbert von Karajan/DG 410 873-2GH
LSO/Geoffrey Simon/Chandos CHAN8310/11
Cleveland O/Riccardo Chailly/Decca 414 159-2DH

1812:OVERTURE OP49/ CAPRICCIO ITALIEN OP45/ MAZEPPA: COSSACK DANCE
Cincinatti Symphony Orchestra
Conductor: Erich Kunzel
Telarc CD80041
DDD Running time: 35.16
Performance: ★ ★   Recording: ★ ★ (★)

In its LP format, this recording gained considerable notoriety for its 'digital cannons', whose explosive discharge was reckoned to be the final test of pickup cartridge 'tracking' ability. The performance was actually mixed down from three separate recordings, the cannons and bells being added to the basic orchestral track through the Soundstream computer editing system.

It remains a 'sonic spectacular' on Compact Disc, and the warning about playback level should be heeded if you value your loudspeakers! Although musically the disc is no more than adequate, it is of course for its sound that most will want it, but note the poor playing time first.

Artistically, the best *1812* currently on CD remains Colin Davis' on Philips, while Eduardo Mata on RCA offers a fine performance of the intoxicating *Capriccio Italien*.

Other recordings on CD:
(*1812: Overture* Op49)
(see above)
(*Capriccio Italien* Op45)
Dallas SO/Eduardo Mata/RCA RCD14439
Chicago SO/Daniel Barenboim/DG 400 035-2GH
Dresden Staatskapelle/Neville Marriner/ Philips 410 047-2PH
Moscow RSO/Vladimir Fedoseyev/JVC Melodiya 880 009
IPO/Leonard Bernstein/DG 415 379-2GH
Detroit SO/Antal Dorati/Decca 414 494-2DH

SUITE FROM THE BALLET LE LAC DES CYGNES (SWAN LAKE) OP20
SUITE FROM THE BALLET CASSE-NOISETTE (THE NUTCRACKER) OP71a
Israel Philharmonic Orchestra
Conductor: Zubin Mehta
Decca 410 551-2DH
DDD Running time: 47.25
Performance: ★ ★   **Recording:** ★ ★ ★

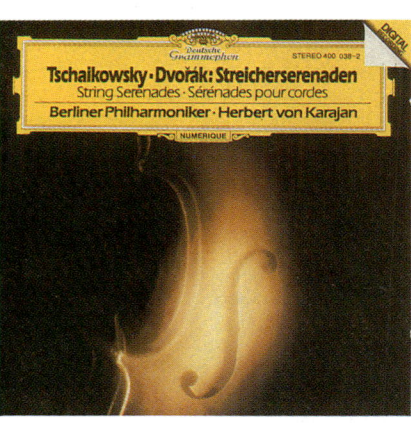

The Decca recording team have obtained better results than most from the unforgiving acoustic of the Mann Auditorium, Tel Aviv. The result is an altogether more open and spacious sound than we are accustomed to, one that remains clear and smooth throughout the range. The balance is very natural, if slightly over-wide and lacking some height, and the tonal quality is excellent. The violin and 'cello solos in *Swan Lake* come over delightfully well, as does the celesta in the *Dance of the Sugar Plum Fairy*.

With fine playing from the Israeli orchestra, there is much to enjoy in these performances, although they lack just a little in character.

Anyone wanting a coupling of the *Swan Lake* suite with that from *Sleeping Beauty*

can do no better than Riccardo Muti's outstanding recording with the Philadelphia. Superbly played and vividly recorded, it is on EMI CDC7 47075-2.

Other recordings on CD:
(*Nutcracker Suite* Op71a)
Cleveland O/Lorin Maazel/Telarc CD80068
BPO/Herbert von Karajan/DG 410 873-2GH
Minnesota O/Leonard Slatkin/Pro Arte CDD121
ASMF/Neville Marriner/Philips 411 471-2PH
Boston Pops O/John T Williams/Philips 412559-2PM
(*Swan Lake suite* Op20)
Philadelphia O/Riccardo Muti/EMI CDC7 47075-2

SERENADE FOR STRINGS IN C MAJOR OP48
(c/w **Dvořák: Serenade for Strings in E Major Op22**)
Berlin Philharmonic Orchestra
Conductor: Herbert von Karajan
Deutsche Grammophon 400 038-2GH
DDD Running time: 60.29
Performance: ★ ★   **Recording:** ★ ★

The Berlin strings are at their sumptuous best here, and the deep, richly resonant bass and inner clarity of the recording are notable qualities. However, the overall sound is less well defined, and there is a distinct edge to the upper strings.

Karajan tends to emphasise the nobility of the Tchaikovsky rather than its lyrical charm, and the result can be sometimes *too* intense, although undeniably effective in the *Elegia*. The finale is hard-driven indeed, and comes over more as the kind of quasi-neurotic *scherzo* Tchaikovsky might have included in a symphony than the spirited conclusion to what, after all, is essentially a good-natured piece.

With slightly better recording, and a more sympathetic treatment, the Dvořák comes off more agreeably here.

Other recordings on CD:
(Tchaikovsky *Serenade for Strings* Op48)
St Louis SO/Leonard Slatkin/Telarc CD80080
English String O/William Boughton/Nimbus NIM5016
ASMF/Neville Marriner/Philips 411 471-2PH
(Dvořák *Serenade for Strings* Op22)
(see under Dvořák)

GEORG PHILIP TELEMANN
(b. Magdeburg, Germany, 14 March 1681; d. Hamburg, 25 June 1767)

Even by baroque standards, Georg Philip Telemann was a prolific composer with some forty Passion settings to his name, a similar number of operas, and no less than six hundred orchestral works.

Born in Magdeburg, he held a large number of posts as *Kapellmeister* throughout northern Germany: Sorau in Brandenburg from 1704 to 1706; in Bach's home town of Eisenach from 1706 to 1711, then Frankfurt. In 1721, he took over direction of the Hamburg theatre, and the town was to be his base for several years.

Telemann was something of an eclectic: the influence of the Italian and French styles of the day is readily apparent, not least in his use of programmatic titles for many compositions, often of an extremely flowery nature. He also introduced East European elements for the first time.

Some of his finest work is to be found in the *Tafelmusik*, a collection of overtures and concertos published in Hamburg in 1733, and in his own brand of *Water Music*. He was also probably the first composer to compose a complete cycle of cantatas for the church year, and – unlike Bach - have them published, too. Indeed, Telemann, in his day was ranked higher than his contemporary.

Anyone interested in Telemann will find a reasonable selection of his music on Compact Disc.

DER GETREUE MUSIC-MEISTER –
selections: Suite in G minor for Oboe and Basso Continuo DgM62/Three pieces: L'Hiver DgM4, Pastourelle DgM59, Polonois for transverse flute and continuo in D Major DgM50/Sonata in A minor for Oboe and Basso Continuo DgM20/Sonata in F minor for bassoon and continuo DgM31/Four pieces: Air trompette in C Major for trumpet and continuo DgM13, Niaise in E Major DgM35, Flauto Pastorale in E Major DgM28, Napolitana for oboe d'amore and continuo DgM53/Sonata di chiesa in G minor for oboe and basso continuo.
Heinz Holliger: Oboe
Klaus Thunemann: Bassoon
Christiane Jaccottet: Harpsichord
Denon C37–7052
DDD Running time: 49.33
Performance: ★ ★ ★   Recording: ★ ★ ★

The story of Telemann's bi-weekly publication of 'music for the masses' is a fascinating one and this disc offers a contrasting and representative selection from the diverse music Telemann provided for his subscribers. Of particular pleasure are the 'four pieces', among which the *Air trompette* and *Flauto Pastorale* are here played by the oboe, and a splendid sound it makes too.

The most substantial works are the two sonatas, and very fine compositions they prove.

The recorded balance is all that could be wanted in such music, with equanimity between the three players, firm imaging, and a marvellously truthful tone to each instrument.

Six index points only are provided on the disc, but the inset booklet gives elapsed timings for each individual piece so it is easy to locate any item.

Other recordings on CD:
(Suite for Oboe and Continuo DgM62)
Paul Dombrecht/Robert Kohnen/Accent ACC48013D

WATER MUSIC: CONCERTOS IN B FLAT MAJOR, F MAJOR AND A MAJOR
Musica Antiqua Köln
Director: Reinhard Goebel
Archiv 413 788–2AH
DDD Running time: 49.10
Performance: ★ ★ ★   Recording: ★ ★ ★

This is a most persuasive disc of Telemann's music, lovingly played and superbly recorded. Reinhard Goebel and his partners bring lively contrast and a ripe period-instrument sound to these three sparkling concertos, and the whole is enhanced by a bright, spacious acoustic. Clear definition allows each instrumental contribution to be fully appreciated.

Of other Telemann concerto recordings on Compact Disc, those by the Academy of St Martin-in-the-Fields under the direction of Iona Brown can be recommended, although they are not quite as atmospherically recorded as the Archiv issue above. On Philips 410 041–2PH the A minor suite for treble recorder is a particular pleasure. Iona Brown has also recorded a splendid selection of the violin concertos, both directing and taking the solo rôle (Philips 411 125–2PH), while oboist, Heinz Holliger, joins her and the Academy in an enjoyable and well-played concert of five oboe concertos on Philips 412 879–2PH.

GIUSEPPE VERDI
(b. Le Roncole, Busseto, 10 October 1813; d. Milan, Italy, 27 January 1901)

The greatest of 19th Century Italian operatic composers was born into the none-too-prosperous family of a licensed victualler in a village about sixty miles from Milan. His musical education came first from the local church organist (Verdi himself was a competent player by the age of twelve) and later in Milan, under Vincenzo Lavigna, senior accompanist at La Scala.

In 1834, he returned home to marry the daughter of a local grocer who had encouraged his career all along, and for four years held his old teacher's post of organist and choirmaster. But the urge to compose was great, and by 1840 he had written two operas, one successful, one a failure. But it was nothing compared to the tragedy to come as, first, his two children, then his wife died in the space of two years.

Somehow, he recovered from these blows to write *Nabucco* which, in 1842, marked out Verdi as a composer of international stature. Fame brought fortune, and a large estate (not far from the impoverished surroundings of his childhood) which was to be home for the rest of his life.

He married again in 1859 to the singer Giuseppina Strepponi. He also became actively involved in the Italian independence movement, more than once using an historical subject in his operas to make a contemporary comment, and, for a spell, sitting in the new Italian parliament.

The period 1850-71 saw the creation of many of his best-loved operas, from *Rigoletto*, through *Traviata*, *Il Trovatore*, and *Don Carlos*, to *Aida*, the latter appropriately enough first performed at the Cairo Opera House.

But it was 1874 before his next major work, the Requiem, and 1879 when he began the first of his two supreme operatic masterpieces, the incomparable *Otello* and *Falstaff*. His last compositions were the *Quattro Pezzi Sacri (Four Sacred Pieces)*, and Giuseppe Verdi died an Italian national hero in 1901.

Here, we are only concerned with the compilations of overtures and preludes from the operas.

LA FORZA DEL DESTINO: SINFONIA/
AIDA: PRELUDIO/ATTILA: PRELUDIO/
LUISA MILLER: SINFONIA/LA
TRAVIATA: PRELUDIO (ATTO 1)/
PRELUDIO (ATTO 3)/UN BALLO IN
MASCHERA: PRELUDIO/NABUCCO:
SINFONIA/I VESPRI SICILIANI:
SINFONIA
Vienna Philharmonic Orchestra
Conductor: Giuseppe Sinopoli
Philips 411 469-2PH
DDD Running time: 51.52
Performance: ★ ★ ★
Recording: ★ ★ ★

Of the three compilations of overtures and preludes from the opera currently in the Compact Disc catalogue, Sinopoli's is the best recorded, and probably the most attractive selection.

Like his rivals, Chailly on Decca and Abbado on RCA, he includes the four-best-known overtures: *Forza del Destino*; *Luisa Miller*; *Nabucco*; and *I Vespri Siciliani*, and augments them with preludes from *Aida*, *Attila*, *La Traviata*, (Acts 1 and 3), and *Un Ballo in Maschera*, giving a fairly generous and representative programme.

He also scores with the marvellous playing (and gorgeous sound) of the Vienna Philharmonic. Chailly's National Philharmonic is given a more vivid sound by Decca, and Abbado's RCA recording cannot quite match the Philips in weight and clarity, although it is worth noting that Abbado includes a rarity in the form of the discarded original overture to *Aida*.

A disc which will hopefully tempt the unconverted to sample Verdi's operas in full: they are, of course, fully discussed in our companion volume.

Other recordings on CD:
(various overtures and preludes)
National Philharmonic O/Riccardo Chailly/
    Decca 410 141-2DH
LSO/Claudio Abbado/RCA RCD31378

RALPH VAUGHAN WILLIAMS
(b. Down Ampney, Gloucestershire, 12 October 1872; d. London, 26 August 1958)

Listening intently, Vaughan Williams rehearses the orchestra of the Leith Hill Festival, once a notable event in Britain's musical calendar, its existence down to V-W's own zeal.

Vaughan Williams enriched British musical life as few others have done, not only with the abundance of music that came from six decades of composition, but through his dedicated research into folk song; a devotion to the work of his forebears, the Tudor composers – particularly Byrd and Tallis – and Purcell; and by his enthusiastic contribution to the active musical life of the nation.

Yet it is difficult to nominate one work that could be said to typify Vaughan Williams: he encompassed a broad range of utterance, from pastoral whimsy to harsh, uncompromising images of the modern age. The only thing that was certain was that the next composition was unlikely to resemble the last. Each of his nine symphonies, for example, is quite individual.

The son of a country vicar, Vaughan Williams was educated at Charterhouse, Cambridge and the Royal College of Music, where he studied under those stalwarts of the English school, Parry and Stanford. Possibly more influential was the short but productive period spent with Ravel in Paris during 1908: a succession of outstanding works appeared in its wake, including the *Tallis Fantasia* which brought his widest recognition to date.

Equally valuable was his friendship with Gustav Holst, whom he met in student days at the RCM, and who accompanied Vaughan Williams on many expeditions around the country collecting folk songs.

After serving in the First World War, Vaughan Williams was appointed a professor at the Royal College of Music. He was now one of the leading figures of the British musical scene, and continued to produce a succession of marvellous compositions, not least the 'masque for dancing', *Job*, which contains some of the noblest melodies in English music. His trilogy of wartime symphonies, Nos 4, 5 and 6 were similarly outstanding, while the Seventh Symphony,

Sinfonia Antartica, drew on the music he had provided for the film, *Scott of the Antarctic*.

Throughout all Vaughan Williams' diverse compositions, the sense of a deep, inherited tradition is ever present, more so than in any other English composer, even Elgar.

On CD, Vaughan Williams has received miserly treatment: the symphonies, *Job*, the great choral works, even the well-known A.E. Housman settings, *On Wenlock Edge*, are all unrepresented. At least it offers something to look forward to!

FANTASIA ON A THEME BY THOMAS TALLIS/OBOE CONCERTO*/ CONCERTO GROSSO/FANTASIA ON GREENSLEEVES/FIVE VARIANTS OF DIVES AND LAZARUS
Maurice Bourgue: Oboe*
English String Orchestra
Conductor: William Boughton
Nimbus NIM5019
DDD Running time: 61.46
Performance: ★ ★ ★   Recording: ★ ★ ★

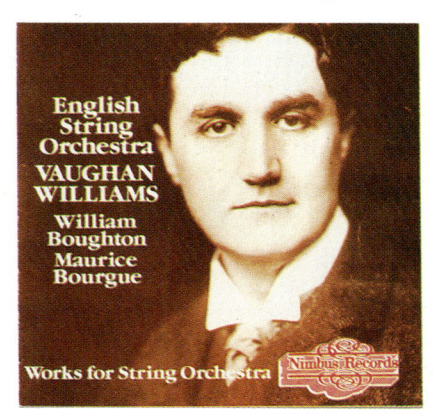

A generous programme that couples Vaughan-Williams' most famous composition, the *Tallis Fantasia* of 1910 with two concertos from the last fifteen years of his life. Much shorter, but by no means makeweights, are the delightful *Fantasia on Greensleeves*, and the set of variations on the ancient British folk-tune, *Dives and Lazarus*, which inhabits very much the same deeply spiritual, almost mystical world as the *Tallis*.

It was the latter which put Vaughan-Williams at the forefront of English music following its highly successful first performance in Gloucester Cathedral in 1910. Its emotive juxtaposition of old and new musical forms, its inspired orchestration, and the sense of mystery and awe which it evokes have assured its status as one of the masterpieces of 20th century music.

Although designed for performance in a cathedral – specifically Gloucester – the acoustic of the Great Hall of Birmingham University proves an adequate substitute for a vaulted Gothic nave. The recording is an excellent example of the success of Nimbus' 'single-point' microphone technique, and the performances are wholly sympathetic, if a little under-characterized in the two concertos.

Other recordings on CD:
(*Tallis Fantasia* only)
St Louis SO/Leonard Slatkin/Telarc CD80059
ASMF/Neville Marriner/ASV CD DCA518
(*Fantasia on Greensleeves*)
St Louis SO/Leonard Slatkin/Telarc CD80080

THE WASPS: OVERTURE/SERENADE TO MUSIC (orchestral version)
(c/w Delius: Summer Night on the River/On Hearing The First Cuckoo in Spring/Summer Evening/Air and Dance)
London Philharmonic Orchestra
Conductor: Vernon Handley
Chandos CHAN8330
DDD Running time: 45.43
Performance: ★ ★ ★   Recording: ★ ★ ★

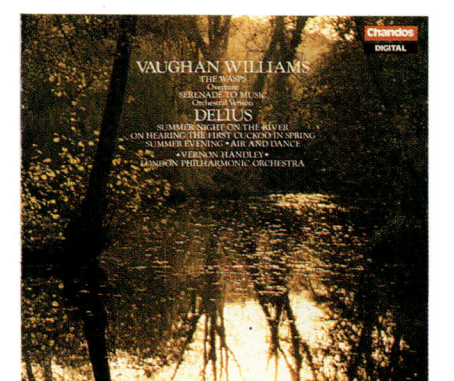

The overture has become the most-played item from Vaughan-Williams' lively score written to accompany a production of Aristophanes' play, *The Wasps*. It contains some fine melodies, not least the noble, very English tune which graces the central section.

No less lovely is the opening theme of the *Serenade to Music*, originally scored for sixteen vocal soloists performing a Shakespearian text. The difficulty of obtaining that number of good singers persuaded the composer to draw up an alternative version for orchestral forces only, and it is that which the LPO plays here very persuasively.

The Delius, also, is ravishingly performed and recorded, and it was imaginative programming to include alongside the popular masterpieces *On hearing the first cuckoo* and *Summer night on the river*, the rare but delectable *Summer Evening* and *Air and Dance*. It all makes for one of the most enjoyable issues of English music.

Other recordings on CD:
(Delius only)
Bournemouth Sinfonietta/Norman del Mar/ Chandos CHAN8372

ANTONIO VIVALDI
(b. Venice, Italy, 4 March 1678; d. Vienna, Austria, 28 July 1741)

Italy in the 17th and 18th Centuries was the land of the violin, of the great makers of the instrument – the Amatis, Guarneris and Stradivaris – and the great composers for it, among them Corelli, Torelli and, with the majority of his 450 or so known concertos written for strings, Antonio Vivaldi.

His father, Giovanni Battista Vivaldi, was a violinist of note and his son's first teacher. Most likely, Antonio was born in Venice; he certainly spent his youth there, also studying with Giovanni Legrenzi, organist and choirmaster at St Mark's, where he was later employed as a violinist.

At twenty-eight, he was ordained a priest and, because of the colour of his hair, became known as *Il prete rosso (The red priest)*, a nickname which has stuck down the ages. It seems Vivaldi suffered from asthma, and also enjoyed some distinctly un-priestly activities, and it is likely that the former was the excuse but the latter the true reason for him being adjudged incapable of saying Mass.

It is impossible to predict the direction his career might have taken had that decision not been made, for he now moved to a post where a requirement for a regular quota of new music produced much of the corpus of concertos for which he is now best remembered.

Venice, at this time, had no less than four large schools-cum-convents taking care of the welfare and education of young girls who were orphaned, or illegitimate, or from poor families. In 1704, Vivaldi joined the staff of one of them, the Ospedale della Pietà, five years later becoming its head violin teacher and, in 1716, being appointed *Maestro di concerti*, a condition of which was that he compose twelve fresh concerted works each month for the use of the school's pupils.

Vivaldi never severed his connection with the Pietà, although he accepted other posts in Venice and beyond, and is thought to have toured Germany, France and Austria at various times. He certainly directed the centenary celebrations of the Amsterdam Theatre in 1738, and it is interesting to note that several of his collections of concertos were first published from that city, the very first, *L'estro armonico (The Harmonic Rapture)* Op3, being one of them.

He is believed to have died on a visit to Vienna in 1741 and, like that of Bach (for whom Vivaldi was a model in many respects), his music was almost entirely neglected for a century.

Today, the catalogue serves him better than any Baroque composer other than Bach (and, possibly, Handel). The explosion in recordings of his works in recent years has been astonishing, and there is a good choice on Compact Disc, too, although it is surely time for a moratorium on *The Four Seasons!*

While his talent and artistry was of the highest order, Vivaldi has come in for a good measure of criticism. Dallapiccola's notorious remark about 'the same concerto written five hundred times' is typically pungent, but hardly fair. Vivaldi was not composing for posterity: he was writing music for the diverse abilities of his pupils. Given that, it is a measure of his genius that so much has survived to enjoy the stature and appeal it does today.

Venice, an evening view across the harbour alongside the Riva Schiavoni towards the elegant church of Santa Maria della Salute. Little has changed much since the 17th century when Antonio Vivaldi spent his childhood and virtually all his career within this 'floating city'.

VIVALDI

VIOLIN CONCERTOS OP8 (IL CIMENTO DELL'ARMONIA E DELL'INVENTIONE): selections
NO 7 IN D MINOR RV242/NO8 IN G MINOR/RV332/NO9 IN D MINOR RV236/ NO10 IN B FLAT MAJOR RV362 (LA CACCIA)/NO11 IN D MAJOR RV210/ NO12 IN C MAJOR RV178
Vienna Concentus Musicus
Principal violin: Alice Harnoncourt
Jürg Schaeftlein: Oboe
Conductor: Nikolaus Harnoncourt
TelDec ZK8.43094
ADD Running time: 52.25
Performance: ★ ★ ★   Recording: ★ ★

These performances of the last six of the Op8 concertos date from 1977 and, although the recording has lost none of its spaciousness, clarity or definition, there is a lean and lightweight quality to the sound compared with the best of today's 'original instrument' recordings.

However, that does little to detract from some very compelling playing. Both the humorous and the lyrical qualities of these works are revealed, and while all the readings are satisfying, there is little doubt that the Twelfth Concerto, with its oboe solo and delightful contribution from the chamber organ is a highspot.

Notwithstanding the minor criticisms of the recording, this remains an immensely enjoyable Vivaldi selection.

VIOLIN CONCERTOS OP8 NOS1-4 (THE FOUR SEASONS)/NO1 IN E MAJOR RV269 (SPRING)/NO2 IN G MINOR RV315 (SUMMER)/NO3 IN F MAJOR RV293 (AUTUMN)/NO4 IN F MINOR RV297 (WINTER)
Alan Loveday: Violin
Academy of St-Martin-in-the-Fields
Director: Neville Marriner
Argo 414 486-2ZH
ADD Running time: 42.49
Performance: ★ ★ ★   Recording: ★ ★ ★

Despite the huge increase in competing alternatives since it was recorded in 1970, the Academy's excellent *Four Seasons* remains just about the best of the modern instrument versions. Certainly, the Compact Disc transfer displays a marked improvement over the recording's last LP incarnation. It sounds sweeter and cleaner than before, and the lithe, well-shaped, no-nonsense performances (with a superb solo contribution from Alan Loveday) are, if anything, more refreshing sixteen years on.

Other recordings on CD (modern instruments – selection):
Scottish CO/Jaime Laredo/Pickwick IMP Red Label PCD800
Piero Toso/I Solisti Veneti/Claudio Scimone/Erato ECD88003
I Musici/Philips 410 001-2PH

12 CONCERTI GROSSI OP3 (L'ESTRO ARMONICO) (THE HARMONIC RAPTURE)
The Academy of Ancient Music
Director and continuo: Christopher Hogwood
L'Oiseau-Lyre 414 554-20H2 (2 discs)
AAD Running time: 95.36
Performance: ★ ★ ★   Recording: ★ ★ ★

Always one of the Academy's finest achievements on LP, this set of the Op3 concertos makes a similarly desirable Compact Disc issue. The lively, well-articulated and authoritative performances are matched by a superbly natural and well-balanced recording. Hogwood directs the proceedings with typical style, alternating between harpsichord and organ in the continuo rôle. The 'period' sound is nicely captured, and both the recording technicians and artists are to be congratulated here.

Unquestionably, one of the most successful of any of the Academy's fresh, vital explorations of the Baroque repertoire, this is a most enjoyable box.

Published in Amsterdam in 1711, *L'Estro Armonico* constituted Vivaldi's first collection of concertos, and was dedicated to the appreciative Grand Prince Ferdinand.

Other recordings on CD (complete):
I Musici/Philips 412 128-2PH2

VIOLIN CONCERTOS OP8 (IL CIMENTO DELL'ARMONIA E DELL'INVENTIONE) (THE TRIAL BETWEEN HARMONY AND INVENTION): selections
**NO5 IN E FLAT MAJOR RV253 (LA TEMPESTA DI MARE) NO6 IN C MAJOR RV180 (IL PIACERE)/
NO7 IN D MINOR RV242/NO8 IN G MINOR RV332/NO9 IN D MINOR RV236/ NO10 IN B FLAT MAJOR RV362 (LA CACCIA)**
Simon Standage: Violin
English Concert
Director (from the harpsichord):
Trevor Pinnock
CRD Records CRD 3410
ADD Running time: 51.58
Performance: ★ ★ ★   Recording: ★ ★ ★

Recordings such as this prove how rewarding it can be to explore further the Op8 set of concertos, of which *The Four Seasons* form the initial quartet. The English Concert offers a generous quota from the other concertos here, including three more of the named works. There is no mistaking the 'raging of the sea' in No5, or the gallop of the hunt in No10. *Il Piacere (Pleasure)* is, however, a more elusive evocation.

These are vigorous and lively performances, vividly but naturally recorded in just the right acoustic. That there is no lessening of interest throughout the six works says much for the enthusiasm the English Concert brings to them, even if they sometimes miss a little of their romance.

VIVALDI

CONCERTOS FOR STRINGS AND CONTINUO: IN G MINOR RV152/IN B FLAT MAJOR RV166/IN D MINOR RV127/IN G MAJOR RV145/IN D MAJOR RV121/IN E MINOR RV133/IN A MINOR RV161/IN F MAJOR RV142/IN G MAJOR RV151 (CONCERTO ALLA RUSTICA)
I Musici
Philips 411 035-2PH ·
DDD Running time: 43.02
Performance: ★ ★ ★
Recording: ★ ★ (★)

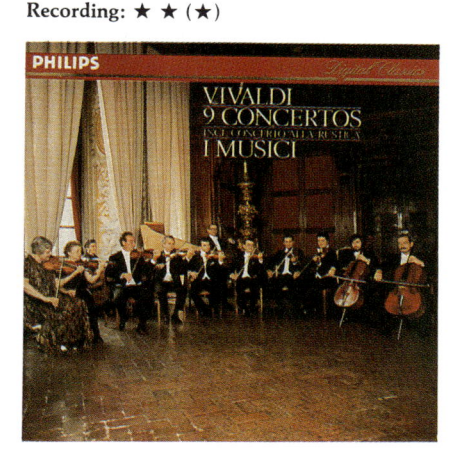

Vivaldi wrote some forty *concerti a quattro*, four-part string concertos which were among the forerunners of the symphony and string quartet, and in them freely explored the potential of the ensemble. Nine of the finest examples are featured here in highly enjoyable performances from I Musici.

The recording offers a broad sound picture, sufficiently transparent in texture clearly to display the part-writing, which adds to the interest. Overall, the sound quality is very good, if a touch dull in the upper register.

Apart from the popular *Concerto alla rustica*, this issue has the field to itself in these works at present.

VIOLIN CONCERTOS OP8 NOS1-4 (THE FOUR SEASONS)/NO1 IN E MAJOR RV269 (SPRING)/NO2 IN G MINOR RV315 (SUMMER)/NO3 IN F MAJOR RV293 (AUTUMN)/NO4 IN F MINOR RV297 (WINTER)
John Holloway: Violin
Taverner Players
Director: Andrew Parrott
Denon C37-7283
DDD Running time: 40.09
Performance: ★ ★ ★   Recording: ★ ★ ★

There are few period instrument recordings of the *Four Seasons* as stylish and unmannered as this. Tonal quality throughout the ensemble is very good, and John Holloway's contribution deserves special mention. The recording is well-imaged, but also convincingly integrates players and acoustic. And, of course, with a good, lively acoustic, the ensemble of just fourteen players can produce a range and depth of sound the equal of many a larger group.

It is difficult to imagine *any* recording of the *Seasons* bringing freshness to the ear, but this one succeeds in doing just that, both through its performances and its piquant sonorities.

Other recordings on CD (period instruments – selection):
Simon Standage/English Concert/Trevor Pinnock/Archiv 400 045-2AH
Christopher Hirons/AAM/Christopher Hogwood/L'Oiseau-Lyre 410 126-2OH
Nils-Erik Sparf/Drottningholm Baroque Ens/BIS CD-275

VIOLIN CONCERTOS: IN D MAJOR OP8 NO11 RV210*/IN C MAJOR OP8 NO12 RV178*/FLUTE CONCERTO IN D MAJOR RV429‡/'CELLO CONCERTO IN B MINOR RV424§
(c/w C. P. E. Bach: Harpsichord Concerto in G Major Wq43 no5†)
Simon Standage: Violin*
Stephen Preston: Flute‡
Anthony Pleeth: 'Cello§
English Concert
Director (and harpsichord soloist):
Trevor Pinnock†
CRD Records CRD3411
ADD Running time: 53.06
Performance: ★ ★ ★   Recording: ★ ★ ★

In the days before they were signed to the German Archiv label, the English Concert made a number of 'original instrument' recordings for the British CRD label, and very good they were, too. For this issue, CRD have selected some 'plums' from those sessions.

Simon Standage is the excellent soloist in two of the Op8 violin concertos, while Stephen Preston's playing of the D minor flute concerto is pure delight (he uses a Schuchart flute from around 1730). No less enjoyable is Anthony Pleeth in the late B minor 'Cello Concerto.

Completing the programme, a brilliant harpsichord concerto from 1771 by that most

VIVALDI

influential of Bach's sons, Carl Philipp Emanuel. As the other works here, it is finely recorded, in a pleasantly open and resonant acoustic (frankly preferable to the sound Archiv have often granted this ensemble).

Other recordings on CD:
('Cello Concerto RV424)
Heinrich Schiff/ASMF/Iona Brown/Philips 411 126-2PH

STRING CONCERTOS: IN A MINOR FOR TWO VIOLINS OP3 NO8 RV552*/IN D MINOR FOR TWO VIOLINS AND 'CELLO OP3 NO11 RV565*‡/IN B MINOR FOR FOUR VIOLINS AND 'CELLO OP3 NO10 RV580*§††/IN F MAJOR FOR THREE VIOLINS RV551*†
Jaime Laredo*, John Tunnell*, Paul Manley†, Brian Thomas§: Violins
Haflidi Hallgrimson: 'Cello‡
Scottish Chamber Orchestra
Director (from the violin): Jaime Laredo
Pickwick Imp Red Label PCD809
DDD Running time: 40.50
Performance: ★ ★ ★   Recording: ★ ★ ★

These are exhilarating performances of some of Vivaldi's finest creations, three taken from the set entitled *L'Estro Armonico* Op3 of 1712, and the fourth, the very rare three-violin concerto, the unusual ensemble of which prompted Vivaldi to some highly original, ear-catching effects.

With an excitingly detailed recording (excellent imaging and inner clarity) set in a open, reverberant acoustic, this budget-price issue makes an excellent introduction to Vivaldi at his most imaginative and entertaining.

Other recordings on CD:
(Concerto for three violins RV551-selection)
Itzhak Perlman/Isaac Stern/Pinchas Zukerman/NYPO/Zubin Mehta/CBS MK36692
Solisti Italiano/Denon C37-7401
(Concertos Op3 Nos8, 10, 11 RV552, RV580, RV565)
AAM/Christopher Hogwood/L'Oiseau-Lyre 414 554-20H2
I Musici/Philips 412 128-2PH2
Solisti Italiano/Denon C37-7401 (Nos8, 10 only)
(Concerto Op3 No8 RV5521)
Isaac Stern/Pinchas Zukerman/St Paul CO/CBS MK37278
(Concerto Op3 No10 RV580)
AAM/Christopher Hogwood/L'Oiseau-Lyre 410 553-20H

OBOE CONCERTOS: IN C MAJOR RV452/IN D MINOR RV454/IN C MAJOR RV446/IN A MINOR RV463*/IN C MAJOR RV447*/CONCERTO FOR OBOE AND BASSOON IN G MAJOR RV545
Heinz Holliger: Oboe
Klaus Thunemann: Bassoon
I Musici
Philips 411 480-2PH
ADD*/DDD Running time: 58.54
Performance: ★ ★ ★   Recording: ★ ★ ★

Both the 1975 analogue and more recent digital recordings were made at one of Philips' favourite venues for chamber music, La Chaux-de-Fonds in Switzerland. In truth, there is very little difference between the two.

The presentation is consistently natural, both in terms of tonal quality and sound-stage. The concertos are among Vivaldi's most imaginative efforts, among them the lyrical RV454 which appears as the ninth violin concerto of Op8.

Holliger's performances, marvellously accompanied by I Musici, are similarly inspired.

Other recordings on CD:
(Concertos RV447 and RV463 only)
Maurice Bourgue/I Solisti Veneti/Claudio Scimone/Erato ECD88031

'CELLO CONCERTOS: IN F MAJOR RV411 (RV412)/IN A MINOR RV418/IN B MINOR RV424/IN G MAJOR RV413/IN C MINOR RV401
Heinrich Schiff: 'Cello
Academy of St Martin-in-the-Fields
Director: Iona Brown
Philips 411 126-2PH
DDD Running time: 46.43
Performance: ★ ★   Recording: ★ ★

Vivaldi's thirty-or-so 'cello concertos are an important constituent of the literature for the instrument, but it is difficult to imagine many listeners being won over to them by these performances whose lack of dynamic contrast cannot be entirely blamed upon the composer. He was able to inject a fair amount of variation and imagination into the basic fast-slow-fast format, but not enough of it is evident here.

That said, the playing is enjoyable enough, but the feeling persists that Vivaldi is not being done justice. The 'cello is balanced forward of the orchestra, but nevertheless sounds natural and well-integrated.

Other recordings on CD:
('Cello Concerto in B minor)
Anthony Pleeth/English Concert/Trevor
 Pinnock/CRD 3411

**OBOE CONCERTO IN A MINOR OP7
NO5 RV461**
**(c/w Haydn [attrib.]: Oboe Concerto in C
Major HVIIg:C1/A.Marcello : Oboe
Concerto in D minor)**
Derek Wickens: Oboe
Royal Philharmonic Orchestra
Conductor: Elgar Howarth
ASV CD DCA1003
ADD Running time: 43.45
Performance: ★ ★ ★   Recording: ★ ★ ★

Titled *The Classical Oboe*, this issue is first-and-foremost a tribute to the skills of Derek Wickens, not just in coping with the technical demands of the solo parts in these concertos, but their expressive requirements too. Throughout, his is playing of the utmost refinement and beauty, a delight to listen to in these three 18th Century concertos.

The excellent Vivaldi concerto dates from around 1716–17, while a feature of that by Alessandro Marcello is its exquisite and haunting *adagio*, which fully exploits the 'yearning' quality of the oboe: disarmingly beautiful music, this, as evidenced by the number of CD versions available.

Whether by Haydn or not (its authenticity has never been established), the C Major concerto has many of his hallmarks, and completes this very well-recorded programme in rousing fashion.

Other recordings on CD (selection):
(Vivaldi: Oboe Concerto Op7 No5 RV461)
Maurice Bourgue/I Solisti Veneti/Claudio
 Scimone/Erato ECD88031
(Marcello: Oboe Concerto)
Collegium Aureum/Pro Arte CDD215
Michaela Petri/ASMF/Kenneth Sillito/
 Philips 412 630–2PH (trans. recorder)
Evelyn Rothwell/Pro Arte O/John
 Barbirolli/PRT PIVCD8374

**FLUTE CONCERTOS OP10: NO1 IN F
MAJOR RV433 (LA TEMPESTA DI
MARE)/NO2 IN G MINOR RV439 (LA
NOTTE)/NO3 IN D MAJOR (IL
GARDELLINO)/NO4 IN G MAJOR RV435/
NO5 IN F MAJOR RV434/NO6 IN G
MAJOR RV437**
Stephen Preston: Flute
The Academy of Ancient Music
L'Oiseau-Lyre 414 685–2OH
ADD Running time: 51.26
Performance: ★ ★ ★   Recording: ★ ★ ★

Based upon the evidence of the earliest known score of these concertos for *flauto traversier*, this recording employs just one string player per part; in other words the supporting 'orchestra' consists only of a string quartet and harpsichord (or in the case of the First and Fifth concertos, a chamber organ). This 'chamber' treatment works very well indeed, especially with the ripe tonal quality of the period instruments (or copies of them).

Stephen Preston, using a Schuchart flute from the early 17th Century, proves an imaginative and stylish soloist, although it would be impossible for any flautist to convey the *'raging of the sea'* that the sub-title of the first concerto demands. These are fine performances, with a recording to match.

Other recordings on CD (selection):
Michaela Petri/ASMF/Iona Brown/Philips
 412 874–2PH

**WIND CONCERTOS: IN C MAJOR FOR
TWO FLUTES RV533*/IN D MINOR FOR
TWO OBOES RV535‡/IN F MAJOR FOR
TWO HORNS RV539§/FOR TWO
TRUMPETS IN C MAJOR RV537**/IN C
MAJOR FOR TWO OBOES AND TWO
CLARINETS RV560‡†**
David Nicholson, Sheena Gordon: Flutes*
Robin Miller, Maurice Checker: Oboes‡
Frank Lloyd, Harry Johnstone: Horns§
Michael Laird, Peter Franks: Trumpets**
Lewis Morrison, Lorna Cook: Clarinets†
Scottish Chamber Orchestra
Director (from the violin): Jaime Laredo
Pickwick IMP Red Label PCD811
DDD Running time: 41.26
Performance: ★ ★ ★   Recording: ★ ★ ★

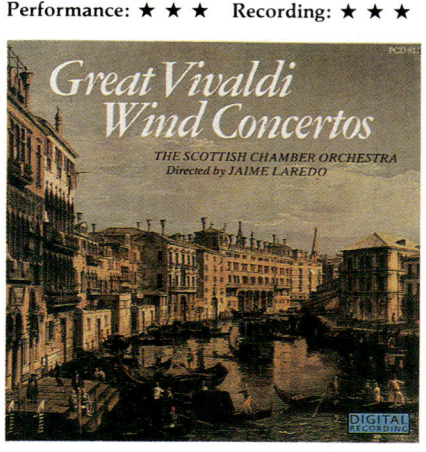

Despite the violin's predominance in 18th Century Italian music, the study of wind instruments was certainly encouraged during Vivaldi's tenure at the Pietà. He left a number of concertos for double wind instruments of which the programme here is an enjoyably diverse selection featuring flutes, oboes, horns and trumpets, in addition to the C Major for oboes and clarinets. In opting for the upper octave, the horn players in RV539 set themselves a task which they overcome triumphantly.

The recording is admirably clear, the balance finely judged for each instrumental combination, that for the two-horn concerto a particular success. The whole is smooth, yet lively, and all round, this is an extraordinarily fine issue.

Other recordings on CD (selection):
(Concerto for two flutes RV533)
Stephen Preston/Nicholas McGegan/AAM/
 Christopher Hogwood/L'Oiseau-Lyre 414
 588–2OH
(Concerto for two horns RV539)
Jacky Magnardi/André Both/I Solisti
 Veneti/Claudio Scimone/Erato ECD88009
(Concerto for two trumpets RV537)
Michael Laird/Ian Wilson/AAM/
 Christopher Hogwood/L'Oiseau-Lyre/410
 553–2OH
John Wallace/James Miller/Philharmonia/
 Christopher Warren-Green/Nimbus
 NIM5017

RICHARD WAGNER
(b. Leipzig, Germany, 22 May 1813; d. Venice, Italy, 13 February 1883)

There can have been few more influential composers than this high priest of romanticism. It was an influence that extended not only to those who revered both man and music, but to those who *so* disliked everything Wagner stood for (some French composers, for example) that they did their utmost to find a musical language that was its total antithesis.

Loved or hated, Wagner nevertheless bestrides the last decades of the 19th Century just as Beethoven had done the first. With him, romanticism reached its zenith, in terms of scale, opulence of sound, and sensuality. A counter-reaction was both inevitable and necessary.

Even now, Wagner provokes extreme reactions, some as much connected with his personality as with his music. His anti-Semitism still precludes its performance in Israel, yet there is a very real chance that, owing to an extra-marital affair on the part of his mother, he may well have been half-Jewish, which would have come as a shock to some of his mid-20th Century admirers in Germany.

His musical interest developed late. There were two early operas and, while living an impoverished existence in Paris, the first of note: *Rienzi*. He returned to Germany, enjoyed success with *Tannhäuser* and *Lohengrin*, and then began working on his supreme achievement, the quartet of operas known as *Der Ring des Nibelungen*, although not completing it until twenty-five years and two tempestuous love affairs later. In between, he wrote undoubtedly his most musically adventurous and perenially influential work, *Tristan und Isolde*.

Wagner's last work was the deeply spiritual 'sacred festival drama', *Parsifal*, of 1882, based upon the Grail legend. Exhausted, he retired to Venice to recuperate, but died there after a series of heart attacks.

Wagner's life and work are, of course, more fully covered in our complementary volume, *Opera on Compact Disc*. Only the popular orchestral selections from the operas are discussed here.

OVERTURES: RIENZI/TANNHÄUSER/ DIE MEISTERSINGER VON NÜRNBERG: PRELUDE TO ACT ONE/PARSIFAL: PRELUDE
Vienna Philharmonic Orchestra
Conductor: Karl Böhm
Deutsche Grammophon 413 551-2GH
ADD Running time: 49.10
Performance: ★ ★ (★)
Recording: ★ ★ (★)

Böhm's Rienzi is a noble and dignified Roman indeed, as he sets the most stately tempo for the overture to Wagner's first major opera. The end result, however, is most persuasive, as the seamless transition from the sacred to the profane of *Tannhäuser*. The rather portly and pompous manner of the *Meistersinger* prelude is equally convincing, but it is in the hushed communion of *Parsifal* that Böhm is at his most intense: a spellbinding performance.

The grandeur of these readings may not suit all tastes in Wagner playing, but it is difficult to resist the sumptuous beauty of the Vienna orchestra in this form, and the recording offers generally natural, well-terraced perspectives in an expansive acoustic.

Other recordings on CD (selection):
(Overture to *Rienzi*)
BPO/Klaus Tennstedt/EMI CDC 7 47030-2
Minnesota O/Neville Marriner/Telarc
  CD80083
(Prelude to *Die Meistersinger*)
BPO/Klaus Tennstedt/EMI CDC 7 47030-2
Minnesota O/Neville Marriner/Telarc
  CD80083
CSO/Georg Solti/Decca 411 951-2DH
BPO/Herbert von Karajan/DG 413 754-2GH
(Overture to *Tannhäuser*)
BPO/Klaus Tennstedt/EMI CDC 7 47030-2
BPO/Herbert von Karajan/DG 413 754-2GH

TANNHÄUSER: OVERTURE AND VENUSBERG MUSIC/DIE MEISTERSINGER VON NÜRNBERG: PRELUDE TO ACT THREE/ TRISTAN UND ISOLDE: PRELUDE AND LIEBESTOD
Berlin Philharmonic Orchestra
Conductor: Herbert von Karajan
Deutsche Grammophon 413 754–2GH
DDD Running time: 49.51
Performance: ★ ★ (★)
Recording: ★ ★

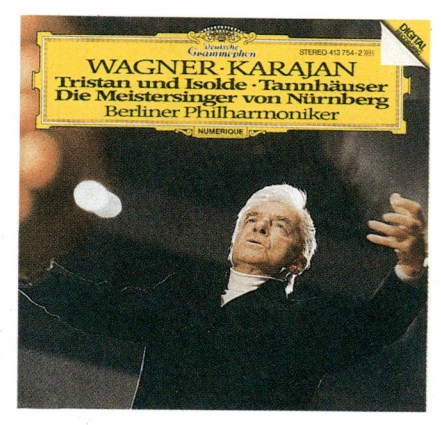

WAGNER

The *Prelude and Liebestod* from *Tristan* can rarely have been played with the kind of sumptuous sensuality Karajan and the Berliners can muster. It is the most successful item here, both in terms of performance and recording.

The *Tannhauser* overture is certainly brilliant and exciting, but is not helped by the rather cramped and unatmospheric sound, and the very bright edge to the upper strings, which become distinctly screechy in the *Venusberg* bacchanale. DG's engineers have been getting better sound than this in Berlin for the past couple of years.

Other recordings on CD:
(*Tannhäuser: Overture* – selection)
VPO/Karl Böhm/DG 413 551–2GH
(*Tristan und Isolde: Prelude and Liebestod*– selection)
CSO/Georg Solti/Decca 411 951–2DH

EXCERPTS FROM DER RING DES NIBELUNGEN: DAS RHEINGOLD: ENTRY OF THE GODS INTO VALHALLA/DIE WALKÜRE – RIDE OF THE VALKYRIES, MAGIC FIRE MUSIC/ SIEGFRIED – FOREST MURMURS/ GÖTTERDÄMMERUNG-SIEGFRIED'S RHINE JOURNEY, SIEGFRIED'S FUNERAL MARCH
Berlin Philharmonic Orchestra
Conductor: Klaus Tennstedt
EMI CDC7 47007–2
DDD Running time: 46.29
Performance: ★ ★ ★   Recording: ★ ★

There is no lack of impact or brilliance here, indeed the sound verges on the shrill at times. The brass can be overpowering when at full tilt, but it is all cleanly caught and presented in vivid detail, although a certain dryness robs the strings of some of their richness.

Tennstedt's performances are appropriately intense and highly-charged, and there is no denying this is an exciting recording.

Other recordings on CD:
(*Entry of the Gods into Vahalla, Ride of the Valkyries, Magic Fire Music, Forest Murmurs* – selection)
VPO/Georg Solti/Decca 410 137–2DH
NYPO/Zubin Mehta/CBS MK37785
(*Siegfried's Rhine Journey, Siegfried's Funeral March* – selection)
Philharmonic SO/Carlos Paita/Lodia LO–CD785
NYPO/Zubin Mehta/CBS MK37785

OVERTURE: DER FLIEGENDE HOLLÄNDER/LOHENGRIN: PRELUDES TO ACTS ONE AND THREE/TRISTAN UND ISOLDE: PRELUDE AND LIEBESTOD
Vienna Philharmonic Orchestra
Conductor Karl Böhm
Deutsche Grammophon 413 733–2GH
ADD Running time: :44.42
Performance: ★ ★ ★
Recording: ★ ★ (★)

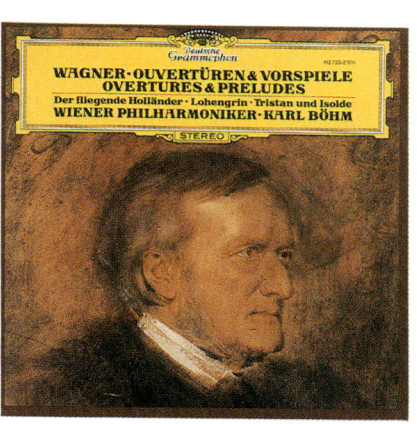

As an illustration of the various facets of Karl Böhm's approach to Wagner, this selection could hardly be bettered, with a powerful, dramatic performance of the overture to *The Flying Dutchman*, a serene account of the first of the *Lohengrin* preludes, and an exuberant, but carefully and effectively-paced, reading of the better-known third. The *Tristan* excerpt exchanges some of Karajan's voluptuousness for a greater nobility and tenderness, which many may prefer.

With superb playing and a much more flattering recording than that given the Berlin Philharmonic in their 1985 digital issue, this is a wholly satisfying reissue which hardly betrays its analogue origins at all. A good 'Wagner sampler'.

SIEGFRIED IDYLL
(c/w Schoenberg: *Verklärte Nacht* **[Transfigured Night]** – orchestral version)
English Chamber Orchestra
Conductor: Vladimir Ashkenazy
Decca 410 111–2DH
DDD Running time: 46.56
Performance: ★ ★ (★)
Recording: ★ ★ (★)

Wagner's birthday present to his wife of just a few months (but mistress of several years) is an apt companion for Schoenberg's musical depiction of Dehmel's poem about the strength and fulfillment true love can bring, although the two works are very different in temperament, the radiant contentment of the *Siegfried Idyll* in sharp contrast to the impassioned extremes of *Verklärte Nacht*. The latter was originally scored for string sextet at its composition in 1899. Schoenberg made a version for string orchestra in 1917, revising it in 1945.

Ashkenazy's deeply-considered performances are given a full-bodied but clear sound (so important in the dense textures of Schoenberg). There is warmth and depth too, and no lack of presence, all of which makes for a most recommendable coupling.

INDEX
of conductors, soloists and orchestras mentioned in main reviews.

A
Abbado, Claudio, 47, 93, 97, 103, 116, 142, 161
Academy of Ancient Music, 16, 26, 76, 81, 82, 101, 102, 103, 107, 170, 173
Academy of St Martin-in-the-Fields, 17, 60, 66, 71, 80, 98, 105, 107, 136, 170, 172
Academy of St Martin-in-the-Fields Chamber Ensemble, 76
Alain, Marie-Claire, 18, 20
Alban Berg Quartet, 30, 110, 138
Albion Ensemble, 87
Aler, John, 87
Ambrosian Singers, 53, 57, 71, 84, 99
Ameling, Elly, 136
Amoyal, Pierre, 162
Amsterdam Baroque Orchestra, 75
Araiza, Francisco, 94
Argerich, Martha, 47, 142, 161
Arrau, Claudio, 29, 49, 50, 89
Ashkenazy, Vladimir, 23, 27, 28, 38, 39, 48, 104, 106, 118, 120, 121, 122, 126, 149, 150, 161, 175
Athena Ensemble, 55
Atlanta Symphony Orchestra and Chorus, 157
Auger, Arleen, 93, 99

B
Baker, Janet, 63
Barbirolli, John, 63
Bate, Jennifer, 67
Battle, Kathleen, 91, 92
Baumann, Hermann, 154
Bavarian Radio Symphony Orchestra, 95, 147
Bavarian State Orchestra, 45
Bayreuth Festival Chorus and Orchestra, 28
Beaux Arts Trio, 109, 125, 138
Bedford, Steuart, 43
Bennett, William, 17, 66, 102
Berlin Philharmonic Orchestra, 29, 35, 39, 45, 59, 70, 71, 92, 94, 95, 113, 147, 151, 152, 154, 155, 161, 163, 174, 175
Bernstein, Leonard, 39, 51, 67, 157
Berry, Walter, 27
Best, Roger, 42
Bilson, Malcolm, 104, 105
Bingham, John, 64
Bishop-Kovacevich, Stephen, 41
Blochwitz, Hans-Peter, 97
Blomstedt, Herbert, 45, 155
Böhm, Karl, 27, 28, 45, 95, 117, 174, 175
Boky, Colette, 65
Bolet, Jorge, 87, 88, 89
Bolton, Ivor, 77
Bonynge, Richard, 131
Borodin Trio, 147
Boston Symphony Orchestra, 156, 162
Boughton, William, 42, 63, 167
Bourgue, Maurice, 167
Bournemouth Sinfonietta, 57, 84
Brandis Quartet, 109
Brendel, Alfred, 28, 88, 105, 139, 142
Brown, Iona, 17, 107, 172
Buchbinder, Rudolf, 33
Burns, Stephen, 158

C
Camerata Bern, 131
Chailly, Riccardo, 131, 162
Chicago Symphony Orchestra, 28, 38, 93, 116
Christ, Wolfram, 35
Chung, Kyung-Wha, 113, 162
Cincinatti Symphony Orchestra, 69, 162
City of Birmingham Symphony Orchestra, 43, 95
City of Birmingham Symphony Orchestra Chorus, 95
Cleveland Orchestra, 59, 112, 118, 142, 162
Coin, Christophe, 82
Collegium Aureum, 108
Collegium Musicum Amstelodamense, 53
Columbia Symphony Orchestra, 37, 102
Concert Association of the Vienna State Opera Chorus, 27
Concertgebouw Orchestra, Amsterdam, 23, 29, 34, 38, 45, 53, 81, 120, 121, 122, 141, 146, 154, 157
Conlon, James, 87
Connell, Elizabeth, 97
Covent Garden, Royal Opera House Orchestra, 162
Czako, Eva, 109
Czech Philharmonic Orchestra, 85, 92

D
Davidovich, Bella, 47
Davis, Colin, 29, 34, 81, 102, 157, 162
de Larrocha, Alicia, 65
del Mar, Norman, 57
Detroit Symphony Orchestra, 51, 69, 158
Dohnanyi, Christoph von, 59
Domingo, Placido, 27
Dorati, Antal, 23, 51, 69, 258
Döse, Helen, 95

Dresden Staatskapelle, 29, 45, 102, 155
Dreyfuss, Huguette, 20
du Pré, Jacqueline, 63
Duchable, François-René, 133
Dutoit, Charles, 65, 124, 125, 127, 129, 133, 156, 157, 161, 162

E
l'École d'Orphée, 77
Edelmann, Otto, 28
Eder Quartet, 83
Ellis, Osian, 102
Enesco, Quatuor, 55
English Baroque Soloists, 17, 101, 104, 105
English Chamber Orchestra, 43, 102, 103, 105, 106, 175
English Concert, 16, 74, 75, 76, 170, 171
English String Orchestra, 42, 63, 167
Evans, Peter, 41

F
Fassbaender, Brigitte, 27, 94
Fenby, Eric, 57
Ferenc Liszt Chamber Orchestra, Budapest, 24
Ferencsik, János, 87
Ferrier, Kathleen, 94
Fischer, Ivan, 87
Fischer-Dieskau, Dietrich, 95
Fitzwilliam Quartet, 31
Forrester, Maureen, 91
Frankfurt Radio Symphony Orchestra, 91
Franz Liszt Chamber Orchestra, Budapest, 80
Frühbeck de Burgos, Rafael, 65
Fujiwara, Mari, 110
Furi, Thomas, 131
Furtwängler, Wilhelm, 28

G
Galway, James, 103
Gardiner, John Eliot, 17, 101, 104, 105
Garland, Roger, 17
Gavrilov, Andrei, 122
Gérecz, Arpad, 109
Gibson, Alexander, 35, 64
Gilbert, Kenneth, 16
Gilels, Emil, 32, 33
Gingold, Hermione, 117
Giulini, Carlo Maria, 94
Giuranna, Bruno, 109
Goebel, Reinhard, 164
Goodwin, Paul, 77
Gothenburg Symphony Orchestra, 113, 149
Grumiaux Trio, 109

H
Hacker, Alan, 108
Hagen Quartet, 137
Haitink, Bernard, 29, 38, 39, 45, 53, 62, 121, 141, 145, 146, 154
Hallgrimsson, Haflidi, 172
Handley, Vernon, 57, 62, 167
Harnoncourt, Alice, 170
Harnoncourt, Nikolaus, 170
Harper, Heather, 93
Harrell, Lynn, 142
Haskil, Clara, 106
Hirons, Christopher, 16
Hodgson, Alfreda, 95
Hoenich, Richard, 65
Hogwood, Christopher, 16, 26, 76, 81, 82, 101, 103, 107, 170
Holliger, Heinz, 164, 172
Holliger, Ursula, 75
Holloway, John, 171
Holmes, Ralph, 57
Höngen, Elisabeth, 28
Hopf, Hans, 147
Horner, Jerry, 147
Howarth, Elgar, 173
Hungarian State Orchestra, 87
Hurford, Peter, 133
Hurst, George, 84

I
I Musici, 171, 172
Inbal, Eliahu, 91
Israel Philharmonic Orchestra, 157, 163
Isserlis, Steven, 41

J
Jaccottet, Christiane, 164
Jansons, Mariss, 160
Janzer, Georges, 109
Järvi, Neeme, 60, 116, 117, 129, 149
Jennings, Patricia Prattis, 133
Jochum, Eugen, 28
Johnson, Emma, 102

K
Kantorow, Jean-Jacques, 110, 126
Karajan, Herbert von see von Karajan, Herbert
Katsaris, Cyprien, 71
Kennedy, Nigel, 62
Kleiber, Carlos, 26, 38
Klemperer, Otto, 94
Kocian Quartet, 109
Kocsis, Zoltan, 54
Kollo, Rene, 93
Kondrashin, Kyril, 59, 87
Kontarski, Alfons and Aloys, 117
Koopman, Ton, 18, 75
Kraemer, Nicholas, 16, 17
Kremer, Gidon, 39
Kubelik, Rafael, 109

Kuhn Children's Chorus, 92
Kunzel, Erich, 69, 162

L
Lamoureux Concerts Orchestra, 105
Laredo, Jaime, 16, 172, 173
Larrocha, Alicia de, 65
Latchem, Malcolm, 17
Leinsdorf, Erich, 158
Leipzig Gewandhaus Orchestra, 40, 136, 154
Leipzig Radio Chorus, 136
Leonhardt, Gustav, 21
Leppard, Raymond, 82, 102
Lesueur, Max, 109
Levi, Yoel, 118
Levine, James, 109
Linde, Hans-Martin, 15
Linde Consort, 15
Lloyd, Peter, 54
Lombard, Alain, 133
London Philharmonic Orchestra, 23, 62, 65, 92, 117, 145, 158, 167
London Symphony Chorus, 97
London Symphony Orchestra, 23, 47, 53, 54, 62, 63, 69, 70, 84, 87, 97, 99, 103, 142, 160
Los Angeles Chamber Orchestra, 158
Los Angeles Philharmonic Orchestra, 51
Lott, Felicity, 57
Loveday, Alan, 170
Ludwig, Christa, 92
Lupu, Radu, 70, 139

M
Ma, Yo-Yo, 29, 62
Maazel, Lorin, 35, 92, 112, 152, 154
Maisky, Mischa, 39
Manley, Paul, 172
Mar, Norman del, 57
Markevich, Igor, 106
Marriner, Neville, 17, 47, 60, 66, 71, 80, 90, 98, 105, 114, 136, 142, 170
Masur, Kurt, 40, 136, 154
Mattila, Karita, 97
Medici Quartet, 64
Mehta, Zubin, 28, 163
Mendelsohn, Vladimir, 110
Meyer, Sabine, 108
Michelangeli, Arturo Benedetti, 48, 54
Minton, Yvonne, 93
Mintz, Shlomo, 21, 116
Mirring, Peter, 155
Montreal Symphony Orchestra, 65, 124, 125, 127, 129, 133, 157, 162
Moroney, Davitt, 18
Mortensen, Lars Ulrik, 16
Murray, Ann, 99
Murray, Michael, 19
Musica Antiqua Köln, 164
Musiciens, Les, 138
Musikverein Quartett, 40
Muti, Riccardo, 106, 131
Mutter, Ann-Sophie, 29, 39, 106

N
Nagai, Yukie, 126
Nash Ensemble, 66
National Philharmonic Orchestra. 37, 131
Neumann, Vaclav, 85, 92
New Irish Chamber Orchestra, 103
New Vienna Quartet, 83
New York 'Y' Chamber Symphony, 92
Norman, Jessye, 27

O
Oborin, Lev, 31
Oistrakh, David, 31
Orchestre National de France, 67
Orlando Quartet, 83, 110, 138
Orpheus Chamber Orchestra, 80
Ortiz, Christina, 69
Oslo Philharmonic Orchestra, 160
Otto, Hans, 19
Ozawa, Seiji, 156

P
Paita, Carlos, 37, 59
Parrott, Andrew, 171
Patzak, Julius, 94
Pay, Antony, 103
Perahia, Murray, 32, 47, 105, 106
Perlemuter, Vlado, 49
Perlman, Itzhak, 151, 156
Philharmonia Orchestra, 26, 27, 62, 98, 99, 104, 106, 114, 127, 131, 149, 150, 161, 162
Philharmonia Quartett, Berlin, 108
Philharmonia Symphony Orchestra, 59
Piguet, Michel, 103
Pinnock, Trevor, 16, 17, 74, 75, 76, 170, 171
Pires, Maria-João, 110, 143
Pittsburgh Symphony Orchestra, 133, 151
Pleeth, Anthony, 171
Pogorelich, Ivo, 118, 143
Pollini, Maurizio, 28, 49, 50, 143
Popp, Lucia, 71, 93

Posch, Alois, 137
Prague Philharmonic Chorus, 92
Pré, Jacqueline du, 63
Preston, Simon, 75
Preston, Stephen, 171, 173
Prêtre, Georges, 99
Previn, André, 23, 40, 53, 54, 62, 69, 70, 84, 114, 121, 133, 151
Prieur, André, 103

R
Rae, Sean, 95
Rattle, Simon, 43, 95, 150
Reichenberg, David, 74
Richter, Sviatoslav, 31, 87
Roberts, Richard, 129
Rogé, Pascal, 124
Rolfe-Johnson, Anthony, 57
Rolla, Janos, 24, 80
Rosenberger, Carol, 158
Rostropovich, Mstislav, 31, 59
Rotterdam Philharmonic Orchestra and Chorus, 87
Rouvier, Jacques, 54, 55, 112, 126
Royal Opera House, Covent Garden, Orchestra, 162
Royal Philharmonic Orchestra. 57, 121, 161, 173
Rozhdestvensky, Gennady, 147

S
St James' Baroque Players, 77
St Louis Symphony Chorus and Orchestra, 91
St Paul Chamber Orchestra, 98
Salomon String Quartet, 107, 108
Sawallisch, Wolfgang, 45
Schaeftlein, Jürg, 170
Schatzberger, Lesley, 108
Schiff, Andras, 40, 137
Schwarz, Gerard, 82, 158
Schiff, Heinrich, 138, 147, 172
Schröder, Jaap, 16, 101, 102
Schwarzkopf, Elisabeth, 28
Scottish Chamber Orchestra, 16, 82, 107, 172, 173
Scottish National Orchestra, 35, 60, 64, 116, 117, 129
Serkin, Rudolf, 103
Shaw, Robert, 157
Shingles, Stephen, 17
Shirley-Quirk, John, 93
Shumsky, Oscar, 107
Sibelius Academy Quartet, 151
Simon, Geoffrey, 127, 160
Sinopoli, Giuseppe, 98, 165
Slatkin, Leonard, 91
Smetana Quartet, 30, 85
Söderström, Elisabeth, 155
Solti, Georg, 23, 38, 93, 136
Staatskapelle Dresden, 29, 45, 102, 155
Standage, Simon, 74, 170, 171
Strasbourg Philharmonic Orchestra, 133
Suisse Romande Orchestra, 156
Suk, Josef, 107
Suk Trio, 60
Szeryng, Henryk, 29

T
Takács Quartet, 24
Talvela, Martti, 93
Tanglewood Festival Chorus, 162
Tate, Jeffrey, 102
Taverner Players, 171
Tear, Robert, 95
Tennstedt, Klaus, 92, 117, 175
Thomas, Brian, 172
Thomson, Bryden, 64
Thunemann, Klaus, 164, 172
Tortelier, Paul, 21
Tortelier, Yan-Pascal, 107
Tourangeau, Huguett, 65
Tuckwell, Barry, 103
Tunnell, John, 16, 172

U
Uchida, Mitsuko, 111
Ughi, Uto, 99
Ulster Orchestra, 64
USSR State Symphony Orchestra, 147

V
Vermeer Quartet, 137
Vienna Boys' Choir, 93
Vienna Concentus Musicus, 170
Vienna Philharmonic Orchestra, 26, 27, 28, 38, 39, 45, 59, 92, 94, 117, 136, 152, 154, 165, 174, 175
Vienna Singverein, 93
Vienna State Opera Choir, 93
Vienna State Opera Chorus Concert Association, 27
Vigay, Denis, 17
Villa, Joseph, 133
von Dohnanyi, Christoph, 59
von Karajan, Herbert, 29, 39, 45, 59, 70, 71, 92, 94, 113, 147, 151, 152, 154, 155, 163, 174

W
Walker, Sarah, 57
Wallfisch, Raphael, 43
Walter, Bruno, 37, 94, 102
Watts, Helen, 95
Wickens, Derek, 173

Z
Zeltser, Mark, 29
Zukerman, Pinchas, 98
Zweig, Mimi, 147

PICTURE CREDITS
Front Cover: Clive Barda
BBC Hulton Picture Library: 14, 35TL, 52, 56, 132, 159, 166; Bettmann Archive/BBC HPL: 22BR, 68, 148; Louvre, Paris/Giraudon/Bridgeman Art Library: 101; Britain on View: 61 (main); J-L. Charmet: 22BL, 78–9 (main), 130; G. Costa: 25, 78 (inset), 119, 123TL, 134, 135; Decca International: title, 120, 123TR; Deutsche Grammophon: rear endpaper (S. Lauterwasser), 97 (Silvia Lelli Masotti); EMI: 10; Mary Evans Picture Library: 46, 86; Peter Herring: 168–9; Mansell Collection; 15, 35TR, 36, 44, 58, 61 (inset), 72–3, 90, 96, 128, 140, 144 (main), 153; Marantz Audio UK: 6–7: Nimbus Records: 8, 9, 11; Philips: front endpaper, half title, 6–7, 79 (inset), 141; Society for Cultural Relations with the USSR: 115, 144 (inset).

176